Oxford Studies in So(
General Editor: Kei(

Meanings of M
in Early Modern England

Meanings of Manhood in Early Modern England

ALEXANDRA SHEPARD

OXFORD
UNIVERSITY PRESS

This book has been printed digitally and produced in a standard specification in order to ensure its continuing availability

OXFORD
UNIVERSITY PRESS

Great Clarendon Street, Oxford OX2 6DP
Oxford University Press is a department of the University of Oxford.
It furthers the University's objective of excellence in research, scholarship, and education by publishing worldwide in

Oxford New York

Auckland Cape Town Dar es Salaam Hong Kong Karachi
Kuala Lumpur Madrid Melbourne Mexico City Nairobi
New Delhi Shanghai Taipei Toronto
With offices in
Argentina Austria Brazil Chile Czech Republic France Greece
Guatemala Hungary Italy Japan South Korea Poland Portugal
Singapore Switzerland Thailand Turkey Ukraine Vietnam

Oxford is a registered trade mark of Oxford University Press
in the UK and in certain other countries

Published in the United States
by Oxford University Press Inc., New York

© Alexandra Shepard, 2003

The moral rights of the author have been asserted
Database right Oxford University Press (maker)

Reprinted 2008

All rights reserved. No part of this publication may be reproduced, stored in a retrieval system, or transmitted, in any form or by any means, without the prior permission in writing of Oxford University Press, or as expressly permitted by law, or under terms agreed with the appropriate reprographics rights organization. Enquiries concerning reproduction outside the scope of the above should be sent to the Rights Department, Oxford University Press, at the address above

You must not circulate this book in any other binding or cover
And you must impose this same condition on any acquirer

ISBN 978-0-19-929934-8

To my parents

ACKNOWLEDGEMENTS

THE idea for this project was inspired by a graduate course taught by John Demos at Yale, and I am grateful to him and to the other participants for introducing me to the challenges of asking awkward questions of the past. Its final shape owes an enormous amount to Keith Wrightson, who supervised my Ph.D. thesis with unstinting insight and encouragement. I wish to thank him for his wisdom, vigilance, generosity, and good humour, without which I would have faltered on numerous occasions. Lyndal Roper was also highly instrumental in supervising parts of the thesis, and I am deeply indebted to her for posing difficult questions and for motivating me to think that I might at least begin to answer some of them. Thanks are also due for her continued enthusiasm for this project. A postgraduate studentship from the British Academy funded my doctoral work, for which I am extremely grateful. I should also like to thank the President and Fellows of St John's College, Oxford, for the opportunity to complete my thesis and to begin postdoctoral work in a secure and stimulating environment. Finally, this book would not have been completed without the award of research leave funded by the Arts and Humanities Research Board, which enabled me to undertake the additional research for new chapters and to redraft the entire manuscript.

The process of reworking and expanding my Ph.D. into this book was aided by the critical rigour of my examiners, Peter Burke and Martin Ingram. I am also indebted to the two anonymous OUP readers for their suggestions and to Keith Thomas for his keen intellectual engagement with this project. On countless occasions Elisabeth Leedham-Green has patiently responded to my questions about the Cambridge university courts, and I should like to thank her for generously sharing her expertise. Thanks are also due to Godfrey Waller and the staff of the manuscripts reading room in the Cambridge University Library. I have benefited enormously from conversations with Catherine Allgor, Susan Amussen, Helen Berry, Alan Bray, Philip Carter, Michèle Cohen, Trish Crawford, David Cressy, Elizabeth Foyster, Laura Gowing, Allegra Hogan, Jennifer Melville, Craig Muldrew, Ulinka Rublack, Tim Stretton, David Underdown, Alison Wall, and Andy Wood, and from feedback in seminars at the Institute of Historical Research, and at the universities of Aberdeen, Cambridge, East Anglia, Oxford, and Sussex. Many colleagues at the University of Sussex have provided support and assistance, and I am particularly grateful to Claire Langhamer, Blair Worden, and Brian Young. Natasha Glaisyer, Margaret Pelling, and Phil Withington have all generously commented on drafts of various chapters, and the final versions owe much to their critical acumen. All remaining errors and blind spots are, of course, my own. I am profoundly indebted to Konstantin Dierks and Sarah Knott, who have read the entire manuscript and provided intellectual anchorage from the book's inception. I am also deeply beholden to them, and to Natasha Glaisyer, for their friendship. My parents and family have provided support in myriad ways, not least by trusting that this project would, eventually, be finished, and by not asking too often whether it was done yet. Finally, I am inexpressibly grateful to Jason Reese, not only for reading the whole thing, but for his patience, constancy, and love, without which we would both have lived with this book for a great deal longer.

Chapter 7 uses material from my article 'Manhood, Credit and Patriarchy in Early Modern England, *c.*1580–1640', *Past and Present*, 167 (May 2000), 75–106, which is reprinted here with kind permission. (World Copyright: The Past and Present Society, 175 Banbury Road, Oxford, England.)

CONTENTS

List of Figures — xi

List of Tables — xi

Conventions and Abbreviations — xii

Introduction — 1

Part I: Modelling Manhood

1. The Constant Age — 21
   Youth and manhood — 23
   One foot in the grave — 38

2. The Imagined Body of 'Man's Estate' — 47
   The ages of man — 54
   A hierarchy of complexions — 58
   'Things not natural': manhood and the environment — 64

3. Models of Manhood — 70
   Manhood, marriage, and domestic conduct — 73
   Manhood and the social order — 87

Part II: The Social Practice of Manhood

4. Youthful Excess and Fraternal Bonding — 93
   The camaraderie of misrule — 96
   Male intimacy, friendship, and illicit sex — 113

5. The Violence of Manhood 127

Judicial punishment and disciplinary violence 132
The gestures of disputed status and the rules of fair play 140

6. Respectability, Sex, and Status 152

The gendered components of honesty and reputation 157
Slanderous debasement 173

7. Credit, Provision, and Worth 186

Credit, worth, and the language of social description 188
Women's provision and alternative household strategies 195
Lone men 205

8. The 'Ancienter Sort' 214

The report of ancient men 221
Ageing, work, and impotence 231

Conclusion: Manhood, Patriarchy, and Gender in Early Modern England 246

Bibliography 254

Index 277

LIST OF FIGURES

1. *Keepe within Compasse; or, The Worthy Legacy of a Wise Father to his Beloved Sonne* (London, 1619), title page — 31
2. *The Mothers Counsell; or, Live within Compasse. Being the Last Will and Testament to her Dearest Daughter* (London, 1630?), title page — 33
3. Differing schemes of the ages of man — 55
4. Language of insult against men in Cambridge, 1581–1640 — 162
5. Language of insult against women in Cambridge, 1581–1640 — 163
6. Categories of insult against Cambridge women, 1581–1640 — 165
7. Categories of insult against Cambridge townsmen, 1581–1640 — 166
8. Categories of insult against Cambridge university members, 1581–1640 — 166
9. Ages of witnesses over 50 in the Cambridge university courts, 1581–1640 — 218
10. Ages of witnesses over 50 in the Lewes archdeaconry court, 1580–1640 — 219
11. Ages of Cambridgeshire witnesses in the Court of Exchequer, 1587–1638 — 220

LIST OF TABLES

1. Defamation litigants in the Cambridge university courts, 1581–1640, by sex and town/gown status — 156

CONVENTIONS AND ABBREVIATIONS

Quotations from manuscript sources remain in the original spelling and punctuation. 'Th' has been substituted for 'y' where appropriate, i/j and u/v have been distinguished, and abbreviations and contractions have been expanded. Dates follow Old Style, but the year is taken to begin on 1 January.

The following abbreviations are used in references to archival sources and secondary works:

Bodl.	Bodleian Library, Oxford
c.	*contra*
CUA	Cambridge University Archives
CUL	Cambridge University Library
DRO	Devon Record Office, Exeter
EDR	Ely Diocesan Records
ESRO	East Sussex Record Office, Lewes
GL	Guildhall Library, London
NRO	Norfolk Record Office, Norwich
OUA	Oxford University Archives
PRO	Public Record Office, London
ser.	series
WSRO	West Sussex Record Office, Chichester

Introduction

THIS book traces the varied meanings of manhood in England between 1560 and 1640 in order to explore their complex relationship with patriarchal norms. Its central argument is that manhood and patriarchy were not equated in early modern England, and should not be elided by gender historians. While men were often better placed to benefit from them, patriarchal imperatives nonetheless constituted attempts to discipline and order men as well as women. Men, like women, might have experienced such imperatives in one or more of three ways: as beneficiaries; as subordinates; and as opponents. In addition, for some men and in certain contexts, patriarchal ideals were largely irrelevant—a point often neglected by gender historians, not least because it is the most difficult to demonstrate. There was no neat scheme to all this: patriarchal ideology itself was muddled, contradictory, and selectively invoked rather than a monolithic system which simply received adherence or rejection. Similarly, the social practice of manhood was enormously diverse, contingent, and contradictory, influenced by and informing distinctions of age, social status, marital status, and context. Access to patriarchal privilege was varied for men as well as women (albeit on profoundly different grounds), and the competing forms of manhood asserted by early modern men could and did undermine patriarchal ideals. By mapping the age-related, class-related, and context-related ways in which early modern men gained from, were subordinated by, resisted, or simply ignored patriarchal dictates, it is possible to assess the distribution of patriarchal benefits not just between men and women, but also between men themselves, in order to comprehend the complex interaction of gender with other determinants of status and identity in early modern society.

A book about manhood no longer needs to begin with a lengthy justification of why we need yet more history written about men. The last decade has witnessed a prolific response to earlier calls for a history of both sexes in general and for a history of masculinity in particular to complement pioneering research in women's history.[1] Many studies are now

---

[1] e.g. Natalie Zemon Davis, '"Women's History" in Transition: The European Case',

in print, collectively surveying a broad chronological, geographical, and thematic expanse.[2] Aiming to particularize male experience (rather than assuming a generically male subject) the history of masculinity contributes an important corrective to the 'sex-blindness of traditional historiography'.[3] In addition, it rejects approaches to male experience as the norm or standard against which female experience is judged, refuting the implication that only women's lives are gendered on account of being variant. That men too are 'carriers' of gender has been firmly established, and the history of masculinity is now an essential sub-field of gender history.[4]

Imbalances of focus still remain, however. One of the most important recent developments to which the history of masculinity can contribute is an appreciation of the multifaceted nature of gender identities beyond the binary opposition of men and women. As Elsa Barkley Brown has argued, we need 'to recognize that all women do not have the same gender'.[5] Such an approach admits the plurality of women's experience rather than viewing women's lives as solely, or even always primarily, determined by gender.[6] Conversely, while the plurality of men's experience has always been assumed, the ways in which this variation was influenced, if not determined, by gender is still only beginning to be understood. To discern the full complexity of the workings of gender in any society we need to be as aware of the gender differences *within* each sex as of those *between* them. Gender means different things for different men and women, and different things during the different stages of the life course. This was particularly true of early modern England where stark hierarchies of age, social status, and marital status were deeply ingrained, interacting with gender hierarchies to produce a complex multidimensional map of

---

Feminist Studies, 3 (1976); Harry Brod (ed.), *The Making of Masculinities: The New Men's Studies* (London, 1987).

[2] e.g. E. Anthony Rotundo, *American Manhood: Transformations in Masculinity from the Revolution to the Modern Era* (New York, 1993); George L. Mosse, *The Image of Man: The Creation of Modern Masculinity* (Oxford, 1996); D. M. Hadley (ed.), *Masculinity in Medieval Europe* (Harlow, 1999); John Tosh, *A Man's Place: Masculinity and the Middle-Class Home in Victorian England* (London, 1999); Hans Turley, *Rum, Sodomy and the Lash: Piracy, Sexuality and Masculine Identity* (New York, 1999); Mathew Kuefler, *The Manly Eunuch: Masculinity, Gender Ambiguity, and Christian Ideology in Late Antiquity* (Chicago, 2001).

[3] Gisela Bock, 'Women's History and Gender History: Aspects of an International Debate', *Gender and History*, 1 (1989), 11.

[4] John Tosh, 'What should Historians do with Masculinity? Reflections on Nineteenth-Century Britain', *History Workshop Journal*, 38 (1994), 180.

[5] Elsa Barkley Brown, 'Polyrhythms and Improvization: Lessons for Women's History', *History Workshop Journal*, 31 (1991), 88. See also Nancy Jay, 'Gender and Dichotomy', *Feminist Studies*, 7 (1981); Mary Poovey, 'Feminism and Deconstruction', *Feminist Studies*, 14 (1988).

[6] For an excellent recent example, see Sara Mendelson and Patricia Crawford, *Women in Early Modern England* (Oxford, 1998).

power relations which by no means privileged all men or subordinated all women.

Such a movement away from a concept of gender defined exclusively in terms of a male–female dichotomy has considerable implications for our understanding of the workings of patriarchy in the early modern period, not least because it requires us to rethink definitions of patriarchy itself. This is by no means a new issue. The historicization of patriarchy has been central to the concerns of both women's history and gender history from their inception, although there has been perennial conflict over its meaning and usage.[7] For many feminist theorists and historians, the defining feature of patriarchy is men's systematic domination of women.[8] Such an approach does not allow for the generational dimension of patriarchy when it is more specifically defined as the government of society by male household heads, involving the subordination of younger men as well as women.[9] In early modern England, patriarchy was literally understood to signify rule by fathers. In one of the earliest dictionaries to be published, Robert Cawdrey defined a 'patriarcke' as the 'chiefe father'.[10] Patriarchy in this sense was central to late sixteenth- and early seventeenth-century political thought which approached kingship in terms of paternal rule, through analogy with the household. As a result, the household itself was viewed as a 'little commonwealth' and categorized as the primary unit of society, within which all individuals should be placed.[11] The maintenance of three basic hierarchies was deemed essential to an ordered household—and, by implication, an ordered society: ideally, husbands should govern wives; masters and mistresses their servants; and parents their children. Such a system privileged male householders, but also accorded married women authority over their servants and children, and subordinated those men as well as women excluded from householding status. While there is no doubt that males were the primary beneficiaries of this model, women were not wholly or unilaterally subordinated by it, and men's gains were by no means uniform.

An emphasis on the consequent multiplicity of gender identities need

---

[7] For a classic statement of the central arguments see Sheila Rowbotham, 'The Trouble with Patriarchy', and Sally Alexander and Barbara Taylor, 'In Defence of "Patriarchy"', both in Raphael Samuel (ed.), *People's History and Socialist Theory* (London, 1981). See also Carole Pateman, *The Sexual Contract* (Cambridge, 1988), ch. 2.

[8] Sylvia Walby, *Theorizing Patriarchy* (Oxford, 1990); Judith M. Bennett, 'Feminism and History', *Gender and History*, 1 (1989); Laura Gowing, *Domestic Dangers: Women, Words, and Sex in Early Modern London* (Oxford, 1996), 4–5.   [9] Walby, *Theorizing Patriarchy*, 19–21.

[10] Robert Cawdrey, *A Table Alphabeticall of English Wordes*, 4th edn. (London, 1617), sig. G3ᵛ.

[11] Gordon J. Schochet, *Patriarchalism in Political Thought: The Authoritarian Family and Political Speculation and Attitudes Especially in Seventeenth-Century England* (Oxford, 1975); Susan Dwyer Amussen, *An Ordered Society: Gender and Class in Early Modern England* (Oxford, 1988), ch. 2.

not sacrifice analysis of relations of power.[12] Both feminist and early modern definitions of patriarchy are necessary if we are to comprehend the complex distribution of authority both between and within the sexes and the ways in which this was mediated by gender. To understand the social practice of patriarchy in early modern England, we need to be far more aware of precisely *which* men stood to gain, *which* women stood to lose, and in *which* contexts. Conversely, we need to identify instances both when women benefited from, and men were barred access to, patriarchal privileges. Finally, it is important to ask whether gender was ever eclipsed by other determinants of status and identity in ways which rendered it temporarily irrelevant.

Recent work on early modern women has made considerable inroads in this respect, looking beyond the ways in which women were victims of patriarchal oppression, and the many ways in which they found agency through active resistance to it, in order to demonstrate how many women themselves exercised, and even benefited from, patriarchal authority in its early modern sense. Demographic reality meant that many women headed households (for example 16 per cent of those listed in the Ealing census of 1599) and so, to a certain extent, occupied patriarchal positions.[13] However, women did not need to act as 'honorary men' to exercise authority. This was particularly true, for example, of the aged wives who were more readily employable than their husbands,[14] or of the respectable matrons and midwives who policed the bodies of unmarried women for signs of illegitimate pregnancy, deriving particular authority from 'the gulf' identified by Laura Gowing between 'married and single, orderly and disorderly, matrons and virgins'.[15] While women's authority in these circumstances may have carried less overall cultural weight than that wielded by the many men in positions of patriarchal privilege, it is

---

[12] For an extreme statement of such concerns, see Joan Hoff, 'Gender as a Postmodern Category of Paralysis', *Women's History Review*, 3 (1994). Cf. Joan Scott, 'Gender: A Useful Category of Historical Analysis', *American Historical Review*, 91 (1986).

[13] K. J. Allison, 'An Elizabethan Village "Census"', *Bulletin of the Institute of Historical Research*, 36 (1963).

[14] Margaret Pelling, 'Old Age, Poverty and Disability in Early Modern Norwich: Work, Remarriage and Other Expedients', and 'Older Women: Household, Caring and Other Occupations in the Late Sixteenth-Century Town', both in ead., *The Common Lot: Sickness, Medical Occupations and the Urban Poor in Early Modern England* (London, 1998); ead., 'Who Most Needs to Marry? Ageing and Inequality among Women and Men in Early Modern Norwich', in Lynn Botelho and Pat Thane (eds.), *Women and Ageing in British Society since 1500* (Harlow, 2001).

[15] Laura Gowing, 'Ordering the Body: Illegitimacy and Female Authority in Seventeenth-Century England', in Michael J. Braddick and John Walter (eds.), *Negotiating Power in Early Modern Society: Order, Hierarchy and Subordination in Britain and Ireland* (Cambridge, 2001), 61. See also ead., 'The Haunting of Susan Lay: Servants and Mistresses in Seventeenth-Century England', *Gender and History*, 14 (2002); Ulinka Rublack, 'The Public Body: Policing Abortion in Early Modern

Introduction 5

possible that these context-related differences between women were as important in determining women's experiences and access to authority as the differences between the sexes.

The differences between men were similarly stark, along many of the same lines. However, their implications have been less well explored by gender historians of the early modern period, who have primarily approached masculinity as a product of relations between men and women.[16] The ground-breaking work of the sociologist R. W. Connell has called for a recognition that 'at any given time, one form of masculinity rather than others is culturally exalted', alerting us to the fact that many variant masculinities existed (and exist) in tension with each other. Consequently men, like women, can be subordinated and marginalized by 'hegemonic' gender constructions which deliver the 'patriarchal dividend' only to the complicit.[17] As John Tosh has emphasized, masculinity 'makes socially crippling distinctions not only between men and women, but between different categories of men—distinctions which have to be maintained by force, as well as validated through cultural means'.[18] However, early modern historians have tended to focus less on the multiplicity of masculinities suggested by such arguments than on the numerous ways in which men too suffered from the demands of patriarchal dictates, even when occupying positions of patriarchal privilege. The early modern period as a consequence has been characterized as one abounding with anxious patriarchs: men dogged by fears that they would fail to achieve patriarchal expectations that were, moreover, arguably impossible.[19]

Germany', in Lynn Abrams and Elizabeth Harvey (eds.), *Gender Relations in German History: Power, Agency and Experience from the Sixteenth to the Twentieth Century* (London, 1996); Linda Pollock, 'Childbearing and Female Bonding in Early Modern England', *Social History*, 22 (1997); ead., 'Rethinking Patriarchy and the Family in Seventeenth-Century England', *Journal of Family History*, 23 (1998). Cf. Pamela Sharpe, 'Dealing with Love: The Ambiguous Independence of the Single Woman in Early Modern England', *Gender and History*, 11 (1999).

[16] Anthony Fletcher, *Gender, Sex and Subordination in England 1500–1800* (London, 1995); Elizabeth A. Foyster, *Manhood in Early Modern England: Honour, Sex and Marriage* (Harlow, 1999). Such an approach is also generally implicit in histories of early modern women.

[17] R. W. Connell, *Masculinities* (Cambridge, 1995), 77–81. See also ead., *Gender and Power: Society, the Person and Sexual Politics* (Cambridge, 1987), 183–8.

[18] Tosh, 'What should Historians do with Masculinity?', 192.

[19] David Underdown, 'The Taming of the Scold: The Enforcement of Patriarchal Authority in Early Modern England', in Anthony Fletcher and John Stevenson (eds.), *Order and Disorder in Early Modern England* (Cambridge, 1985); Katharine Hodgkin, 'Thomas Wythorne and the Problem of Mastery', *History Workshop Journal*, 29 (1990); Anthony Fletcher, 'Men's Dilemma: The Future of Patriarchy in England, 1560–1660', *Transactions of the Royal Historical Society*, 6th ser. 4 (1994); Alan Bray, 'To be a Man in Early Modern Society: The Curious Case of Michael Wigglesworth', *History Workshop Journal*, 41 (1996); Mark Breitenberg, *Anxious Masculinity in Early Modern England* (Cambridge, 1996); Foyster, *Manhood in Early Modern England*.

While it would be wrong to suggest that early modern men were never anxious about proving or asserting their manhood, there is nonetheless a danger of assuming that there were only two options for early modern men: they either achieved manhood in the normative—or hegemonic—mode as dominant patriarchs (in terms of effectively managing a household through controlling themselves and their subordinates) or they failed in this endeavour. Such arguments are often accompanied by two unsettling implications. The first is that men who failed to achieve the dictates of patriarchal manhood were themselves oppressed by patriarchal ideology. At extremes, the men in such accounts are represented as competing with women for victimhood at the hands of patriarchy. Kenneth Lockridge, for example, has argued that even the most consummate patriarchs in early New England suffered acutely from the demands of domestic patriarchy, claiming that 'patriarchy could be a prison for the patriarchs as well as for their women'.[20] The second and related assumption is that men who failed to live up to normative or patriarchal ideals of manhood consequently somehow failed to be men.

The problem with such approaches is that they tend to equate manhood with patriarchy, rendering it impossible to appreciate the full range of male responses to patriarchal imperatives. The men who failed to be patriarchs, either because they did not live up to the expectations of the patriarchal position they occupied (such as the archetypal lazy, thriftless, drunken, wife-beating householder), or because they did not have access to patriarchal manhood (such as the journeyman who never moved beyond dependence on wage labour), nonetheless found plenty of ways in which to assert their manhood. Such men, like unruly women, could be 'domestic dangers', but that did not stop them being men; instead they pursued different codes of manhood which often existed in tension with patriarchal imperatives. It is necessary, therefore, to open up the potential gaps, and tensions, between patriarchy and different varieties of manhood, rather than simply colluding with the normative evaluative schemes of early modern social commentators. While relations between the sexes were a primary site for its definition, manhood was often most resonantly worked out between men. Exploring such contests affords insight into the ways in which meanings of manhood (patriarchal and otherwise) were socially embedded, and, as this book will suggest, increasingly socially specific over the course of the early modern period.

Issues of periodization pose particular difficulties for gender

---

[20] Kenneth A. Lockridge, *On the Sources of Patriarchal Rage: The Commonplace Books of William Byrd and Thomas Jefferson and the Gendering of Power in the Eighteenth Century* (New York, 1992), 90.

historians.²¹ It is difficult both to scrutinize the complex workings of gender in early modern society and to chart more general currents of long-term change. The period between 1560 and 1640 is the main focus here, for both practical and historiographical reasons. A wider timeframe would have precluded a sufficiently detailed survey of a broad range of material pertaining to the construction of varied meanings of manhood. In addition, 1560 to 1640 was a time of rapid, and often unsettling, demographic and economic change which had a profound impact on social—and, as it will be argued here, gender—relations.²² While 1640 was by no means the end point to these changes, they were most acute in the period between 1560 and 1640 when access to resources was fundamentally realigned and the tenor of social relations began to be redrawn. Although largely contained within the chronological parameters of 1560 and 1640, therefore, the details of this study are nonetheless suggestive of much longer-term patterns of change, in which the distribution of patriarchal dividends became increasingly related to distinctions of social position rather than divisions of age or marital status.

What follows comprises two parts, derived from two main bodies of source material. Part I offers a rereading of some of the didactic literature—such as domestic conduct books, guides to health, sermons, and father–son advice—that has been the starting point for so much of the period's gender analysis. Gender constructions were central to the ways in which early modern moral, political, and social commentary made sense of things. Whether explicitly discussed (for example in defences of women or debates over cross-dressing) or whether implicitly suggested by the employment of gender metaphors to discuss wider issues, the different traits expected of women and men provided constant points of reference in prescriptive discourse.²³ While ideals of womanhood contained in such sources have been closely analysed, the ways in which normative codes of manhood were constructed warrant further scrutiny. Despite being littered with words referring to masculinity (such as 'mannish', 'manly', 'masculine') and its antitheses (such as 'womanish', and

---

²¹ Amanda Vickery, 'Golden Age to Separate Spheres? A Review of the Categories and Chronology of English Women's History', *Historical Journal*, 36 (1993).

²² The now classic account is Keith Wrightson, *English Society, 1580–1680* (London, 1982).

²³ For explicit debates, particularly concerning women, see Suzanne W. Hull, *Chaste, Silent and Obedient: English Books for Women, 1475–1640* (San Marino, Calif., 1982); Linda Woodbridge, *Women and the English Renaissance: Literature and the Nature of Womankind, 1540–1620* (Brighton, 1984); Katherine Usher Henderson and Barbara F. McManus, *Half Humankind: Contexts and Texts of the Controversy about Women in England, 1540–1640* (Urbana, Ill., 1985). For gender as a signifier of relationships of power in political debate, see Scott, 'Gender: A Useful Category'; Moira Gatens, *Imaginary Bodies: Ethics, Power and Corporeality* (London, 1996), ch. 2.

'effeminate'), concepts of manhood in advice books rarely received any explicit definition. The prescriptive literature of this period was largely written by and for a comparatively elite group of men, and, unless stated otherwise, it was generally assumed by authors that the reader was male and reasonably well educated.[24] As a result, the bulk of references to manhood and their accompanying associations remained implicit, suggesting shared assumptions between author and reader that are often difficult to discern, and that moreover we should not assume were universally held. Even within the comparatively narrow context of prescriptive literature, manhood was associated with a broad array of attributes, the varied selection of which was shaped by the agenda of different authors, with considerable diversity of emphasis even between works by the same author.[25] Although such works generally laboured to define manhood in patriarchal terms, its meanings were manipulated to serve a range of interests, and prescriptive codes were by no means uniform.

Common themes were undoubtedly present, however. Normative manhood was primarily defined through comparison with a broad range of deviant 'others'. The starkest definitions were usually a product of male/female comparisons, and unsurprisingly these bald assertions of a hierarchy which placed men above women have received the most attention from gender historians. Such formulae claimed reason and strength as the defining attributes of manhood and classed women as comparatively weak and unstable.[26] This basic dichotomy was widely invoked to justify male superiority and to command female obedience. Unlike ideals of femininity, however, most constructions of manhood emerged from comparisons along axes of difference besides gender, and normative meanings were substantially modified, and sometimes considerably undermined, through distinctions drawn between an assortment of

---

[24] e.g. William Guild, *A Yong Mans Inquisition, or Triall. Whereby All Young Men (as of All Ages) may Know how to Redresse and Direct their Waies, According to Gods Word* (London, 1608). Some works which might be expected to have appealed to a unisex audience were sometimes nonetheless exclusively directed to men, such as Alexander Niccholes, *A Discourse of Marriage and Wiving* (London, 1615), which he addressed to 'the Youth and Batchelary of England, hote blouds at high Revels', and *A Discourse of the Married and Single Life. Wherein, by Discovering the Misery of the One, is Plainely Declared the Felicity of the Other* (London, 1621), the preface of which was addressed to 'the Masculine Reader', sig. A3. See also Ann Rosalind Jones, 'Nets and Bridles: Early Modern Conduct Books and Sixteenth-Century Women's Lyrics', in Nancy Armstrong and Leonard Tennenhouse (eds.), *The Ideology of Conduct: Essays on Literature and the History of Sexuality* (New York, 1987).

[25] Cf., e.g., William Gouge, *Of Domesticall Duties* (London, 1622) and id., *The Dignity of Chivalry; Set Forth in a Sermon Preached before the Artillery Company of London* (London, 1626).

[26] Foyster, *Manhood in Early Modern England*, ch. 2; Mendelson and Crawford, *Women in Early Modern England*, ch. 1.

different male stereotypes. Although male/female comparisons implied that patriarchal manhood (in its feminist sense of male superiority over women) was extended to all men, they were extensively qualified by comparisons between men which suggested that many were excluded from its benefits. Despite differences of emphasis, conduct writers identified three principal gateways to patriarchal privilege: age, marital status, and, more obliquely, social status.

Apart from gender, age was the most directly acknowledged difference to inform constructions of normative manhood. Besides being a qualitative set of attributes, manhood was approached in advice literature as a distinct stage in the life cycle. Chapter 1 explores the ways in which accounts of the ages of man placed 'man's age'—or 'man's estate'—at the summit of the life course and defined manhood in relation to youth and old age. Parenting manuals, father–son advice, sermons, and tracts on ageing approached manhood as an ideal to which young men should aspire and from which old men would decay. Manhood was thereby portrayed as the golden mean of existence, although it was also deemed a fleeting phase. Theoretically limited to a mere ten or twenty years of the life cycle it was, as a consequence, restricted to a minority of men at any one time. Chapter 2 focuses on medical representations of manhood which were founded upon a broader range of distinctions between men. Guides to health similarly excluded younger and older men from the bodily equilibrium ideally expected of manhood, but they also appear to have subtly mapped temperamental deviations from the norm onto contours of social status. Emphasizing just how difficult it was to achieve the moderation expected of manhood, such works tended to elide the temperate ideal with concepts of civility and virtue which were implicitly associated with elites. Chapter 3 surveys the domestic conduct literature and advice on marriage in order to re-examine the ways in which manhood was defined along the axis of gender. Although stark male–female dichotomies were frequently invoked to uphold assertions of male superiority (particularly in discussions of the duties of wives), they were considerably qualified by discussions of husbands' duties which primarily emphasized mutuality and the limits of their authority. Normative models of manhood in domestic advice were also drawn from comparing two further sets of male stereotype: the unmarried and the married, and the good and the bad husband, with conduct writers often conceding that bad husbands were more prevalent than good.

Despite their different emphases, all these works sought to define manhood in broadly patriarchal terms of discretion, reason, moderation, self-sufficiency, strength, self-control, and honest respectability. More importantly, they all expressed considerable concern about the ubiquity of male tendencies antithetical to the ordered, rational ideal. At the heart of these representations of manhood lay misgivings that, far from being self-contained exemplars, many men constantly worked against the patriarchal goals of order and control. Advice literature therefore conveyed both assurance and anxiety. The assured tone stemmed from the supposition of men's general capacity for rational, self-governed action superior to that of women which was the foundation for the normative concepts of manhood propagated by these authors. Yet this was overlaid by a dirge of concern about men's failure to live up to patriarchal ideals, which was either attributed to fundamental flaws in men's nature, or to the inadequacies of particular groups of men on the grounds of their age, marital status and, more remotely, social status. While maleness as cultural category was automatically celebrated in terms of superiority, men as a group of people were far less confidently endorsed.

Such anxieties have been ascribed to a general set of male fears about both attaining manliness and sustaining the patriarchal order, particularly through controlling women.[27] As a result the implications of such commentary for relations between men themselves have remained comparatively neglected in preference for consideration of men's subjective experience of patriarchal norms. There is no doubt that didactic literature both drew upon and informed a highly powerful language of social description that was suffused with patriarchal logic. Yet, to presuppose that all men somehow measured their manliness according to a commonly accepted patriarchal gauge risks simply replicating, rather than questioning, the conduct writers' perspective. Their greatest fear appears not to have been that men were failing to be men *per se*, but that they were failing to be men *on the right terms*. Advice writers' anxiety stemmed less from the presence or absence of manliness than from concerns about the terms of manhood itself and the degree to which they coincided with the patriarchal agenda for an ordered society. Just as exhortations to chastity, silence, and obedience for women were primarily prescriptive, so the attributes expected of men were more a rhetorical device than straightforwardly illustrative of early modern manhood. Rather than simply describing commonly held expectations of manhood and womanhood, conduct writers attempted to fix their meanings in patriarchal terms and to coach men as well as women in their corresponding duties.

The degree of contest over meanings of manhood is therefore indirectly revealed by prescriptive attempts to secure them. Both the ways

[27] Fletcher, 'Men's Dilemma'; id., *Gender, Sex and Subordination*; Foyster, *Manhood in Early Modern England*. See also Coppélia Kahn, *Man's Estate: Masculine Identity in Shakespeare* (Berkeley, 1981).

in which man's nature was deemed to undermine the normative ideal and the ways in which certain types of men were described as deviating from it are illustrative of fissures in concepts of manhood and of limits to the authority of patriarchal norms. Part II traces such fissures further by investigating the ways in which different men variously asserted, maintained, and defended their manhood in the course of routine social practice. It is not intended as an investigation of 'reality' to be measured against the ideals outlined in advice books, but is designed to provide a broader perspective on the complexity of early modern meanings of manhood and their relation to patriarchy. Already plagued by dualism, the 'ideal/reality' paradigm is one more dichotomy that gender history can well afford to lose.[28] The advice literature discussed in Part I was a product of reality, rather than somehow separate from and comparable with it. Besides ascribing greater influence and coherence to normative codes than is warranted, attempts to compare them with 'reality' also neglect what Konstantin Dierks has usefully identified as the 'prescriptive force of social practice'.[29] Especially given their own inherent contradictions, conduct books merely articulated strands of identity which might be selectively invoked rather than a comprehensive set of morals for internalization.[30] Men primarily sought validation of their manhood from each other, and the responses of peer groups, superiors, and subordinates were arguably far more influential than the paper images constructed by moralists, however much they chimed or clashed with particular contexts and circumstances.

Gender identities in early modern England were neither static nor given, but the product of social interaction. Part II is therefore concerned with the social processes which conferred, contested, or diminished manhood in its varied meanings. The range of discernible male identities were regularly associated with patriarchal notions of manhood, either as claims to patriarchal authority, or as forms of explicit resistance to its dictates. Yet there is also more fragmented evidence of alternative codes of manhood that were not primarily defined in relation to patriarchal principles, but were instead shaped by expedience and social context. While the contingency of meanings of manhood (and the potential for overlap between

---

[28] Gisela Bock, 'Challenging Dichotomies: Perspectives on Women's History', in Karen Offen, Ruth Roach Pierson, and Jane Rendall (eds.), *Writing Women's History: International Perspectives* (Basingstoke, 1991).

[29] Konstantin Dierks, 'The Social Practice of Letter Writing in America, 1750–1800', unpublished paper, presented to the Graduate Seminar in History 1680–1815, University of Oxford, Mar. 1999. I am grateful to the author for his permission to cite it here.

[30] Gowing, *Domestic Dangers*, 1–12.

them) should not be neglected, early modern articulations of masculinity can nonetheless be broadly categorized as patriarchal, anti-patriarchal (in terms of deliberate counter-codes), or as loosely configured alternatives.

The social practice of manhood in its varied forms is pieced together primarily from court records, ranging in scope from the regulatory activities of London livery companies, quarter sessions, and borough courts, to the disputes brought before ecclesiastical courts, the university courts, and the Court of Exchequer. Although they are not straightforwardly representative of everyday life, court records nonetheless provide the broadest access to a wide range of historical actors, especially given the intensity of litigation (petty, criminal, and civil) in England between 1560 and 1640. It is clearly important to be alert to the ways in which such records were shaped by jurisdictional and procedural demands; depositions (the formal account of witnesses' statements) in particular principally supply evidence of the ways in which stories were narrated in the context of a courtroom rather than direct statements of fact or fixed values.[31] Yet the ideals and identities invoked by men and women in court are nonetheless suggestive, and depositions also contain a wealth of incidental detail pertaining to routine existence, thus providing the closest available point of contact with the lived experience of many early modern English men and women whose voices would not otherwise have entered the historical record.[32]

At the heart of Part II lies a case study of Cambridge, primarily derived from the court records of the university. These neglected sources are extraordinarily rich owing to the extent of the university's jurisdiction in Cambridge and to the civil law procedure employed by its courts.[33] By the later sixteenth century the university's jurisdiction was at its broadest, stretching far beyond its own members into the moral, commercial, and criminal lives of many townspeople. In addition to upholding its regulatory authority over the market and various petty crimes, the university was entitled to hear all personal pleas (except felony or mayhem, and in suits involving landed property) brought by or against its members and its servants. The cases heard by the university courts therefore spanned a wide cross-section of business that elsewhere would have been separately administered by several different courts. In addition, because, like church

[31] Natalie Zemon Davis, *Fiction in the Archives: Pardon Tales and their Tellers in Sixteenth-Century France* (Cambridge, 1988); Gowing, *Domestic Dangers*, chs. 2, 7.
[32] Malcolm Gaskill, *Crime and Mentalities in Early Modern England* (Cambridge, 2000), ch. 1.
[33] For a detailed account of the university's jurisdiction, the legal procedures it employed, and levels of litigation see Alexandra Shepard, 'Legal Learning and the Cambridge University Courts, c.1560–1640', *Journal of Legal History*, 19 (1998); ead., 'Litigation and Locality: The Cambridge University Courts, 1560–1640', *Urban History* (forthcoming).

courts, they employed civil law procedure, cases were tried on the basis of written rather than oral evidence. This means that depositions were generated not only in defamation and testamentary disputes (elsewhere similarly produced by church courts) but also in cases of debt and assault (elsewhere heard orally—and thus never recorded—in borough courts and quarter sessions). Witnesses' statements therefore provide unusually rich detail of a broad range of disputes all heard within a single legal setting. From the 1580s the vice-chancellor and his commissary, each holding weekly sessions, were handling hundreds of cases every year. The bulk were suits of debt or injury brought by or against Cambridge inhabitants who were in some way (often tenuously) connected to the university. By the 1630s, biennial levels of one case per household are not implausible. Although households were not evenly represented, plaintiffs were nonetheless drawn from a broad social spectrum, in proportions which, apart from the under-representation of labourers, roughly matched the overall occupational structure of the town.[34]

The extent to which any case study is representative is an inherent problem, but it is perhaps an especially pressing issue with Cambridge. The presence of the university generated structural and social peculiarities which were unmatched except in Oxford and parts of London. A disproportionate number of comparatively elite young men created an abnormally top-heavy social structure, a greater-than-usual demographic preponderance of youths, and a distorted sex-ratio. University men (except heads of colleges) were expected to be celibate, and they lived in an almost exclusively male world. Furthermore, it could be argued that their presence and behaviour in the town, particularly in regard to the university's extensive powers, generated levels of conflict unparalleled in degree or kind. While all of this might seem to offset the merits of the university's exceptionally rich archive, Cambridge's peculiarities are actually extremely informative. By comparing the concerns of town and gown brought before the university courts, it is possible to discern ways in which meanings of manhood were linked to differences of age

[34] Of 716 cases entered in the act books of the vice-chancellor's and commissary's courts between 1632 and 1634, roughly 10% were brought by university members. If the estimated population of the town in the early 1630s (7,750) is divided by Nigel Goose's estimate of the average household size in Cambridge (4.13), and the number of cases entered in the act books excluding 10% is divided by this figure, the result is 0.33. The university's jurisdiction extended over roughly one-third of the households in Cambridge, suggesting biennial levels of one case per household. In this sample, approximately 450 households were involved in initiating the 716 suits. For population figures in Cambridge see Nigel Goose, 'Household Size and Structure in Early-Stuart Cambridge', *Social History*, 5 (1980), 353, 363. For comparable levels of litigation in borough courts, see Craig Muldrew, *The Economy of Obligation: The Culture of Credit and Social Relations in Early Modern England* (Basingstoke, 1998), 216–42.

and social status. The presence of scholars amongst litigants and witnesses provides a highly visible status differential which, when systematically traced, reveals how different notions of manhood both competed and overlapped according to context. In addition, the importance of the universities in early modern England should not be overlooked. Expanding rapidly in the late sixteenth and early seventeenth centuries they became the training ground of the country's political and clerical elite, whose consequent bearing and attitudes were carried far beyond the city limits of Oxford and Cambridge.[35] Finally, the state had a vested interest in the universities and their products. Directives from the Crown treated the universities as 'nurseries to bringe up youthe in the knowledge and feare of God and in all manner of good learnynge and vertuous educacion ... where by the state and common wealthe maie receive hereafter greate good'.[36] The universities were thus treated as bastions of idealized manhood whose orderly government held national significance.

Even though they were not always typical, the experiences of university men cannot therefore be written off as insignificant. They should also not be allowed to obscure the many ways in which Cambridge was similar to other early modern urban communities. Categorized as a 'second-rank' town it was an important centre of trade situated at the meeting point of major highways and served by the river Cam.[37] Linked to London, King's Lynn, York, Coventry, Newmarket, and Huntingdon, and with a favourable agricultural hinterland, it was a regional centre for the exchange of grain, fish, coal, hogs, and horses. It also hosted two important annual fairs: Barnwell Fair, which drew traders from a regional level, and Sturbridge Fair, which was of national significance. The late sixteenth and early seventeenth centuries were a period of expansion for Cambridge, as elsewhere in England. Between the 1560s and 1620s

[35] Mark H. Curtis, *Oxford and Cambridge in Transition, 1588–1642* (Oxford, 1959); Lawrence Stone, 'The Educational Revolution in England, 1560–1640', *Past and Present*, 28 (1964); id. (ed.), *The University in Society*, 2 vols. (Princeton, 1974), vol. i, ch. 1. For the social status of students during this period of expansion see Joan Simon, 'The Social Origins of Cambridge Students, 1603–1640', *Past and Present*, 26 (1963); David Cressy, 'Education and Literacy in London and East Anglia 1580–1700', unpublished Ph.D. thesis (Cambridge, 1972), ch. 7. For subsequent careers, see John Venn and J. A. Venn, *Alumni Cantabrigienses: A Biographical List of All Known Students, Graduates and Holders of Office at the University of Cambridge, from the Earliest Times to 1900*, 4 vols. (Cambridge, 1922–54).

[36] Privy Council to the University of Cambridge, 29 July 1593, in *Records of Early English Drama: Cambridge*, ed. Alan H. Nelson, 2 vols. (Toronto, 1989), i. 348. See also Hugh Kearney, *Scholars and Gentlemen: Universities and Society in Pre-industrial Britain, 1500–1700* (London, 1970).

[37] Goose, 'Household Size and Structure', 351, with reference to the classification of towns outlined in Peter Clark and Paul Slack, *English Towns in Transition 1500–1700* (Oxford, 1976), 25–32.

Introduction

the town's population roughly trebled, largely as a consequence of rapid immigration, which generated acute concerns about overcrowding, poverty, and plague typical of this period.[38] Cambridge should not therefore be regarded as fundamentally different or cut-off from the rest of early modern England: it shared similar economic and social circumstances with other provincial towns, and its place within extensive trading networks permitted its citizens broader—sometimes national—horizons.

Many of the resultant preoccupations of Cambridge inhabitants were represented in the litigation they brought to the university courts. The majority of litigation heard by the vice-chancellor and commissary involved townsmen and women who were disproportionately represented (in comparison to university members) amongst the large numbers of litigants resorting to the university courts for relatively cheap and speedy justice.[39] Admittedly, some of these cases were born of tensions between town and gown, although the nature and extent of town–gown conflict has been both oversimplified and exaggerated, and was secondary to most disputes.[40] The vast majority of actions brought before the university involved petty wranglings between townspeople typical of day-to-day community relations that would have been clearly recognizable to men and women throughout England.[41] As corroboration, evidence from a broad geographical spread and a wide range of different courts has been consulted and is included alongside the Cambridge case study in order to test its findings and to set them into wider relief. Nonetheless, the Cambridge material occupies the foreground, since it affords the sort of rich and intricate detail necessary to reconstruct the mundane processes of asserting identity within a local context.

The meanings of manhood implicit in social practice were enormously

---

[38] M. C. Siraut, 'Some Aspects of the Economic and Social History of Cambridge under Elizabeth I', unpublished M.Litt. thesis (Cambridge, 1978); Nigel Goose, 'Economic and Social Aspects of Provincial Towns: A Comparative Study of Cambridge, Colchester and Reading, c.1500–1700', unpublished Ph.D. thesis (Cambridge, 1984); id., 'Household Size and Structure'.

[39] University members were involved in 16.7% of cases heard by the university courts between 1580 and 1640, while the university comprised roughly one-third of the total population of Cambridge. For a precise breakdown of the distribution of suits, see Shepard, 'Litigation and Locality'.

[40] Rowland Parker, *Town and Gown: The 700 Years' War in Cambridge* (Cambridge, 1983). Cf. Alexandra Shepard, 'Contesting Communities? "Town" and "Gown" in Cambridge, c.1560–1640', in Alexandra Shepard and Phil Withington (eds.), *Communities in Early Modern England: Networks, Place, Rhetoric* (Manchester, 2000).

[41] For general accounts of comparable litigation in early modern England see, e.g., J. A. Sharpe, '"Such Disagreement betwyx Neighbours": Litigation and Human Relations in Early Modern England', in John Bossy (ed.), *Disputes and Settlements: Law and Human Relations in the West* (Cambridge, 1983); Martin Ingram, *Church Courts, Sex and Marriage in England, 1570–1640* (Cambridge, 1987); Muldrew, *The Economy of Obligation*.

varied, and contingent upon age, status, and context in ways which often competed with each other and clashed with patriarchal expectations of order. The most explicit counter-codes of manhood were expressed in the rites of youthful misrule. Chapter 4 examines the ways in which young men contested patriarchal notions of manhood rooted in thrift, moderation, and self-control with a culture of excess. Youthful rioting, drinking, gambling, and sexual prowess was largely performed for and validated by their peers, and this chapter will focus on the fraternal bonds which facilitated young men's inversions of patriarchal norms. While these links were sufficiently important to overcome distinctions of social status, they were also brittle and fleeting because of fears surrounding male intimacy. An element of competition was therefore present between men even at this most homosocial phase of the life course. Context-related tensions between codes of manhood that were more incidental, but no less complex, are suggested by the broader patterns of male violence explored in Chapter 5. Violence was both a tool for enforcing the patriarchal imperatives of household and social order and one of the primary means of undermining them, either by lending weight to counter-codes of manhood, or, more commonly, featuring in assertions of manhood claimed independently of (and without reference to) a patriarchal agenda. As a form of regulation and correction, as a demonstration of male strength and authority, and as a method of territorial demarcation, violence conferred manhood in ways which both bolstered and countered patriarchal codes of order and which also served alternative codes of manhood according to the status and context of those involved.

Chapters 6 and 7 explore the ways in which men asserted and disputed honesty, credit, and worth in the course of slander and debt litigation. While the insults alleged in defamation suits suggest that reputation was more multifaceted for men than for women, there was nonetheless a considerable degree of overlap in their respective concerns, with the substance of suits depending on age and status as well as gender. It is also clear that male litigants were less concerned with proving their honesty either in purely sexual or economic terms than with disputing their social standing through various points of comparison with other men. Evidence from debt litigation confirms the extent to which male status was competitively gauged between men. Patriarchal imperatives of male provision and self-sufficient mastery were regularly invoked, suggesting that appraisals of manhood rooted in economic independence, and heading and maintaining a household, were commonplace. However, evidence of women and children's extensive (and sometimes primary) contributions to the household economy suggests that patriarchal manhood in these terms was a privilege which many men could not afford, if not a chimera. In addition, from the later sixteenth century, increasing numbers of men and women were either excluded from householding positions or chose to adopt alternative family strategies. For these men and women patriarchal behavioural codes were irrelevant, except as the substance of social critiques levelled by their 'betters', suggesting the emergence of deepening fissures between concepts of manhood along class lines.

The final chapter returns to questions of age. Old age often compounded class distinctions, and, in contrast with youth, it was more likely to be a period of gender convergence than a leveller of social status. The experiences of old men, and their continued access either to patriarchal dividends or to competing codes of manhood, varied considerably according to means and physical capacity. There is considerable evidence of older men continuing to hold office, and to support themselves and their households, into very advanced years. Others pursued alternative survival strategies in common with younger men of limited means. Many, however, resumed positions as dependants, either through retirement arrangements with kin, or by resorting to charity and poor relief, limiting, if not precluding, access to the autonomy commonly associated with manhood.

There was, then, enormous variation in men's experiences and assertions of male identity. This book seeks to assess the associated meanings of manhood in early modern England and their complex relationship with patriarchy. It pursues a multi-relational model of gender identities that goes beyond the male–female dichotomy and which does not assume that men failed to achieve manhood if they did not reap the full patriarchal dividend. This enables a fuller exploration of the ways in which gender interacted with other determinants of status to shape the social distribution of power. While there is no denying that men were the primary beneficiaries of patriarchal dictates, many also claimed manhood in ways which actively resisted, indirectly undermined, or simply ignored them. The consequent disparities between meanings of manhood were most clearly linked to variables of age and marital and social status, although they were also profoundly contingent on context and therefore often contradictory. Tracing such links affords a fuller assessment of the impact of patriarchy in early modern England, as well as the considerable scope for manoeuvre beyond its dictates. And by identifying the variations in meanings of manhood, and their relation to the uneven distribution of patriarchal dividends, it becomes possible to construct a more sophisticated model of early modern social change which takes account of the variations within, as well as between, the sexes.

PART I

Modelling Manhood

I
The Constant Age

> The fift age is virile or manly, and the constant media, betweene flourishing young age and old age; Yet doth it not so participate of either, as that it is intemperate or infected thereby.[1]

MEANINGS of manhood in early modern England were as dependent on perceptions of difference between men themselves as between men and women. Solely focusing on gender differences risks neglecting the ways in which gender interacted with the many other status distinctions operating in early modern England. One of the most important of these differences was age. Manhood was defined as a distinct phase in the life course, besides being more generally associated in prescriptive texts with an array of attributes tending to virtuous and ordered conduct. Distinguishing manhood or 'man's age' from both youth and old age was a frequently deployed device in the construction of normative definitions of manhood in a wide range of advice literature and social commentary. The importance of age in defining and regulating access to manhood was far more readily admitted by conduct writers than differentials of social status, and it provides a valuable starting point for the examination of prescriptive constructions of patriarchal manhood and the ways in which they hinged upon distinctions between men that denied many access to its benefits.

There was no clear corpus of texts discussing age in early modern England, which instead featured as a common theme across a range of genres. Youth and old age were often represented as paradigmatic of the human condition in relation to questions of sin, virtue, and morality, as well as being treated more specifically as particular phases of the life course. This chapter therefore includes material from a variety of works, although it focuses principally on direct discussions of age rather than the more abstract formulations of moral commentary. Youth, and the problems associated with it, received lengthy attention in domestic

---

[1] Tobias Whitaker, *The Tree of Humane Life; or, The Bloud of the Grape. Proving the Possibilitie of Maintaining Humane Life by the Use of Wine* (London, 1638), 44.

advice literature and parenting manuals. Many of these were penned by puritan clergy, although the most frequently reprinted parenting guide of the period was Plutarch's *De Educatione Puerorum*, published in several Latin editions and in two English translations (one of which was by Sir Thomas Elyot). The bulk of printed advice relating to youth, however, was directed towards young men themselves rather than to their parents. While some authors used entertaining ditties and cautionary tales to convey their lessons, such as William Averell's *A Dyall for Dainty Darlings* (1584) or Francis Lenton's *The Young Gallants Whirligigg* (1629), the majority of such texts were more overtly didactic and were aimed primarily at the privileged ranks of young gentlemen. Richard Brathwait, for example, began *The English Gentleman* (1630) with a section entitled 'Youth', and James Cleland's intended audience was evident from the title of his tract, *The Instruction of a Young Noble-Man* (1607). From the beginning of the seventeenth century, an increasingly popular vehicle for the instruction of elite young men was father–son advice, much of which was inspired by James I's precepts penned for his son, Prince Henry, which were produced in Welsh, Latin, and Swedish as well as in numerous English editions.[2] Similarly in demand was *Sir Walter Raleighs Instructions to his Sonne and to Posterity*, which went through eight editions in the four years after its initial publication in 1632. While such works were often more optimistic about the promise of youth than the jeremiads issued by godly divines, they nonetheless drew a sharp distinction between youth and manhood, and overwhelmingly portrayed the latter rather than the former as the pinnacle of the life course.

Discussions of old age, while not as prevalent as works directly addressing youth, contained just as vivid imagery and were similarly reliant on comparisons with both youth and manhood. Contrasting metaphors of old age as either a reward for godliness or the punishment of sin sometimes appeared in funeral sermons, and they were also central to direct debates on the relative merits of old age versus youth.[3] Old age (as well as youth and manhood) was also defined chronologically and temperamentally in medical works, which will be discussed more fully in Chapter 2.

[2] James I, *Basilikon Doron; or, His Majesties Instructions to his Dearest Sonne, Henry the Prince* (London, 1603). See also W. Lee Ustick, 'Advice to a Son: A Type of Seventeenth-Century Conduct Book', *Studies in Philology*, 29 (1932); Louis B. Wright, *Advice to a Son: Precepts of Lord Burghley, Sir Walter Raleigh, and Francis Osborne* (Ithaca, NY, 1962), introduction. For an early 16th-century precursor, see Thomas Lupset, 'An Exhortation to Young Men', in *Complaint and Reform in England*, ed. William Huse Dunham Jr. and Stanley Pargellis (New York, 1938). See also *Peter Idley's Instructions to his Son*, ed. Charlotte D'Evelyn (London, 1935).

[3] e.g. *A Two-fold Treatise, the One Decyphering the Worth of Speculation, and of a Retired Life. The Other Containing a Discoverie of Youth and Old Age* (Oxford, 1612).

The most sustained representations of ageing, however, are to be found in formal defences of old age. Most were deeply indebted to Cicero's *De Senectute*, which was first published in English translation by Caxton in the late fifteenth century, and which went through two subsequent English editions in the sixteenth century, the last of which was translated by the physician, poet, and divine Thomas Newton in 1569.

Across this range of works, both youth and old age were frequently approached as periods of instability attributed either to a surfeit of vitality or to its absence. In contrast to the excesses of youth and the deprivations of old age, manhood was designated the 'firmest age', characterized by the ability to control youthful energies without yet being threatened by their debilitating decline.[4] That youth and old age were approached as 'other' to manhood illustrates the importance of age as a determinant of early modern hierarchies of masculinity. Although the superiority of maleness as a cultural category was not jeopardised by such distinctions, the implicit contest between the generations was more salient to the construction of manhood as a phase in the life course than any comparison between the sexes. Discussions of generational difference served to define patriarchal manhood, and firmly claimed it for the middle-aged householder. On the rare occasions when any of its features were extended to the younger or 'ancienter' sort it was generally on account of their superior social status, which suggests that gentility could sometimes override distinctions of age and more readily confer aspects of patriarchal status. Such processes of differentiation bring to light many of the attributes both claimed for and renounced by patriarchal constructions of manhood. The characteristics associated with young and old men are in turn suggestive of the ways in which they were mostly deemed unworthy claimants of patriarchal privilege and of the criteria for their exclusion from the full patriarchal dividend.

YOUTH AND MANHOOD

> Beate downe the evill: raise the just:
> Learne best thy selfe to know[5]

Authors of parenting manuals and domestic advice in early modern England agreed that there was no more dangerous age than youth. While this was deemed to be as true for girls as boys, conduct books tended to dwell at greater length on the perils associated with young men than young

---

[4] *The Office of Christian Parents: Shewing how Children are to be Governed throughout All Ages and Times of their Life* (Cambridge, 1616), 44.
[5] *Keepe within Compasse; or, The Worthy Legacy of a Wise Father to his Beloved Sonne* (London, 1619), sig. Bᵛ.

women, and youth as a social category was usually treated in generically male terms.[6] Male youth was widely characterized as an age of extremes, marked both by an unrivalled capacity for spirited and courageous action and a seemingly unlimited potential for vice. According to many models of the ages of man this hazardous stage, sometimes subdivided into two or three separate phases, spanned a full two decades of the life cycle.[7] Readers of *The Office of Christian Parents* (1616) were warned that between the ages of 14 and 28 a young man's entire future was at stake. Although it was the time when he was 'most sensible, full of strength, courage and activenes', without sufficient direction and constant vigilance he would be 'easily drawne to libertie, pleasure, and licentiousnes':

> which if they take deepe rooting in this age, they will hardly or never be remooved; and so all the good, and all the joy, and all the honour of our child, is turned into evill, sorrow, and shame, and the poore young man laid open to the snares of the devill, to be holden at his pleasure with the tight chaine of his raging concupiscence[8]

This was a common theme. Young men were in control of neither their minds nor their bodies. By humoral analogy, youth was a 'hot office', 'sliding and slippery', 'naturally inclined [to] great intemperaunce', and prone to 'inordinate affections, absurd actions . . . extravagant courses, and preposterous progressions, and aversions'.[9] Needing stringent bridling, youth was 'heedlesse', 'like an untamed colt', 'an affecter of all licentious liberty', and full of 'wilfulnesse, and selfe conceit'. Youth was 'drunke with pleasure, and therefore dead to all goodnesse', the age 'set upon the very pinacle of temptations' requiring constant vigilance and direction to avoid permanent shipwreck on the rock of vice.[10]

---

[6] See also Hilda L. Smith, *All Men and Both Sexes: Gender, Politics, and the False Universal in England 1640–1832* (Philadelphia, 2002), ch. 1.

[7] See Fig. 3, p. 55 below. See also Paul Griffiths, *Youth and Authority: Formative Experiences in England, 1560–1640* (Oxford, 1996), 19–34.   [8] *The Office of Christian Parents*, 135–6.

[9] *The Foure Ages of Man* (London, 1635); Plutarch, *A President for Parentes, Teaching the Vertuous Training up of Children and Holesome Information of Yongmen* (London, 1571), sig. D2ᵛ; Bartholomaeus Battus, *The Christian Mans Closet. Wherein is Conteined a Discourse of the Training of Children. Nowe Englished by W. Lowth* (London, 1581), fo. 84; Francis Lenton, *The Young Gallants Whirligigg; or, Youths Reakes* (London, 1629), title page.

[10] Arthur Newman, *Pleasures Vision: With Deserts Complaint and a Short Dialogue of a Womans Properties, betweene an Olde Man and a Young* (London, 1619), 13; William Guild, *A Yong Mans Inquisition, or Triall. Whereby All Young Men (as of All Ages) may Know how to Redresse and Direct their Waies, According to Gods Word* (London, 1608), 26; Richard Brathwait, *The English Gentleman: Containing Sundry Excellent Rules how to Accommodate Himselfe in the Manage of Publike or Private Affaires* (London, 1630), 2; *A Discoverie of Youth and Old Age*, 4, 5; W.P., *The Prentises Practise in Godlinesse, and his True Freedome* (London, 1613), fo. 41. For images of shipwrecked youth, see, e.g., Guild, *A Yong Mans Inquisition*, 27; Thomas Sheafe, *Vindiciæ Senectutis; or, A Plea for Old-Age* (London, 1639), 98.

Notions of youth as 'contested territory' not only informed advice literature directed at young men and their parents, but were also paradigmatic of the battles between good and evil that defined the human condition.[11] Metaphors of (male) youth featured prominently in conversion literature, catechisms, sermons, and religious drama, a common subject of which was the parable of the prodigal son.[12] Emblematic of the fraught pathway to salvation, youth was characterized as the period in which an individual was suspended between the contrasting prospects of virtue and reprobation. Thus in his *Portraitur of the Prodigal Sonne*, Samuel Gardiner distinguished between two 'sortes' of people: 'The one of them orderlie and of good government . . . the other exorbitant, refractorie and disloyall, gadding abroad after his owne fancies.'[13] The characteristics of these two 'sorts' paralleled the qualities distinguishing staid manhood from unsettled youth according to the imperatives of socially functional conduct. Critics of youth were insistent upon their exclusion of young men from manhood in these terms. According to Thomas Sheafe, until 'mans age' or maturity, 'a man is not a man'—from which status 'the youth' was firmly excluded 'though he strut it out, and thinke there is no man-hood to be found but in himselfe'. Another (anonymous) tract similarly claimed that 'unbridled youth wil runne it selfe forth of breath, in running ryot, accounting that the greatest grace, to live ungratiously; and that life to be manlike, which is altogether beastly: thus inverting the course of all things'.[14]

Such concerns suggest that the terms of manhood were deeply contested along the lines of age, and very differently conceived by middle-aged and young men—a point which will be explored further in Chapter 4, since the conduct literature only tells us part of this story. One of the main preoccupations of conduct books was to deny young men access to manhood unless it was approached on their authors' terms. Advice to young men was founded on an exaggerated distinction between the qualities associated with youth and manhood, which pinned disruptive vice on the former and patriarchal virtue on the latter. The depravities of youth were rehearsed relentlessly, and, by implication, dissociated from

---

[11] Griffiths, *Youth and Authority*, 54–61. See also Ilana Krausman Ben-Amos, *Adolescence and Youth in Early Modern England* (New Haven, 1994), ch. 1.

[12] e.g. Richard Brathwait, *The Prodigals Teares; or, His Fare-Well to Vanity* (London, 1614); William Cowper, *A Mirrour of Mercie; or, The Prodigals Conversion, Full of Comfortable Consolations* (London, 1614); Samuel Crooke, *The Guide unto True Blessednesse; or, A Body of the Doctrine of the Scriptures, Directing Man to the Saving Knowledge of God*, 2nd edn. (London, 1614); R. Wever, *An Enterlude Called Lusty Iuuentus* (London, 1565).

[13] Samuel Gardiner, *Portraitur of the Prodigal Sonne* (London, 1599), sig. B3v.

[14] Sheafe, *Vindiciæ Senectutis*, 103; *A Discoverie of Youth and Old Age*, 6.

manhood. In turn, conduct writers variously claimed the patriarchal attributes of discretion, self-control, thrift, order, and respectability for 'man's age' in what appear to be attempts to fix definitions of manhood in these terms. Young men were therefore instructed to serve out their minority in submissive obedience rather than pursue alternative—and, in this context, wrong-headed—forms of prowess. Although the rewards of maturity were more positively emphasized in some texts, particularly those penned by fathers to their sons, they were nonetheless conditional upon access to a patriarchal position and conformity to the normative codes of patriarchal behaviour.

The main vices for which young men were excoriated were related to intemperance and pride. Lust, drunkenness, anger, and idleness were demonized as particular pitfalls stemming from an incapacity for self-control, while the vanities of flamboyant dress and swaggering gesture betrayed a contemptuous disregard of position. Young men were depicted as 'polluted' with 'the burning lustes of the carnall affections', which, combined with their own surfeit of heat, generated an explosive bodily concoction.[15] According to Richard Turner, the 'Venerious youngsters' of this 'blood-warme age' (i.e. youth) were 'set on fire', so consumed by the need to 'drench their itching' that this 'sulpherous flame' spilled forth from their bodies in a process analogous to ejaculation itself:

> This is the Age that makes my spleene to swell
> With laughter, and my gall to leave her cell:
> Which being vomited up, about doth flye,
> Bespurtling every body that stands nigh.[16]

Young men as well as young women were counselled in the virtues of chastity, although moralists betrayed expectations that such advice was less likely to be heeded by young men. William Martyn cautioned his son at Oxford to protect 'your virgin chastitie' as 'the wife of your youth' by steering clear of the 'impudent and whorish inticements' he was likely to encounter, and *The Office of Christian Parents* bemoaned that while men ought, like women, to 'keep the vessels of their body undefiled' before marriage, this was becoming less and less customary.[17] Some attempted to deter young men by emphasizing the physically debilitating consequences of 'whoring': 'Lechery is no other thing then a furious Passion, shortning

---

[15] Guild, *A Yong Mans Inquisition*, 25.
[16] Richard Turner, *Youth Know Thy Selfe* (London, 1624), sigs. A3ᵛ–A4.
[17] William Martyn, *Youths Instruction* (London, 1612), 57; *The Office of Christian Parents*, 23. See also, e.g., Battus, *The Christian Mans Closet*, fo. 93; Sir Walter Raleigh, *Sir Walter Raleighs Instructions to his Sonne and to Posterity* (London, 1632), 14–15.

the life, hurting the Understanding, darkening the Memorie, taking away the Heart, spoyling Beauty, weakning the joints, ingendring *Sciatica*, Gouts, Giddinesse in the Head, Leprosie, and Pox.'[18] In this context, sexual dalliance was deemed to endanger rather than enhance manhood, auguring mental torpor, premature ageing, and irreparable disfigurement.

Drunkenness was depicted as similarly enfeebling to both mind and body. While excessive drinking was more readily admitted as a vice to which men of all ages might succumb (not least those of the 'meaner sort'), young men were portrayed as being especially allured by its attractions.[19] They were also deemed particularly vulnerable to its hazards because of their inherent bodily instability. The 'artificiall heat' of wine 'putteth fire to fire', diminishing a young man's capacity for action by wasting the body's natural heat and overpowering the mind.[20] In respect to drink, therefore, youthful heat was like a tinderbox awaiting ignition, and drunkenness was 'nothing else but a voluntary madness'.[21] Linked to anger, bad company-keeping, and idleness, drunkenness was also condemned by advice writers because of its associated dangers. Anger was similarly characterized as 'madness', and because 'The heat of their age doth scarse suffer young men to keepe measure' young men were deemed especially vulnerable. Conduct writers emphasized that it was through restraint, rather than a rash response to insult, that a young man might 'shew himselfe invincible'. Anger, by contrast, was designated 'unnaturall, uncivill, unreasonable . . . base, cowardly, and miserable . . . foolish, desperate, and dishonourable'.[22] This kind of hot-headedness was linked in turn to the corrupting influence of bad company. *The Fathers Blessing*, an adaptation of James I's advice to his son, Prince Henry, warned: 'Be no company keeper, Gaimster, or such like, for both are the wasters of the pretious treasure of time: besides, hee that is wholly possest of either, is not master of himselfe or his owne substance.'[23] Idleness was deemed

---

[18] Patrick Scot, *Omnibus & Singulis. Affording Matter Profitable for All Men, Alluding to a Fathers Advice or Last Will to his Sonne* (London, 1619), 81. See also James Cleland, *The Instruction of a Young Noble-Man* (Oxford, 1612), 207–8.

[19] For general diatribes against drinking, see, e.g., B.H., *The Glasse of Mans Folly, and Meanes to Amendment, for the Health and Wealth of Soule and Body*, 2nd edn. (London, 1615); Thomas Young, *Englands Bane; or, The Description of Drunkennesse* (London, 1617).

[20] Raleigh, *Instructions to his Sonne*, 86–7.

[21] *Keepe within Compasse*, sig. C7ᵛ. See also Thomas Nash, *The Anatomie of Absurditie: Contayning a Breefe Confutation of the Slender Imputed Prayses to Feminine Perfection, with a Short Description of the Seuerall Practises of Youth, and Sundry Follies of Our Licentious Times* (London, 1589), sig. D4ᵛ.

[22] *The Office of Christian Parents*, 181, 183, 187. See also Martyn, *Youths Instruction*, 82. Cf. Elizabeth Foyster, 'Boys Will Be Boys? Manhood and Aggression, 1660–1800', in Tim Hitchcock and Michèle Cohen (eds.), *English Masculinities 1660–1800* (Harlow, 1999).

similarly threatening to manhood: 'Hee is not worthy the name of man that spends a whole day in pleasure.'[24]

Advice writers and moralists therefore cast the follies of youth in terms of an absence of self-control which they laboured to equate with unmanliness. By contrast, self-mastery was claimed as the defining feature of manhood, and youthful deviations from this rational ideal were further stigmatized as bestial. It was a commonplace that drunkenness was a 'beastly' vice because it undermined men's reason. Raleigh warned that wine 'transformeth a Man into a Beast', and Lenton that drunkards were 'more like beasts then men'. Young depicted the brutish mutation suffered by drinkers by categorizing drunkenness into nine stages, each corresponding with an animal as the inebriate descended the scale of depravity.[25] According to conduct manuals, this kind of excess not only resulted in the forfeiture of rational manhood; it brought about complete transfiguration. Hence the drunkard could be described as 'having no more of a man but the shape'.[26] The effects of anger were similarly depicted: anger was like a 'furious serpent', and, according to William Gouge, caused 'the heart to swell againe, and as it were fire to come out of the eies, and thunder out of the mouth'.[27] The excesses of drink and bile were portrayed as having a literally monstrous impact.

Gender analogies were also employed to condemn ungoverned appetites. Young men not only risked becoming beast-like through indulgence; they were in grave danger of becoming effeminate. Parents were warned that lenient upbringing could produce sons 'effeminately prone to all manner of vice', and that sloth would make their bodies 'dull, fainte, and effeminate'.[28] The fate of Alexander the Great was used as a cautionary example: because of his surrender of manliness in exchange for Persian riches and luxury, he and his son Ninus 'lived more abject than any shamelesse woman, dissipating and wasting . . . goods'.[29] Dancing and music were also characterized as unmanly in these terms. The puritan hack Philip Stubbes's main complaint against such pursuits was that they

[23] *The Fathers Blessing; or, Second Councell to his Sonne. Appropriated to the Generall, from that Perticular Example his Majestie Composed for the Prince his Sonne* (London, 1616), 22.
[24] *Keepe within Compasse*, sig. C6.
[25] Raleigh, *Instructions to his Sonne*, 81; Lenton, *Young Gallants Whirligigg*, 9; Young, *Englands Bane*, sigs. F2ᵛ–F3ᵛ.
[26] *Muld Sacke; or, The Apologie of Hic-Mulier* (London, 1620), sig. C2.
[27] *The Office of Christian Parents*, 187; William Gouge, *Of Domesticall Duties* (London, 1622), 174.
[28] *A Discourse of the Married and Single Life. Wherein, by Discovering the Misery of the One, is Plainely Declared the Felicity of the Other* (London, 1621), sig. A7; Battus, *The Christian Mans Closet*, fo. 43ᵛ.
[29] Plutarch, *A President for Parentes*, sig. C5ᵛ. See also, e.g., John Preston, *The Patriarchs Portion; or, The Saints Best Day. Delivered in a Sermon at the Funerall of Sir Thomas Reynell* (London, 1619), 34.

'womannisheth the minde', claiming:

> if you wold have your sonne, soft, womannish, uncleane, smoth mouthed, affected to bawdrie, scurrilitie, filthie rimes, and unsemely talking: brifly, if you wold have him, as it weare transnatured into a woman, or worse, and inclyned to all kind of whordome and abomination, set him to dauncing school, and to learn musicke, and than shall you not faile of your purpose.[30]

Immoderate dress was condemned as having a similarly degenerative impact. Young men were not to be 'delicately and effeminately appareled' since it worked against nature and turned them into women. Barnaby Rich complained that 'the yong man in this age, that is not *strumpet* like attired, doth thinke himselfe quite out of *fashion*'.[31] In Rich's eyes, gaily attired gallants were not only at risk of resembling women; they were in danger of being mistaken for the worst sort of women.

These kinds of unmanly degeneration were portrayed in terms of a distinct hierarchy of descent from man to woman to beast. Although this hierarchy transcended distinctions of age, it was frequently invoked in discussions of youthful misdemeanours. Hence one warning against the excesses of apparel and leisure to which youth were prone declared that 'Idlenes and disguised cloathes makes men women, women beasts, and beasts monsters.'[32] The further a youth slipped down this hierarchy, the looser his grip on reason became since it was reason that primarily distinguished a man from both woman and beast in this gendered version of the great chain of being.[33] By invoking the stigma of effeminacy conduct writers adopted a far more potent critique than mere unmanliness. Effeminacy, and its further corruption into bestiality, were the labels given to men's excessive or unchecked behaviour that diverted them from their rational purpose.[34] Conduct writers repeatedly insisted that the youthful vices they detailed disqualified young men from claiming manhood, and in doing so equated manhood with reason, temperance, and self-control

---

[30] Philip Stubbes, *The Anatomie of Abuses: Contayning a Discoverie, of Vices in a Verie Famous Ilande called Ailgna* (London, 1583), sigs. O4ᵛ, O5.

[31] Plutarch, *A President for Parentes*, sig. H7ᵛ; Barnaby Rich, *My Ladies Looking Glasse. Wherein may be Discerned a Wise Man from a Foole, a Good Woman from a Bad* (London, 1616), 21. See also Brathwait, *The English Gentleman*, 25; and David Kuchta, 'The Semiotics of Masculinity in Renaissance England', in James Grantham Turner (ed.), *Sexuality and Gender in Early Modern Europe: Institutions, Texts, Images* (Cambridge, 1993).

[32] *Keepe within Compasse*, sig. C8.

[33] For women's place in this hierarchy, see Margaret R. Sommerville, *Sex and Subjection: Attitudes to Women in Early-Modern Society* (London, 1995).

[34] Alan Bray, 'To be a Man in Early Modern Society: The Curious Case of Michael Wigglesworth', *History Workshop Journal*, 41 (1996). See also Hitchcock and Cohen (eds.), *English Masculinities*, 3–6.

and labelled deviation from these virtues in antithetical terms of unmanliness, beastliness, or effeminacy.

While denouncing many of the consequences of misdirected youthful vigour, advice books did not, however, desire its entire suppression which smacked of 'Stoicke insensible stupiditie'.[35] The moderation expected of manhood involved not only self-conquest, but also self-command. Thus, according to Brathwait, the Stoic was as much an offender as the Libertine, and moderation itself should be moderate.[36] A young man's capacity for spirited action was ideally harnessed during manhood, and thus redirected towards patriarchal ends, rather than being rejected altogether. Advice on youth was therefore not solely concerned with suppressing youthful fervour and misplaced bids for manhood. It ultimately aimed to coach young men in their duties and interests as adult males by directing their energies towards appropriate action and by promising its associated dividends.

This was a particular feature of the father–son advice that emerged as a printed genre from the early seventeenth century. Often published posthumously, these precepts from beyond the grave instructed young men in their responsibilities as adults, and treated youth more as a porous antechamber to manhood than as an entirely separate state of being. This was especially true of the advice penned by aristocratic authors such as Lord Burghley and Sir Walter Raleigh, whose sons might have expected to 'act ... upon the stage of the World'.[37] Such texts were concerned with the expediency of establishing influence and maintaining privilege, in contrast with more religiously minded tracts which focused more squarely on moral duties.[38] Yet all father–son advice, in common with other didactic texts concerning youth, predominantly emphasized the ideal of *balance* as young men assumed manhood. Balance was required both externally, in terms of handling social and political interaction, and internally, in terms of directing the potentially chaotic natural impulses associated with youth, with frequent warnings that the former was predicated on the latter.

Balance, according to these texts, was the precondition of manhood, and, as such, was primarily conceptualized in terms of discretion, control, and containment. This was the organizing principle of the anonymous tract *Keepe within Compasse; or, The Worthy Legacy of a Wise Father to his Beloved Sonne* which went through ten editions in the eleven years after its first publication in 1619. The title page illustrated its theme with a diagram establishing the boundaries of virtuous practice in religion, conversation, diet, and apparel, thus circumscribing the vices of atheism, luxury, glut-

[35] James I, *Basilikon Doron*, 97.
[36] Brathwait, *The English Gentleman*, 347.
[37] Scot, *Omnibus & Singulis*, sig. B^v.
[38] Ustick, 'Advice to a Son'.

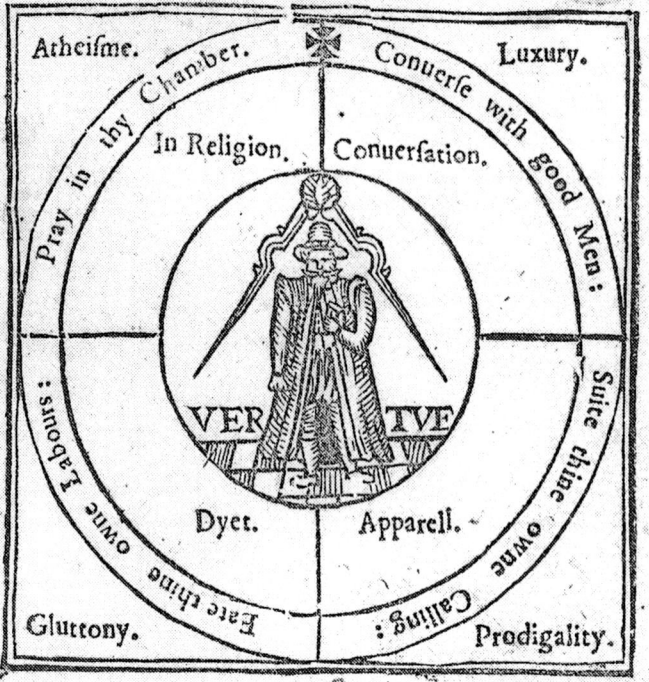

Fig. 1. *Keepe within Compasse; or, The Worthy Legacy of a Wise Father to his Beloved Sonne* (London, 1619), title page, Bodleian Library, University of Oxford, 8° K 12 Th (1)

tony, and prodigality (Fig. 1). These boundaries were to be maintained and defended respectively with unwavering faith and private prayer; with honest friendship and moderate action; by living according to one's means; and through the temperate avoidance of immoderate excess. In this way a young man might both govern his disorderly impulses, and carefully establish himself within a complex network of social relations.

While containment was by no means purely advocated as a male-specific quality, it was elaborated very differently along the axis of gender. This is illustrated by the much rarer female counterpart to *Keepe within Compasse*, which was identically structured, and published as *The Mothers Counsell; or, Live within Compasse. Being the Last Will and Testament to her Dearest Daughter*.[39] A lesson in (female) 'modesty' as opposed to (male) 'virtue', *The Mothers Counsell* sought to contain young women within the bounds of chastity, temperance, humility, and beauty, thus safeguarding them from wantonness, madness, pride, and 'odiousness' respectively (Fig. 2). The advice of the two tracts converged in a number of ways, particularly in exhortations to piety and temperance. The latter was even advocated to both sexes in precisely the same terms of bridling with reason 'the vice of sensuality, and all other grosse affections of the minde'.[40] In this context, therefore, women as well as men were accorded the capacity for rational self-government. However, there was considerable divergence in the way that these tracts stigmatized deviation from this ideal, with female waywardness condemned as madness and male excess as prodigality. A woman's intemperance was primarily figured in terms of disobedience, with the consequent derangement of herself and society, since an 'outragious woman' was a 'fierce beast and a dangerous foe... to a Commonwealth'. The solution was a firm husband to maintain rational control, rather like the sharp bit needed to tame a 'rough stirring Horse'.[41] While similarly exhorted to self-control, therefore, women were ultimately expected to be governed by men in adult life to some degree as they had been by parents in childhood.

The dividend of manhood on the other hand was freedom from youthful subordination acquired through the exertion of self-government, not least because men's capacity for self-control was the justification for their control over others (particularly women). While independence in

---

[39] M.R., *The Mothers Counsell; or, Live within Compasse. Being the Last Will and Testament to her Dearest Daughter* (London, 1630?).
[40] *Keepe within Compasse*, sig. C; *The Mothers Counsell*, 12–13.
[41] *The Mothers Counsell*, 17, 15. For the use of animal imagery to describe women's bridling by marriage, see Laura Gowing, *Domestic Dangers: Women, Words, and Sex in Early Modern London* (Oxford, 1996), 25–6.

Fig. 2. *The Mothers Counsell; or, Live within Compasse. Being the Last Will and Testament to her Dearest Daughter* (London, 1630?), title page, Bodleian Library, University of Oxford, Mal. 450 (2)

women was routinely stigmatized as dangerous and disorderly, men were instructed how to manage their independence, with discredit attached merely to its misdirection. Thus the patriarchal interests of men served as a carrot to entice them to perform their duties, while women were generally goaded with the stick of male dominance. Conduct books commanded self-government as the price of manhood, but they were also forthcoming about the many rewards for those who aspired to function in the commonwealth as 'pillars of the land'.[42] Fathers were also encouraged to invest in such rewards: 'A godly father can leave behind him no monument more excellent then his sonne, the very lively Image of his maners, vertues, constancie, wisdome, and godlinesse.'[43]

Although independence was touted as the prize of adult males, it should be noted that it was not unlimited, particularly in association with distinctions of social status. This was barely acknowledged by authors of father–son advice, however. One of the principal duties expected of young men as they learned the ropes of adulthood was to know their place in relation to other men. This was not a new set of expectations, but rather the continuation of a process of socialization which in childhood had placed enormous emphasis on the respect owed by youth to age.[44] The difference in adulthood was that the primary axis of deference shifted (and, for some men, narrowed in degree) from differentials of age to differentials of rank. While this was also true for women, it was masked by the conduct literature's frequent insistence on gender as the principal determinant of women's 'place', particularly in adulthood. With a similar degree of distortion, men's 'place' was discussed almost exclusively in terms of their relationships with other men, despite the fact that some men were required to defer to women in positions of authority.[45] In this way, many advice writers denied women's agency in relationships either with men or with other women, and appropriated the arena of socially and politically significant action solely, and inaccurately, for men.[46] Yet when it came to delineating the degrees of deference governing relationships between men, conduct writers also ignored the extent to which adult men

---

[42] *The Office of Christian Parents*, 98. On the importance of ensuring a child's future contribution to the commonwealth, see also John Dod and Robert Cleaver, *A Godly Form of Householde Government: For the Ordering of Private Families* (London, 1612), 272.

[43] Battus, *The Christian Mans Closet*, fo. 42. See also William Averell, *A Dyall for Dainty Darlings, Rocks in the Cradle of Securitie* (London, 1584), sig. E1ᵛ.

[44] Keith Thomas, 'Age and Authority in Early Modern England', *Proceedings of the British Academy*, 62 (1976); Griffiths, *Youth and Authority*, ch. 2.

[45] See, e.g., Katharine Hodgkin, 'Thomas Wythorne and the Problem of Mastery', *History Workshop Journal*, 29 (1990); Andy Wood, *The Politics of Social Conflict: The Peak Country 1520–1770* (Cambridge, 1999), 24–5.

[46] For the extent of this inaccuracy, see, e.g., Amy Louise Erickson, 'Common Law versus

subordinated *each other* on the grounds of rank, principally because they assumed an elite readership. While advising young men to be considerate of their place in relation to other men, they catered to the expectations of and aspirations to privilege amongst their readers. As a consequence they did not fully explore or even acknowledge the fact that the balance between deference owed and deference commanded, in relations with other men, at least, was tipped comparatively unfavourably for the majority.

William Cecil, Lord Burghley, advised his son (and the numerous other gentlemen who subsequently purchased or copied his precepts[47]) to be acutely aware of his place in relation to other men, and to reflect this in his attitudes and gestures towards them: 'Towards thy superiours be humble yet generous, with thy equals familiar, yet respective, towards inferiours shew much humility and some familiarity, as to bow thy body, stretch forth thy hand, uncover thy head, and such like popular compliments.' According to Cecil, the first was necessary for advancement, the second for securing a reputation for good breeding, and the third for maintaining 'popularity'.[48] Humility was here associated with gain: on the one hand it oiled the wheels of preferment when expressed towards superiors, and on the other hand it secured loyalty when directed towards inferiors. In the latter case it was effective because the social distance separating the gentry and their 'inferiors' was so great that it was paradoxically reinforced by gestures that temporarily ignored its existence (which, presumably, was

---

Common Practice: The Use of Marriage Settlements in Early Modern England', *Economic History Review*, 2nd ser. 43 (1990); Ilana Krausman Ben-Amos, 'Women Apprentices in the Trades and Crafts of Early Modern Bristol', *Continuity and Change*, 6 (1991); Patricia Crawford, 'Public Duty, Conscience, and Women in Early Modern England', in John Morrill, Paul Slack, and Daniel Woolf (eds.), *Public Duty and Private Conscience in Seventeenth-Century England: Essays Presented to G. E. Aylmer* (Oxford, 1993); Garthine Walker, 'Women, Theft and the World of Stolen Goods', in Jenny Kermode and Garthine Walker (eds.), *Women, Crime and the Courts in Early Modern England* (London, 1994); Sara Mendelson and Patricia Crawford, *Women in Early Modern England* (Oxford, 1998), chs. 5–7; Diane Willen, 'Women in the Public Sphere in Early Modern England: The Case of the Urban Working Poor', *Sixteenth Century Journal*, 19 (1988); Patricia Crawford, '"The Poorest She": Women and Citizenship in Early Modern England', in Michael Mendle (ed.), *The Putney Debates of 1647: The Army, the Levellers, and the English State* (Cambridge, 2001); Laura Gowing, 'Ordering the Body: Illegitimacy and Female Authority in Seventeenth-Century England', in Michael J. Braddick and John Walter (eds.), *Negotiating Power in Early Modern Society: Order, Hierarchy and Subordination in Britain and Ireland* (Cambridge, 2001); and Ch. 7 below.

[47] For evidence of the circulation of father–son advice between elites, see Linda A. Pollock, 'Living on the Stage of the World: The Concept of Privacy among the Elite of Early Modern England', in Adrian Wilson (ed.), *Rethinking Social History: English Society 1570–1920 and its Interpretation* (Manchester, 1993).

[48] William Cecil, *The Counsell of a Father to his Sonne, in Ten Severall Precepts* (London, 1611), 8th precept.

precisely the effect Burghley intended).

When the disparity in status was so great, expressions of humility towards lower-ranking men came with little social cost, particularly as advice regarding its expression was hedged with provisos. Thus, in a tract somewhat derivative from Burghley's precepts, John Norden recommended courtesy towards inferiors but cautioned against over-familiarity, just as he also advised against excessive self-abasement towards superiors with carriage that was 'too awfull'. Moreover, the degree of familiarity towards inferiors had distinct social and spatial boundaries, evident in Norden's suggestion 'neither let drudges, as horse-keepers or labourers, or such like come neere thy person, or thy table, for either their rude behaviour or ill smell will bee offensive'.[49] In this instance, 'drudges' were not even accorded recognition as inferiors to whom feigned familiarity might be extended. Such advice taught elite young men how to signal their place within the social hierarchy through appropriate speech and bearing and by maintaining topographies of rank. There was no direct consideration of how lower-ranking men might assert their position since it was assumed that they had none; they featured merely as the 'inferiors' or 'drudges' from whom their social superiors desired to maintain sufficient distance. Expressions of humility by such men—feigned or otherwise—were not expected to yield nearly such high returns, since the demands of deference were more likely to be exacted to their cost than claimed to their benefit. The men accorded political and social agency in these tracts were therefore confined to a minority; furthermore, their position was deemed a consequence not only of the subordination of women, but also of the subordination of other men. This was advice for young men who were on a fast track to adult male authority and who could expect the highest returns from the patriarchal dividend.[50] Yet also implicit in such advice was the assumption that the majority of men needed to know their place and be resigned to it. For these men, if they had access to them at all, such profits of assuming maturity were restricted to deference exacted primarily from household subordinates and across a narrower spectrum of other men.

The extent of a man's adult autonomy and independence was also contingent upon his means. Beyond the social and political interests acknowledged in father–son advice was a set of economic concerns that were deemed central both to the successful management of relationships with other men and to the preservation of social status. Such precepts advocated the maintenance of distance and, importantly, economic inde-

[49] John Norden, *The Fathers Legacie. With Precepts Morall, and Prayers Divine* (London, 1625), sigs. A4^v, A7^{r-v}.   [50] Thomas, 'Age and Authority', 213.

pendence from other men, in contrast to advice emphasizing social and political connection. Thus Sir Walter Raleigh's instructions to his son cynically promoted 'shunning alwayes such as are poore & needie' when selecting friends.[51] With their emphasis on the demands of 'friendship', such tenets were predominantly concerned with relationships between equals rather than between inferiors and superiors, and focused particularly on relationships of trust.[52] One of the principal exhortations of fathers to sons was that they should live within their means, thus maintaining not only their place, but also their independence. This required both the avoidance of excessive expenditure and the protection of one's estate from the demands of friends in need or the wiles of flatterers and sycophants. When writing about the dangers of unnecessary financial obligations to others, advice writers frequently employed images of slavery which presaged an inversion of the hierarchy upon which elite status rested: the world would indeed be turned upside down if those of gentle status were to become bondsmen. Elite young men were similarly cautioned against jeopardizing their credit by acting as sureties. According to Raleigh, suretyship was a 'Manslayer, or enchanter', and Cecil advised against it on the grounds that 'he that payeth an other mans debts, seekes his owne decay'.[53] While encouraged to build social and political links, particularly with their superiors, genteel sons were simultaneously advised to ensure economic independence by avoiding all ties that were a risk to their credit. Although this kind of balancing act was most cynically espoused by noble advisers such as Raleigh and Burghley, an emphasis on economic autonomy as a fundamental attribute of adult masculinity was commonplace, not least in marital advice, as we shall see below.

Father–son advice therefore sought to instruct young men in the rights and responsibilities of patriarchal manhood, offering admission to those who followed its many tenets. Freedom from the yoke of parental discipline was conditional upon learning self-mastery and upholding meanings of manhood in terms of rational discretion and self-government. The resultant independence was to be carefully safeguarded through circumspection in relationships with other men. Speech was particularly important in this regard. While one of the rewards of patriarchal masculinity was to be accorded a voice in social and political affairs, this privilege was to be exercised with the utmost caution. Martyn warned his

---

[51] Raleigh, *Instructions to his Sonne*, 2.

[52] For a fuller discussion of the expectations of friendship and the limits of trust, see pp. 122–4 below.

[53] Raleigh, *Instructions to his Sonne*, 65; Cecil, *Counsell of a Father*, 7th precept. See also *The Fathers Blessing*, 25.

son that although 'The tongue is one of the least members in the bodie, yet if she bee not restrained and governed by wisedome and by good discretion, she will make a man captive and slavish to the greatest woe.'[54] While there was much to be gained from admission to patriarchal manhood, advice writers therefore also emphasized that such men also had a great deal to lose, not least the claim to manhood itself. In attempting to fix the terms of manhood according to patriarchal principles, the excesses associated with youth were universally condemned. Yet while all adult males were expected to pay the price of self-government for manhood, the rewards were not unilaterally extended to all adult males. Conduct books belied the degree to which the patriarchal dividends were unevenly distributed, since the autonomy and influence to which young men could aspire was considerably affected by social status as well as behaviour. The youth–manhood dichotomy was a useful device for the general attribution of rational behaviour to adult males, but it also masked the fact that the scope for and rewards from such action varied extensively.

ONE FOOT IN THE GRAVE

> But it may be thou art an old man, & hast one foote in the grave already; then I say ... Thou art not to be reckoned among them that live, nor among them that be dead [55]

Old age was represented in a variety of ways in tracts on longevity and defences of age, conduct books and sermons, although negative portrayals were rarely absent. Across a range of genres, 'drouping old age' was depicted as 'the dregges onely and powder of mans life', 'a continuall disease', or like 'living death'. Old men were 'pettish' and crazed, discussed through analogy to desolate cities or 'bare ruined choirs'.[56] As the forerunner to death, old age was approached as a product of the Fall, and like birth's entrance to 'lifes *tragedie*', the aged exit was painful and difficult: 'we come in with [a] moane and go out with a groane'.[57] Drawing

---

[54] Martyn, *Youths Instruction*, 97–8. See also Raleigh, *Instructions to his Sonne*, 52–4; Scot, *Omnibus & Singulis*, 56–8; *The Fathers Blessing*, 17–18; Cleland, *Instruction of a Young Noble-Man*, 184–91; Simon Robson, *A New Yeeres Gift. The Courte of Civill Courtesie: Assembled in the Behalfe of All Younge Gentlemen, to Frame their Behaviour in All Companies* (London, 1577). Cf. Jane Kamensky, 'Talk Like a Man: Speech, Power, and Masculinity in Early New England', *Gender and History*, 8 (1996).

[55] Richard Eaton, *A Sermon Preached at the Funeralls of that Worthie and Worshipfull Gentleman, Master Thomas Dutton of Dutton, Esquire* (London, 1616), 13.

[56] André Du Laurens, *A Discourse of the Preservation of the Sight: Of Melancholike Diseases; of Rheumes, and of Old Age*, trans. R. Surphlet (London, 1599), sig. A3^v; Sampson Price, *The Two Twins of Birth and Death. A Sermon. Upon the Funeralls of Sir W. Byrde* (London, 1624), 9; John Reading, *The Old Man's Staffe, Two Sermons Shewing the Onely Way to a Comfortable Old Age* (London, 1621),

on a long tradition of such representations,[58] moral commentary treated ageing as an analogy for the misery of the human condition in general, and as a reminder that *all* life was a prelude to death: '*Old age . . . is a disease* evill enough of it selfe: yea our life it selfe is a disease, and a deadly disease, a disease unto death.'[59] While such representations in many ways transcended gender differences, suggesting a degree of gender convergence in old age, the generic aged stereotype, like the paradigmatic youth, tended to be male. When elderly women were specifically portrayed, authors scaled misogynist heights that were not offset by the redeeming features of wisdom and gravity typically extended to old men.[60] Medical writers expected women to grow older more quickly than men 'by reason of the weakenes of their bodies and of their [idle] manner of living', and moralists represented their ageing as a doubly harsh punishment.[61] According to the archdeacon George Hakewill, for example, old women suffering from gout or baldness 'have forfeited the priviledge of their sexe by their owne visciousnesse, and having together with their modesty put off their womanhood, they are deservedly plagued with mens diseases'.[62]

Although negative associations were largely inescapable, old men were at least accorded some positive attributes, even if these were often

---

3; William Hunnis, *Hunnies Recreations: Conteining Foure Godlie and Compendious Discourses, Intituled Adams Banishment: Christ his Crib. The Lost Sheepe. The Complaint of Old Age* (London, 1595), 53; Henry Cuffe, *The Differences of the Ages of Mans Life* (London, 1607), 121; Simon Goulart, *The Wise Vieillard, or Old Man* (London, 1621), 53; Hallett Smith, 'Bare Ruined Choirs: Shakespearean Variations on the Theme of Old Age', *Huntington Library Quarterly*, 39 (1976).

[57] George Ferebe, *Lifes Farewell; or, A Funerall Sermon. At the Funerall of John Drew Gentleman* (London, 1615), 20. For old age as a consequence of the Fall, see, e.g., Goulart, *The Wise Vieillard*, 22–3, 30; Reading, *The Old Mans Staffe*, 3.

[58] David H. Fowler, Lois Josephs Fowler, and Lois Lamdin, 'Themes of Old Age in Preindustrial Western Literature', in Peter N. Stearns (ed.), *Old Age in Preindustrial Society* (New York, 1982); Georges Minois, *History of Old Age: From Antiquity to the Renaissance*, trans. Sarah Hanbury Tenison (Cambridge, 1989); Alicia K. Nitecki, 'Figures of Old Age in Fourteenth-Century English Literature', in Michael M. Sheehan (ed.), *Aging and the Aged in Medieval Europe*, Papers in Medieval Studies 11 (Toronto, 1990); Pat Thane, *Old Age in English History: Past Experiences, Present Issues* (Oxford, 2000), chs. 2–3.

[59] Thomas Gataker, *Pauls Desire of Dissolution, and Deaths Advantage* (London, 1620), 7. See also id., *Abrahams Decease. A Meditation on Genesis 25.8. Delivered at the Funerall of Mr. Richard Stock* (London, 1627), 41–2.

[60] Lynn Ann Botelho, 'Provisions for the Elderly in Two Early Modern Suffolk Communities', unpublished Ph.D. thesis (Cambridge, 1996), 9–17; ead., 'Old Age and Menopause in Rural Women of Early Modern Suffolk', in Lynn Botelho and Pat Thane (eds.), *Women and Ageing in British Society since 1500* (Harlow, 2001), 43.

[61] Du Laurens, *A Discourse of the Preservation of the Sight*, 177. See also James Hart, *KAINIKH; or, The Diet of the Diseased* (London, 1633), 9.

[62] George Hakewill, *An Apologie or Declaration of the Power and Providence of God in the Government of the World* (Oxford, 1630), 169–70.

approached as compensation for other failings. As a result, commentators on the male ageing process were ambivalent about the degree to which old age nullified manhood. As with discussions of youth, old age was often defined in relation to manhood, and generally contrasted unfavourably with it. At its worst, old age was portrayed in terms of total deterioration, returning men to childhood. At its best, old age was represented as preserving, and even improving, some of the qualities said to distinguish man's estate. Such contrasts shed further light on the ways in which normative manhood was defined, as well as the ways in which its achievement was deemed conditional upon age. Just as conduct writers excluded disorderly young men from claiming patriarchal manhood, so accounts of ageing were reluctant to extend all—or even any—of its privileges to the end of the life course.

Defences of old age frequently emphasized its merits compared with youth. Such works ingested Cicero's protest that old age 'hath in it so greate authoritye, that it is muche more to be esteemed and is farre moore woorthe then all the vaine pleasures of headye and rashe Adolescencye'.[63] Free from the lasciviousness, self-conceit, ambition, impulsiveness, and vanity of youth, old age afforded constancy, moderation, 'exquisite judgement', wisdom, and virtuous contemplation.[64] Favourable comparisons with manhood, on the other hand, were rarer, and often ran counter to platitudes about old age rehearsed elsewhere. William Gouge, providing a preface to his former tutor's vindication of old age, favoured old age not only above 'distempered *youth*' but also, and unusually, above 'disordered manage'.[65] Sheafe continued this theme by suggesting that although old age was the 'Winter' of man's life, this was nonetheless the best season, 'when all the profits arising from the husband-mans labours and charges, are come into his barnes and store-houses':

As therefore at this time of the yeere, the barne is full of corne, the hive of honey and waxe; as then the fleece is laid up ready for warme winter cloathing, and all the other provision, by the thriving *Pater-familias*, is stored up for the necessary use of the house: and as then the Ants heape is growne great for succour and food: so to Old-men all the forenamed good things come in, and crownes this age with all manner of blessings.[66]

This contrasted dramatically with the more common depiction of 'the *winter season*' as 'colde and troublesome' and a fitting analogy for 'the

---

[63] Marcus Tullius Cicero, *The Worthye Booke of Old Age Otherwyse Entituled the Elder Cato, now Englished* (London, 1569), fo. 46ᵛ.
[64] *A Discoverie of Youth and Old Age*, 25. See also Sheafe, *Vindiciæ Senectutis*, especially 95–103.
[65] Sheafe, *Vindiciæ Senectutis*, sig. A7.
[66] Ibid. 165–6.

cumbersome coldnesse of the latter end of our life'.[67]

Unlike Sheafe's rosy image, positive depictions of male ageing were more likely to extend attributes of manhood into old age than to contrast the final stages of the life course favourably with the 'constant age'. This was evident in the subdivision of old age into different stages. Some health tracts distinguished between 'flourishing old age'—sometimes described as 'fresh, or greene old age'—and decrepitude.[68] Treatises more directly concerned with ageing often posited three divisions. According to Goulart's *Wise Vieillard*, in the initial stage after manhood, between 50 and 60 years, 'a man is yet lusty, strong, and youthfull':

> And though that after fifty yeares the strength of nature doth wane, and by little and little doth abate and grow weake, yet wee see that men at that age and after, untill they bee threescore and five yeeres old and upwardes, are fit persons to bee imployed in publike places of charge and command, as well for their counsell and wisedome to direct, as for their ability and valour to execute and performe.

Even between 65 and 80 years 'old men may be fit to be counsellours of estate, and directours and governours of families'. Only after that were they 'fit for nothing but to sit in a chaire in their chamber'.[69] This was by far the most generous chronological extension of authority into old age. Du Laurens, for example, claimed that men were 'fit for to governe common weales' until they were 70, when they became 'incumbred with many small disadvantages', while Whitaker only admitted a ten-year period between the ages of 50 and 60 during which old men 'may doe the Republique good service, and execute offices as other men', beyond which 'by reason of naturall imbecillity, they cannot deserve of the Common-wealth'.[70]

Advocates of the concept of flourishing old age therefore saw it as a continuation of many of the features of patriarchal manhood, excepting those associated with bodily strength. Old men were depicted as assets in public life: 'one of the pillars wherewith politics are supported', literal *senators* or aged counsellors.[71] Their contribution lay primarily in their 'ripenesse of judgement': the rational discretion that was one of the most

---

[67] Cuffe, *The Differences of the Ages of Mans Life*, 116. See also, e.g., Nicolas Abraham de La Framboisière, *An Easy Method to Know the Causes and Signs of the Humour Most Ruleth in the Body* ([London?], 1640), 6.

[68] William Vaughan, *Directions for Health, both Naturall and Artificiall* (London, 1617), 214; Hart, *KAINIKH*, 12. See also Sir Thomas Elyot, *The Castel of Helth* (London, 1561), fos. 10ᵛ–11.

[69] Goulart, *The Wise Vieillard*, 24–5.

[70] Du Laurens, *A Discourse of the Preservation of the Sight*, 174–5; Whitaker, *The Tree of Humane Life*, 44–5.

cherished attributes of manhood. Wisdom, 'the beauty and vigor of the mind', was claimed as one of the prizes of old age, equipping elderly men for continued public service.[72] Wisdom was often depicted as a product of temperance, which, as we have seen, was also associated with maturity. Old men were portrayed as being untroubled by the hasty impulses and burning lusts of youth which were 'blotted out' by age. In particular they were deemed (and expected to be) chaste, free from the 'tyrannous motion' of the 'voluptuous Love' that dogged young men, which tracts on longevity counted as a blessing: 'O noble and excellent gift, wherwith Old age is soe blessed, if it take frome us that thing, which is in youth most vicious & detestable.'[73] Similarly, old men were represented as being largely immune to the debilitating dangers of drink. Unlike the ignition to youthful riot, wine was 'the old mans milke', a beneficial source of heat and comfort for their phlegmatic bodies. According to one regimen, 'one may geve an olde manne as much wine to drinke as he can beare without hurte'.[74] Furthermore, while youth was stereotyped as careless of salvation, old age was heralded as a period for religious reflection and pious deeds. Some authors approached contemplation of virtue as the labour of old age. While 'somewhat debilitated in bodily strength' old men were nonetheless expected to 'prove vigorous in the indowments of the soule'.[75]

Although pious conduct was often represented as a pleasurable task and a rewarding feature of longevity, authors also emphasized that 'pietie, justice or upright dealing, charity or brotherly love' were *duties*, 'beseeming and requirable in the ancienter sort of persons in every thing they doe'.[76] As young men's access to patriarchal manhood was contingent on their adherence to its tenets, so old men's continued claims to it in terms of wisdom and authority, temperance and piety, were dependent upon their appropriate behaviour. While emphasizing the respect owed to the aged, concomitant on the fifth commandment and 'in regard that they carrie upon them, as it were a print of Gods eternitie', even the most staunch defenders of old age nonetheless stressed that the honour due to

---

[71] Sheafe, *Vindiciæ Senectutis*, sig. B; Goulart, *The Wise Vieillard*, 27–8. See also Cicero, *The Worthy Booke of Old Age*, fo. 11ʳ⁻ᵛ.

[72] Goulart, *The Wise Vieillard*, 87; Reading, *The Old Man's Staffe*, 11. See also *A Discoverie of Youth and Old Age*, 25–7.

[73] Goulart, *The Wise Vieillard*, 51; Vaughan, *Directions for Health*, 231–2; Cicero, *The Worthy Booke of Old Age*, fo. 26ᵛ.

[74] Whitaker, *The Tree of Humane Life*, 30; *Regimen Sanitatis Salerni*, trans. Thomas Paynell (London, 1575), fo. 53ᵛ. See also Du Laurens, *A Discourse of the Preservation of the Sight*, 186–7.

[75] Sheafe, *Vindiciæ Senectutis*, sig. A7. See also *A Discoverie of Youth and Old Age*, 24.

[76] Goulart, *The Wise Vieillard*, 1.

age was conditional.[77] 'Dishonor not thou thy gray haires, if thou wouldst have others honour them' warned one preacher, with the further bidding: 'remember thou art old, become thine Age'. It was therefore incumbent on old men to be 'sober, grave, meeke, sound in the fayth, abounding in charitie, patience, and wisedome' if they sought entitlement to gerontocratic dignity.[78]

In addition, it was frequently emphasized that old men were only eligible to the proverbial 'crown of glory' conferred on the aged if they had lived righteously in the past. Elaborating the theme that a virtuous life breeds a contented old age, moralists and writers on health and longevity insisted that honour and comfort were due only in the old age of 'a *good* man'.[79] Thus, for Sheafe, 'Honourable age' was not a product of years alone but of virtuous living, and, as a result, many were ineligible:

There are many that in the former part of their life, have wasted their rationall powers, in lewdnesse, or at lest in idle extravagant courses. These are not OLD-MEN rightly so called: nor (indeed) men at all: but ... evill beasts and slow bellies, such, having lived in pleasures, were dead while they lived: their Sun is gon downe at noone ... their old-age is past, before it comes.[80]

Such admonitions embellished the commonplace that the discomforts associated with old age were the product of a misspent youth. 'Sensuall men' were warned that they risked shortening their lives by ten years, and another author declared that from as early as 35 the 'riots, surfets, sore labours, bearing of extreame burdens, wrestling, actes venerous with the abuse of youth, wil then spring forth, to the detriment of age and sodaine decay of life, in especiall of drunkards'.[81]

The link between a riotous youth and the physical and mental decay associated with age was not always maintained, however, and a persistent range of stereotypes depicting the calamities of ageing indicate that it was often automatically characterized negatively. Gruesome descriptions of the physical failings of age suggest that the potential extension of some

---

[77] John Dod and Robert Cleaver, *A Plaine and Familiar Exposition of the Ten Commandements* (London, 1618), 248.
[78] Reading, *The Old Mans Staffe*, 24, 31; Goulart, *The Wise Vieillard*, 198–9.
[79] Reading, *The Old Mans Staffe*, 8 (my emphasis). See also Cicero, *The Worthy Booke of Old Age*, fos. 7–8ᵛ.
[80] Sheafe, *Vindiciæ Senectutis*, sig. B8. See also, e.g., Gataker, *Abrahams Decease*, 51–5; Dod and Cleaver, *A Plaine and Familiar Exposition of the Ten Commandements*, 250; William Clever, *The Flower of Phisicke. Wherein is Comprehended a True Method for Mans Health: With Three Bookes of Philosophie for the Due Temperature of Mans Life* (London, 1590), 92.
[81] 'A Treatise of Temperance and Sobrietie', in Leonardus Lessius, *Hygiasticon; or, The Right Course of Preserving Life and Health unto Extream Old Age*, trans. N. Ferrar (Cambridge, 1634), 27; William Bullein, *The Government of Health* (London, 1595), fo. 12.

of the attributes of manhood such as wisdom and temperance did little to offset the debilitation associated with old age. Given the numbers of illnesses connected with ageing, it is hardly surprising that many authors viewed it as 'nothing els but a kinde of sicknes' and a disease in its own right.[82] According to Elyot, the aged should expect 'Difficultee of breath, reumes with coughes, strangulyon [sic], and difficultee in pyssynge, ache in the joyntes, dyseases of the raynes, swymminges in the head, palseies, itchyng of al the body, lacke of sleepe, moysture in the eyes and eares, dulnesse of syght, hardnesse of hearynge, tysicknes, or shortnes of breath.' Other complaints included dry and wrinkled skin, hard flesh, weak digestion, dry bowels, trembling nerves, feeble hands, bowed legs, and rotten teeth.[83] In addition, as the 'road way to death', old age stripped men not only of their bodily strength, but also of their memories and their wits, to the extent that 'age leaveth unto man only of man the name'.[84] The implied disqualification of the aged from manhood was compounded by depictions of age in terms of a return to childhood: 'all the actions both of the bodie and minde are weakened and growne feeble, the sences are dull, the memorie lost, and the judgement failing, so that then they become as they were in their infancie'.[85] Although such representations were often reserved for decrepitude rather than 'flourishing' old age, they are suggestive of the potential disdain and even hostility that could be brought to bear on the aged.

A series of unflattering characteristics associated with elderly males also suggested that they were not always approached as founts of wisdom, moderation, and pious dignity. Old men were routinely depicted as covetous, jealous, and suspicious, and derided for being fearful, gloomy, and over-talkative. Even defences of old age presumed covetousness was one of its features, disagreeing merely over whether or not it should be excused.[86] Having had extensive experience of people's wiles, old men were represented as suspicious and burdened by grudges. Suspicions of false-dealing made them distrustful not only of other men but also of their own families, 'by reason that they still feele sharpe goades in their mindes, and grievous woundes in their bodies, either for that their children mis-

[82] *A Discoverie of Youth and Old Age*, 31.

[83] Elyot, *Castel of Helth*, fo. 81; Francis Bacon, *The Historie of Life and Death. With Observations Naturall and Experimentall for the Prolonging of Life* (London, 1638), 276–8; William Morray, *A Short Treatise of Death in Sixe Chapters: Together with the Aenigmatic Description of Old Age and Death, Written Ecclesiastes 12* (Edinburgh, 1633), 43.

[84] Goulart, *The Wise Vieillard*, 23; Hunnis, *Hunnies Recreations*, 53.

[85] Du Laurens, *A Discourse of the Preservation of the Sight*, 175. See also, e.g., *The Foure Ages of Man*; Thomas Cogan, *The Haven of Health* (London, 1636), 186.

[86] Cf. Goulart, *The Wise Vieillard*, 70–1; and Sheafe, *Vindiciæ Senectutis*, 111–12.

governe themselves, or their wives behave themselves usurpingly', suggesting that a further smart suffered by old men was their relinquished control over others as well as themselves.[87] One of the explanations for their tendency for prattling like 'chirping Grashopper[s]' was that they were otherwise powerless: 'knowledge, the onely thing old age can bragge of, cannot be manifested but by utterance'. Yet old men's conversation was frequently derogated as tedious because 'their manner is always to commend times past, and ever to bode and presage that the times to come will bee worse and worse'.[88]

Such representations suggest that any extension of the qualities of patriarchal manhood into old age was, at best, extremely qualified. Although the gerontocratic ideal received considerable lip service, most authors begrudged prolonging the attributes of manhood too far into old age, or allowing old men too much distinction in their own right. Even when they were being rejected, images of decrepitude, physical decay, and mental incapacity often outweighed claims to wisdom, gravity, and temperance. Furthermore, such positive claims were not extended to all old men. While some were deemed capable of continued public service and household government, this was contingent upon their unblemished living and physical capability (if not strength). It was also conditional upon access to office and sufficient means of support—although the fact that such assets were beyond the reach of many remained unacknowledged, masking the distinctions of social status that informed most discussions of ageing in print.

Both youth and old age came off badly in comparisons with manhood, whether explicitly or implicitly drawn. Although occasionally celebrated in their own right, on the one hand for vigour and spirit, and on the other hand for gravity and wisdom, youth and old age were more usually represented as two troublesome extremes on either side of the middle—and preferable—way of manhood. The young and the old were condemned for being ungoverned in their speech. The young were prodigal and wildly optimistic, the old were covetous and tediously gloomy. The young could not govern their bodies, the old were debilitated by disease. The young were headstrong and wilful, the old were fearful and timid. The young were lustful, the old were lust*less*. The young could not control their unruly impulses; the old had none to control. Their self-mastery was by default, rather than by design. The claims of both young and old

---

[87] Goulart, *The Wise Vieillard*, 76. See also Cuffe, *The Differences of the Ages of Mans Life*, 131.
[88] Bacon, *The Historie of Life and Death*, 282; Cuffe, *The Differences of the Ages of Mans Life*, 132; Goulart, *The Wise Vieillard*, 76.

to autonomy were contingent upon their good behaviour, and to a largely unacknowledged degree upon their means, for which they could well be obliged to others.

By implication the men enjoying 'man's estate' were in control. They were masters of themselves, of others, and of resources. Rational speech and discreet bearing, moderation, bodily strength, and even-headedness were claimed for 'man's age' as authors laboured to fix the meanings of manhood in these terms. The 'manly age' was therefore the 'constant age': achieving a perfect balance between passion and discretion, it was represented as the golden mean between the deviations of youth and old age.[89] By presenting these attributes of normative manhood as conditional upon age, conduct writers excluded young men and old from its benefits unless they were endowed with sufficient social status or virtue to transcend the disadvantages of their years. Such distinctions therefore worked to subordinate both the young and the old and to limit access to claims to patriarchal manhood in terms of rational discretion, bodily stature, authority, and self-control. Yet, as we shall see in the next two chapters, they also involved the considerable simplification—if not denial—of the many other differences between men which informed normative constructions of manhood. Age differentiation also sidestepped concerns about the failure of many adult men to perform the duties expected of them and the difficulties associated with governing both themselves, and others.

[89] Du Laurens, *A Discourse of the Preservation of the Sight*, 174.

2
The Imagined Body of 'Man's Estate'

> Mans differing motions are the jar in question.
> The Combatants are *Passion*, and *Discretion*:
> Each striving to be chiefe in the desire.
> Or, if you please to straine it any higher,
> Then here you, partly, may behold the strife
> Betweene the Flesh, and Spirit in this Life.[1]

ONE of the fundamental building blocks of early modern patriarchal ideology was the assertion of men's superior physical and intellectual capacities. This was expressed both generically, in terms of humanity's relation to the rest of the animal kingdom, and particularly, in terms of a gendered hierarchy of being that ranked males above females. This hierarchy was an early modern commonplace present in a wide range of genres; one context in which it was most clearly articulated was in the varied medical literature of the period which discussed the form, functions, and properties of the human body. As with depictions of youth and old age, the generic body idealized by medical writers was almost always assumed to be male, whereas female bodies and the qualities associated with them generally only received explicit attention as deviations from a routinely invoked male norm. So, for example, one particularly popular tract explained that women had less body hair, fewer teeth, shriller voices, narrower chests, and more ill humours than men.[2] Women's relative imperfection was generally explained either in Aristotelian terms as a freakish accident of nature—as 'a man hurt'—or in Galenic terms as the necessary condition of a second sex fashioned for reproductive purposes.[3] More often, women's bodies only appeared in a fragmented form (particularly in discussions of reproductive functions), while some authors declined altogether to discuss female anatomy on the grounds of

---

[1] *The Foure Ages of Man* (London, 1635), title page.
[2] *The Problemes of Aristotle, with Other Philosophers and Phisitions* (Edinburgh, 1595), sigs. A6ʳ–7, B8ᵛ, C5, D2, E3ᵛ.
[3] Ibid., sig. Hᵛ; Ian Maclean, *The Renaissance Notion of Woman: A Study in the Fortunes of Scholasticism and Medical Science in European Intellectual Life* (Cambridge, 1980), ch. 3.

decency.[4] It is therefore not difficult to see how medical discourse featured as one of the central strands in the construction of female inferiority by denigrating and fragmenting the female body in comparison with an ideal male norm—a point which has been widely highlighted by historians of early modern women.[5] In contrast to women, men were characterized as the beneficiaries of bodily perfection, capable of achieving a balanced and temperate constitution. This, crucially, was the bodily basis of the link between masculinity and reason which in turn provided the justification for men's claim to social and political precedence in manhood.

Comparatively unexplored, however, are the terms in which the ideal male standard itself was constructed. This chapter argues that the notion of male perfection was neither assiduously maintained nor universally extended to all men. As an ideal it was claimed most definitively in direct comparisons with women. Yet such comparisons only comprised a fraction of most medical texts, which tended to dedicate the majority of their pages instead to the problems associated with bodies that were implicitly and often explicitly male. It would be mistaken to suggest that the male body was uniformly represented simply as the apex of human existence. While a normative rational and controlled male body was certainly invoked, the predominant emphasis of many medical texts was on the difficulties associated with achieving this ideal. Although the superior qualities of manhood were frequently asserted, they were not always assumed to exist. Instead, medical works tended to emphasize the considerable extent of bodily instability suffered by men as well as women, albeit on different grounds, and stressed the degree of effort required to overcome the obstacles to an even-tempered existence.

Furthermore, while the perfectly temperate body of the adult male was

---

[4] e.g. John Banister, *The Historie of Man, Sucked from the Sappe of the Most Approved Anathomistes* (London, 1578), sig. B1ᵛ, p. 85. See also Sir Thomas Elyot's demurral from writing about menstruation in the 'vulgare tongue' in *The Castel of Helth* (London, 1561), fo. 64, and the lengthy apology for writing about women's generative organs in English in Helkiah Crooke, *Mikrokosmographia: A Description of the Body of Man*, 2nd edn. (London, 1631), 197.

[5] Patricia Crawford, 'Attitudes to Menstruation in Seventeenth-Century England', *Past and Present*, 91 (1981); Lucinda McCray Beier, *Sufferers and Healers: The Experience of Illness in Seventeenth-Century England* (London, 1987), 213–15; Londa Schiebinger, *The Mind Has No Sex? Women in the Origins of Modern Science* (Cambridge, Mass., 1989), 161–5; Anthony Fletcher, *Gender, Sex and Subordination in England 1500–1800* (London, 1995), ch. 2; Olwen Hufton, *The Prospect before Her: A History of Women in Western Europe*, i: *1500–1800* (London, 1995), 39–44; Margaret R. Sommerville, *Sex and Subjection: Attitudes to Women in Early-Modern Society* (London, 1995), ch. 2; Sara Mendelson and Patricia Crawford, *Women in Early Modern England* (Oxford, 1998), 18–30; Gail Kern Paster, 'The Unbearable Coldness of Female Being: Women's Imperfection and the Humoral Economy', *English Literary Renaissance*, 28 (1998). For theories of women's inferior rational capacity see Genevieve Lloyd, *The Man of Reason: 'Male' and 'Female' in Western Philosophy* (Minneapolis, 1984).

occasionally invoked in comparisons with the female body, it was most vividly constructed through implicit comparisons with other, inferior, versions of the male body. Men's bodies were represented through endless distinctions, comparisons, divisions, and subdivisions, whereas women's bodies appeared only partially, in fragmented form, with scant acknowledgement of the variations between them. As Moira Gatens has argued, 'the selection of a particular image of the human body will be a selection from a continuum of differences'.[6] The spectrum of difference invoked in guides to health involved hierarchies of male bodies as well as the gender hierarchy which placed males above females. Medical tracts treated the contribution of gender difference to constructions of manhood almost as cursorily as texts discussing age. The ideal male body being 'imagined' in these texts, therefore, was by no means consistent; it involved frequent slippage between the archetype occasionally suggested by male–female comparisons and the numerous different categories of the male body ranked according to age, humoral complexion, environment, and social status.

As a consequence, the broad range of variations between men's bodies detracted from the normative ideal of manhood by suggesting the degree of male as well as female deviation from it. Men's bodies appeared unable to comply with the rational containment expected to accompany adult masculinity, or 'man's estate'. Yet this potential contradiction was diverted by many medical tracts which grafted male deviation from the ideal onto hierarchies of age and social status. Ultimately, the most striking claim embedded within such works was that aspirations to the temperate ideal were restricted to an elite minority variously distinguished by their moral, religious, and, more implicitly, their social superiority. While these suppositions were incidental, and wholly in line with the assumptions of a genteel readership, they nonetheless illustrate the fundamental tension which lay at the core of patriarchal ideology. On the one hand male superiority was claimed for all men in male–female comparisons. On the other hand, patriarchal ideology delineated a more exclusive set of privileges which excluded many men on the grounds of age, social status, and moral and bodily temperament. While many medical texts laboured to deny the plurality of women's experiences by emphasizing gender as the primary determinant of their (deviant) identity, men were more likely to be subcategorized in terms of age, status, and temperament, and as a result patriarchal privilege was implicitly reserved for those who also exercised social privilege.

[6] Moira Gatens, *Imaginary Bodies: Ethics, Power and Corporeality* (London, 1996), p. vii.

This chapter will focus on the ways in which men's bodies were characterized as unstable and problematic in contrast to the normative ideal of temperate, reasoned control, and on the consequent ranking of different types of male body in areas of early modern medical writing. Just as there was not a distinct medical 'profession' in early modern England, so also there was no clear-cut corpus of medical works. In terms of both content and authorship, printed works addressing health and disease spanned a range of fields: they overlapped with religious exhortation, moral philosophy, and astrology, and they were written by clergymen, lawyers, and civil servants as well as by established physicians. They ranged from heavily illustrated tomes on the intricate details of human anatomy (largely written by and for practising surgeons) to pocket-sized collections of recipes and remedies.[7] Such publications constituted an expanding field. Paul Slack has estimated that 392 editions of 153 medical tracts were produced in English between 1486 and 1604. By this time it is possible that one such book was in use for every twenty people, although Slack suspects that their readership was chiefly confined to the gentry.[8] This chapter focuses primarily on textbooks on health and regimens since they offer the most expansive accounts of the body in terms of a normative ideal against which both health and disease were to be judged. The frequent reprinting of many of these works, often over the course of several decades, suggests that they endured as a highly marketable subgenre throughout the period between 1560 and 1640.[9]

One of the best-known examples is Thomas Elyot's *Castel of Helth* which, after its initial publication in 1539, exercised considerable influence over Elizabethan tracts, and went through seventeen editions by the early seventeenth century. Defending himself from insinuations that the publication of a tract on physic was beneath the dignity of a knight, Elyot maintained that he was serving the interests of the commonwealth, thus reflecting the broader relevance of medicine to the humanist educative agenda which sought to instil virtue in the body as well as the mind. The *Castel of Helth* espoused Galenic pathology, newly shored up by humanist scholarship, which approached health in terms of maintaining the body's humoral stability according to each individual's innate temperament and circumstances. According to humoral theory, all matter consisted

---

[7] Cf. Crooke, *Mikrokosmographia*, and John Partridge, *The Widowes Treasure, Plentifully Furnished with Secretes in Phisicke* (London, 1585).

[8] Paul Slack, 'Mirrors of Health and Treasures of Poor Men: The Uses of the Vernacular Medical Literature of Tudor England', in Charles Webster (ed.), *Health, Medicine, and Mortality in the Sixteenth Century* (Cambridge, 1979), 239, 258–61.

[9] Ibid., 243. See also Margaret Healy, *Fictions of Disease in Early Modern England: Bodies, Plagues and Politics* (Basingstoke, 2001), ch. 1.

of the four elements, each of which was associated with a combination of qualities: air (hot and wet); fire (hot and dry); earth (cold and dry); and water (cold and wet). In the human body these four elements were associated, respectively, with blood, yellow bile, black bile, and phlegm, which were in turn linked to four bodily temperaments or humours: sanguine, choleric, melancholic, and phlegmatic. There was a distinct hierarchy of bodily qualities and their associated humours. Although all four qualities were necessary for a body to function, different proportions produced differences in bodily capacity according to temperament, age, and gender. Heat and moisture were life-giving, while coldness and dryness sapped energy. Thus gender difference was accounted for in terms of women's comparative coldness and moistness in relation to men who were, in contrast, privileged by their relative heat and dryness. Other differences were also delineated. Sanguine bodies were characterized as more healthy and vigorous than melancholic ones. Young bodies were represented as dangerously overpowered by heat and moisture, while the sluggishness of old age was accorded to a surfeit of coldness and dryness. Additional differences in bodily complexions were attributed to the impact of external influences such as diet, exercise, emotional demands, the environment, the climate, the season of the year, and even the time of day.

By the time of its final reprinting in 1610, the *Castel of Helth* was decidedly unrepresentative of the medical pluralism that had emerged in England by the later sixteenth century.[10] While many of its Elizabethan counterparts were more eclectic in content, Galenic theory continued to feature heavily in textbooks on health which were some of the 'stock medical works by the traditionalists', often resisting newer, Paracelsan approaches that treated disease as a separate entity rather than as a product of bodily imbalance.[11] That they were failing in this regard is suggested not only by the inclusion of chemical remedies in regimens, but also by their increasingly embattled tone. Thus in his reassertion of humoral theory Thomas Walkington acknowledged: 'I know the *Paracelsian* will utterly condemn my endeavour for bringing the foure Humours on the stage again, they having hist them off so long ago.'[12] Such works were by no means obso-

---

[10] Sue Carol Lorch, 'Medical Theory and Renaissance Tragedy', unpublished Ph.D. thesis (Louisville, Ky., 1976); Charles Webster, 'Alchemical and Paracelsian Medicine', in id. (ed.), *Health, Medicine, and Mortality*; id., 'William Harvey and the Crisis of Medicine in Jacobean England', in Jerome J. Bylebyl (ed.), *William Harvey and his Age: The Professional and Social Context of the Discovery of Circulation* (Baltimore, 1979).

[11] Allen G. Debus, *The English Paracelsians* (London, 1965), 77; Walter Pagel, *Paracelsus: An Introduction to Philosophical Medicine in the Era of the Renaissance* (Basel, 1958), 137–8.

[12] Thomas Walkington, *The Optick Glasse of Humors. Wherein the Foure Complections are Succinctly Painted Forth* (London, 1607), sig. A3ᵛ.

lete, however, and continued to flourish alongside and incorporate newer approaches, not least because humoral pathology served the entrenched interests of established physicians well beyond the mid-seventeenth century.[13] Many authors emphasized their desire to disseminate guidance on the preservation of health, even if only to enable the selection of a good physician over a scurrilous quack or empiric.[14] Most regimens and guides to health were, therefore, directed towards two main interest groups: physicians—the elite ranks of early modern medical practitioners—and those wealthy enough to purchase their services.[15]

Littered with Latin and Greek quotation and classical examples emphasizing the link between bodily containment and ethical living, the content of such works suggests that they may have been approached by an elite readership as a minor branch of conduct literature. The physician Thomas Cogan's regimen, produced in eight editions between 1584 and 1636, was 'Chiefly gathered for the comfort of Students' in order to coach young gentlemen how to rule appetite with reason and achieve a measured existence.[16] Health and morality were closely linked in such works, and the exemplary body frequently epitomized the man of virtue. The 'perfectly and exactly temperate' body celebrated by the eminent humanist and Dutch physician Levine Lemnius in his *Touchstone of Complexions* clearly embodied the traits expected of a gentleman. In appearance it displayed 'a kinde of heroicall grace and amiablenesse', and its perfect balance enabled both rational and civil action. Such finely tuned bodily equilibrium was linked to a superior quality of mind: 'His memory is stedfast and holding fast . . . his minde quick, sharpe and industrious, wisely and circumspectly dealing in every thing that he taketh in hand.' This in turn produced 'honest and vertuous' manners and conversation informed by 'singular and excellent' wit and 'good judgement and con-

---

[13] Owsei Temkin, *Galenism: Rise and Decline of a Medical Philosophy* (Ithaca, NY, 1973), ch. 3; Lester S. King, 'The Transformation of Galenism', in Allen G. Debus (ed.), *Medicine in Seventeenth-Century England* (Berkeley, 1974); Charles Webster, *The Great Instauration: Science, Medicine and Reform 1626–1660* (London, 1975), ch. 4; Andrew Wear, 'Galen in the Renaissance', in Vivian Nutton (ed.), *Galen: Problems and Prospects* (London, 1981); A. W. Sloan, *English Medicine in the Seventeenth Century* (Durham, 1996); Healy, *Fictions of Disease*, ch. 1.

[14] e.g. Philip Barrough, *The Methode of Phisicke, Conteyning the Causes, Signes, and Cures of Inward Diseases in Mans Body from the Head to the Foote* (London, 1583); E.D., *The Copy of a Letter. The Former Part Conteineth Rules for the Preservation of Health* (London, 1606); James Hart, *KAINIKH; or, The Diet of the Diseased* (London, 1633).

[15] Margaret Pelling and Charles Webster, 'Medical Practitioners', in Webster (ed.), *Health, Medicine, and Mortality*.

[16] Thomas Cogan, *The Haven of Health* (London, 1636), title page and sig. ¶4.

sideration', free from all 'rashnesse' and 'ill affections'.[17] Such attributes were the stock in trade of courtesy books, and were central to lessons on gentlemanly conduct.[18]

This temperate, rational model was by no means uniformly expected of men by medical writers, however. One of the most striking aspects of humoral accounts of the body is their emphasis on how difficult the ideal was to achieve, especially given the body's temperamental changeability. The bodies described in these terms were not static but in an almost constant state of flux. An even-tempered bodily complexion was not a given—even for (gentle)men—but a largely unrealizable standard used both to gauge illness and health and to account more generally for differences in physical and emotional potential. Paradoxically, constructions of the normative male body therefore conveyed a sense of its considerable limits, both in terms of the likelihood of its achievement, and because of its supposed inapplicability to many early modern men. Echoing accounts of age which privileged manhood as the pinnacle of the life course, medical writers nonetheless represented 'man's estate' as a distinctly limited phase, sometimes only spanning a decade of the life course. In addition there were many perceived dangers to the bodily stability of adult men, derived both from internal natural weaknesses and external environmental threats. While the idealized body of man's estate was potentially undermined by such dangers, they were often accounted for in terms of a hierarchy of manhood which worked to exclude 'inferior' men from the ideal, thereby retaining it only for a select group of men, often as an apparently self-evident justification for their gentle status. Although of little direct concern to medical writers who were mostly well placed in relation to such ideas, these constructions of manhood are suggestive of the ways in which patriarchal ideals were socially refracted, and far from uniformly applied to early modern men.

---

[17] Levinus Lemnius, *The Touchstone of Complexions Expedient and Profitable for All such as be Desirous and Carefull of their Bodily Health*, trans. Thomas Newton (London, 1633), 52, 57, 54–5.

[18] e.g., Henry Peacham, *The Complete Gentleman*, ed. Virgil B. Heltzel (Ithaca, NY, 1962), ch. 17; Richard Brathwait, *The English Gentleman: Containing Sundry Excellent Rules how to Accommodate Himselfe in the Manage of Publike or Private Affaires* (London, 1630), section 7 on 'Moderation'. See also Anna Bryson, 'The Rhetoric of Status: Gesture, Demeanour and the Image of the Gentleman in Sixteenth- and Seventeenth-Century England', in Lucy Gent and Nigel Llewellyn (eds.), *Renaissance Bodies: The Human Figure in English Culture c.1540–1660* (London, 1990), and pp. 30–4 above.

THE AGES OF MAN

As we have seen in Chapter 1, one of the clearest hierarchies of masculinity was based on age. The differences between the ages of man were central to humoral theory which approached the life course as series of temperamental shifts. Although medical writers occasionally applied such divisions to both sexes,[19] the various stages of the life course were usually conceptualized in terms that were male specific, particularly as the attributes of each stage were closely related to the normative male sex role expected of it. Medical accounts of the ages of man drew upon astrological and moral traditions as well as humoral theory, and varied in their structure and complexity. They ranged from simple tripartite divisions into childhood, manhood, and old age to systems detailing up to twelve stages.[20] With the exception of Henry Cuffe's account of *The Differences of the Ages of Mans Life*, authors rarely acknowledged the existence of rival systems, despite the considerable disparity between them not only in terms of the numbers of life-cycle stages but also in terms of their duration (Fig. 3). According to Elyot and Bullein manhood was all but over by 35 or 40, whereas for most other authors this was the time when it was just beginning.[21] Texts which approached ageing according to multiples of sevens—the 'climactericall' years—differed further over whether 49 should be accounted either the pinnacle or the end of manhood.[22] This suggests that the ages of man were as much functionally as chronologically defined, especially by authors who omitted chronological tags in preference for an emphasis on the physical or social attributes expected of the different stages.[23]

Across this diversity of approach there was a common emphasis on both 'lusty' or 'staid' youth as well as manhood as the high points in the life course. In more complex schemes, the prime of youth (distinguished by many authors from adolescence or the 'stripling age') enjoyed some

---

[19] e.g. the scheme in J. A. Comenius, *Orbis Sensualium Pictus*, 3rd edn. (1672), illustrated in Mendelson and Crawford, *Women in Early Modern England*, 76.

[20] Elizabeth Sears, *The Ages of Man: Medieval Interpretations of the Life Cycle* (Princeton, 1986); John Winter Jones, 'Observations on the Origin of the Division of Man's Life into Stages', *Archaeologia*, 35 (1853).

[21] Elyot, *Castel of Helth*, fos. 10ᵛ–11; William Bullein, *The Government of Health* (London, 1595), fos. 11–12.

[22] Cf. William Vaughan, *Directions for Health, both Naturall and Artificiall* (London, 1617), 221–2; Cogan, *Haven of Health*, 193.

[23] e.g. William Clever, *The Flower of Phisicke. Wherein is Comprehended a True Method for Mans Health: With Three Bookes of Philosophie for the Due Temperature of Mans Life* (London, 1590), 69–71.

Four-part schemes

Elyot *Castel of Helth*		Goeurot *The Regiment of Life*		Bullein *The Government of Health*	
adolescence	to 25	childhood	to 25	childhood	to 15
youth	25–40	youth	25–35	youth	15–25
old age	40–60	middle age	35–50	'the lustie state of life'	25–35
decrepit age	60+	old age	50+	old age	35+

Seven-part schemes

Lemnius *Touchstone of Complexions*		Vaughan *Directions for Health*		Hart KAINIKH	
infancy	to 7	infancy	to 7	infancy	to 7
childhood	7–15	childhood	7–14	childhood	7–14
puberty	15–18	'strippling age'	14–22	youth	14–21
adolescence	18–25				
youth	25–35	young man	22–34	'staied youth'	21–35
man's age	35–50	man's age	34–60	manhood	35–45/49
old age	50/65+	flourishing old age	60–74	green old age	49–62/63
		decrepit old age	74+	decrepit old age	63–97

Fig. 3. Differing schemes of the ages of man

of the qualities that inaugurated manhood, suggesting that the medical literature was comparatively generous in its extension of manly qualities to young men. In such schemes it was children and adolescents who were primarily excluded from aspirations to bodily equilibrium on the grounds of their excessive heat and moisture. Childhood was a 'tender state' witnessing a gradual shift in temperament as the child aged into a more 'wilfull and slippery' adolescent.[24] As heat became increasingly overpowering at puberty, and in the absence of the dryer and colder qualities associated with maturity, it was an uncontainable source of great disruption, both to young bodies and to the society in which they lived. 'Striplings' of 14 or 15 years old were characterized as 'nimble, active, wanton, unmodest, malepert, sawcy, proud, without wit, and much given to toying and playing', all of which stemmed from 'the boyling of their blood within them, which boyleth up, and as it were seetheth in their Veines, even as new Wine, Ale, or Beere spurgeth and worketh in the Tunne'.[25] In contrast, the prime of youth was marked by the gradual tempering of such hot impulses and for some authors it witnessed the 'lustie' peak of the male physique.[26] However, like the conduct literature discussed in Chapter 1, health tracts also expressed considerable ambivalence towards the physical vitality attributed to young men, and most authors ultimately expressed their preference for the greater mental discretion associated with manhood or the 'myddle age'.[27] While the hot vigour of youth was frequently celebrated, it was nonetheless also approached as a continued source of instability which could easily overpower the brain and hinder capacity for rational action.

Attaining 'man's estate' on the other hand was represented as the assumption of a bodily inheritance, marked by a humoral shift into 'the most constant and setled part of our life, as having our life-qualities most firme and in greatest mediocritie'. Manhood was associated with moderation and constancy, since this was the stage when the body's heat was sufficiently tempered without yet facing the threat of extinction, and although the body's heat and moisture were beginning to wane, the passionate impulses and emotions associated with these qualities were less likely to distract men from their appropriate callings or divert their minds from the powers of reason. Accordingly, 'man's age' was like 'the *Autumne* or *Harvest*, when after the manifold turmoiles and dangers of our forespent life, the good giftes and indowments of our minde (as we see it fall out in the fruites of Nature) receive a kind of seasonable and timely ripeness'.[28] Autumn was the season of melancholy, and the celebration of manhood in these terms corresponded with late sixteenth- and early seventeenth-century preoccupations with the virtues of a melancholic

---

[24] Bullein, *Government of Health*, fo. 10ᵛ; Lemnius, *Touchstone of Complexions*, 46.
[25] Lemnius, *Touchstone of Complexions*, 156–7. See also Gail Kern Paster, 'Nervous Tension: Networks of Blood and Spirit in the Early Modern Body', in David Hillman and Carla Mazzio (eds.), *The Body in Parts: Fantasies of Corporeality in Early Modern Europe* (London, 1997).
[26] e.g. Clever, *Flower of Phisicke*, 69; Bullein, *Government of Health*, fo. 11ᵛ.
[27] Jehan Goeurot, *The Regiment of Life*, trans. Thomas Phayer (London, 1546), fo. 3.
[28] Henry Cuffe, *The Differences of the Ages of Mans Life* (London, 1607), 119, 116.

temperament.[29] Medical writers therefore also endorsed manhood as the summit of the life cycle above the sanguine season of youth: 'man is in his full ripenesse ... [and] his minde advisedly, carefully, and wisely dealeth in everything that he enterpriseth'.[30] According to the Galenic model, such integrity was based in a humoral shift in the body which kept the qualities of heat and moisture sufficiently balanced by coldness and dryness so that they were 'aswell tempered as their nature possibly can be'.[31]

While celebrating this even-tempered equilibrium of manhood, medical discussions of the ages of man also approached it as a fleeting phenomenon. In whichever way 'man's estate' was defined chronologically, what is most striking about medical discussions of age is their unanimous limitation of manhood itself to a mere ten or fifteen years of the life cycle. The one more generous exception was the poet William Vaughan's scheme which allowed twenty-six years for the peak of 'mans age'.[32] For many others, ten years was the maximum period of time designated to manhood. Threatened on one side by the potentially chaotic heat of youth, manhood was also quickly overshadowed by decrepitude in later years, which was approached in terms of an undesirable decline. Although occasionally associated with gravity and authority, old age was more often depicted in terms of lost capacity, specifically caused by diminishing heat, and it was frequently likened to a return to childhood.[33] So, for example, the aged were depicted by Vaughan as sharing children's natural fearfulness which made them 'againe play the babies'.[34] Ageing was expected to be particularly acute if it followed an excessive youth which had overspent the body's vital spirits. As the physician Tobias Venner stated this particular commonplace, 'a riotous youth breedeth a miserable age, full of paines and loathsome maladies'.[35] Despite concessions of a period of 'flourishing' (as opposed to 'decrepit') old age by some authors, ageing was more often treated as a 'calamitie', or 'a great and troublesome sicknesse' and thus a disease in its own right.[36]

Although manhood was presented as the pinnacle of the life cycle,

---

[29] Michael MacDonald, *Mystical Bedlam: Madness, Anxiety, and Healing in Seventeenth-Century England* (Cambridge, 1981), 150–64. I am indebted to David Lederer for this observation.
[30] Lemnius, *Touchstone of Complexions*, 47.
[31] Cuffe, *The Differences of the Ages of Mans Life*, 116.
[32] Vaughan, *Directions for Health*, 214.
[33] Keith Thomas, 'Age and Authority in Early Modern England', *Proceedings of the British Academy*, 62 (1976), 245.
[34] Vaughan, *Directions for Health*, 249.
[35] Tobias Venner, *Via Recta ad Vitam Longam; or, A Plaine Philosophicall Demonstration of the Nature, Faculties, and Effects of All such Things as by Way of Nourishments Make for the Preservation of Health* (London, 1628), 170.
[36] Clever, *Flower of Phisicke*, 70; Vaughan, *Directions for Health*, 51. See also pp. 41–4 above.

medical discussions of the ages of man therefore also suggested its considerable limits. However much it was cited as the justification for men's superiority over women, the heat associated with manhood was neither a lasting nor an unqualified benefit. Ambivalence towards youth's 'lustiness', for example, suggests that both men and women's minds were deemed to encounter bodily hazards, although as a result of different causes: whereas women's powers of reason were considered to be diminished by an excess of coldness and moisture, it was men's greater heat that often threatened their ability to behave rationally. Of course, such reservations were never expressed in direct comparisons of the sexes. Moreover, it was assumed that men at least had the greater potential for both vigorous and rational action, even if its achievement was limited, whereas evidence of substantial heat in women was routinely deemed to be problematic, if not monstrous, reflecting a double standard at work in concepts of the humoral economy.[37] Thus humoral logic was considerably stacked in favour of patriarchal principles, and served to reinforce social norms. Yet the moderation expected of even-tempered manhood was nonetheless limited to a brief spell of the life cycle—no more than ten or fifteen years—constructed in terms of a hierarchy of age which subordinated both the old and the young on the grounds of bodily incapacity. Moreover, the degree to which moderation was achieved depended on the character of individual humoral complexions. Even amongst those who were reaping the harvest of manhood there was a considerable spectrum of temperaments which resulted in a range of behavioural characteristics, both positive and negative. Each of the four complexions involved an element of deviation from the ideal of the temperate man, and their elaboration involved the further demarcation of hierarchical distinctions between men, further circumscribing achievement of 'man's estate'.

A HIERARCHY OF COMPLEXIONS

Despite being privileged above the other stages in the life course, man's estate, once achieved, by no means guaranteed a balanced temperament. The temperate ideal topped eight other possible humoral complexions: simple (moist, hot, dry, cold) and compound (sanguine, choleric, melancholic, phlegmatic). The vast majority of bodies, therefore, even if male and mature, were not free of unruly and excessive impulses and needed serious regulation and discipline if they were to aspire to moderation.

[37] Paster, 'The Unbearable Coldness of Female Being'.

The Imagined Body of 'Man's Estate'

Most authors concurred that perfect humoral temperance was a rarity, if not an impossibility; a temperate complexion was 'a thyng very seldome sene amonge men', and generally served as a standard from which most deviated rather than a realistic set of expectations for all men.[38] This, in turn, provided the basis for the further elaboration of hierarchies of masculinity, which were constructed through the comparison of the different humoral complexions, and through discussions of the internal relationships between different bodily organs. Beyond the temperate ideal, each complexion had negative as well as positive connotations, and, in discussions of the differences between them, the imagined body of man's estate was further splintered into a range of subordinate categories which subtly interacted with conceptions of the social order.

Both the simple and compound complexions were clearly ranked in terms of appearance and character as well as health. According to Lemnius's *Touchstone of Complexions*, a hot complexion was 'the first in order' since 'for conservation of health it be better then the rest', and 'whosoever is of that Complexion and constitution, is of stature comely, and of shape and beauty agreeable and consonant to manly dignity'. Conversely, a cold complexion placed a man at the opposite end of the spectrum as 'the worst of all others, and furthest from that state which is perfectest and best'. Besides suffering from ill health, obesity, and sluggishness, cold men were blighted with weak characters, and were likely to be branded as womanish or effeminate: 'Such persons have faltering tongues, and nothing ready in utterance, a nice, soft, and womannish voyce, weake, and feeble faculties of nature, ill memory, blockish wit, doltish minde, courage (for lacke of heat and slendernesse of vitall spirit) fearefull and timorous, and at the wagging of every straw afraid.'[39]

This logic was also applied to individual bodily organs. A man's virility, for example, was dictated by the temperature of his testicles. Once again, the degree of heat determined the hierarchy. If hot, a man displayed 'Great appetite to the act of generacyon. Ingendryng men children [with] Heare soone growen about the members.' Conversely cold 'genitoryes' caused diminished 'puissance', evident in a lack of pubic hair, limited sexual appetite, and (if successful in conception) the spawning of female children.[40] The contrast between hot and cold temperaments therefore opened up a sliding scale of manhood, conceived in gendered terms. Topping the hierarchy were the lusty, valiant men, literally and metaphorically fired up to courageous action. At the bottom of the scale were

---

[38] Goeurot, *Regiment of Life*, sig. Aᵛ.
[39] Lemnius, *Touchstone of Complexions*, 61, 97, 104.
[40] Elyot, *Castel of Helth*, fo. 7ʳ⁻ᵛ.

the men undignified by heat, accorded the insult of being little better than women: 'for the most part persons effeminate, nice, tender, without courage and spirit, sleepy, slothfull, weaklings, meycockes, and not apt nor able to beget any children'.[41]

Yet there were other hierarchies at work, beyond those conceived in gendered terms. The majority of medical discussions of the complexions focused on the four humours, since it was agreed that most bodies were characterized by a combination of qualities rather than just one. These compound complexions were also ranked according to their degree of heat, and with similar implications for 'placing' men on grounds of age and status—as one regimen put it, 'the sayde foure humours governe and rule everyone in his place'.[42] The details of the character types of the four humours were frequently rehearsed, often infused with analogies corresponding to perceptions of social hierarchies. The sanguine complexion was 'the princeliest and best of all', characterized by 'promptnesse of minde, quicknesse in device and sharpnesse in practice, which by daily use and exercise attaineth in the end to wisedome, knowledge and experience of many things'.[43] Yet sanguine men also risked being overcome by their hot blood. According to Lemnius, therefore, without sufficient education, 'They that be *meere* Sanguine ... are commonly dolts and fooles, or at least, not greatly cumbred with much wit.' Such men were not much better than animals: 'In many men there is a great resemblance and affinity in nature with other Beasts, and the further that these digresse from the purity of temperament, the lesse sway in them beareth reason, judgement, understanding, willingnesse to doe good, wisedome, and discretion.' Even a sanguine complexion, therefore, did not guarantee rational capacity in a man. Instead the body's susceptibility to unruly impulses was frequently emphasized. The 'vitall spirit' associated with 'the force and power of blood in mans body' was a double-edged sword, and was the source of as much disruption as virtue. Without education and training in civility, therefore, such men were more likely to feature in the commonwealth as asses rather than exemplars.[44]

As even greater deviations from the temperate ideal, the other three compound complexions were similarly discussed in terms of their drawbacks and limitations. The choleric man was represented as quarrelsome, 'stoute stomaked', ambitious, and 'desirous of honor ... by reason that superfluos heate maketh mans minde prove to arrogance and foole hardi-

---

[41] Lemnius, *Touchstone of Complexions*, 130.
[42] Goeurot, *Regiment of Life*, sig. A^v.
[43] Walkington, *Optick Glasse of Humors*, fo. 58; Lemnius, *Touchstone of Complexions*, 159–60.
[44] Lemnius, *Touchstone of Complexions*, 155 (my emphasis), 159.

nes'.[45] Despite being 'lively, dapper, quicke, [and] nimble', choleric types were caricatured as being meddlers and wily like foxes. Unchecked, they were 'unconstant, crafty, deceitfull, subtle, wily, cogging ... and so fickle of word and deed, that a man may not well and safely deale with them, nor trust them, as persons to whom there is no more hold then is of a wet Eele by the tayle'. The less laudable aspects of manhood were further elaborated in discussions of phlegmatic and melancholic complexions. Although melancholy was celebrated by a number of English physicians, according to Lemnius the coldness and dryness of the melancholic could also leave him 'voide of reason, foolish, block-headed, doltish, dull, and doting'.[46] Phlegmatics were similarly disabled: 'They are of a dull wit ... they are fearefull, covetous, and given to heape up riches, and are weake in the act of venerie.' As a result of their coldness and moistness, 'The manners and mind, and all the motions of the body flow with heavinesse and sloth.'[47]

According to such accounts the rational discretion expected of man's estate was seriously undermined by a range of inferior bodily conditions. Many men either lacked the heat ideally associated with manhood or were insufficiently in control of it. As in discussions of age, men's superior heat was not solely referred to as an unqualified benefit. While possessing the capacity for valiant action, men with hot complexions also risked being 'greatly given to lechery and whore-hunting, and thrall to all other pleasures of the body'. They were also prone to dishonesty and riotous living: 'they many times become cogging shifters, crafty coozeners, slye make-shifts, nimble conveiers, and foisting filchers, troublesome and seditiously natured, unconstant, wavering, fraudulent ... untrusty, and factious'. As a consequence, heat needed bridling. This could be achieved through a careful regime of diet and exercise, and, more significantly, with 'civill and vertuous education'—something that was beyond the reach of the majority.[48] Thus the venery associated with hot bodies ungoverned by civil manners corresponded to the disruption feared from the unruly and uneducated lower orders. Men's bodies, therefore, were not rated simply in meritocratic terms, but were ranked within the confines of contemporary assumptions about the social order, as physical inferiority was grafted onto social inferiority. This was made explicit by Claude Dariot who reserved the sanguine, or 'greatest', complexion for 'Noblemen,

---

[45] *Regimen Sanitatis Salerni*, trans. Thomas Paynell (London, 1575), fo. 142.
[46] Lemnius, *Touchstone of Complexions*, 206, 208, 224.
[47] *The Problemes of Aristotle*, sig. F8; Nicolas Abraham de La Framboisière, *An Easy Method to Know the Causes and Signs of the Humour Most Ruleth in the Body* ([London?], 1640), 7.
[48] Lemnius, *Touchstone of Complexions*, 72.

Bishops, prelates, Judges, Lawyers, honest men, just, true, benevolent, liberall, faithfull, milde, godly, shamefast, magnanimous, religious, dignities, spirituall offices, principalities... rich men, honorable, faithfull and happie'. In contrast, phlegmatics included a motley crew of vagabonds, 'common people', servants, fools, mothers, and wives.[49]

Discussions of the relationship between the internal organs used terms similarly suggestive of the analogies of inclusion and exclusion through which the imagined bodily ideal of man's estate was constructed. That individual organs were associated with special characteristics was clear in discussions of the particular bodily seats of each humour (the sanguine liver; the choleric gall bladder; the melancholic spleen; and the phlegmatic lungs). Consequently, the temper of individual parts of the body could determine a person's overall character: 'if you looke unto Man-kind, you shall find some that have the stomach of an Estrich; others that have the heart of a Lyon: Some are of the temper of a Dog, many of a Hog, and an infinite number of as dull and blockish a temper as an Asse'.[50] It was important, therefore, to maintain an ordered relationship between the various internal organs in order to avoid debilitation by the brutish tendencies associated with different parts of the body. The Dutch physician Lemnius' account of this bodily order was by far the most vivid. In his discussion of the liver, he likened the body to a commonwealth of interconnected members, each of which had an office to perform. The liver itself, as the originator of 'natural spirit' (which in turn nourished the body's 'vital spirit'), was analogous to the clergy; the stomach corresponded to the magistrates and peers; and the entrails were likened to the merchants and 'traffickers' of the commonwealth, some of whom were prone to deceit. Finally, the anus was compared with the 'poore Commonality, lowest in degree', who were identified as the 'Drudges, Porters, Saylers, Coblers, Tinkers, Carters, Tipplers, handy Artificers, filthy Bawdes, Butchers, Cookes, Botchers, and such like'.[51]

Other authors used metaphors of monarchy to discuss the workings of the body, some privileging the brain, others crowning the heart as the principal ruler. So, perhaps appropriately for the physician to James I, to Helkiah Crooke the body was like a royal household in which the 'Rationall facultie' of the brain presided over the lower orders of the heart and liver, 'and therefore ... these lower and inferiour faculties, must be

---

[49] Claude Dariot, *A Breefe and Most Easie Introduction to the Astrologicall Iudgement of the Starres*, trans. Fabian Wither (London, 1598), sigs. D2^v and E^{r-v}. Interestingly, this category also included historians.
[50] Crooke, *Mikrokosmographia*, 5.
[51] Lemnius, *Touchstone of Complexions*, 17–19.

serviceable and obedient to the higher, as to the Queene and Prince of them all'.[52] An earlier depiction of the heart, in a compilation by Thomas Vicary (surgeon to several sixteenth-century English monarchs), had used similar imagery, claiming that 'as a Lord or King ought to be served of his Subjects that have their living of him, so are all other members of the body subjects to the Heart: for they receive their living of him, and they doe service many wayes unto him againe'.[53] Most frequently, however, such imagery was applied to the general relationship between the body and the mind, although this was sometimes also likened to a marital bond. According to Lemnius, therefore, it was necessary 'to keepe as it were an equall poize of matrimoniall consent and agreement together betweene them, as it were betweene man and wife'.[54]

Whether the images of government selected were republican, monarchical, or domestic, they all held both metaphorical and metonymical significance.[55] The ideal body of man's estate was imagined through appeals to difference, and its construction informed and was informed by the contested hierarchies not only of age and sex but also of the social and political order. Analogies which likened the body to a household or a commonwealth served metaphorically to deprecate the disenfranchised: women, children, servants, and the 'lower orders'.[56] Metonymically, this implied that they were deemed incapable of bodily equilibrium and the even-tempered behaviour associated with it. As we have seen, the bodies delineated by the medical literature were rarely female, and authors were in no doubts about women's limited capacity for rational or spirited action. In these mainstream, conservative tracts, women were definitely excluded from assuming the imagined body of man's estate. Yet so were the many ranks of men who were poorly positioned in the hierarchy of complexions or who were insufficiently able to bridle or overcome the body's inevitable instability. Often rationalized in terms of the social order, the normative, temperate body of man's estate was, therefore, appropriated as an indicator of elite status by the men who, perhaps not coincidentally, had been educated to read and write these kinds of texts:

[52] Crooke, *Mikrokosmographia*, 13.
[53] Thomas Vicary, *The English-mans Treasure with the True Anatomie of Mans Body* (London, 1633), 36. See also Christopher Hill, 'William Harvey and the Idea of Monarchy', Gweneth Whitteridge, 'William Harvey: A Royalist and no Parliamentarian', and Hill's response, all in Charles Webster (ed.), *The Intellectual Revolution of the Seventeenth Century* (London, 1974).
[54] Lemnius, *Touchstone of Complexions*, 120.
[55] Cf. Gatens, *Imaginary Bodies*, ch. 2.
[56] For anthropomorphic representations of the commonwealth see David George Hale, *The Body Politic: A Political Metaphor in Renaissance English Literature* (The Hague, 1971); Leonard Barkan, *Nature's Work of Art: The Human Body as Image of the World* (New Haven, 1975), ch. 2.

'for we see the common sort and multitude, in behaviour and manners grosse and unnurtured, whereas the Nobles and Gentlemen (altering their order and dyet, and digressing from the common fashion of their pezantly Country-men) frame themselves and theirs to a very commendable order, and civill behaviour'.[57]

The temperate ideal of manhood, then, was here imagined as the exclusive birthright of only a very select cohort. Such assumptions similarly infused the moral philosophy and political thought of the period. Rationality was portrayed as 'the fruit of education and character', and in the context of the polity the capacity for its achievement was limited to statesmen alone, whose temperate rule was necessary to bridle the unruly impulses of the populace.[58] The imagined body of man's estate was therefore constructed on the basis of differences not just between men and women but also between men themselves. Only a privileged few could aspire to 'the highest and happiest temperance ... when the mind in naturall propertie is provided to all good deedes and perfect workes, and ... nothing may hinder or entercept the honest intent thereof'.[59]

'THINGS NOT NATURAL': MANHOOD AND THE ENVIRONMENT

Even if a man was well placed in relation to such aspirations of temperance, his body was perceived to be constantly under threat from external influences. 'The things that hinder and crush it, and which doe weaken, alter, and corrupt the temperament that naturally is in us, are not few,' cautioned Lemnius:

> although there be in the body of man many good furnitures, and in the minde sundry excellent ornaments, yet notwithstanding, the life of man is subject every where, and in all places to innumerable casualties, mis-haps and inconveniences, and is on each side beset and torne in pieces with such a number of miseries and by-reckonings, as every way weaken and appaire the perfect vigour and lusty state thereof.[60]

Such mishaps came in many forms. Referred to as the 'non-naturals', the potentially hazardous external sources of 'distemperaunce' included air, diet, sleeping habits, exercise, and 'affectes of the mynde'.[61] Also import-

---

[57] Lemnius, *Touchstone of Complexions*, 26.
[58] Susan James, 'Reason, the Passions, and the Good Life', in Daniel Garber and Michael Ayers (eds.), *The Cambridge History of Seventeenth-Century Philosophy*, 2 vols. (Cambridge, 1998), ii. 1378.
[59] Clever, *Flower of Phisicke*, 63.   [60] Lemnius, *Touchstone of Complexions*, 45, 152.
[61] Elyot, *Castel of Helth*, fos. 11ᵛ, 64.

ant was the impact of the seasons and the climate. All of these factors threatened to undermine the operation of a man's rational discretion at any moment, and their discussion in the medical literature is indicative of the degree to which all bodies were portrayed as continually susceptible to disruption and in need of fortification in the form of civil education.

The physical environment was deemed to have an enormous influence on the body.[62] Air, climate, and topography were all important. Wholesome air that was 'meanely cold' and 'meanely moist' nurtured and produced bodies distinguished by 'an acute wit, a sound and lively colour, a stable integritie of the head, quicke sight, perfect hearing, sound smelling, clear voyce, and no difficultie of breathing, or unlustinesse of the limmes'. Yet there were numerous pollutants: boggy fenland, barren moors, low valleys, and places with standing water all produced corrupt vapours which, according to the physician Tobias Venner, made their inhabitants 'dull, sluggish, sordid, sensuall [and] plainly irreligious'.[63] Certain winds were believed to have unwholesome properties, with the south wind bringing 'yll vapours' and the wind from the west being 'verye mutable, whyche nature doeth hate'. Only the east wind was 'temperate & lusty'. Health tracts such as Elyot's cautioned their readers to avoid corrupt air—particularly when it was a product of offensive living habits attributed to 'Muche people in small roume liynge uncleanelye and sluttyshely' in overcrowded towns—an association which not only linked ill health with poverty but also viewed it as the consequence of immorality.[64]

Similarly influential were the climate and the seasons. Extremes of hot and cold produced men of different complexions, and climate was often cited as the cause of different 'racial' or national characters. Thus men bred 'neere to the Pole Articke and Icie Sea' were characterized as 'very huge and strong bodied' yet 'for wit and learning, meere Dolts and Asseheads'. Asian men, on the other hand, were typecast as less manly, being 'fairer, greater, more gentle, feareful, effœminate, and unapt to warre for the temperature of the ayre'. Europeans placed themselves somewhere between these two poles, claiming superiority as 'cruell, of hauty courage, bold, upright or honest, and given to warre', which illustrates the ways in which racial as well as social categories could be

[62] Andrew Wear, 'Making Sense of Health and the Environment in Early Modern England', in id. (ed.), *Medicine in Society: Historical Essays* (Cambridge, 1992).
[63] Venner, *Via Recta ad Vitam Longam*, 3, 4, 9. See also Bullein, *Government of Health*, fos. 29ᵛ–31ᵛ. For continued concerns about air quality after the Restoration, see Mark Jenner, 'The Politics of London Air: John Evelyn's *Fumifugium* and the Restoration', *Historical Journal*, 38 (1995).
[64] Elyot, *Castel of Helth*, fo. 12. See also Venner, *Via Recta ad Vitam Longam*, 2; Healy, *Fictions of Disease*, 37–40.

invoked in constructions of the imagined body of man's estate.[65] Less lastingly influential on the body were the changes in temperature which accompanied the different seasons. The time of year in general was also influential from an astrological perspective, as each month, day, and hour was regulated by the stars and the planets.[66] Such influences required careful monitoring and could be balanced and combated only through a strict regimen of diet and exercise.

Dietary principles were more central to much of the period's advice about health. Given that foods were believed to contain varying degrees of heat, moisture, dryness, and coldness, they could be used to maintain or restore bodily equilibrium. Yet just as they could provide a source of humoral balance, food and drink were also potentially debilitating if the wrong quantities and qualities were consumed, and it was in discussions of food and drink that the body's mutability was most acutely stressed. Written for a privileged audience, health tracts rarely discussed the problems of deprivation, but instead stressed the dangers of excessive consumption. Overburdening the stomach was deemed to be particularly threatening. Different constitutions required different diets according to the temperature of each individual's stomach, although this also varied in line with connotations of social difference. The digestive problems of social elites seemed not to have troubled the 'meane people [who] worke for a living, and are not pampered with full and daintie fare', or the 'Rustickes' who, according to Thomas Cogan, had stomachs like ostriches 'that can digest hard yron'.[67] For those for whom it was an option, however, inappropriately varied consumption caused both long-term health problems as well as temporary debilitation. If the body was not 'rustickly strong' too many dishes threatened to upset its balance, temporarily dethroning the powers of reason.[68] Food and drink could add fire to the blood, and its excessive consumption was another incitement to bodily riot: 'For even as in a civill tumult, and sedicious uproare among the common people, the Magistrate hath much adoe to appease and mollifie the wilfull peoples rage and heavinesse: so likewise reason is not able easily to subdue the lewd affections, and unbridled motions, that grow by immod-

[65] Lemnius, *Touchstone of Complexions*, 25; Banister, *Historie of Man*, sig. B3.
[66] See, e.g., Thomas Moulton, *The Mirrour or Glasse of Health* (London, 1580), chs. 4–6; Vaughan, *Directions for Health*.
[67] Gualterus Bruele, *Praxis Medicinæ; or, The Physicians Practice: Wherein are Contained Inward Diseases from the Head to the Foote* (London, 1632), 363; Cogan, *Haven of Health*, 31. Cogan similarly designated beans as 'meate for Mowers ... and for ploughmen, but not for studentes', and animal fat as digestible only by 'country men', 29, 130.
[68] Venner, *Via Recta ad Vitam Longam*, 169. See also Elyot, *Castel of Helth*, fo. 45; Cogan, *Haven of Health*, 168–73.

erate gurmandize, surfet and drunkennesse.'[69] Employing the same logic, Hart declared that a drunkard forfeited his manhood: 'it unmans a man; and of a reasonable man maketh him worse than an unreasonable beast [and] expelleth all vertue out of the mind'. He went on to claim that this was doubly demeaning of gentlemen who 'so far to wrong themselves, as in Tavernes and Tap-houses to become a companion to any base varlet, swill-bowle, tosse-pot and pot-companion', since they thereby relinquished not only their manhood but also their social position—once again confirming the expectation that moderate behaviour was the mark of the gentleman.[70]

Excessive emotion was accorded a similarly blood-boiling impact, and was discussed as yet another obstacle to the achievement of rational discretion. This was particularly true for men, who were victims as well as beneficiaries of their comparative heat, since it was heat that was the driving force behind the passions and that mobilized the body's vital spirits to rebellious and unbridled action. If this heat became overpowering, the mind's primacy was once again toppled. Just as a man who was exposed to a harmful environment risked bodily mutation, so a man who abandoned himself to his senses encouraged internal chaos by surrendering reason to passion. Elyot warned that the emotions inspired by extreme anger, the loss of a friend, or the death of a child were all potentially debilitating: 'For if they be immoderate, they doo not onely annoye the bodye and shorten the lyfe, but also they do appaire, and somtyme lose utterly a mans estimacyon. And that much more is, they bryng a man from the use of reason, and somtime in the dyspleasure of almyghtye God.' More positive emotions such as joy were also potentially deadly, and Elyot similarly cautioned against 'inordynate gladnesse'.[71] Lust was also discussed in these terms. Simply catching a glimpse of a woman could completely upset the body's equilibrium:

if he fortune to espy any pretty Wench, or beautifull Damsell, that liketh his fantasie, his minde is straightwaies enflamed and set on fire with unlawfull desire of her person, for the satisfying of his unbridled concupiscence: and by reason of the store of humours and concourse of spirits resorting thither from every part of his body; his privities undecently swell, and his member of generation becommeth stiffe, so that many times it hapneth, mans minde to be overcome and drowned in fleshly concupiscence.[72]

---

[69] Lemnius, *Touchstone of Complexions*, 16.
[70] Hart, *KAINIKH*, 131, 135.
[71] Elyot, *Castel of Helth*, fos. 64, 70. See also *The Problemes of Aristotle*, sig. F3ᵛ; Venner, *Via Recta ad Vitam Longam*, 225.
[72] Lemnius, *Touchstone of Complexions*, 22–3.

For all its distinguishing features, the rational discretion expected of manhood was an extremely delicate faculty, likely to be overcome at almost every turn. Such descriptions of the numerous dangers posed by emotional responses, diet, and the environment indicate that man's estate was not characterized simply by rational moderation—as discussions of the differences between the sexes would suggest—but by the repeated failure to live up to this ideal. According to Lemnius, the only man ever to have attained such bodily supremacy was Christ.[73] While many medical writers were somewhat less pessimistic when encouraging temperance in their readers, they nonetheless betrayed repeated assumptions that aspirations towards its achievement were limited at most to a social elite.

Medical writers constructing the ideal body invoked a series of hierarchies associated with gender, age, social status, and, less frequently, national character. The relative significance and intrinsic structure of these several hierarchies was by no means uniform across guides to health and regimens. Commonly implicit, however, was the assumption that bodily merit corresponded with social position, and it provides an example of the ways in which patriarchal and social privilege could be mutually constitutive. Those deemed able to achieve or aspire to the ideal were often limited to a very select group of men who were either sufficiently trained in civility or who were accorded an innate bodily superiority, often implicitly as a consequence of their social position. While mature men of a temperate or hot complexion, sufficiently educated to deflect environmental threats to their bodily stability, were repeatedly idealized in health tracts, their authors also reflected that they were a rarity, betraying assumptions that the moderation deemed 'manly' in this context was socially exclusive.

While the principle of generic male superiority was certainly propagated by early modern medical literature, therefore, the construction of the temperate ideal entwined descriptions of the male body with images of the social order in ways which rendered it more socially specific. Employing a vocabulary of social, as well as sexual, difference the ideal body imagined by medical writers flattered their elite male readership and encouraged them to aspire to the civic virtue associated with gentility. Despite being claimed as the central property of man's estate, rational discretion was implicitly lacking in the majority of men, and constantly under threat for the minority who might aspire to it. Consequently, the moralization of health involved a tacit critique of the numerous men who were excluded from accomplishing it on the grounds of age, tempera-

[73] Lemnius, *Touchstone of Complexions*, 58–9.

ment, ignorance, or their 'rustic' constitution, which in turn highlights the tension between the generic privileging of males and the particular privileging of certain men along various axes of difference besides gender. Just as maintaining a healthy body was approached as a constant labour, so attaining the ideal of rational discretion associated with manhood was portrayed as a precarious enterprise requiring considerable skill and training, if not innate virtue, that was deemed beyond the reach of many.

3
Models of Manhood

THE self-government expected of manhood was the basis of men's claims to authority. Men could not govern others if they were unable to govern themselves. This idea was most clearly—and most inclusively—articulated in domestic conduct literature and marital advice which focused on the successful management of the household. In such works, the household was represented as the primary site of male authority both because the stability of the commonwealth was deemed to depend on its proper ordering, and because it was anticipated (increasingly erroneously) that the vast majority of adult males would become household heads. Heading a household was associated with the mastery not only of a man's self, but of his subordinates and his resources, and in this way it was often equated with manhood itself. Heading a household was presented as the greatest portion of the patriarchal dividend to which all adult males might aspire, and it was often approached as the precondition of men's political involvement within the wider community. Involving the authority of husbands over wives, fathers over children, and masters over servants, it linked manhood to patriarchy in both its early modern and its feminist senses: the household was the primary structural locus of male supremacy in terms of fatherly rule, and the marital relations at its core were the justification for men's subordination of women.

Marriage was privileged as the primary bond upon which a household was founded in the domestic conduct literature penned by puritan clergymen such as William Gouge and John Dod with Robert Cleaver. That such works enjoyed an enduring readership is suggested by their frequent reprinting. Dod and Cleaver's *Godly Form of Householde Government* went through nine editions in the thirty-two years after its initial publication in 1598, and Gouge's *Of Domesticall Duties* went through three editions between 1622 and 1634. Readership of such works, however, which were of considerable size and expense, was in all likelihood restricted to the better off and to the most committed aspirants to godliness.[1] A related genre

---

[1] For an example of the latter category, see Paul S. Seaver, *Wallington's World: A Puritan Artisan in Seventeenth-Century London* (Stanford, Calif., 1985), 79.

comprised a series of briefer tracts focusing solely on the duties of marriage, some of which were later absorbed into lengthier works. Perhaps the best-known example is Edmund Tilney's *A Brief and Pleasant Discourse of the Duties in Mariage, Called the Flower of Friendshippe*, which, after going through nine editions between 1568 and 1587, was extensively borrowed in Dod and Cleaver's *Godly Form of Householde Government*.

As master of the revels in the royal household, Tilney was unlike other authors of marital advice, who were mostly eminent preachers of a puritan disposition. Henry Smith, for example, whose *A Preparative to Mariage* went through four editions within a year of its first publication in 1591, had earned the epithet 'silver-tongued Smith' from his success as a preacher in London in the 1580s, which possibly accounts for the subsequent demand for his tract. Smith and Tilney were nonetheless similar in one respect; both wrote their tracts without any direct personal experience of marriage, since Tilney did not marry until 1583 and Smith did not marry at all. The majority of authors about whom such information is available were married when they published their advice, however. With the exception of William Crompton, a puritan minister who drafted *A Wedding Ring, Fitted to the Finger of Every Paire that Have or Shall Meete in the Feare of God* (1632) at the age of 33 and around the time of his own marriage, most authors were in their late forties and had several years' personal experience of marital relations. The puritan divine William Whately had been married for seventeen years when his first tract on marriage was published in 1617 (*A Bride Bush; or, A Direction for Married Persons*) and for twenty-three years by the time his second discussion of the topic appeared in print (*A Care-Cloth; or, A Treatise of the Cumbers and Troubles of Marriage*). Several works addressing marriage were published in sermon form, either as wedding sermons or for general edification.[2] Many were derivative from the homily 'On the State of Matrimony', which was reprinted countless times alongside the other Elizabethan homilies in the later sixteenth and early seventeenth centuries, designed as the weekly staples of parish preaching. While at least most of the lengthier works were likely to have been limited to an audience of social elites, therefore, the general ideas they espoused would not have been unfamiliar to sermon-gadders or to the mass of churchgoers who listened to homilies read from parish pulpits.

Moralists' lengthy discussions of the respective duties of husband and wife illustrate some of the ways in which manhood was distinguished from womanhood and thus directly defined along the axis of gender. Although

---

[2] e.g. Robert Abbot, *A Wedding Sermon Preached at Bentley in Darby-Shire* (London, 1608); Thomas Taylor, *A Good Husband and a Good Wife: Layd Open in a Sermon* (London, 1625).

sermons and advice literature represented the hierarchy separating husband and wife as the least acute form of household subordination, they nonetheless appear to have exaggerated the differences between men and women in order to bolster men's patriarchal authority. In one such comparison John Dod and Robert Cleaver claimed that a woman's duties resided solely in 'shamefastnes', whereas 'A man needeth many things: as wisedome, eloquence, knowledge of things, remembrance, skill in some trade or craft to live by, justice, courage and other things and qualities moe, which were too long to rehearse.'[3] It is therefore unsurprising that domestic prescription has provided the cornerstone for much of the gender analysis of the early modern period, particularly since it outlined such a restrictive set of behavioural options for women.[4]

Evidence of their considerable contradiction by women in a variety of contexts has led historians to conclude that these roles were as much a product of prescriptive fantasy as of routine social practice.[5] The roles outlined for men were similarly prescriptive rather than purely descriptive, and they need to be analysed with comparable caution rather than taken at face value. While approaching the subordination of women as one of the primary features of patriarchal manhood, moralists also expressed abundant concern that this was neither a straightforward task nor an unlimited benefit. Separate sections addressing the duties of husbands and the duties of wives differed considerably when discussing the limits of a husband's power. While wives were urged to concede absolute authority to their husbands (except in matters of conscience) husbands

[3] John Dod and Robert Cleaver, *A Godly Form of Householde Government: For the Ordering of Private Families* (London, 1612), 350.

[4] See, e.g., Kathleen M. Davies, 'Continuity and Change in Literary Advice on Marriage', in R. B. Outhwaite (ed.), *Marriage and Society: Studies in the Social History of Marriage* (London, 1981); Suzanne W. Hull, *Chaste, Silent and Obedient: English Books for Women, 1475–1640* (San Marino, Calif., 1982); Katherine Usher Henderson and Barbara F. McManus, *Half Humankind: Contexts and Texts of the Controversy about Women in England, 1540–1640* (Urbana, Ill., 1985); Ann Rosalind Jones, 'Nets and Bridles: Early Modern Conduct Books and Sixteenth-Century Women's Lyrics', in Nancy Armstrong and Leonard Tennenhouse (eds.), *The Ideology of Conduct: Essays on Literature and the History of Sexuality* (London, 1987); Anthony Fletcher, *Gender, Sex and Subordination in England 1500–1800* (London, 1995), chs. 6, 11.

[5] See, e.g., Margaret J. M. Ezell, *The Patriarch's Wife: Literary Evidence and the History of the Family* (Chapel Hill, NC, 1987); Susan Dwyer Amussen, *An Ordered Society: Gender and Class in Early Modern England* (Oxford, 1988); Linda Pollock, '"Teach Her to Live under Obedience": The Making of Women in the Upper Ranks of Early Modern England', *Continuity and Change*, 4 (1989); Alison Wall, 'Elizabethan Precept and Feminine Practice: The Thynne Family of Longleat', *History*, 75 (1990); Tim Stretton, 'Women, Custom and Equity in the Court of Requests', in Jenny Kermode and Garthine Walker (eds.), *Women, Crime and the Courts in Early Modern England* (London, 1994); Anthony Fletcher, 'Men's Dilemma: The Future of Patriarchy in England, 1560–1660', *Transactions of the Royal Historical Society*, 6th ser. 4 (1994); Sara Mendelson and Patricia Crawford, *Women in Early Modern England* (Oxford, 1998).

were repeatedly warned against the over-zealous exaction of subjection. When addressing women, or women's roles, advice writers upheld the patriarchal basis of order in terms of men's almost unlimited authority; when addressing the beneficiaries of this system they emphasized that claiming unlimited authority would be little short of disastrous. This suggests that there were as many internal contradictions *within* prescriptive accounts of male authority as between prescription and practice.

Domestic advice also emphasized that maintaining authority over household subordinates—and particularly wives—was a constant labour, rather than a given, with many perilous pitfalls. Although women were blamed for many of the potential failings of household order, husbands were represented as doubly culpable, condemned for the forfeiture of their authority over others as well as over themselves. Conduct writers emphasized the contingency of household order upon men's self-government and added their voice to the chorus rehearsing the difficulties associated with the self-containment expected of manhood. While undoubtedly according male householders considerable authority, domestic conduct manuals were more concerned with ensuring that they performed the corresponding duties, and were as preoccupied with male deviations from the ideal as with the ideal itself. Conduct writers were as concerned with directing men's behaviour as that of women's—if not more so—since they were far from confident that men would pay the price of privilege and perform the roles expected of them. Once again this constituted an attempt to fix the meanings of manhood in patriarchal terms of wisdom, reason, discretion, moderation, self-sufficiency, and, above all, honest respectability. Conduct writers insisted that it was not only the terms of manhood that were at stake, but the entire social order.

MANHOOD, MARRIAGE, AND DOMESTIC CONDUCT

[T]hey are but very fooles, that judge and thinke matrimonie to be a dominion.[6]

Marriage was represented as a serious undertaking in early modern England for men as well as women. Its routine association across a variety of genres with the adjectives 'honest' and 'complete' suggests it transformed the way a man viewed himself and was perceived by society. Married men had a greater claim to trustworthiness. According to one commentator, honesty was the 'portion' which men 'get by their

---

[6] Dod and Cleaver, *A Godly Form of Householde Government*, 215.

wives'—which was perhaps an early version of the colloquial characterization of marriage as 'making an honest man' of the groom.[7] Even more comprehensive in its claims was the expectation that marriage made a man 'complete'. One of the most lyrical exponents of this idea declared marriage to be the 'absolute greatest action of a mans whole life':

> by this so excellent [act], so honourably accounted of amongst all men are thy wilde and unbridled affections reduced to humanity and civility, to mercy and clemency, and thou thy selfe called backe to looke into thy selfe, and to understand the substance and truth of things, and therefore he that hath no wife is said to be a man unbuilt that wanteth one of his ribbes, a sleepe as *Adam* was till his wife was made, for marriage awaketh the understanding as out of a dreame; and he that hath no wife is said to be a man in the midst of the sea, perishing for want of this ship to waft him to shore.[8]

Like images of young men as shipwrecked or unable to steer a safe course through stormy seas, the unmarried man was portrayed as directionless, insensible, and out of control. Furthermore he was incomplete. Wives here were accorded far more than a civilizing influence: they were portrayed as the means by which a man became whole. Marriage, here, was the gateway to manhood.

It was a widely held view that marriage was essential to the achievement of patriarchal manhood in early modern England. One ballad, for example, asked, 'what were you but a skip-jacke, before you had a wife?'[9] As 'the ancientest calling of men', marriage both conferred status within the context of the household and elevated a man's position in the wider community. It was by 'beeing matched in mariage schoole' that young men became 'profitable membres in the common weale'.[10] That marriage was central to patriarchal privilege is clear from Sir Thomas Smith's exclusion of young men from yeoman status: 'commonly wee doe not call any a yeomen till he be married, and have children, and as it were have some authoritie among his neighbours'. Sir Francis Bacon also warned that unmarried men were bad subjects, being 'light to runne away' like

---

[7] Ester Sowernam, *Ester hath Hang'd Haman; or, An Answere to a Lewde Pamphlet Entituled, the Arraignment of Women* (London, 1617), 23. John Paige wrote in 1651 of his 'late change from a bachelor to an honest man', *The Letters of John Paige, London Merchant, 1648–1658*, ed. George F. Steckley, London Record Society Publications, 21 (London, 1984), 36.

[8] Alexander Niccholes, *A Discourse of Marriage and Wiving* (London, 1615), 13, 6.

[9] J. A. Sharpe, 'Plebeian Marriage in Stuart England: Some Evidence from Popular Literature', *Transactions of the Royal Historical Society*, 5th ser. 36 (1986), 83.

[10] Henry Smith, *A Preparative to Mariage. The Summe Whereof was Spoken at a Contract, and Inlarged After* (London, 1591), 4; Plutarch, *A President for Parentes, Teaching the Vertuous Training up of Children and Holesome Information of Yongmen* (London, 1571), sig. *5ᵛ.

fugitives.[11] Marital status transcended hierarchies of age since married men were accorded higher status than their elders who were still single.[12]

Marriage was synonymous with manhood in these contexts because it symbolized the transition from a dependent minority to social and political maturity. Although many male householders were excluded from the franchise, their position was nonetheless accorded political significance since the household was approached both as the primary unit of society and as a microcosm of the polity. According to William Gouge, 'a conscionable performance of houshold duties, in regard of the end and fruit thereof, may be accounted a publicke worke'.[13] Ignoring the existence of many female household heads, domestic advice instead elaborated the stereotype of the male householder as the 'Chiefe Governour' of his 'little commonwealth'.[14] Although this involved the government of three sorts of subordinate—wife, servants, and children—moralists were most preoccupied with the relationship between husband and wife. This was because the marriage bond was regarded as the fount of all others, and it was contingent upon husbands and wives to set a good example. It was also because it involved the subtlest of hierarchies, since 'of all degrees wherein there is any difference betwixt person and person, there is the least disparitie betwixt man and wife'. By implication, 'that small inequalitie which is betwixt the husband and the wife' could be easily subverted.[15]

The solution envisaged by domestic conduct writers was the allocation of distinct roles to husband and wife through which the gender hierarchy and social harmony should be maintained. The primary duties of both spouses were directed towards maintaining the husband's authority. According to William Whately, the two 'proper' duties of a husband were to 'governe or rule' and to maintain his wife, whereas those of his wife were to 'acknowledge her inferioritie' and to 'carry her selfe as an inferiour'. A wife was expected to know her place; a husband was expected to keep her in it. While easing the emphasis on the man's authority when he summed up the particular duties of husbands as 'Wisdome and Love', William Gouge nevertheless declared that all the wife's duties should stem from subjection and the acknowledgement of 'an husbands

---

[11] Sir Thomas Smith, *De Republica Anglorum*, ed. Mary Dewar (Cambridge, 1982), 76. Sir Francis Bacon, *The Essayes or Counsels, Civill and Morall*, ed. Michael Kiernan (Oxford, 1985), 25.
[12] William Whately, *A Care-Cloth; or, A Treatise of the Cumbers and Troubles of Marriage* (London, 1624), 61. [13] William Gouge, *Of Domesticall Duties* (London, 1622), 18.
[14] Dod and Cleaver, *A Godly Form of Householde Government*, 19; Gouge, *Of Domesticall Duties*, 18.
[15] Gouge, *Of Domesticall Duties*, 271. See also Ste B., *Counsel to the Husband: To the Wife Instruction* (London, 1608), 40.

superioritie'.[16] A wife's role was defined solely in terms of her husband's needs: she was to submit herself willingly in reverent obedience, faithfully performing his directions with mildness and modesty imbued with love, fear, and loyalty, remembering that he had 'absolute authoritie, over the woman in all places'.[17]

The husband was frequently cast through bodily analogy as the head to his wife's body, the fount of reason directing their joint concerns. By claiming that 'The husband is made the head, and the wife resembled to the bodie', moralists reiterated the association of rational discretion with manhood and ungoverned passion with womanhood.[18] As a consequence men, once again, were granted powers of speech—the conduit of reason—serving as household representatives beyond the domestic sphere: 'For that as the trumpeters owne voice is nothing so loud or so strong, as the sound that it yeeldeth when it passeth through the trumpet: so every action in the family shall gaine it selfe more weight . . . and carry more authoritie with it, when it passeth through the husband's hands and is ratified and sealed as it were with his seale.' By contrast the speech of a wife (and other subordinates) lacked substance and legitimacy, and wives were cautioned not to be like 'those women that will do all of their owne head'.[19] Largely untroubled by considerations of social status, such comparisons afforded the most comprehensive appropriation of reason for adult males, further encouraging its coupling with manhood.

In addition to their emphasis on the husband's patriarchal authority, advice manuals outlined a strict division of labour between spouses that they deemed essential for a household's credit (in both social and economic terms) and harmonious functioning. Dod and Cleaver rehearsed the most expansive version of this common theme, which is worth quoting in full:

The dutie of the Husband is to get goods: and of the Wife to gather them together, and save them. The dutie of the Husband is to travell abroad, to seeke living: and the Wives dutie is to keepe the house. The dutie of the Husband is to get money and provision: and of the Wives, not vainely to spend it. The dutie of the Husband is to deale with many men: and of the Wives to talke with few. The dutie of the Husband is to be entermedling: and of the wife, to be solitary and

---

[16] William Whately, *A Bride Bush; or, A Direction for Married Persons* (London, 1623), sig. A4ᵛ; Gouge, *Of Domesticall Duties*, sig. Aᵛ.

[17] Edmund Tilney, *A Brief and Pleasant Discourse of the Duties in Mariage, Called the Flower of Friendshippe* (London, 1568), sig. E1. See also, e.g., Gouge, *Of Domesticall Duties*, 267–348; Whately, *A Bride Bush*, 189–216.

[18] Ste B., *Counsel to the Husband*, 42. See also, e.g., Samuel Hieron, *The Bridegroome* (London, 1613), 17.

[19] Thomas Gataker, *Marriage Duties Briefely Couched Togither* (London, 1620), 16.

withdrawne. The dutie of the man is, to be skilfull in talke: and of the wife, to boast of silence... The dutie of the Husband is to bee lorde of all: and of the wife, to give account of all: The dutie of the husband is, to dispatch all things without dore: and of the wife, to oversee and give order for all things within the house.[20]

According to such instructions, a husband's duty was to provide, by 'getting money' through 'intermeddling' with other men, and a wife's duty was to protect such provision and her own honour, thereby safeguarding the welfare and good name of the household. A wife's honour was contingent upon her being solitary, silent, and withdrawn, while her husband should be locked into a web of commercial concerns and familiar with other men's business. Male duties were characterized as active and acquisitive; female duties were not so much passive as defensive. This division of labour was a commonplace of domestic conduct literature, if not of many couples' experience.[21] Drawing on classical models, and in particular Xenophon's *Oeconomicus*, advice writers seemed to have taken comfort in prescribing rigidly separate duties for husband and wife.[22] While it would be a mistake to class these roles strictly in terms of 'public' and 'private' owing to the moralists' emphasis on the public significance of the household, they nonetheless reinforced associations of manhood with authority, acquisition, discretion, and negotiation and denied women's possession of such skills and rights to independent action.

Moralists also betrayed considerable concern that this was an ideal that was extraordinarily difficult, if not impossible, to realize, and dwelt at far greater length on the threats deemed to undermine it than on the patriarchal blueprint itself. As a consequence, although marriage was deemed to prove manhood, didacts also emphasized the degree to which it could endanger it. The threats associated with marriage were manifold. Beyond misogynist reprisals for women's failings, conduct manuals emphasized that love was a potential hazard to manhood while nonetheless being one of the husband's fundamental duties, suggesting that the nature of patriarchal authority itself was contradictory and inherently problematic. While reserving autonomy for the husband, conduct manuals also betrayed his considerable dependence upon his wife. Finally, men were vulnerable to their own weaknesses, which in turn undermined their authority and prevented them from performing the duties expected of them. Although domestic advice dwelt extensively on men's mastery

---

[20] Dod and Cleaver, *A Godly Form of Householde Government*, 167–8. This is an expanded version of Tilney, *Flower of Friendshippe*, sig. C5ᵛ.   [21] See Ch. 7 below.
[22] Sarah B. Pomeroy, *Xenophon*, Oeconomicus: *A Social and Historical Commentary, with a New English Translation* (Oxford, 1994), 76–87. See also Joan Thirsk, 'Making a Fresh Start: Sixteenth-Century Agriculture and the Classical Inspiration', in Michael Leslie and Timothy Raylor (eds.), *Culture and Cultivation in Early Modern England: Writing and the Land* (Leicester, 1992).

of others, it also emphasized that this was predicated on their mastery of themselves. While advice writers expected this in principle, they seemed less confident of its performance in practice. In addressing wives' duties and in comparing the roles of husbands and wives, conduct manuals upheld the tenets of male superiority. Yet when the duties of husbands were considered in isolation, their capacity for wielding authority with rational discretion was by no means treated as a given, but as a constant and extremely challenging labour.

Conduct manuals frequently deflected attention from men's failings by blaming women for many of the dangers posed to patriarchal manhood by marriage. Despite unanimity about the importance of marriage, advice writers rarely recommended it with unmitigated enthusiasm and images of marital fulfilment were seldom unqualified. As one author declared, 'man is imperfect without a wife, unhappy without a good one'.[23] Marriage was far more often portrayed as fraught with dangers for men than as a source of either delightful completion or unlimited authority, and one particularly scathing author advised his readers that it was better avoided altogether.[24] Extensive advice was published about how to choose a wife, littered with warnings that if the choice was misguided a man risked spending the rest of his days in unceasing hell. The very first piece of guidance offered by William Cecil to his son was to 'use great providence and circumspection in the choice of thy wife: for from thence may spring all thy future good or ill'.[25] For a man there was 'no greater plague, nor torment to his minde then to be matched with an untoward, wicked, and dishonest Woman'. Employing the imagery of thraldom, Dod and Cleaver claimed 'it were better for him to be a slave to some honest man, then a husband to such a wife'.[26] The implicit paradox was that although a man gained a distinct element of independence through marriage, it was deemed to be continually at risk from his relationship with his wife.

Women were censured for usurping their husbands' authority either through assertiveness or by reducing them to a love-induced submis-

---

[23] William Crompton, *A Wedding-Ring, Fitted to the Finger of Every Paire that Have or Shall Meete in the Feare of God* (London, 1632), 6.

[24] *A Discourse of the Married and Single Life. Wherein, by Discovering the Misery of the One, is Plainely Declared the Felicity of the Other* (London, 1621).

[25] William Cecil, *The Counsell of a Father to his Sonne, in Ten Severall Precepts* (London, 1611). See also *The Fathers Blessing; or, Second Councell to his Sonne. Appropriated to the Generall, from that Perticular Example his Majestie Composed for the Prince his Sonne* (London, 1616), 28; Sir Walter Raleigh, *Sir Walter Raleighs Instructions to his Sonne and to Posterity* (London, 1632), ch. 2.

[26] *The Court of Good Counsell. Wherein is Set Downe How a Man Should Choose a Good Wife and a Woman a Good Husband* (London, 1607), sig. B1; Dod and Cleaver, *A Godly Form of Householde Government*, 167.

Models of Manhood 79

sion. Concerns about the potential emotional demise that accompanied love stemmed from broader anxieties that any surrender to passion was unmanly, and were often expressed through humoral analogy in similar terms to guides on health. Love upset the humours: it inflamed the heart inducing an excess of heat which could, without strict vigilance, overthrow the reason associated with manhood. As one author complained:

> I wish distressed Lovers such a blisse,
> To understand and know what reason is,
> But all in vain, love in another kinde,
> By violence thrusts reason from the minde.[27]

Women were caricatured as 'the cracke of a Mans wit' and 'reasons Torture', and men were cautioned against 'too much' love.[28] The usual gender analogies were employed as warnings. Women were accorded bewitching capacities with an emasculating impact. Thus the 'uxorious man' was depicted as preferring his wife over the world, 'with which idole he is so effeminately bewitcht' that he could be 'no good commonwealths man'.[29] Similar language was used to condemn women who appropriated male authority, inverting the gendered chain of being: 'Women grow mankind, men effeminate', and, in turn, 'a mankinde woman or a masterly wife' was represented as 'even a monster in nature'.[30] According to Gouge, a man who yielded to his wife was a 'milke-sop' and thus perverted nature, with the inference that he was as dependent upon her as he had once been upon his mother's breast.[31]

Images of slavery were also commonly used to caution husbands against ceding the breeches. Verses on the 'miserie of love' declared that 'It makes the man most free become a slave.' Patrick Hannay likewise warned that the potential 'servitude' suffered by husbands with dominant wives 'disvalues man'.[32] Perhaps the most extreme condemnation of such situations accorded them a degenerative impact:

> I scorn as much to stoop to women kinde;

---

[27] Humfrey Crouch, *Loves Court of Conscience... Wherunto is Annexed a Kinde Husband's Advice to his Wife* (London, 1637), sig. A5ᵛ.

[28] Nicholas Breton, *An Olde Mans Lesson and a Young Mans Love* (London, 1605), sig. D2ᵛ; Hieron, *The Bridegroome*, 20.

[29] Francis Lenton, *Characterismi; or, Lentons Leasures* (London, 1631), sig. B9ʳ⁻ᵛ. See also warnings about women's 'Artfull bewitching' in Niccholes, *A Discourse of Marriage*, 23.

[30] Crouch, *Loves Court of Conscience*, sig. B3ᵛ; Gataker, *Marriage Duties*, 10.

[31] Gouge, *Of Domesticall Duties*, 286. See also Ste B., *Counsel to the Husband*, which blamed any inversion of roles on men being 'effeminate', 43.

[32] Henry Chillester, *Youthes Witte; or, The Witte of Grene Youth* (London, 1581), 42–3; Patrick Hannay, *A Happy Husband; or, Directions for a Maide to Choose her Mate. As Also, a Wives Behaviour towards her Husband after Marriage* (London, 1619), sig. B3.

For if I should, then all men would me hate,
Because from manhood I degenerate.
And surely I should have the love of no man:
Which to prevent, and to avoid ill speeches,
I'le look to that thou shalt never wear the breeches.[33]

According to these verses losing authority over women amounted to relinquishing both manhood and admittance to male society. Such representations served to reinforce the patriarchal blueprint by emphasizing the dangers of an inverted gender hierarchy, and by scapegoating women for any breakdown in male authority.

Although misogynist representations of deviant women and corresponding fantasies of tamed wives often deflected attention from men's faults, conduct writers by no means depicted husbands as blameless.[34] More importantly, advice books did not advocate heavy-handed husbanding as a solution to the apparent dangers posed by women. Indeed, domestic advice conveyed a far more complex and contradictory set of messages beyond the emphasis on the imperative of male control. Alongside portrayals of women as temperamentally unruly and needing to be tamed, conduct manuals also stressed the limits of patriarchal authority in lengthy discussions of a husband's extensive duties towards his wife, and of the importance of mutuality within marriage. Husbands' duties were just as rigorously expounded as those of wives, often at greater length, with the implication that the burden of ensuring a successful marriage rested more with husbands than with wives.[35] According to Gouge, it was 'a farre more difficult and hard matter to governe well than to obey well'.[36] A husband and wife's duties were by no means equal, yet early modern commentators were in considerable doubt as to which obligation was the more exacting.

While advice to women stressed their duty of unconditional obedience except in matters of conscience, advice to husbands repeatedly warned that a wife's obedience was to be earned rather than expected. Far from a one-way exaction, marriage was a 'reciprocall debt' with *both* partners bound to each other in 'indebted benevolence'.[37] According to Henry Smith, 'The husband saith, that his wife must obay him because he is her

---

[33] Crouch, *Loves Court of Conscience*, sig. B2^{r-v}.

[34] For stereotypes of the tamed wife see Linda Woodbridge, *Women and the English Renaissance: Literature and the Nature of Womankind, 1540–1620* (Brighton, 1984), ch. 8.

[35] e.g. in Dod and Cleaver, *A Godly Form of Householde Government*, 120 pages were devoted to husbands' duties compared with 26 pages on the duties of a wife; similarly in Whately, *A Bride Bush*, six chapters as opposed to one.

[36] Gouge, *Of Domesticall Duties*, 22.

[37] Whately, *A Bride Bush*, 2, 14.

better, therefore if he let her be better than himselfe, he seemes to free her from her obedience, and binde himselfe to obey her.'[38] Great emphasis was placed on a husband's responsibility to justify his position in the household, leading by example and thus vindicating the gender order. Whately therefore advised the husband 'to exceede his wife as much in goodnesse, as he doth in place':

> Let his wife see in him, such humilitie, godlinesse, wisdome, as may cause her very hart to confesse, that there is in him some worth and dignity, something that deserveth to be stooped unto: let him walke uprightly, Christianly, soberly, religiously in his family, and give a good example to all in the houshold: then shall the wife willingly give him the better place, when she cannot but see him, to be the better person.[39]

Similarly, William Gouge argued that adultery in men was far worse than in women because of 'how much the more it appertaineth to them to excell in vertue, and to governe their wives by example'.[40] Even when the double standard was maintained that 'the cause of contention may be in the husband, but the fault of contending, is surely in the wife', the husband was nonetheless advised to 'give not occasion by foolishnes to be despised, nor by overmuch severitie to be hated or feared'.[41]

Conduct manuals warned husbands that the biggest threat to their authority was their own tyrannous delusions. Moralists constantly reiterated the inadvisability of simply asserting dominance. Dod and Cleaver stressed that an over-simplistic approach to male authority was perilous:

> such husbands as doe bragge, and thinke themselves able to rule, and over rule their wives: by that time they have proceeded and gone a little further, they shall well feele and perceive themselves to be beguiled, and finde that thing to be most hard and intricate, the which to be done, they esteemed most light and easie.[42]

Similarly, Gouge cautioned husbands to avoid 'the over-bold and over-heady pretended manhood' caused by irrational jealousy and heavy-handed husbanding, and Whately advised against 'big lookes, great words, and a fierce behaviour'. This same logic was applied to men who subjected their wives to the violence of an 'unmanlike fist'.[43] In the

---

[38] Smith, *A Preparative to Mariage*, 62.
[39] Whately, *A Bride Bush*, 100.
[40] Gouge, *Of Domesticall Duties*, 219. See also *The Court of Good Counsell*, sig. C3ᵛ.
[41] Ste B., *Counsel to the Husband*, 70, 88.
[42] Dod and Cleaver, *A Godly Form of Householde Government*, 215.
[43] Gouge, *Of Domesticall Duties*, 417–18; Whately, *A Bride Bush*, 100; id., *A Care-Cloth*, 45. This theme was also heavily emphasized by the homily, 'On the State of Matrimony', in *Certain Sermons or Homilies Appointed to be Read in Churches in the Time of Queen Elizabeth of Famous Memory* (London,

context of marital advice, manhood was forfeited not only by weak husbands, but also by overbearing tyrants. While such advice sought to maintain men's authority over women, it paradoxically emphasized that their position of dominance was best achieved without domination.

This point was developed further in the considerable attention given to the importance of love as the basis for a husband's authority. While men were cautioned against too much love, they were also advised against its total suppression. Moralists did not handle this issue in terms of a consolation with which to temper the realities of male dominance, but as the central crux upon which a successful relationship rested.[44] According to Pauline doctrine, the love required of men for their wives was seen as analogous to that of Christ for his Church—that is, unconditional and forgiving. It demanded of a husband that he 'delight in his wife intirely', not through self-interest, but with 'respect to the *object* which is loved, and the good it may doe thereunto, rather then to the *subject* which loveth, and the good that it may receive'.[45] This exhortation of a loving commitment of husbands to their wives stemmed from the conceptualization of marriage primarily as a union of two persons into one flesh. Dod and Cleaver claimed that husband and wife should be 'of one heart, will, and mind', and Gouge portrayed the relationship almost as a continuum of being, rather than a conjunction of two individuals: 'A man is *glued* to his wife. The metaphor setteth forth the *neerenesse* of a thing as well as the *firmnesse* of it: for things glued together are as one intire thing.'[46] Consequently a man was exhorted to think of his wife as an 'other selfe' or a 'second selfe', using the same imagery applied in other contexts to perfect, and equal, friendship.[47]

Just as this emphasis on a husband's duty to love his wife as himself tempered depictions of the authoritarian patriarch, so the corresponding emphasis on mutuality diminished men's claims to autonomy within marriage. Moralists cautioned that a husband subsumed his credit and livelihood with his wife to the extent that his dependence upon her was

---

1890), 537–8. See also Martin Parker's ballad, *Hold your Hands Honest Men for here's a Good Wife hath a Husband that Likes her, in Every Respect, but Onely he Strikes her, then if you Desire to be Held Men Compleat, what ever you doe your Wives doe not Beat* (London, 1634).

[44] Cf. Fletcher, 'Men's Dilemma'.

[45] Gouge, *Of Domesticall Duties*, 360, 415. See also, e.g., 'On the State of Matrimony', 539–40; Abbot, *A Wedding Sermon*.

[46] Dod and Cleaver, *A Godly Form of Householde Government*, 229; Gouge, *Of Domesticall Duties*, 115.

[47] Taylor, *A Good Husband*, 25; Niccholes, *A Discourse of Marriage*, 5. See also Gouge, *Of Domesticall Duties*, 391; Smith, *A Preparative to Mariage*, 26. For parallels with descriptions of 'entire' friendship, see below, pp. 123–4.

inescapable. This was clear in the most alarmist warnings to men of the dangers of marriage, which declared that 'the Husband that is not beloved of his wife, holdeth his goods in danger, his house in suspition[,] his credite in Ballance, and also sometimes his life in perill'.[48] Unless blessed with considerable resources, a successful household was not something a man could create easily on his own, even if it was advocated as one of his fundamental responsibilities as an adult male. While the strict division of labour propounded by moralists denied the extent of women's contribution to the household economy, it also overemphasized the importance of their reputation to its credit. So Dod and Cleaver insisted that 'It is to be noted, and noted againe, that as the provision of houshould dependeth onely on the Husband: even so the honour of all dependeth onely of the woman: in such sort, that there is no honour within the house, longer then a mans wife is honorable.'[49] Given the ways honour and reputation could be gendered in early modern England, this invoked a fundamental double standard, which could nonetheless leave men in a disturbingly precarious position.[50] Resting a household's reputation upon a wife's sexual honour deflected attention from the possibilities of men's waywardness. Yet by locating the fault with women and often ignoring the threats posed by adulterous men to marital stability and domestic order, household honour was left nominally and somewhat precariously (not to mention unrealistically) balanced in the hands of women.

Advice literature therefore contained a paradoxical set of messages for husbands. Marriage was approached simultaneously as a threat to manhood and an intrinsic part of its achievement. Although wives were advised to be unconditionally obedient, husbands were constantly warned of the limits of their authority. A man was advised to retain sufficient distance from his wife, since he was in danger of becoming 'effeminately' overcome by ungoverned love, yet a husband's love was acclaimed as the principal tool with which a successful marriage could be

---

[48] Dod and Cleaver, *A Godly Form of Householde Government*, 166. See also Tilney, *Flower of Friendshippe*, sig. B6; Niccholes, *A Discourse of Marriage*, 4.

[49] Dod and Cleaver, *A Godly Form of Householde Government*, 168. According to Jacqueline Eales, this was a particular concern of advice written by clerics. However, it was promoted in a variety of genres beyond such conduct books. Cf. Jacqueline Eales, 'Gender Construction in Early Modern England and the Conduct Books of William Whately (1583–1639)', in R. N. Swanson (ed.), *Gender and Christian Religion*, Studies in Church History 34 (Woodbridge, 1998) and Elizabeth A. Foyster, *Manhood in Early Modern England: Honour, Sex and Marriage* (Harlow, 1999), ch. 2.

[50] Keith Thomas, 'The Double Standard', *Journal of the History of Ideas*, 20 (1959); Laura Gowing, *Domestic Dangers: Women, Words, and Sex in Early Modern London* (Oxford, 1996); Foyster, *Manhood in Early Modern England*, ch. 3; Coppélia Kahn, *Man's Estate: Masculine Identity in Shakespeare* (Berkeley, 1981).

achieved. Moreover, a husband was warned against becoming dependent on or beholden to his wife, yet the model of marriage, with its emphasis on mutuality, meant that his credit (and therefore his livelihood) hinged upon the reputation of his wife. It appears, therefore, that there were as many discrepancies within prescriptive codes as there might have been between prescription and practice.

That there were gaps between prescription and practice was more readily admitted by moralists, as has already been suggested by their preoccupation with unruly wives and tyrannical husbands. Although often reluctant to concede the fictions of a double sexual standard which focused the blame for marital infidelity on women, advice writers did grant that men themselves posed dangers to domestic stability. Perhaps the greatest underlying agenda of the conduct literature was to coach men in their marital duties, precisely because they were seen to work against household order. Despite being the beneficiaries of prescriptions which accorded men authority and control over women, men were portrayed by advice writers as being equally, if not more, prone to fail in their duties as women, with similarly disruptive consequences. Dod and Cleaver made no secret of the extent of men's inadequacies in ensuring domestic stability, claiming that 'if at this day, a due survey should be taken of all Men and Women, throughout his Majesties dominions, there would be found in number moe women that are faithfull, religious, and vertuous then men'.[51] Similarly, Whately warned that no man was free from fault, and that a woman could not expect to find a husband free from at least one of the following 'disorders':

Some men are churlish, sowre, & unkind; some, wrathfull, passionate, and furious; some hard, miserable, and niggardly; some wastefull, riotous, and unthriftie; some uncleane, unsatiable, and ranging after other women; some suspicious, mistrustfull, and jealous of their owne wives; some rash and harebrained; some fond and giddie; some simple; some subtill; some idle; some toylesome; some carking; some careless.[52]

Just as men were expected to have many attributes, so they were prone to many faults. According to the moralists, women were not the only 'domestic dangers' requiring instruction in the principles of order.

Besides the bitter tyrant, the character of the spendthrift particularly concerned advice writers. Characterized in familiar terms as 'beast-like', owing to his propensity for 'Drunkennesse, gaming, [and] ill company keeping', he contravened his calling to provide for his family. Such mis-

[51] Dod and Cleaver, *A Godly Form of Householde Government*, 232.
[52] Whately, *A Care-Cloth*, 44, 43.

placed prodigality was a popular topic in domestic advice, and men were stereotyped as singularly prone to flightiness and dissipation:

> Many men spend day after day, like a bird that flieth up and downe, as it falleth out, from tree to tree, from twigge to twigge: they goe from place to place, but know not for what end: as they meet with any company, so they abide as long as the company tarrieth, and then seeke after other company, and are ready to goe with any to Ale-house, Taverne, Play-house, Bowling alley, or other like places.[53]

The thriftless husband persisted with the vices elsewhere associated with youth, and as a result he was deemed to forfeit his manhood. The stereotype of the spendthrift was coupled with descriptions of 'light' men, portrayed as having 'no stampe nor impression of gravity, or discretion', favouring instead 'a kinde of puerilitie and boyishnesse'.[54] Besides being likened to boys, such men opened themselves to the censure often reserved for rogues or 'yong and lusty vagrants' who, according to Dod and Cleaver, were worse than dogs and undeserving of the name or company of men because of their idleness and mischief. Moralists emphasized that in contrast to the 'bondage' of gluttony and drunkenness, work was liberating and manly. It made those who laboured 'with their owne handes... big and mightie', and it also 'quickeneth and maketh them like men' who directed the work of others.[55]

Besides idleness, perhaps the greatest offence committed by such men in moralists' eyes was their forfeiture of rational self-control, and, by implication, their manhood. According to Whately, 'The bitter man is like a frantike head, very troublesome; the unthrifty man as a scald head, very fulsome; the light man, the jester, like a giddy head, very ridiculous.' All three types had abandoned reason and as a result could not rule.[56] Men who could not govern themselves were unfit to govern others, and unworthy of claims to superiority. Conduct writers warned that men who made themselves contemptible by 'profanenesse, riotousnesse, drunkennesse, lewdnesse, lightnesses, [and] unthriftinesse' surrendered their authority. Men's self-government was therefore approached as a precondition of successful household management and of access to the full patriarchal dividend: 'hee is a Husband of a Wife, a Father of Children, and a Maister of Servants, and therefore had neede of government in

---

[53] Whately, *A Bride Bush*, 103; Gouge, *Of Domesticall Duties*, 256.
[54] Whately, *A Bride Bush*, 104.
[55] John Dod and Robert Cleaver, *A Plaine and Familiar Exposition of the Ten Commandements* (London, 1618), 245; *Xenophons Treatise of Householde*, trans. G. Heruet (London, 1573), fos. 5ʳ–6, 16ᵛ.
[56] Whately, *A Bride Bush*, 104.

himselfe that must governe all these'.[57] As the justification for their authority, a superior capacity for rational action was firmly claimed for men. Moralists discussing marriage, like medical writers discussing moderation, nevertheless betrayed considerable concerns about the ubiquity of male tendencies antithetical to the ideal.

There was far less scope in domestic advice literature to attribute such faults to 'other' kinds of men, on the basis of either age or social status. Instead, the primary distinction was between stereotypes of the good husband and the bad husband. Such contrasts were as important in constructions of normative manhood as the comparison between husbands and wives and their respective duties. A good husband was to be 'judicious, a man of understanding, able to manage the affairs of his generall, and particular calling'. His vocation was to be 'wisedome, knowledge, experience, sobriety, Christian care, [and] to provide for his charge'.[58] Such claims reflect further attempts to fix the meanings of manhood in terms of rational discretion, thrift, industry, and self-control both through positive association and by labelling deviations from this ideal in terms of effeminacy, bestiality, and servile bondage.

Rather than simply claiming superiority for husbands, moralists were more preoccupied with bidding men not to abuse it. Imperatives of female subordination were accompanied by warnings about the limits of male authority, and men were exhorted to govern themselves before they could claim the right to govern others. While householding men were undoubtedly its greatest beneficiaries, the patriarchal model of manhood detailed in domestic advice was nonetheless designed to constrain men as well as women. The attributes of normative manhood were emphasized not only as the justification for men's authority, but also precisely because the nature and extent of that authority was ultimately unclear. Even at its prescriptive source, the patriarchal model of manhood associated with marriage was full of contradictions. Marriage marked a rite of passage into householding maturity for men, yet paradoxically it posed as much of a threat to manhood as the guarantee of its achievement. Love endangered manhood, yet it was the necessary foundation of marriage and a husband's authority. Furthermore, this authority was limited by the extent of men's (largely unacknowledged) dependence upon their wives, as well as threatened by their own tendencies to disorder. The extensive concern of moralists with male deviations from the ideal reflected not only tensions between prescription and practice, but contests over the meanings of manhood itself.

[57] Gouge, *Of Domesticall Duties*, 355; Niccholes, *A Discourse of Marriage*, 44.
[58] Crompton, *A Wedding-Ring*, 33.

MANHOOD AND THE SOCIAL ORDER

> Oh if the head and severall members of a family would be perswaded every of them to be conscionable in performing their own particular duties, what a sweet society, and happy harmony would there be in houses? ... Necessary it is that good order be first set in families: for as they were before other polities, so they are somewhat the more necessary: and good members of a family are like to make good members of Church and common-wealth[59]

Ultimately, domestic advice attempted to outline a template for the maintenance of an ordered society, and was therefore the product of a distinct social and political agenda. This was at heart a patriarchal project, prescribing not only a strict differentiation of roles between men and women, but also crucial distinctions between members of the same sex, particularly on the basis of age, marital status, and, less directly, social status. Privileging men above women, the patriarchal blueprint also privileged some men above others, based on assumptions about their ability to discipline both themselves and others. The nominal extension of the patriarchal dividend to all men in invocations of a gender order which ranked men above women was repeatedly qualified by references to the many other hierarchies at work in early modern society. As a result, there was a tension between assertions of generic male superiority which implied the extension of privilege to all men, and concerns to maintain an ordered society that necessitated the disciplining and therefore subordination of many men as well as women. Conduct writers appeared extensively concerned that such subordination was often insufficiently maintained. Furthermore, they expressed considerable anxiety that the extension of authority to men in patriarchal positions also risked being undermined by their failure to perform the duties expected of them.

The differences between men that were most readily acknowledged by conduct writers of various genres were those based on age and marital status. Normative, or patriarchal, manhood was constructed through contrasting 'man's age' with youth and old age, and married men with their unmarried counterparts. The attributes of reason, discretion, wisdom, self-government, moderation, strength, self-sufficiency, and honesty were reserved for men of adult years who had achieved householding status through marriage. The exceptions to this rule were the men who enjoyed sufficient social status to override these other distinctions, which

---

[59] Gouge, *Of Domesticall Duties*, fo. 2ᵛ.

in turn is suggestive of the potential impact of social status differentials between men. This was rarely explicitly acknowledged by conduct writers who generally assumed an elite readership. Implicit assumptions remained, however, which are telling, such as the association of deviations from the temperate ideal with lower-ranking occupations and the link between the prodigality and idleness of deviant married men and vagrancy.

The patriarchal exemplar outlined by conduct writers in its various different forms was therefore a product of its authors' social concerns, and often appealed to aspirations of gentility and civility. Rational discretion and the bodily control associated with temperance were linked to Ciceronian concepts of virtue that underpinned notions of gentility, and the golden mean of patriarchal manhood chimed with the ideals of civic as well as aristocratic culture.[60] The extreme analogies of deviance which conduct writers were willing to invoke—in terms of effeminacy, bestiality, and servility—suggest that their definitions of manhood were neither always adhered to nor broadly shared. An obvious point of tension was between young men and adults: that moralists laboured so hard to deny any link between the excesses of youth (such as heavy drinking, lustfulness, and prodigality) and manhood suggests that they were viewed precisely in this way by their protagonists. Similarly, concerns about married men's deviations from the patriarchal model suggest the existence both of competing interpretations of the limits and duties of patriarchal authority and of alternative meanings of manhood disconnected from this prescriptive agenda.

It appears evident that, by representing manhood as conditional on age, marital status, behaviour, and, more implicitly, social status, moralists were attempting to fix the meanings of manhood in their terms, denying the legitimacy of competing definitions which were classified in terms of failure rather than acknowledged as alternative forms of manhood. Conduct writers advocated limited access to the patriarchal dividend, variously excluding men on the grounds of age, marital status, and social status. Claiming again and again that those who were excluded from or who deviated from the ideal failed to be men was a rhetorical device aimed both to establish definitions of manhood in exclusively patriarchal terms and to encourage men either to adopt self-discipline or to submit to the authority of others. Rather than simply extending the benefits of

---

[60] Blair Worden, *The Sound of Virtue: Philip Sidney's* Arcadia *and Elizabethan Politics* (New Haven, 1996), 23–37; Jonathan Barry, 'Civility and Civic Culture in Early Modern England: The Meanings of Urban Freedom', in Peter Burke, Brian Harrison, and Paul Slack (eds.), *Civil Histories: Essays Presented to Sir Keith Thomas* (Oxford, 2000).

patriarchal privilege to adult males, therefore, moralists sought to coach them in the behaviour required for the maintenance of an ordered society. As a result, conduct writers implied that men posed as much of a menace to patriarchal order as women, even if they stood to benefit more from its dictates. As will become apparent in the next section, although the ideals of patriarchal manhood undoubtedly informed the language of social description, attempts to fix meanings of manhood exclusively in these terms enjoyed, at best, a very qualified success.

PART II

The Social Practice of Manhood

4
Youthful Excess and Fraternal Bonding

IN August 1593, the vice-chancellor of the university of Cambridge examined several witnesses about the havoc wreaked by a group of 'nightwalkers'. Two constables' assistants confessed that after leaving the Falcon at about ten or eleven o'clock they had met with a group of scholars from Queens' College. According to the constables' men, the scholars were posing as the proctor's watch—the university's policing body which nightly searched the streets of Cambridge—and therefore they had decided to join them. They also admitted that the students had been disguised, some with false beards 'like players berds', some with scarves over their faces, and some with caps over their heads. Thus adorned they rang the bell of the Cross Keys with a rapier and demanded beer. Their disguise did not fool Agnes Haull, the tavern's maid, who attempted to keep them out, 'for that she kneewe that the proctor was not there (the which shee sayeth shee tooke to be soe for that they kept sutche a laughinge & a stirre whereupon they sayed they were the proctor[)]'. Her attempts failed, however, as they 'brake open the doore', pushed inside, 'flourishinge with there naked swordes', and blew out the candles lighting the room. Then, having called for beer and been refused, the young men 'brok out with terrible oathes', and after finally obtaining some drink, 'one of them dreewe out a shillinge & woulde have had the sayed Agnes kisse yt & when shee refused soe to doe he dreewe out his rapyer & sayed he wooulde thrust her throughe yf shee woulde not kisse yt'. They also swore at her master and pushed his wife down the stairs when she attempted to remove their disguises. Another witness complained that they had created further disturbance by tolling the church bell. When he had admonished them that 'yt was noe fitt tyme of the night to disquiet neighbours' they called him rascal and 'Cloggheaded cookowlde', tore down the lattice on his chamber window, and broke his shop windows, causing over 20*s.* worth of damage.[1]

These were the actions of young men performing rituals of bravado through which they temporarily claimed dominance. By masquerading as

[1] CUL, CUA, Examination of Agnes Haull et al., V.C.Ct.III.2, no. 249.

the proctor's men, flourishing their swords and demanding beer, forcing deference to their spending power, breaking windows, and insulting all whom they encountered, this coterie of nocturnal revellers openly flouted the rules expected to govern their behaviour, leaving a trail of offence and destruction. Their actions suggested that the perpetrators, most of whom were to take holy orders (and who included two future bishops), were above the codes of conduct expected of them.[2] Inverting the supposition that men should work by day and sleep at night, they conformed to legal definitions of nightwalking which associated such behaviour with idleness and dishonesty.[3] The participants additionally asserted manhood by subverting official rites of violence. Claiming the authority of university proctors, they pursued precisely the disorderly kinds of action that the proctors were charged to prevent.

Arguably the boldest resistance to patriarchal concepts of order was performed by young men, many of whom espoused potent inversions of normative meanings of manhood. Youthful rituals of misrule indulged routine aspects of male sociability to excess; misappropriated the authority of adult males; and subverted patriarchal imperatives of order, thrift, and self-control. In their bids for manhood, young men embraced precisely the kinds of behaviour—violent disruption, excessive drinking, illicit sex—condemned by moralists as unmanly, effeminate, and beastlike. While such critiques were often levelled at youthful miscreants, who in addition risked severe punishment for their misdeeds, the governors of the university and of other institutions charged with the socialization of young men more frequently condemned their behaviour as 'common' or undignified, implicitly ranking codes of manhood according to distinctions of social status. Yet there is also evidence that at times youthful misrule was tolerated and even implicitly condoned by those in authority over them. Although the active resistance performed by young men was in many ways the most serious attack on patriarchal norms, therefore, it was not necessarily taken the most seriously by men wielding patriarchal power, not least because many adult men recognized and even endorsed the potent meanings of manhood to which it was linked. It is possible that alternatives to patriarchal codes could, in many instances, be deemed

[2] John Davenant, BA, of Queens' College, later became Lady Margaret Professor of Divinity and then Bishop of Salisbury. George Montaigne, MA, of Queens' College, was subsequently chaplain to James I, Dean of Westminster, Bishop of Lincoln, Bishop of London, Bishop of Durham, and briefly served as Archbishop of York before his death in 1628. John and J. A. Venn, *Alumni Cantabrigienses: A Biographical List of All Known Students, Graduates and Holders of Office at the University of Cambridge, from the Earliest Times to 1900*, 4 vols. (Cambridge, 1922–54).

[3] Paul Griffiths, 'Meanings of Nightwalking in Early Modern England', *Seventeenth Century*, 13 (1998), 213.

less threatening when articulated along divisions of age than of social status. Central to youthful exploits was the role of the group, which facilitated young men's disruptive assertions of manhood in ways which often cut across boundaries of social status and geographical origin. This kind of fraternal bonding alerts us to the importance of links between men in conferring male identity. Male bonding has been identified as a natural propensity, with comparable significance to relations between the sexes, and as such it has not received sufficient historical analysis.[4] It was a particularly significant feature of male youth culture in early modern England, because it both validated claims to manliness and provided a largely unacknowledged source of intimacy during this most homosocial phase of the life course. Recent research in men's studies is helpful in establishing the potential range of such bonds, and the contrasting dynamics governing them. A crucial distinction is made between comradeship and friendship. Comradeship is defined in terms of shared activity (likened to 'parallel play') while friendship involves reciprocal disclosure and mutual trust.[5] The collective action of comrades presupposes 'the loss of an individual sense of self to a group identity', and rests on transient and temporary loyalties. On the other hand, the intimacy established between friends is based upon 'an individual's intellectual and emotional affinity to another individual' and ideally constitutes what Aristotle deemed 'complete' friendship, devoid of competition and mistrust.[6]

This distinction between comradeship and friendship provides a useful compass for navigating the range of early modern bonds adopted by young men and contemporary attitudes towards them, although it perhaps requires more nuances than allowed by the prescriptive agenda of men's studies' nascent phases which sought to encourage deeper bonds of friendship between men. Rather than effecting the loss of self-identity, group action in early modern England could provide opportunities to develop particular aspects of selfhood through affiliation to a group identity. Furthermore, although such processes of self-exploration by elective affinity to the group could be transient, they could also be a powerful basis for lifelong identities. Friendship, on the other hand, could often be

---

[4] Lionel Tiger, *Men in Groups*, 2nd edn. (London, 1984). See also Eve Kosofsky Sedgwick, *Between Men: English Literature and Male Homosocial Desire* (Baltimore, 1985).
[5] Larry May and Robert A. Strikwerda, 'Male Friendship and Intimacy', in eid., *Rethinking Masculinity: Philosophical Explorations in Light of Feminism* (Baltimore, 1992), 97.
[6] Peter Lyman, 'The Fraternal Bond as a Joking Relationship: A Case Study of the Role of Sexist Jokes in Male Group Bonding', in Michael S. Kimmel (ed.), *Changing Men: New Directions in Research on Men and Masculinity* (Newbury Park, Calif., 1987), 160; May and Strikwerda, 'Male Friendship and Intimacy', 101.

far removed from the Aristotelian ideal, and not necessarily more lasting than group loyalties. Even if it is a little less clear cut than its abstract definition, the distinction between comradeship based on group identity, and friendship derived from direct personal affinity, is nonetheless helpful in approaching the spectrum of potential relations between young men and the dynamics governing them—not least because the Aristotelian ideal of 'entire' or complete friendship was frequently invoked in early modern discussions of friendship, and because fraternal camaraderie was so central to young men's assertions of manhood.

This chapter begins by investigating the ways in which young men subverted patriarchal concepts of manhood rooted in thrift, order, and self-control through rituals of excess. While there were attempts to contain the extent of such youthful disorder, there appears to have been more scope for disruption by young men than by young women, suggesting that the potency of such assertions of manhood was broadly recognized, however hard conduct writers and men in authority laboured to deny and contain it. (By contrast, young women more frequently encountered warnings that deviations from behavioural codes, and particularly expectations of chastity, would result in their permanent 'ruin'.) Secondly, this chapter explores the fraternal bonds upon which such counter-codes of manhood depended, and argues that despite the rhetoric emphasizing the importance of male friendship, the more transient rituals of male camaraderie were deemed preferable to (and in some ways less dangerous than) intimate friendships between men, since they facilitated unacknowledged intimacy without surrendering a degree of competition and independence for the participants. Male intimacy associated with individual friendships on the other hand was regarded with fear and suspicion. Just as distinctions between male stereotypes were pivotal to constructions of normative manhood, so relationships between men, and their careful regulation, were central to the establishment of male identity in early modern England. This was especially true for young men whose manhood was proved primarily amongst their peers, and often in opposition to their elders.

THE CAMARADERIE OF MISRULE

Episodes of nightwalking were not unusual in early modern Cambridge. The proctor's watch was frequently impersonated and parodied by young men drawn from the town as well as the university. Town lads were reported to have paraded the streets in scholars' gowns, 'fighting and quarreling with such as they mett: Knockinge att menns doores and saieinge they were Proctors', and, on a separate occasion, were heard shouting 'as yf they had counterfett broken lattin'.[7] Smashing glass, pulling up poles, breaking window lattices and demolishing men's work stalls all featured in such nocturnal escapades. Arrogant posturing and sexual insult were also common occurrences in further violation of the symbols of the established male order. Scholars were admonished for 'being in company with others that brake downe glasse windowes' and for 'riotting & swaggering in the towne'; a group of servants was examined for throwing stones and breaking windows, and for playing rough music, exhorting one of their neighbours to hang up his horns; and in a similar incident several students were sued for making 'a great hodiloghe & noyse & hoopeinge & halloweinge with singeinge of badd songes, [running] up & downe the streates like mad men', singing 'yt ys at the best: when Cuckoulds be at rest' and breaking several windows.[8]

Nor were such episodes unfamiliar in other provincial towns.[9] Two servants from Rye were put in the stocks for 'beatinge and misusinge the watche of the towne', and 'certeine lewde youthes' were bound to appear before the Staffordshire justices 'for assaultinge the Kinges watche', which 'triumphe' they celebrated by 'a bibbinge & quaffinge of their ale at the markett Crosse'.[10] In Leicester, an 'Acte for Nyght Walkers' was first passed in 1553 to stop the offences caused by 'dyvers Idell ryottous & evyll disposed persons who ys not content all the day to sytt in Innes, Tavernes, alle housys & other vyttulyng housys to ther gret costes & loss of tyme, but lykewyse wyll do the same all the nyght with walkyng in the strettes [with] moche truble to the well dyssposyd people that wold take ther naturall rest'. Reiterated on several subsequent occasions, this Act apparently failed to prevent further disruption after the nine o'clock curfew.[11] The bellman of Devizes was instructed to stop 'the breaking up of houses, shoppes or warehouses by nightwalkers and other disordered and ydle persons', and several servants from Midhurst (Sussex) were presented by their churchwardens for ringing the church bells 'almost all the

---

[7] CUL, CUA, V.C.Ct.III.32, no. 181; Depositions regarding Gill and Clarke, 'nightwalkers', V.C.Ct.III.2, no. 228. See also Comm.Ct.I.18, fo. 80.

[8] Emmanuel College, Cambridge, Emmanuel College Archives, Admonitions Book, 1586–1775, CHA1.4.A, fo. 3ᵛ; Trinity College, Cambridge, Trinity College Archives, Admissions and Admonitions, 1566–1759, p. 435; CUL, CUA, V.C.Ct.III.8, no. 63; V.C.Ct.III.2, no. 260. See also V.C.Ct.III.14, nos. 88, 92; *Mark Charlton c. William Rogerson*, V.C.Ct.III.2, no. 211; V.C.Ct.III.17, no. 99; Comm.Ct.I.18, fo. 80.

[9] Griffiths, 'Meanings of Nightwalking', 223–8.

[10] ESRO, Rye 1/5, fo. 26; *The Staffordshire Quarter Sessions Rolls*, v: *1603–1606*, ed. S. A. H. Burne (Kendal, 1940), 237–8.

[11] *Records of the Borough of Leicester. Being a Series of Extracts from the Archives of the Corporation of Leicester*, iii: *1509–1603*, ed. Mary Bateson (Cambridge, 1905), 73, 154, 162, 194.

night... very disorderly so that we could not sleep quietly in our beds'.[12] In the metropolis, as elsewhere, masters were concerned to keep their servants and apprentices out of trouble at night. Thus William Lyndesley, a cooper's servant, was threatened with imprisonment, on account that he, 'getting a sworde which he usuallie kepte under his bed, did use diverse and sundrie nights to lye furthe of his masters house, and to haunt such companies as were farre unbeseeminge a good servaunt, and very prejudiciall to the good of his said master'.[13] The rituals of youthful misrule were also widely associated with forms of moral regulation—particularly of sexual behaviour—both across England and further afield.[14]

Nightwalkers shouting sexual insults postured as self-appointed moral arbiters and, rather than simply subverting patriarchal imperatives of order and self-control, appropriated the regulative stance of those in authority. A harrowing example of such misappropriation is provided by a case brought to the Cambridge university courts in 1594 which involved a motley crew of students and marginal inhabitants of the town collectively mimicking the violence of officials. A group of scholars had been roaming the town after dark together with a Dutchman, one Cliburne 'of Newcastle', and Marmaduke Toulson the baking man from the White Horse, when they came across a woman hiding under a hedge. They took her to Smoke Alley (where, as they were informed, they would find 'evill rule') in an attempt to identify her as a prostitute. Having failed, they led her into the fields and (as one witness recounted) decided on her 'punishment':

four say that shee should be whipt &c the newcastle man said shee should be whipt, who made her put of all her clothes to her smocke & the dutchman then gettinge hold of her hands bad bind her hands: some answered they could not gett off her clothes & so her hands were not bonded. [S]hee willingly put of all but her smocke & than the Newcastle man bad her put off that, which shee refused, but lay down in the mier & the ... Newcastle man tare yt down to her Middle. & then shee sittinge in the myre ... the Northern man toke his girdle & gave her 2

---

[12] Griffiths, 'Meanings of Nightwalking', 224; *Churchwarden's Presentments (17th Century). Part 1. Archdeaconry of Chichester*, ed. Hilda Johnstone, Sussex Record Society 49 (Lewes, 1948), 126.

[13] GL, Coopers' Company, Court Minutes, 1567–96, MS 5602/1, fo. 161. See also Joan Lane, *Apprenticeship in England, 1600–1914* (London, 1996), ch. 9.

[14] Bernard Capp, 'English Youth Groups and "The Pinder of Wakefield"', and Steven R. Smith, 'The London Apprentices as Seventeenth-Century Adolescents', both in Paul Slack (ed.), *Rebellion, Popular Protest, and the Social Order in Early Modern England* (Cambridge, 1984). See also Natalie Zemon Davis, *Society and Culture in Early Modern France* (Cambridge, 1987), ch. 4; Michael Mitterauer, *A History of Youth*, trans. Graeme Dunphy (Cambridge, Mass., 1993), ch. 4; Norbert Schindler, *Rebellion, Community and Custom in Early Modern Germany*, trans. Pamela E. Selwyn (Cambridge, 2002), 201–12.

or 3 lashes with yt: then came 2 or 3 more of the company, & toke dirt & sh[it?] at her.[15]

Such brutality, besides being a perverse source of titillation, served many functions in asserting manhood, facilitated, endorsed, and conferred by the group. It appropriated the power of officials who routinely punished women of suspicious character in this way by whipping them, similarly stripped to the waist, often on the back of a cart.[16] By choosing to flog the unknown woman, the men mimicked forms of judicial punishment designed to shame and humiliate in order to demonstrate their power. They distanced themselves from her sexually, and instead claimed an alternative form of dominance which was not theirs to exercise. This incident was a display of strength and power which was probably meant to impress the gathered male company as much as the female victim (possibly more so). Those who declined to endorse or participate in their actions were ostracized, as in the case of one witness who claimed that when he refused to help shove the woman into the water, 'the supposed proctor of the company called [him], thrust at him with his halbart & bad him gette him home for he was none of this company'.[17]

Less extreme regulative rituals, whereby the perpetrators nonetheless derived prestige from their humiliation of others, were an integral part of student life. Like the Shrove Tuesday disorders associated with London apprentices, college-based festivities of licensed misrule involved the exuberant appropriation of regulative authority.[18] In Trinity College, it was a standard part (although increasingly contested) of the bachelors' Christmas festivities to abuse and taunt any disliked college servant by stocking him in the college hall. This was explicitly couched in terms of punishment. In 1620 a Bachelor of Arts claimed that such an incident had been provoked by the under-butler's 'proude carriage', asserting that the bachelors had 'a libertie from time to time in their Christmas merriments or sports to punish misdemeanours and faults then and there committed by servants of the Colledge and other inferiour officers'.[19] The

---

[15] CUL, CUA, V.C.Ct.III.2, no. 254.

[16] See, e.g., the vice-chancellor's order that Faith Madison, found 'lewde and incontinent', should be 'whipped through the Towne at a Carts arse untill the bloode followe uppon her shoulders naked', CUL, CUA, V.C.Ct.I.9, fo. 38ᵛ. See also below, p. 134.

[17] CUL, CUA, V.C.Ct.III.2, no. 253.

[18] Smith, 'The London Apprentices'; Paul Griffiths, *Youth and Authority: Formative Experiences in England, 1560–1640* (Oxford, 1996), 147–61.

[19] CUL, CUA, *Henry Goche and Edward Beeston c. Richard Meredith*, V.C.Ct.II.22, fo. 11, and V.C.Ct.III.24, no. 48. For the full dispute, including many discussions of this custom, see also V.C.Ct.III.24, nos. 45–7, 49, and V.C.Ct.II.22, fos. 1, 3. College servants were regularly bludgeoned by students. See, e.g., Trinity College Archives, Admissions and Admonitions, 398, 400;

celebrations on All Saints' Day seem to have involved similar affronts, as suggested by Thomas Bigge's confession to 'disorderly and outrageous' behaviour 'in stocking & striking diverse persons both a man & his wife & others & pouring water on them, being in the stocks'.[20] Here scholars dispatched regulation and correction which they were more used to receiving than administering. That such incidents were part of the festivities of licensed misrule suggests that the university occasionally sanctioned students' appropriation of regulative violence in recognition of their incipient authority as elite males, although college authorities were concerned to limit the extent of abuse and disorder. In 1608, for example, it was ordered in Trinity College that 'uppon over greate liberty taken by the Bachellours this present yeare, that heareafter, they shall have no authoritye in them selves, to make sporte, at all Saynte daye, Chrismas, & the feast of purification, but they shalbe licenced therunto by the Master if he be present, or by the vice Master, & senior deane, when the Master is absent'.[21]

For the most part, however, such rituals were primarily endorsed by young men's peers. They were an expression of the collective power and identity of the group which temporarily eclipsed the profiles of its individual members. Derived from an 'erotic of shared danger', the fraternal bonds of comradeship linking the group conferred a form of manly status far removed from the prescribed codes of conduct.[22] Through such collective activity, individual men could temporarily claim authority and prowess which was ordinarily denied to them. It is no coincidence that the majority of nightwalkers appear to have been young men who occupied subordinate positions due to either their age or social status. In this context, manhood was conferred by the group, through both its facilitation of collective disorder and its approbation of the actions of individual perpetrators. The group enabled young men either to appropriate or subvert forms of violent behaviour which ordinarily enforced patriarchal authority (such as the regulative discipline of university proctors) and to assert counter-codes of manhood.

This was similarly true of the ways in which young men took up the rituals of male drink culture and pushed them to disruptive extremes. The excessive consumption of alcohol was often integral to such subversive displays of bravado, and collective drinking was one of the primary

St John's College, Cambridge, St John's College Archives, Orders and Admonitions, 1627–1780, C5.1, fo. 193ᵛ.

[20] Trinity College Archives, Muniment Conclusion Book, 1607–73, 20.
[21] Ibid. 7.
[22] Lyman, 'The Fraternal Bond', 160.

lubricants of young men's fraternal bonding and comradeship, involving elaborate rituals as group revellers with a disruptive agenda transformed and inverted regular patterns of male conviviality into the extremes of intemperate debauchery. While such rituals were not age specific, they were clearly age related, occupying a central place in male youth culture. At a mundane level, drink was a marker of accord and friendship between men, associated with 'good fellowship'.[23] Wine or beer was often used to seal an agreement, and much bargain-making was performed in alehouses and confirmed with a toast. When the brewer William Pickering agreed in 1635 to see to the repairs of a malthouse he was renting from John Byatt, he 'tooke a glasse of wyne, & drunke unto the sayd John Byatt... [saying] well then you & I shall never fall out about them'. Often a token sum was exchanged 'in earnest' to bind an agreement, and it was customary for this to be spent on drink as a symbolic seal of the transaction. So in 1597, when Francis Phillips bargained with Thomas Emons in a Cambridge tavern for 120 quarters of malt, the agreement was sealed with a groat, which Emons 'did spend... there in wyne'.[24] Drink featured similarly in patching up quarrels. Pledging a health symbolized the restoration of harmony and concord. In 1594, John Scorye claimed that the grocer Robert Harvey had forgiven him for his insulting behaviour, since Harvey had accepted his apology and had 'called for beere & drunke to him the sayd Skorie and the sayd Skorie pledged him & dranke with him'.[25] Drinking pledges also featured as part of the processes of informal reconciliation to prevent quarrelling parties from going to law. Such drinking rites were part of men's everyday exchange, and ideally served to oil their networks of credit and community.

Drinking was also a routine part of male sociability, especially from the mid-sixteenth century when, according to Peter Clark, the alehouse began to replace the churchyard as the locus of communal recreation and 'traditional neighbourliness was transmuted into new-style drinking

---

[23] Keith Wrightson, 'Alehouses, Order and Reformation in Rural England, 1590–1660', in Eileen and Stephen Yeo (eds.), *Popular Culture and Class Conflict, 1590–1914: Explorations in the History of Labour and Leisure* (Brighton, 1981); id., 'The Puritan Reformation of Manners, with Special Reference to the Counties of Lancashire and Essex, 1640–1660', Ph.D. thesis (Cambridge, 1974), chs. 4–5; Peter Clark, *The English Alehouse: A Social History 1200–1830* (London, 1983), 156; J. A. Sharpe, *Crime in Seventeenth-Century England: A County Study* (Cambridge, 1983), 52.

[24] CUL, CUA, *William Pickering c. John Byatt*, V.C.Ct.II.25, fo. 60; *Thomas Emons c. Francis Phillips*, Comm.Ct.II.8, fo. 35ᵛ. See also Thomas Gataker's complaint that 'every bargaine [is made] over a Wine-pot', *The Decease of Lazarus Christ's Friend. A Funerall Sermon. At the Buriall of John Parker Merchant* (London, 1640), sig. A4.

[25] CUL, CUA, *Robert Harvey c. John Scorye*, V.C.Ct.III.4, no. 87. See also *Thomas Field, MA c. Ralph Dawson*, V.C.Ct.II.1, fo. 203.

camaraderie'.²⁶ This was a male-dominated atmosphere, although it should be emphasized that alehouses and their drinking festivities were not an exclusively male preserve. Evidence of women's involvement in alehouse culture, as both purveyors and consumers, can occasionally be glimpsed. In 1602, for example, four young men examined on suspicion of misrule confessed that they had been drinking wine 'in the Company of divers young mayds which they had lost at stoole ball to'. Married women were also present in alehouses, and not always in the company of their husbands, as suggested by an injury suit alleging that the saddler John Alcocke had defamed Richard Pindar while drinking at the Pheasant Cock in Cambridge. In the company of Michael Homes (a brewer), Ursula Fox, and Mary Longworthe (both married to tailors), Alcocke recounted the sexual exploits of their mutual friend Richard Pindar. He then challenged Mary Longworthe to tell Pindar's wife of his infidelity, goading, 'Marrye I will geve the ... a pinte of wyne to tell her of yt.'²⁷ Women were also occasionally punished for drunkenness,²⁸ although such examples of women's involvement in alehouse conviviality are relatively few when compared with the far greater prominence of men's drinking rituals in the records.²⁹ In addition women present in or connected to alehouses were clearly vulnerable to slurs couched in terms of unchastity. Dorothy Dugresse, the wife of a French teacher, entered two suits in the Cambridge university courts to refute accusations that she 'did shew hir arse in an alehouse' as part of drunken revelry.³⁰ Similar abuse was suffered by Rachel and Elizabeth Humbletoft from their neighbour Elizabeth Newman, who declared to them that 'your father keepes a base blinde alehouse or taphouse and you shalbe hung up for signes to it: you stand at the doare to traule in guests and schollers', further claiming that

---

²⁶ Peter Clark, 'The Alehouse and the Alternative Society', in Donald Pennington and Keith Thomas (eds.), *Puritans and Revolutionaries: Essays in Seventeenth-Century History Presented to Christopher Hill* (Oxford, 1978), 64.

²⁷ CUL, CUA, *Office* c. *Whyckham et al.*, V.C.Ct.I.5, fo. 247; *Richard Pindar* c. *John Alcocke*, Comm.Ct.II.8, fos. 5ᵛ–6. For other instances of married women in alehouses, with or without their husbands, see, e.g., *Minutes of the Norwich Court of Mayoralty 1632–1635*, ed. William L. Sachse, Norfolk Record Society 36 (Norwich, 1967), 128; *The Case Book of Sir Francis Ashley J.P., Recorder of Dorchester, 1614–1635*, ed. J. H. Bettey, Dorset Record Society 7 (Dorchester, 1981), 48; GL, Armourers and Brasiers' Company, Court Minutes, 1559–1621, MS 12071/2, 60.

²⁸ e.g. Elizabeth Blakey, ESRO, Rye 1/5, fo. 18ᵛ; Alice Legate and Cecely Symonds, *Minutes of the Norwich Court of Mayoralty 1632–1635*, 169.

²⁹ Wrightson, 'Alehouses, Order and Reformation', 7–8; Clark, *The English Alehouse*, 131–2; Griffiths, *Youth and Authority*, 209–12.

³⁰ CUL, CUA, *Dorothy Dugresse* c. *Mary Westly*, V.C.Ct.II.32, fo. 112. See also *Dorothy Dugresse* c. *Tabitha Reynolds*, V.C.Ct.II.32, fo. 108ᵛ; *Tabitha Reynolds* c. *Dorothy Dugresse*, V.C.Ct.II.32, fos. 127, 130*ʳ⁻ᵛ.

Rachel had 'played the wanton and bin incontinent with some scholler or schollers'.[31]

This is not to argue that men's drinking patterns went uncriticized, but to suggest that the associations surrounding men and women's consumption of alcohol could be profoundly different. Women occupied a more peripheral status at alehouse gatherings, and they were often denied the unselfconscious enjoyment of drinking which was automatically accorded to men.[32] Men not only sat more comfortably with the routine habits of sociability exercised within the alehouse, but they also adopted particular, gender-specific drinking practices which held important meanings of manhood. Beyond cementing ties of neighbourhood and community, drinking was also a central feature of the dramatic rituals of male bonding, as young men in particular pushed everyday patterns of alehouse conviviality to extremes in profligate displays of manly prowess.

The collective consumption of excessive quantities of alcohol was an intrinsic part of male youth culture and of the rites of passage into manhood. This is most vividly illustrated by the drinking habits adopted by many students which were based upon extravagant and exaggerated consumption. When students were punished for drinking, the amount spent on beer was often noted, with the implication that the primary offence was exorbitance as much as disorder. Two members of Emmanuel College were admonished in 1616 for 'disorder in drinking namly xvj*d.* at one tyme in Middletons house', and in 1633 John Callis of the same college was punished for 'frequent haunting [of] Tavernes Innes & alehouses in the compony of other scholers, & mispending his commencement mony, & other monyes'.[33] In 1611, when Sir Girling and Befaithful Asser of Emmanuel were disciplined for spending 5*s.* in an alehouse and 'for drunkennes at the Casle ... where they spent xviij*d.*', such expenditure would have procured at least two kilderkins of double beer, ensuring considerable inebriation.[34]

Besides being an assault on the ideal of thrift, such excessive consumption was in direct contravention of the demeanour prescribed for scholars by the university, whose official rhetoric placed a heavy emphasis on the gravity and civility expected of its members. The Emmanuel College

---

[31] CUL, CUA, *Thomas and Elizabeth Newman* c. *Rachel Humbletoft*, V.C.Ct.III.28, no. 22.

[32] The same appears to have been true of women's subsequent participation in coffeehouse culture. See Brian Cowan, 'What was Masculine about the Public Sphere? Gender and the Coffeehouse Milieu in Post-Restoration England', *History Workshop Journal*, 51 (2001).

[33] Emmanuel College Archives, Admonitions Book, fos. 8, 10ᵛ. See also the presentment of John Yaxley, CUL, CUA, Comm.Ct.I.18, fo. 41ᵛ.

[34] Emmanuel College Archives, Admonitions Book, fo. 3ᵛ.

statutes, for example, decreed that 'every pupil be always occupied, so far as may be, either in the worship of God, or in the study of good learning, or in the cultivation of distinguished manners'. Learning and virtue went hand in hand in these official expectations of young men, since (as the same statutes emphasized) 'it is of little profit that men be learned unless they be good also'.[35] In his capacity as chancellor of the university of Cambridge, William Cecil was similarly concerned with the well-ordered behaviour of students (as he was later to be with that of his own son).[36] In preparation for the Queen's visit in 1564, he requested that two things 'may specyally appeare' in the university: 'Order/ and lernyng. and for order I meane bothe for religioun and Civyll behavor.'[37]

Drunkenness was the antithesis of these expectations, and, in common with the central government and other local authorities, the university was increasingly preoccupied with it from the early seventeenth century. A decree against 'excess in drinking, drunkennes and taking Tobacco', issued by the vice-chancellor in 1607, complained that:

> there is too much practice grown in these latter years amongst scholars of this university (not heard of in former better times) in excessive drinkings, foul drunkenness, and taking tobacco in taverns and shops too commonly and immodestly frequented, to the dishonour of God, great scandal of the university at home and abroad, waste of expense besides hurt of body and mind, and evil example from those that profess learning and sobriety.[38]

University authorities were particularly concerned to quash the public display of such behaviour, both within colleges, as with the admonition of a student of St John's for having been 'much distemperd in drink to the notorious scandall & offence of many boath publiquely in Chappell & Hall', and beyond, such as the 'unseasonable' drinking flaunted by two scholars 'excessively in a chamber next to the open street to the offence both of the colledge & also of the town'.[39] In 1626, under pressure from Charles I for better discipline in the universities, the vice-chancellor insti-

---

[35] *The Statutes of Sir Walter Mildmay Kt Chancellor of the Exchequer and One of her Majesty's Privy Councillors, Authorised by him for the Government of Emmanuel College Founded by him*, trans. Frank Stubbings (Cambridge, 1983), 76, 62. See also Sarah Bendall, Christopher Brooke, and Patrick Collinson, *A History of Emmanuel College, Cambridge* (Woodbridge, 1999), 23–30.

[36] See above, pp. 35–7.

[37] *Records of Early English Drama: Cambridge*, 2 vols., ed. Alan H. Nelson (Toronto, 1989), i. 227–8.

[38] Charles Henry Cooper, *Annals of Cambridge*, 5 vols., vol. v, ed. J. W. Cooper (Cambridge, 1842–1908), iii. 27.

[39] St John's College Archives, Orders and Admonitions, fo. 192ᵛ; Emmanuel College Archives, Admonitions Book, fo. 8. See also the admonitions of Francis Fotherby, Roger Wingfield, and Phineas Cochraine, Trinity College Archives, Conclusion Book, 17 (from back).

gated special weekly sessions to restore ordered behaviour, which were particularly concerned with the regulation of excessive drinking.[40]

It is clear, however, that for the groups of young men indulging in rituals of excessive drink culture such behaviour held entirely different meanings, however much their elders sought to label it as scandalous, wasteful, or riotous. As a deliberate inversion of prescribed norms, the collective misrule of drunken revelry rejected expectations of frugality, order, and control, facilitating an entirely oppositional bid for manhood. That such behaviour underpinned youthful assertions of manhood was clearly articulated in an exchange between scholars charged with nightwalking in 1608. '[B]einge thirstie to drinke' a group had gone into the town in search of beer. Having consumed 18*s*.' worth, the evening ended in a brawl which was apparently caused by wounded pride. When Newman refused his companion Sir Holmes's challenge to 'drinke whole potts', Holmes retaliated by calling him a 'drunken Rogue'. At the suggestion that he could not rival Holmes's consumption, Newman deflected the challenge onto another of their company, asking 'what he was', to which came the emphatic reply 'a man'. Newman responded again with a different challenge: 'then said newman go with me who goinge into the Churchyard fell to buffetts. then the rest lepping over the wall fell all to buffetts a great while with fists.'[41] The challenge to drink 'whole pots', like the challenge to the field, was a test of strength and a measure of manhood. Far from being uncontrolled, as suggested by its critics, such behaviour was carefully contrived in order to serve very different principles of self-fashioning.

Such heavy nocturnal drinking functioned as a form of initiation into the manhood of excess. Letters to tutors divulged parental anxieties about sons being led astray in this fashion, which echoed conduct writers' warnings about the dangers of bad company and 'too much libertie'. Writing on behalf of Sir Randle Crewe, Ellis Wynn emphasized Crewe's concern that his son should 'avoyde the company of Tobacco takers, Drinkers and Swaggereres', claiming that 'The young gent is by nature of a modest sober and cyvill conversacion and no doubt will so contynewe if evell company draw hym not from it.'[42] Many students and some of the younger fellows were admonished for leading others on. In contravention of a decree in his college statutes prohibiting members from

---

[40] Cooper, *Annals*, iii. 182–3; CUL, CUA, '1626 Monday Courts begunn by Dr Gostlyn', V.C.Ct.I.49. See also Comm.Ct.I.18.

[41] CUL, CUA, V.C.Ct.III.14, no. 105.

[42] St John's College Archives, John Darcy to Owen Gwyn, 15 Sept. 1615, D94.144; Ellis Wynn to Owen Gwyn, 26 Apr. 1616, D105.282. See also Thomas Edwards to Owen Gwyn, D94.463.

engaging 'in drinking parties and carousals', Robert Booth of Emmanuel was admonished in 1615 for his third offence of drunkenness and also for 'thereby corrupting divers of our Colledge to the great grief and offence of us all'.[43] Mr Hakluyt of Trinity College was likewise punished for 'the misleading [of] a young scholler of the house & often intisuing him unto the taverns'.[44] Younger students were also sent over walls and out of windows into town to fetch beer, thus earning themselves a place in drinking circles and a chance to prove their courage.[45]

Despite official pronouncements against excessive drinking and the frequent punishment of those indulging in collective misrule, there is also evidence that at times the excesses of young men were tolerated and even condoned by their elders as harmless sport, or at least only a temporary form of deviation attributable to inexperience. Fathers of troublesome sons sought exculpation for their offspring by accounting for their misbehaviour in terms of '*iuuenilia delicta*', or as an inevitable and unavoidable product of 'the heate of youth', looking more kindly on their indiscretions than the conduct writers who sought to label such behaviour in terms of effeminacy, beastliness, degeneracy, or thraldom. One father jokingly alluded to his own 'wild and rude Carriage in times past' when seeking preferment for his son, and it is likely that many of the senior members of the university had their own memories of debauched student days that made them somewhat forgiving of their charges.[46] This suggests that the meanings of manhood to which such behaviour was linked were broadly recognized in contrast to patriarchal codes and sometimes accommodated within them.

One clear example of the university's toleration of student immoderation is provided by evidence of rowdiness at college plays. On occasion this could take on riotous proportions, such as the fracas between students of Trinity and St John's colleges in 1611 which began when a Johnian playgoer was struck with a torch by a Trinity stage-keeper, and ended only after several St John's members had been pelted with stones from the Trinity Great Gate and the battlements on the wall behind Trinity's chapel had been clubbed to pieces. As the depositions confirm (some sixty in all), such extensive damage was the calculated product of careful long-term planning rather than the temporary emergence of ungoverned youthful aggression.[47] Stones and water had been collected

---

[43] *Statutes of Sir Walter Mildmay*, 62; Emmanuel College Archives, Admonitions Book, fo. 4.
[44] Trinity College Archives, Admissions and Admonitions, 396. See also 397.
[45] e.g. Trinity College Archives, Conclusion Book, 25.
[46] St John's College Archives, Robert Goffe to Owen Gwyn, D105.140; Thomas Fairfax to Owen Gwyn, D105.136; Richard Tray to Owen Gwyn, D94.17.
[47] For a full transcription of the case, see *Records of Early English Drama*, i. 424–86. See also

as ammunition as much as two weeks in advance of the riot. Rumours had been circulating for some days: Trinity men had warned their friends and siblings at St John's not to go to the plays; clubs had been placed at the ready, and those of a more peaceful bent had had time to make their own preparations: 'Sir Mason warned a schoolfellowe of his . . . to take heed for that there would be some hurlie burlie, addinge that hee for his parte had locked upp some 3 or 4 Clubes which hee would not lend.'[48] This deposition is a reminder that the possession of weapons was as routine, and uncontested, for students as their ownership of books. The events themselves were conducted in the manner of an overblown duel, as a Trinity stage-keeper, armed with his sword and dagger, yelled into the darkness, 'where be these rogish cowardes or Jonians/ yf there be any of you that dares aunswer me come forth', to which the response came, 'there is them that dare aunswer you'.[49] The rioters were concerned to prove their worth as men through demonstrations of strength and territorial supremacy, and the honour of their respective colleges provided them with a convenient excuse. Collective action gave licence to assertions of dominance by individual rioters, and a chance to prove their manhood in terms of courage and bravery. Ultimately, college rivalry was not the only precipitating factor; it provided a pretext for those involved who were seeking to be regarded as manly by their peers.

It is worth noting that the Great Gate riot of 1611, although extreme, was not unprecedented or entirely exceptional. Similar incidents (on a smaller scale) occurred at plays in 1595, 1601, and 1607.[50] Although these skirmishes invoked censure and punishment from the vice-chancellor, there is other evidence to suggest that disruption at college plays was also routinely tolerated, if not implicitly condoned. Despite outlawing public plays and entertainments within a five-mile radius of Cambridge on the grounds that they drew students from their books and encouraged lewd and unseemly behaviour, student plays within colleges were not only sanctioned, but in some colleges required by statute.[51] Yet college accounts suggest that these plays provided a regular forum for the kind of 'unseemly' behaviour condemned in public plays. Between 1560 and 1640

J. W. Clark, *The Riot at the Great Gate of Trinity College, February 1610–11*, Cambridge Antiquarian Society, Octavo Series 43 (Cambridge, 1906).

[48] *Records of Early English Drama*, i. 481.
[49] Ibid. 438.
[50] Ibid. 359, 385, 407.
[51] e.g. at St John's College 'at least six dialogues, festival or literary spectacles' were to be performed between Christmas and Epiphany, with several other comedies and tragedies scheduled for between Epiphany and Lent, *Records of Early English Drama*, ii. 712. See also Alan H. Nelson, *Early Cambridge Theatres: College, University and Town Stages, 1464–1720* (Cambridge, 1994).

the eight colleges which have left records spent over £26 on repairing windows which had been smashed during plays. By 1567 Trinity College had begun to take the precaution of removing the window panes before a performance and then replacing them again afterwards, and by 1598 they were employing men to watch the glass windows during the comedies. It was not only windows that were broken. Clocks, cressets, trestles, forms, locks, walls, and doors all suffered the abuse of playgoers. What is surprising is the apparent absence of any attempt to reform behaviour at plays (except on the occasion of a royal or official visit) and the routine acceptance of such extensive damage.[52]

In this context, therefore, disorder was tolerated by the very same authorities who also stressed the virtue of sedate and orderly carriage in young men. Such evidence demands to be understood in terms of licensed misrule in the same way that the ritual of 'barring out' in early modern schools has been explained by Keith Thomas.[53] The disorder at college plays and its toleration speaks of the recognition by the university that its authority, and its official code of male conduct, had limits. Like the pseudo-regulative violence of college festivities, the disruption condoned at college plays was a compromise reached over competing forms and expressions of manhood. By sanctioning rowdy behaviour at private plays, the colleges could at least attempt to contain student violence. However, there was more here than a mere disparity between ideal and practice gaining a grudging recognition from the ideologues. It was also an acknowledgement of the potency of meanings of manhood derived from violence and excess—which were sometimes claimed in other contexts by the same authorities who sought to limit their pursuit by their charges.

This was perfectly evident in the university's own assertions of regulatory power within the town. In its demonstrations of university authority the proctor's watch, which nightly policed the town searching for suspicious persons and nocturnal revellers, depended on similarly violent assertions of manhood. The proctor's watch was a forbidding group, comprised of large numbers of young men, heavily armed, and backed by weighty institutional authority. In 1600, a young woman, terrified by the sudden appearance of the watch at her master's threshold, described them as 'a greate cumpanye . . . some of them haveinge longe staves, & some others of them haveinge other things which she did see glister & brighte', while another witness in the same case deposed that they carried 'clubbs, longe staves, swords, rapiers, & suche other

[52] See, e.g., *Records of Early English Drama*, i. 620–1.
[53] Keith Thomas, *Rule and Misrule in the Schools of Early Modern England* (Reading, 1976).

weapons'.[54] The proctor's watch was usually headed by the senior proctor's appointed deputy, whose authority was symbolized by his possession of the proctor's staff which was a weighty and formidable weapon, designed as much to inflict harm as to designate status. His company seems to have largely been made up of willing and available colleagues (both graduate and undergraduate), and assisted by scholars' servants from the town.[55]

The watch was far more than a regulative band; it was first and foremost an embodiment of masculine self-assertion and display. It involved possessing the streets of the town after dark, claiming them with clanking weapons, raucous voices, and exaggerated strutting and parade. The proctor's activities were often referred to as 'jetting', a term which held both positive and negative connotations in university orders. Jetting was predominantly associated with ostentatious parade, holding meanings of boastful vaunting and pomposity. Yet it was condemned by the university only when misappropriated by unlicensed scholars, since it was an expected part of the demeanour of the proctor's watch, as implied by orders of 1561: 'That no scholler be out of his college in the night season, or goe a Jetting and walke the streets in the night season, unlesse he goe with the Proctors'.[56] It is unsurprising that the distinction between the watch and unauthorized nightwalkers was often unclear, especially since the watch was regularly charged with similar kinds of violent excess, such as smashing windows and initiating fights, complained of in nightwalkers.[57]

Definitions of and responses to unruliness were not entirely consistent, therefore, and the same kinds of behaviour could inform competing codes of manhood. Nor should we assume that all students earned or even desired inclusion in the types of fraternal camaraderie discussed above. The processes by which some were excluded from collective misrule are difficult to discern, since it was usually a student's inclusion in such groups that warranted observation in disciplinary records. A few students remained deliberately aloof from their more rambunctious associates, refusing to endorse the manhood of excess. Simonds D'Ewes,

---

[54] CUL, CUA, *Edward Dodson* c. *Richard Senhouse*, V.C.Ct.II.3, fos. 2ᵛ, 4ᵛ.

[55] e.g. the company which assisted Richard Senhouse (appointed deputy proctor by Mr Woodcock in 1600) 'were suche as were verye neere the sayd mr woodcocke, & one of them lyeinge in his chamber'. They were all scholars or students of St John's, and were also accompanied by 'the buttlers boye of the same house called Durham', CUL, CUA, V.C.Ct.II.3, fos. 10ᵛ, 11ᵛ.

[56] Cooper, *Annals*, ii. 162. This use of the term 'jetting' pre-dates the *Oxford English Dictionary*'s earliest record from 1689.

[57] e.g. CUL, CUA, *John Price* c. *John Loader*, V.C.Ct.III.17, no. 99. For town complaints against the watch, see also Cooper, *Annals*, ii. 548–56.

weary of 'that swearing, drinking, rioting, and hatred of all piety and virtue' amongst his Cambridge cohort, recalled that he had been 'fain to live almost a recluse's life, conversing chiefly in [his] own College with some of the honester fellows', resolving to avoid 'the unnecessary society of all debauched and atheistical companions (which then swarmed there)'. John Milton recorded a similar critique of his peers' play-acting, observing that when they 'made their sport' they 'thought themselves gallant men' whilst he 'thought them fools'.[58] It is impossible to know how many young men actively dissociated themselves from the pursuit of collective misrule, although if we are to believe D'Ewes it was a very small minority. It is likely that those with less resolve to maintain their distance from such groups, yet who did not fit in with their excesses, were the subject of scorn and hostility. Possibly this lay at the root of an incident of 1622, recorded in the Trinity College Conclusion Book. Christopher Oxley, George Horsey, and Edward Salmon confessed that they had 'very disorderly and at unseasonable times gone to schollers chambers violently to take them out of their logeing and to abuse them in their persones'.[59] Perhaps such abuse had taken place because the scholars had been unwilling or unable to endorse the perpetrators' bids for manly status.

While the camaraderie of misrule did not unite the entire student body in a shared culture of excess it could nonetheless temporarily override barriers of social status. Counter-codes of disruptive masculinity were not limited to any one social group.[60] Amongst undergraduate offenders it was not merely the privileged ranks of fellow-commoners (social elites who took their meals with the fellows), but all types of student who were involved in the antics of misrule. Of the 102 students admonished at Emmanuel College between 1586 and 1640, 8 per cent were scholars—young men who by statute were required to be 'distinguished by . . . honesty, and outstanding capacities, [and] persons of proved ability and good promise . . . who intend to take up Theology and the sacred ministry'.[61] Roughly a third (30 per cent) obtained a Master's degree, an almost

---

[58] *The Autobiography and Correspondence of Sir Simonds D'Ewes, Bart., during the Reigns of James I and Charles I*, ed. James Orchard Halliwell, 2 vols. (London, 1845), i. 141–2, 121; John Milton, *Apology* (1642), in *Records of Early English Drama*, ii. 859. For evidence of Samuel Ward's internalization of a moral code rooted in order and self-control while studying at Cambridge, see *Two Elizabethan Puritan Diaries*, ed. M. M. Knappen (Chicago, 1933).

[59] Trinity College Archives, Conclusion Book, 18.

[60] Cf. Anna Bryson, 'The Rhetoric of Status: Gesture, Demeanour and the Image of the Gentleman in Sixteenth- and Seventeenth-Century England', in Lucy Gent and Nigel Llewellyn (eds.), *Renaissance Bodies: The Human Figure in English Culture c.1540–1660* (London, 1990); Merry Wiesner, '*Wandervögels* and Women: Journeymen's Concepts of Masculinity in Early Modern Germany', *Journal of Social History*, 24 (1991).

[61] *Statutes of Sir Walter Mildmay*, 74.

definite indication of a subsequent intention to take holy orders, and one became first a Doctor of Divinity and then a fellow of the college. The nocturnal habits of 'haunting the town' and drunken carousal were therefore not restricted to the fellow-commoners or pensioners who had less need of a degree and fewer pretensions to clerkly virtue. Nor were they restricted to the rich: 23 per cent of offenders were sizars—the poorer students who earned their keep by waiting on the fellows and wealthier residents of the college. The social boundaries which determined the hierarchies of college life could sometimes be overcome by fraternal bonds of misrule. In such instances, the meanings of manhood attached to the competitive processes of social differentiation were jettisoned in favour of those derived from identification with the group.

The attractions of collective disorder and the counter-code of manhood it entailed were by no means limited to students. As is already clear from cases of nightwalking, young men from Cambridge and elsewhere were similarly active in group revelries, both mimicking the watch and performing their own rituals of informal regulation. Excessive drinking held similar attractions for servants as for scholars, as suggested by a list of complaints lodged in 1632 by a physician about his apprentice. It was not only the amount of alcohol consumed which disturbed this master, but the manner in which it was drunk:

in his drinking he is most unreasonable and unsatiable somtimes to shew his vallor in that wickednes he hath set a can of thre pints to his head & drink it off he saith it was all most full & that he drunk indeed a quart or above & many times ordinarily drinketh a pint at a time.[62]

In contravention of associations with dissolution and disruption, for this apprentice the flamboyant consumption of large quantities of alcohol was a means of claiming 'valour'. Such heavy drinking and the disruptive behaviour that accompanied it were central features of the 'bachelor's social round' in wide recognition that it conferred a form of manhood that was most potently claimed by and often broadly expected of young men.[63]

Drunkenness and its associated exploits were not exclusive to young men, and could overcome distinctions of age as well as social status. This is clear from the extent to which nocturnal misrule in Cambridge involved combinations of young men from both the town and the university, and included older participants. Questioned by the vice-chancellor about the company with whom he 'drank & carded etc', John Binnes

[62] CUL, CUA, V.C.Ct.III.32, no. 59.
[63] Griffiths, *Youth and Authority*, 200–13.

named twenty other men, including students from three different colleges, and the tapsters of the White Swan, the White Horse, and the White Lion. A nightwalking incident of 1616 similarly involved students from several colleges, two college servants, a labourer, and Thomas Diggles, 'servant to one Mr Langley a dauncer who kept at the redd lyon'.[64] Such links were not unusual, as students and young men from the town built up extensive (although often fleeting) networks that facilitated fraternal camaraderie. In an affray of 1592, which was ostensibly a clash between scholars and the male inhabitants of the neighbouring village Coton, the scholars were accompanied on a hunting spree by several men from the town. They included one Thomas Beanes, a servitor of King's College; Robert Flamson, the son of a baker who was the keeper of the Ram Inn; Richard Rust, a tailor; Richard Bacon, a singing man from King's College; and one 'Hodson's man' with his master's dogs. A marginal note at the bottom of one of the examinations spelt out the situation quite clearly: 'thus townsmen and ther sons keep misrule in the felds as well as schollers but all goeth in the name and slander of schollers and the universitie'. The bonds between this particular group may well have been more firmly established, since Rust and Bacon were heavily punished by the vice-chancellor for regularly receiving scholars into their houses along with stolen meat which they dressed and ate together.[65]

The broader involvement of a range of men in such episodes of youthful misrule suggests that alternative forms of manhood held considerable potency beyond the ranks of young men, and that the sources of prowess that appealed to male youths could also inform older men's assertions of manhood, albeit in ways that were not so explicitly anti-patriarchal. Implicit in the university's critique of unruly behaviour in students was that it was beneath their dignity, and therefore associated with socially related as well as age-related codes of manhood. The Gonville and Caius College statutes, for example, banned their members from going to entertainments in public houses or to bull-baitings, bear-baitings, and dog fights, not only because they made 'dumb beasts out of human beings', but also because they were deemed 'stupid performances for a stupid rabble': 'these things are rather appropriate to a stupid and fickle crowd, to that degree they are unsuitable for men of liberal studies'.[66] The university's responses to youthful misrule often also admitted the resonance of alternative meanings of manhood, however much they attempted to dissuade students of their merits. On certain occasions, the university con-

[64] CUL, CUA, V.C.Ct.III.17, no. 76; V.C.Ct.I.8, fo. 261.
[65] CUL, CUA, V.C.Ct.III.2, no. 233. See also nos. 234, 237–8.
[66] *Records of Early English Drama*, ii. 1146.

doned and even employed some of the characteristics of counter-codes of manhood, such as violence at college plays or the aggressive posturing of the proctor's watch. This is further evidence of the contradictions inherent in the practice of patriarchal manhood and the degree to which it was contested along varied axes of difference between men.

MALE INTIMACY, FRIENDSHIP, AND ILLICIT SEX

The group's facilitation and celebration of a counter-code of manhood was particularly central to the rituals of youthful misrule. The group offered a temporary forum for role-playing as its members colluded in a joint enterprise of disruptive and excessive display which was best achieved collectively. In response to their dependent status as young men, coteries of nocturnal revellers asserted independence from the rules expected to govern their behaviour. In their drinking practices, groups of young men played on the ties of male sociability and pushed them to extremes which temporarily suspended ordinary rules of neighbourly interchange. Through violent attacks on other men and their property, they ridiculed established expectations of manhood with assertions of dominance founded upon inverse assumptions of disorder. The group was a vehicle for these forms of manly adventure, which sought a type of transient heroism through courting the dangers of misrule. The participants were bonded to each other less by mutual knowledge or intimacy than by a collective desire for prowess on these terms. As a consequence, fraternal bonds could narrow divisions of status and allegiance which ordinarily separated students of different backgrounds, town and gown, and, occasionally, young men and their elders. These were not the bonds of friendship, however. The status and personalities of participants in the camaraderie of excess were ultimately irrelevant beyond a desire to perform and applaud this alternative theatre of manhood.

The fraternal bonds enabling the camaraderie of excess were nonetheless not devoid of potential intimacy. Especially where sport and violence were concerned, group bonding enabled close bodily contact which could remain unacknowledged and therefore undemanding. In this way the homosocial and the homoerotic could be subtly, and unthreateningly, elided.[67] Collective disturbances often entailed physical abandon, such as that displayed by 'divers unrulie and disordered schollers and students' who, according to a complaint of 1618, trampled 'wheate and Rye in

[67] Sedgwick, *Between Men*; Bruce R. Smith, *Homosexual Desire in Shakespeare's England: A Cultural Poetics* (Chicago, 1991), ch. 2.

the feildes; and [made] greate spoyle thereof by lyeinge and tumblinge therein'.⁶⁸ The culture of excessive drinking could also engender its own, curious, intimacies, albeit still under the guise of competition. It is hard to know how else to make sense of a case noted by the Dorchester justice of the peace Sir Francis Ashley in 1617. Having spent around 7*s*. on beer during a Sunday drinking session which began before morning prayer and continued into the evening, the servant Thomas Ford and a butcher named Patye, in the presence of the third member of their company (and, presumably, the rest of the alehouse), each 'pist both at once into a chamber pott and then one dranke upp the one haulfe and thother the other haulfe, and because one of them should drinke lesse than thother, they measured it out by glasse fulls'.⁶⁹ This ritual, through sharing bodily substances, is likely to have established a temporary sense of kinship between the men involved.

Perhaps less unusual was the physical intimacy afforded by violence. Although violent interplay often revolved around the expression of group rivalries, it also served to bind opponents through its celebration of male strength and its facilitation of close bodily contact.⁷⁰ So, for example, after being examined about the affray involving scholars and the inhabitants of Coton in 1592, one of the participants claimed that after much opposition and aggressive posturing the exchange between the scholars and villagers had taken quite a different and harmless course. He insisted that towards the end of the dispute, 'both partes entred into a frendly conference and went about to wrastle in a frendly manner'.⁷¹ Regardless of its veracity, this statement's significance lay in its attempt to pass off fighting as a friendly affair: a routine part of male sociability. This was a common defence, which suggests that the boundaries between friendly familiarity and aggressive contest were both blurred and consequently often crossed during men's interaction. A witness in a lengthy dispute in 1594 between Robert Prance and John Carowe (both gentlemen) deposed that he had initially mistaken Carowe's gestures to betoken intimacy, saying that when he saw Carowe pull Prance's gown he thought 'that they had ben at some familiar talke together', before realizing that Carowe was in fact gripping Prance menacingly in his arms.⁷²

---

[68] CUL, CUA, Order to prevent scholars trampling grain, V.C.Ct.III.23, no. 55.

[69] *Case Book of Sir Francis Ashley*, 45.

[70] For a discussion of the 'brotherhood of bloodshed' in early modern German towns, see Lyndal Roper, *Oedipus and the Devil: Witchcraft, Sexuality and Religion in Early Modern Europe* (London, 1994), ch. 5.

[71] CUL, CUA, V.C.Ct.III.2, no. 234. See also *Thomas Redditt c. John Cutchey*, V.C.Ct.II.1, fo. 28.

[72] CUL, CUA, *Robert Prance c. John Carowe*, V.C.Ct.II.1, fo. 28.

Wrestling—indeed 'friendly' wrestling—was a proof of strength and a form of intimacy between men, as well as an expression of contest. So a witness testifying to the strength of John Nightingale in 1618 explained to the vice-chancellor that Nightingale 'had not bene sicke but only a griefe in minde which trobled him and said tri my strength for I am as strong as you and so I . . . founde him by makeing a triall by wresling'.[73]

It is difficult to tease out the broader implications of such defences which aimed to downplay the seriousness of violent interchange. However, even when violent clashes resulted in injury, they seem sometimes to have been an extension of a more routine aspect of men's aggressive joviality and fraternity. Wrestling, for example, necessitated a curious combination of rivalry and familiarity. It enabled the bodily intimacy of physical contact without surrendering the dynamic of competition which was expected to govern men's relations with each other and which underpinned their claims to autonomy and independence. The resulting intimacy was fleeting, disguised, and incidental (and therefore unacknowledged). Paradoxically, an extensive way in which men achieved close physical contact with each other was under the guise of contest and hostility. Rivalries may often have been expressed playfully in jest; nonetheless it was rare for competitive overtones to be entirely abandoned in favour of mutual friendship and affection.

This paradox is not hard to explain given early modern fears about unconstrained male intimacy. Notions of friendship between men in early modern England invoked a spectrum of complex associations spanning the highly formalized public gestures of patronage to the symbolic depravity of sodomy.[74] Close contact between men, in the form of either friendship or homosexual intimacy, was considered dangerous. Although the distinctions between the two phenomena (friendship and homosexuality) could occasionally be blurred, there were different fears surrounding each which in turn may have had a significant impact on the ways in

---

[73] CUL, CUA, *Thomas Jugg* c. *Mark Nightingale*, V.C.Ct.III.22, fo. 62. The trial of strength was necessitated by Mark Nightingale's accusation that Jugg had poisoned his brother John.

[74] Alan Bray, 'Homosexuality and the Signs of Male Friendship in Elizabethan England', *History Workshop Journal*, 29 (1990); Lisa Jardine, 'Companionate Marriage Versus Male Friendship: Anxiety for the Lineal Family in Jacobean Drama', in Susan D. Amussen and Mark A. Kishlansky (eds.), *Political Culture and Cultural Politics in Seventeenth-Century England* (Manchester, 1995); Alan Bray and Michel Rey, 'The Body of the Friend: Continuity and Change in Masculine Friendship in the Seventeenth Century', in Tim Hitchcock and Michèle Cohen (eds.), *English Masculinities 1660–1800* (Harlow, 1999). See also Naomi Tadmor, '"Family" and "Friend" in *Pamela*: A Case-Study in the History of the Family in Eighteenth-Century England', *Social History*, 14 (1989); ead., *Family and Friends in Eighteenth-Century England: Household, Kinship and Patronage* (Cambridge, 2001).

which men viewed and maintained male bonds. These concerns were particularly acute for young men who occupied a primarily homosocial world for a prolonged period before marriage.

According to Alan Bray's path-breaking study of Renaissance homosexuality, same-sex relations between men were ubiquitous in the 'established social institutions' of sixteenth- and seventeenth-century England, and most pertinently the household and the education system. Despite the symbolic significance attached to sodomy as a criminal breakdown of sexual order, homosexuality occurred 'on a massive and ineradicable scale' due to a vast discrepancy between image and practice. Such a discrepancy was the product both of early modern social-structural circumstances and of pre-eighteenth-century attitudes to the nature of sexuality. Due to the constraints of a marriage pattern which was predicated on the economically independent nuclear family, the majority of early modern men and women married comparatively late in their life cycle, if at all. As a consequence same-sex relations provided a potential sexual outlet, particularly for young men who found themselves largely in all-male environments. In addition, Bray argues, homosexuality had not yet been typified by a dominant discourse as the exclusive inclination of a deviant subculture, but was instead viewed as a sin to which all men were potentially prone: it was an act, rather than a category of identity.[75] Homosexuality, at one end of a continuum of male sexuality, was approached (beyond its symbolic portrayal) in some of the same terms as other forms of unrestrained lust as an effeminate loss of control over appetite and the indulgence of excessive and destructive lechery.[76]

The Cambridge records are frustratingly mute when searched for evidence supporting Bray's thesis of extensive homosexual activity.[77] Open references to same-sex relations were recorded in only two extant instances throughout the entire period between 1560 and 1640. Both were the subject of defamation litigation heard by the vice-chancellor and do not impart much reliable information about routine practices, particularly as both might be construed as accusations of pederasty rather than homosexuality. Interestingly, both involved allegations of illicit sex with women as well as men. Estimating his injury at £50, Theophilus Field (a doctor of Divinity of Pembroke Hall) entered a suit in 1611 against

[75] Alan Bray, *Homosexuality in Renaissance England* (London, 1982), 74, 79. Cf. Joseph Cady, '"Masculine Love," Renaissance Writing, and the "New Invention" of Homosexuality', in Claude J. Summers (ed.), *Homosexuality in Renaissance and Enlightenment England: Literary Representations in Historical Context* (New York, 1992).

[76] Alan Bray, 'To be a Man in Early Modern Society: The Curious Case of Michael Wigglesworth', *History Workshop Journal*, 41 (1996).

[77] Bray himself was forced to argue from silence and relied entirely on the literary evidence of

Alexander Reade (another fellow of the college) following a highly contentious conversation that had occurred between the two men in the fellows' garden. According to Field's allegations, Reade had accused him of pursuing his sexual predilections for both women and men to the disgrace of his vocation as a man of holy orders. Initially Reade suggested that Field had committed indiscretions with 'lasses & wenches' whom he had 'kept' and 'maintained', vividly describing one episode as follows: 'thou diddest cast of thy Cassocke and through it downe & diddest say ... lye there Preist, & so thou didest go Close to a wench in a Corner of the kitchin Chimnye, & on[e] passing by the, did say thus unto ye ... Ah: will you never leave these doinges[?]' Field had renounced his calling, symbolically removing his priestly garb, in order to satisfy his lust. The accusations did not end here, however. Reade had continued 'that he could object to him mr ffeild nott onlye lasses or wenches but allso boyes'.[78]

The subsequent exchange between the two men, as recounted in Field's allegations, is of particular interest. Reade asked Field whether his 'late servaunt did never lye with him'. Field denied it, saying that 'to his remembrance' the servant in question (Thomas Smith) had not 'layne with him', adding in his allegations that he had responded in this way 'of purpose to drawe the said Read on further to knowe whether he Reade did speake those speaches of him selfe or where he Reade hadd hard them'. When Reade repeated the accusation, Field altered his strategy, and '(further to drawe some further matter from the said Reade touching the premisses) seemed to graunt that his said man servaunt had layne with him'. All this elicited was the further insult from Reade that Field 'was the skome of his order & Rancke, & that he was a contemptible and odious ffellowe'.[79]

Field's tactics in his allegations are intriguing. First, he seems to have been constructing a defence for having admitted to bedding his servant, through implying that he was merely trying to draw out Reade's sources. Secondly, Field's initial denial of the event was qualified with the statement that *as far as he could remember* he had not lain with Thomas Smith, with the possible implication that such intimacy was a common enough occurrence for such a memory slip to be plausible. The case is further

---

satirical verse in referring to homosexual practice in the universities, *Homosexuality in Renaissance England*, 51–3.

[78] CUL, CUA, *Theophilus Field* c. *Alexander Reade*, V.C.Ct.III.16, no. 75. Cf. Aubrey's story about Richard Corbest, Bishop of Oxford, and his chaplain, John Lushington, casting off their hats and gowns before a drinking spree, John Aubrey, *Brief Lives and Other Selected Writings*, ed. Anthony Powell (London, 1949), 288. I am grateful to Keith Thomas for this reference.

[79] CUL, CUA, *Theophilus Field* c. *Alexander Reade*, V.C.Ct.III.16, no. 75.

complicated by its possible connection to college politics concerning the comparative standing of Field and another fellow, Mr Collins.[80] The accusation of same-sex relations did not receive any mention beyond Field's allegations, and the case appears ultimately to have been dropped since no depositions were taken and no outcome was recorded. The imputation of same-sex relations was in all likelihood a by-product of a different dispute, acting as ammunition in a malicious attack. Its veracity seems to have been secondary to the concerns both of the litigants and of the court.

The other surviving accusation of same-sex practices generated more serious consequences, and was the central issue of several injury cases brought by Robert Hutton, a Bachelor of Divinity and fellow of Trinity College. He sued three of his pupils for alleging that he had 'committed the act of buggery' with them by enticing them 'to that sinn'. These claims had culminated when one of them, Walter Lassells, exhibited a bill of indictment against Hutton both at the gaol delivery sessions in Cambridge and at the assizes of 1589, alleging that Hutton had 'committed most unnaturall sinnes and abuses with and against the bodies of Martin Turner Henry Wharton and my selfe'. Hutton's subsequent litigation in the vice-chancellor's court was successful, at considerable cost to his opponents. All three students were forced to recant and confess that the allegations were untrue and maliciously imputed 'by the instigacion of the devell'. Turner was condemned to pay 300 marks in damages as well as Hutton's legal costs, and was to be kept in prison until the full sum was paid. Lassells, the main perpetrator, was similarly condemned with a higher charge of £500 damages. Wharton escaped a pecuniary sentence, on the grounds that he had been tricked by Lassells into adding his name to the bill of indictment without knowing what it was.[81] The situation in which Robert Hutton sought to defend himself was similar to that experienced by Theophilus Field. The allegations of homosexual advances seem to have been the product of more generally hostile circumstances, and were related to another case involving the same three students for spreading malicious rumours that Hutton had been sighted on his bed 'hard at yt' with his maid, Ann House.[82] Walter Lassells was once again the main perpetrator and seems to have borne a serious grudge against his tutor. Whether this animosity was connected to any actual sexual contact

---

[80] See, in the same case, V.C.Ct.III.17, no. 2; Comm.Ct.II.17, fo. 48ᵛ.

[81] CUL, CUA, *Robert Hutton c. Walter Lassells, Martin Turner and Henry Wharton*, V.C.Ct.I.2, fos. 20ᵛ–30ᵛ.

[82] CUL, CUA, *Ann House c. Walter Lassells*, Comm.Ct.II.3, fo. 191ᵛ. See also fos. 190–193ᵛ, 217.

between the two men is impossible to know. What is interesting is that such allegations were made so rarely. Defamation litigation involving imputations of sexual incontinence by university members nearly always concerned fornication or adultery with women from the town.[83] Possibly a tacit understanding existed between men that imputations of same-sex contact were taboo, and were thus associated with singular hostility and malice.

Such evidence sheds little light on the extent of same-sex relations within the university, therefore, let alone beyond its college walls. University members (and undergraduates in particular) were expected to remain within an all-male world, and their living arrangements were certainly conducive to close, and possibly intimate, physical contact. According to a royal injunction, women were generally banned from college chambers apart from in exceptional circumstances.[84] Consequently, the Emmanuel College statutes decreed that 'none shall hold secret converse with a woman anywhere, especially in any of the rooms of the said College, which we desire no woman ever to enter, if she be alone ... except in time of sickness, in a manner known and approved of the Master or his deputy'. Trinity College ordered in 1625 that 'noe woemen under the age of 50 yeares or thereabouts, & they also of honest fame & respect & approved honestie, shall come into the Colledge to make bedds or doe any other service for ffellowes & schollers'. The College also decided that in the interests of maintaining a bachelor community, 'noe maried man [was to] bee admitted to be a servant to the Colledge in the Backhouse except the Master Baker'.[85]

Such measures were far from successful. Trinity College was forced on more than one occasion to reiterate its injunction against 'intertaining of yong women to dresse up chambers, and doe other Services for Scholars', since its previous orders had not been heeded—'to the Scandall of this Societie'.[86] The university's concern to identify prostitutes and banish them from the town; the numerous paternity suits brought against its members; and a few cases of clandestine marriage between students and local women are all evidence that illicit sexual contact with women was possible. In 1631, Charles I was so concerned that students had dishonoured the university's reputation by undertaking 'contracts of

---

[83] See below, pp. 168–72.

[84] Cooper, *Annals*, ii. 169–70.

[85] *Statutes of Sir Walter Mildmay*, 62; Trinity College Archives, Conclusion Book, 87, 125. See also Cooper, *Annals*, iii. 182.

[86] Trinity College Archives, Conclusion Book, 143. See also the warnings to Rebecca Moncaster, Annis Wilkinson, Alice Swindon, Ann Allison, May Tompson, and Ann Chambers not to go to any colleges to make beds, CUL, CUA, V.C.Ct.I.49, fo. 13ᵛ.

marriage with women of mean estate and of no good fame' that he issued a set of orders to prevent taverners and victuallers from allowing 'any daughter or other woman in his house to whom there shall resort any scholars . . . to mispend their time or otherwise to misbehave themselves or to engage themselves in marriage without the consent of those that have the guardiance and tuition of them'.[87] Women bore the brunt of the blame, and it was they rather than the students who were to be punished for such offences by banishment from the town.[88]

Despite official portrayals of university members as the hapless victims of lascivious money-grabbing harlots, there is plentiful evidence that they could be determinedly active in pursuit of sexual gratification from townswomen. In an adultery case of 1598, it was claimed that Hugh Baguley (a young fellow of St John's College) had convinced Robert Bales's wife that if she denied his sexual advances he would hang himself. Baguley had also forced Robert Bales into a deed of gift whereby he bound all his goods to Baguley in order to prevent Bales from taking legal action against his wife's infidelity.[89] Students, like London apprentices, sought casual sex in 'suspicious houses' after curfew as part of their nocturnal recreation.[90] Such pursuits were heralded as a form of manly prowess by those who bragged of their conquests, as in a lengthy adultery case brought against William Coville of Queens' College and Bridget Edmunds in 1596, in which it was alleged that Coville had boasted to a friend that 'the swetest sport that ever he had with [Bridget Edmunds] was in the chayre'.[91] A young draper's apprentice in London indulged a similar form of self-congratulation when, having been found 'in naked bed' with a maid-servant, he 'often and openly made his avaunte and boste of hys said unthrifty demeanor among mens servants of our Companye'.[92]

It is possible that young men suffered considerable peer pressure to appear heterosexually active. Anthony Fletcher has argued that 'to establish himself as a man' in early modern England a boy was required to engage fully in 'a youth culture where manhood was learnt by drinking,

---

[87] Cooper, *Annals*, iii. 221.

[88] e.g. orders for the banishment of Susanna Pratt, Anna Barton, Margrett Larkin, Maria Finch, CUL, CUA, Comm.Ct.I.18, fos. 34ᵛ, 35, 39, 54ᵛ.

[89] CUL, CUA, *Hugh Baguley* c. *Robert Bales*, V.C.Ct.II.2*, fos. 6ᵛ–8.

[90] See, e.g., the admonition of Waterhous, Broxop, and Acrinby, Emmanuel College Archives, Admonitions Book, fo. 8. Griffiths, *Youth and Authority*, 213–21.

[91] CUL, CUA, *Office* c. *Bridget Edmunds and William Coville*, V.C.Ct.III.5, no. 69. See also pp. 171–2 below.

[92] William Herbert, *The History of the Twelve Great Livery Companies of London*, 2 vols. (London, 1834–6), ii. 424. See also G. R. Quaife, *Wanton Wenches and Wayward Wives: Peasants and Illicit Sex in Early Seventeenth Century England* (London, 1979), 54; Laura Gowing, 'Gender and the Language of Insult in Early Modern London', *History Workshop Journal*, 35 (1993).

fighting and sex'. This last component, sexual prowess, was, according to Fletcher, 'the most telling test of manhood'.[93] A case of 1601 is suggestive of the contempt lobbed at university men regarding their bachelor existence. On seeing his master's house searched by the proctor's watch, William Loudham claimed that the deputy proctor was maliciously causing aggravation 'because he could not have his lust satisffied: for yf he ... might have had his lust satisffied or his pleasure uppon the maides or goodwyfe of the howse or might have had mens wyves sent for into the Towne to him, this trouble had not bene'.[94] In contrast to the codes of celibacy established by official regulations and moralists' exhortations to chastity, powerful counter-codes of male sexual prowess and bravado were frequently asserted and maintained. These different ideals existed in an uneasy tension, since young men indulging in illicit sexual activity put at risk their attainment of respectability and preferment, as suggested by their initiation of defamation litigation to counter accusations of fornication or adultery. It is likely that many young men responded to these conflicting demands through bragging words rather than actual deeds.[95]

The evidence above confirms that at least some young men of the university were not wholly restricted to male company and without recourse to illicit sex with females. This does not rule out the concurrent practice of same-sex relations, however. Although university life did not preclude heterosexual activity for the more determined, the majority of students were mostly confined to their colleges in unremittingly close physical proximity to other men, as 'men set apart'.[96] The consequent attractions of fraternization were actively discouraged at Emmanuel College, in a ruling that sought to prevent 'the visitation of students' rooms' and 'the frequent converse of the young upon idle matters'. Fellows were appointed to police students' rooms nightly to check against any untoward 'frivolities and foolishness'.[97] However, bed-sharing was an unquestioned aspect of the living arrangements of universities (as well as households), and regardless of efforts to separate young men socially, the familiarity of bed-fellows was routinely assumed. In a list of questions for his opponent's witnesses in an injury suit, Gamaliel Toulson asked 'whether [any] be Chamber fellowe bedfellowe fellow pupills unto the same Tutor of the

---

[93] Anthony Fletcher, *Gender, Sex and Subordination in England 1500–1800* (London, 1995), 92–3.
[94] CUL, CUA, *Simon Tyndall c. William Loudham*, V.C.Ct.I.5, fo. 150.
[95] Bernard Capp, 'The Double Standard Revisited: Plebeian Women and Male Sexual Reputation in Early Modern England', *Past and Present*, 162 (1999), 72–4.
[96] Victor Morgan, 'Country, Court and Cambridge University, 1558–1640: A Study in the Evolution of a Political Culture', 4 vols., Ph.D. thesis (East Anglia, 1984), vol. ii, ch. 6.
[97] *Statutes of Sir Walter Mildmay*, 69.

party producent and his verie entire and speciall freind and most lovinge unto and most familiar with him'.[98] Whether such sleeping arrangements were conducive to sexual relations is another matter. Once again, the records are tantalizingly silent, although the temporary suspension of two fellow-commoners of St John's for 'seducing young schollers' suggests that the power relations between older and younger members were open to abuse.[99]

Being forced to argue from silence, it is thus impossible to verify Bray's thesis (however compelling it is to do so).[100] Regardless of the extent of same-sex relations, the defamation cases brought by fellows against imputations of sodomy are indicative of the suspicion and danger potentially associated with same-sex unions, particularly if they involved a substantial age difference between the parties. That Simonds D'Ewes held such associations is evident from his 'secrett' discourses with a friend in London about 'the sinne of sodomye', observing, 'how frequente it was in this wicked cittye, and if God did not provide some wonderfull blessing against it, wee could not but expect some horrible punishment for it; especially it being as wee had probable cause to feare, a sinne in the prince as well as the people'.[101] Homosexuality certainly seemed to have held more serious implications than the illicit heterosexual activities which the university regularly sought to quash. Furthermore, there is no evidence of the undertones of conquest and prowess which were associated with illicit liaisons with women. Whether habitually practised or not, same-sex relations was a type of intimacy between men which ultimately courted danger and discredit; however unacknowledged on a routine basis, it could too easily be construed as illegitimate and unsafe.

The anxieties associated with men's friendships, in contrast to homosexual relations, were less dramatic, although it was possible for the former to be interpreted as the latter.[102] Male friendship was not without its pitfalls, however, and was approached with ambivalence. The term 'friendship' was applied not only to men's familiarity with equals, but

[98] CUL, CUA, *Gamaliel Toulson c. Godwin Walsall*, V.C.Ct.III.10, no. 53. For the 'love affair' between William Sancroft and his chamber fellow Arthur Bownest, see Bendall et al., *A History of Emmanuel College*, 60–2.

[99] St John's College Archives, Orders and Admonitions, fo. 193. See also the admonition of Mr Hakluyt, Trinity College Archives, Admissions and Admonitions, 396.

[100] For an enthusiastic endorsement of Bray's arguments, see Christopher Hill, 'Male Homosexuality in Seventeenth-Century England', in *The Collected Essays of Christopher Hill*, 3 vols. (London, 1986), vol. iii.

[101] *The Diary of Sir Simonds D'Ewes (1622–1624): Journal d'un étudiant londinien sous le règne de Jacques Ier*, ed. Élisabeth Bourcier (Paris, 1974), 92–3.

[102] Bray, 'Homosexuality and the Signs of Male Friendship'; Jardine, 'Companionate Marriage'.

also to networks of credit and patronage. In credit networks, a man's 'friends' loaned him money, stood surety for him, and lent weight to his dealings with their good word (and thus provided backing with the symbolic promise of their own worth). Yet these actions carried the risks of debt and obligation, and were therefore regarded ambivalently. As we have seen, William Cecil counselled his son to avoid standing surety for a friend, and to trust no one with his credit, cautioning that 'it is a meere folly for a man to enthrall himselfe to his friend further then if just cause be offered, he should not dare to become otherwise thy enemie'. Using the dramatic imagery of slavery, Cecil suggested that friendship could be a double-edged sword.[103] In the context of patronage networks, friendship could be similarly precarious. It was part of a public display of loyalty and alliance, and in elite circles it indicated access to power and influence through close physical proximity to a patron. Powerful 'friends' had to be courted using strategic negotiations of distance and familiarity.[104] Such 'friendship' engendered as much suspicion as trust, and its agents were vulnerable to the volatile character of political alliance.[105]

Friendships between equals, although less politically charged than patronage networks, also held associations of danger. There was a special category of friendship between early modern men, referred to as 'entire' or 'perfect'. Originally an Aristotelian concept, further elaborated in Cicero's dialogue *De Amicitia*, references to 'entire' friendship nonetheless occurred in everyday discourse. A witness being questioned in the vice-chancellor's court about his relationship to both litigants in a suit of 1604 replied that he was 'neyther intire frende to the one nor capitall enymye to the other'—since both extremes of this spectrum of loyalty were regarded as prejudicial to disinterested participation in a case.[106] In *The Mirrour of Friendship* (1584) such entire constancy was set at the pinnacle of men's relations with each other. It was founded upon mutual disclosure and trust and held significant long-term implications of debt and obligation, which qualities distinguished 'perfect' friendship from the incidental variety:

such a number of friendes serve for no other cause, but to eate drinke, walke, and

---

[103] William Cecil, *The Counsell of a Father to his Sonne, in Ten Severall Precepts* (London, 1611). See also above, p. 37.

[104] See, e.g., the elaborate strategies prescribed by Simon Robson, *A New Yeeres Gift. The Courte of Civill Courtesie: Assembled in the Behalfe of All Younge Gentlemen, to Frame their Behaviour in All Companies* (London, 1577).

[105] e.g. the fate of Robert Carr, Earl of Somerset, described by Anthony Weldon in *The Court and Character of King James* (London, 1650), cited by Bray and Rey, 'The Body of the Friend'.

[106] CUL, CUA, *Daniel Rogers, MA c. Francis Caitlin, MA*, V.C.Ct.II.8, fo. 17ᵛ.

talke together: not to succor them in their necessities, with their goods, favour and credits, nor brotherly to reprove them of their vices and faults, where in truth, where is a perfect amitie, neither my friend to me, nor I to my friend ought never to dissemble.[107]

Entire friendship presupposed utmost loyalty and self-denial. Couched in terms of love, the commitment and intensity of such friendships was likened to marriage and often compared favourably to it.[108] A true friend was characterized by one author as 'deere as a good wife, more deere than a brother', and according to another on the death of such a 'mate', his friend 'accounts himselfe but halfe alive'.[109] According to Lisa Jardine, in the late sixteenth and early seventeenth centuries such relationships came to hold an 'erotic charge' which competed with the expectations of companionate marriage, as men's homosocial bonds and marital commitments were more generally seen as mutually exclusive.[110]

Even idealized versions of male friendship did not escape ambivalence, however. The author of *The Mirrour of Friendship* advised his readers that they should 'never discover nor declare to any person all that thou thinkest, nether make any privy how much treasure, or value in goods thou haste'.[111] Although a 'perfect' friend should be prepared to risk death for his 'second self', he should never abandon the vigilant defence of his estate.[112] In this context, friendship never quite escaped association with alliance. Hedged with similar warnings as advice on how to choose a wife, accounts of friendship played on men's fears about relationships of trust. Despite the idealization of 'entire' friendship it could involve the indebtedness and obligations which men were ordinarily anxious to avoid, especially since there was increasing uncertainty about how to detect genuine friendship from falsity.[113]

---

[107] *The Mirrour of Friendship: Both How to Knowe a Perfect Friend, and How to Chose Him*, trans. T. Breme (London, 1584), sig. B4ᵛ. See also Sir Francis Bacon, *The Essayes or Counsels, Civill and Morall*, ed. Michael Kiernan (Oxford, 1985), 80–7.

[108] Smith, *Homosexual Desire*, 35–8.

[109] Francis Lenton, *Characterismi; or, Lentons Leasures* (London, 1631), sig. H; Joseph Hall, *Characters of Vertues and Vices*, in *A Recollection of Such Treatises as have bene Heretofore Severally Published and are now Revised, Corrected and Augmented* (London, 1615), 241.

[110] Jardine, 'Companionate Marriage', 235. On the conflict of marriage with male friendships, see also Linda Woodbridge, *Women and the English Renaissance: Literature and the Nature of Womankind, 1540–1620* (Brighton, 1984), 237–9; Elizabeth A. Foyster, *Manhood in Early Modern England: Honour, Sex and Marriage* (Harlow, 1999), 125–30.

[111] *The Mirrour of Friendship*, sig. C.

[112] The characterization of a 'true friend', in Lenton, *Characterismi*, sig. H. See also James Cleland, *The Instruction of a Young Noble-Man* (Oxford, 1612), 196.

[113] Lorna Hutson, *The Usurer's Daughter: Male Friendship and Fictions of Women in Sixteenth-Century England* (London, 1994).

The extent to which early modern men routinely troubled themselves with pursuing 'perfect' friendships is impossible to estimate. Both contemporary commentary and the historiography on men's friendships tend to concern a minority of elites. Whether such ambivalence about male intimacy was more widely felt is largely hidden from view, although general fears of debt and obligation were commonplace. It is clear, however, that the bonds of entire friendship and the intimacies of same-sex contact were wholly removed from the ephemeral loyalties of fraternal comrades. It is likely that the latter were more appealing to young men in particular, and they certainly served more visible and less ambiguous functions in the assertion of masculine identity. The ties that bound men together in collective homosocial escapades (as opposed to friendship) were transient and without more than the most temporary obligation to applaud and collude in the pursuit of manliness defined in terms of excess, from which all participants were beneficiaries. Such bonds were the basis for assertions of inverted codes of manhood rooted in excess and clamorous misrule. At its extremes fraternal camaraderie permitted and encouraged not only the misappropriation of authority, but also the rejection and inversion of patriarchal codes of conduct in the pursuit of an alternatively defined manhood of immoderation.

The transience of such fraternal bonds was deliberate; participants could enjoy an intense emotional experience in courting danger without acknowledging any long-term involvement with, or obligation to, each other. Although such collective misrule resulted in disruption and disorder, it did not risk the dangers of permanent intimacy or indebtedness. The bonds of comradeship facilitated bids for independence, whereas those of intimate friendship imposed the constraints of dependence and reciprocity. The former offered opportunities for liberation; the latter exacted obligation. Fraternal bonding was therefore both a 'safe' form of male intimacy for its participants who were unhampered by accountability, and a vital part of young men's claims to power located in practices antithetical to the patriarchal values of thrift, order, and self-control. In these assertions of manhood, dominance was founded upon excessive and disruptive displays of strength and abandon, rather than upon patriarchal position. Yet although such fraternal ties of collective misrule often resulted in disorder, and created fissures between men along the fault lines of age and class, they may well have been viewed as far less potentially threatening than the ties of friendship, precisely because the spectre of intimacy between men remained submerged. As Bruce Smith has argued, early modern manhood could be shored up by homophilia as well as homophobia, and this seems to have been the case regarding its homoerotic, rather than homosexual, manifestations.[114] The homosocial infractions of male youth culture contained a largely unacknowledged homoerotic charge that contributed to their potency. This was a central component of the camaraderie of misrule which, unlike acknowledged homosexual behaviour, helped to confer rather than undermine manhood.

Unlike women's transgressions, young men's disorderly assertions of masculinity were sometimes treated as an inevitable annoyance rather than an immediate threat to the patriarchal order. The consequences of unruly behaviour were generally less grave for young men than young women, as the vice-chancellor's decision to banish young women from Cambridge rather than expel their student paramours suggests. It is also likely that the consequences of misrule differed between young men along class lines, although this is harder to discern, particularly as the forms of male camaraderie they adopted were remarkably consistent across all social groups, sometimes even uniting youths from very different backgrounds. A degree of accommodation of men's youthful disorder attests to the potential contradictions intrinsic to patriarchal configurations as well as the potency of counter-codes of manhood. While it might be argued that young men's inversion and misappropriation of patriarchal codes of order ultimately served to reconfirm them, it is my contention that the disruption of youthful misrule constituted a form of anti-patriarchal resistance. According to patriarchal principles which privileged the married and middle-aged, young men should not only be subordinate, but also submissive, quietly and obediently waiting their turn. When young men appropriated patriarchal sources of power they transgressed in doing so, and they also ridiculed and subverted the values of their elders by counter-codes of conduct focused on bravado and excess. In addition, the camaraderie of misrule drew upon alternative sources of male prowess that were by no means age bound, and which existed in tension with patriarchal imperatives along numerous other axes of difference. This, in turn, suggests the endurance of a spectrum of alternative meanings of manhood well beyond youth.

[114] Smith, *Homosexual Desire*, ch. 2.

5
The Violence of Manhood

In December 1594 a quarrel erupted in Cambridge between John Durant, a tanner, and Henry Elwood, a waterman. The quarrel was over Elwood's attempted arrest of one of Durant's friends in his capacity as a constable. Having been called a 'flapte mouthe boye' by Durant, Elwood responded that 'he Elwood was as good a man as he' and threatened to punch him. When Durant asked 'what meanest thowe', Elwood replied that 'yf thy knyfe were awaye thowe shouldest see what I would do by & bye'. As witnesses reported, blows and further threats soon followed. Durant threw down his knife and thrust his hands into his hose, to demonstrate that he had no unfair advantage and that he offered no aggression. Elwood punched him, whereby (as a witness deposed) 'al his face was beblodied'. He then challenged Durant to the field, although when Durant agreed to meet him in Coe Fen, Elwood demurred, and instead issued Durant with the warning 'the next tyme I meete thee I will geve the a sound bocks on thye eare'. But the quarrel did not end here. Seeing the trouble at her gate, Durant's wife ran to her husband's defence, and calling Elwood a scurvy boy, a jack, and a knave, lashed at him with her fists and also tried to strike him with a large stick. Elwood's response was not to Elizabeth Durant, but to her husband, in gibing, 'well durrante lett thy wiffe weare thye breeches, for she is worthie of them, she is the better man'.[1]

According to Henry Elwood, fighting was a man's business, even if, as in this situation, it was as much a matter of bluff as of actual blows. His opinion is borne out by evidence that violent crime in early modern England involved a far greater number of men than women.[2] The records of the Cambridge university courts corroborate a familiar story. Of 151 injury suits alleging assault for which depositions survive between 1581 and 1640, only 27 involved female litigants, and of those only 11 (7 per

---
[1] CUL, CUA, *John Durant* c. *Henry Elwood*, Comm.Ct.II.6, fos. 29ʳ⁻ᵛ, 47ᵛ.
[2] e.g. in 17th-century Essex over 91% of those accused of assault and 84% of those accused of homicide were male, J. A. Sharpe, *Crime in Seventeenth-Century England: A County Study* (Cambridge, 1983), 117–18, 124. For evidence of similar sex-ratios in homicide cases across Europe, see Natalie Zemon Davis, *Fiction in the Archives: Pardon Tales and their Tellers in Sixteenth-Century France* (Cambridge, 1988), 191 n. 21.

cent) were sued as perpetrators of violence. This predominance of male offenders in violent crime is well known, yet too readily taken for granted. Given such a profound gender bias in cases of assault—which involved similarly disproportionate sex-ratios to witchcraft cases (only with the gender balance tipped in the opposite direction)—it is surprising that the 'masculinist context' of violence, in terms of the specifically male interests it underpinned, has not received more analysis.[3] Violence was one of the main props of patriarchy in early modern England, and as such was central to the regulation of social relations between men as well as between men and women. It also informed a range of male identities which existed in tension with patriarchal principles of order. Finally, it was a resource open to appropriation and abuse, and in its most extreme forms violence was deployed by men in ways which deliberately contravened prescriptive tenets of self-government.

Until recently, scholarship directly addressing violence in early modern England has preoccupied with its extent rather than its gendered character or functions in particular contexts. The early modern period has traditionally been characterized as a comparatively violent era marking the turbulent transition from feudalism to capitalism, and the subsequent decline in levels of violence has been associated with a qualitative shift towards less violent cultural norms, often with reference to Norbert Elias's theory of a 'civilizing process'.[4] This approach is epitomized by the now classic assertion of Lawrence Stone that early modern England was 'five times more violence-prone' than the late twentieth century.[5] Although Stone's explanatory framework and the reliability of his evidence have been contested, his critics have nonetheless been primarily concerned with measuring violence over time, using homicide rates as the gauge.[6] With the exception of recent work by Susan Amussen, the focus

[3] Marilyn Lake, 'The Politics of Respectability: Identifying the Masculinist Context', *Historical Studies*, 22 (1986). See also Judith Allen, ' "Mundane" Men: Historians, Masculinity and Masculinism', *Historical Studies*, 22 (1987). Of those indicted for witchcraft by the Home Circuit Assizes, 1560–1709, 89.7% were women, J. A. Sharpe, *Instruments of Darkness: Witchcraft in England 1550–1750* (London, 1997), 108.

[4] Norbert Elias, *The Civilizing Process: The History of Manners and State Formation and Civilization*, trans. Edmund Jephcott (Oxford, 1994).

[5] Lawrence Stone, 'Interpersonal Violence in English Society 1300–1980', *Past and Present*, 101 (1983), 32. For a critique of this approach, to which Stone was responding, see Alan Macfarlane, in collaboration with Sarah Harrison, *The Justice and the Mare's Ale: Law and Disorder in Seventeenth-Century England* (Oxford, 1981).

[6] J. A. Sharpe, 'The History of Violence in England: Some Observations', *Past and Present*, 108 (1985); Lawrence Stone, 'A Rejoinder', *Past and Present*, 108 (1985); J. M. Beattie, *Crime and the Courts in England, 1660–1800* (Oxford, 1986), 132–9; J. S. Cockburn, 'Patterns of Violence in English Society: Homicide in Kent 1560–1985', *Past and Present*, 130 (1991). See also J. M.

of this debate has therefore remained on changing levels of violent crime, rather than on the meanings of violent behaviour in varied contexts.[7] Qualitative, rather than quantitative, approaches to the history of violence in early modern England have been more fruitfully developed in analysis of the rituals of mass protest. With its roots in E. P. Thompson's explication of the 'moral economy' of the crowd, the history of rioting has, more successfully than the history of homicide, shed the associations of barbarism traditionally linked to violent behaviour.[8] However, like the history of homicide, it is biased towards extreme and exceptional forms of unrest. As yet, the history of violence in England has not fully benefited from anthropological approaches which have been so fruitfully adopted to explore the cultural meanings of violence elsewhere in the early modern period, particularly in its mundane rather than extreme forms, and which have highlighted the potent expressive functions of violence in conferring male integrity and authority.[9] In order to understand the links between violence and manhood suggested by the sex-ratios in violent crime, more analysis is needed along these lines of the many routine and often legitimate forms of violence in early modern England. Such links have been partially investigated in research addressing early modern

Beattie, 'Violence and Society in Early-Modern England', in Anthony N. Doob and Edward L. Greenspan (eds.), *Perspectives in Criminal Law: Essays in Honour of John Ll. J. Edwards* (Ontario, 1985). For more qualitative analytical models addressing homicide rates elsewhere in early modern Europe, see Pieter Spierenburg, 'Faces of Violence: Homicide Trends and Cultural Meanings: Amsterdam, 1431–1816', *Journal of Social History*, 27 (1994); Eva Lacour, 'Faces of Violence Revisited: A Typology of Violence in Early Modern Rural Germany', *Journal of Social History*, 34 (2001).

[7] Susan Amussen, 'Punishment, Discipline and Power: The Social Meanings of Violence in Early Modern England', *Journal of British Studies*, 34 (1995).

[8] E. P. Thompson, *Customs in Common* (London, 1991), ch. 4. See also Paul Slack (ed.), *Rebellion, Popular Protest, and the Social Order in Early Modern England* (Cambridge, 1984); John Walter, 'A "Rising of the People"? The Oxfordshire Rising of 1596', *Past and Present*, 107 (1985); id., 'Grain Riots and Popular Attitudes to the Law: Maldon and the Crisis of 1629', in John Brewer and John Styles (eds.), *An Ungovernable People: The English and their Law in the Seventeenth and Eighteenth Centuries* (New Brunswick, NJ, 1980). For the traditional link between violence and barbarism, see the 'Benefits derived by the Common People from the Progress of Civilisation', Thomas Babington Macaulay, *History of England from the Accession of James II*, 5 vols. (London, 1849–61), i. 424–6.

[9] e.g. Elliott J. Gorn, ' "Gouge and Bite, Pull Hair and Scratch": The Social Significance of Fighting in the Southern Back Country', *American Historical Review*, 90 (1985); Garry Marvin, 'Honour, Integrity and the Problem of Violence in the Spanish Bullfight', in David Riches (ed.), *The Anthropology of Violence* (Oxford, 1986); Henk Driessen, 'Gestured Masculinity: Body and Sociability in Rural Andalusia', in Jan Bremmer and Herman Roodenburg (eds.), *A Cultural History of Gesture: From Antiquity to the Present Day* (London, 1991); Edward Muir, *Mad Blood Stirring: Vendetta and Factions in Friuli during the Renaissance* (Baltimore, 1993); Robert C. Davis, *The War of the Fists: Popular Culture and Public Violence in Late Renaissance Venice* (Oxford, 1994).

domestic violence.[10] This chapter explores the relationship between masculinity and violence further by turning its gaze to the routine violent exchanges that took place between men on the streets, in the fields, and within the alehouses of early modern towns and villages.

Attempts to measure levels of violence are problematic because they assume that the meanings attached to violence are static. In addition, the selection of homicide as a gauge (as the form of violent crime least open to multiple interpretations and therefore least likely to conceal a 'dark' figure of unrecorded incidents) assumes a direct correlation between this particular felony and the incidence of violence more generally. In turn, this associates all forms of violence with this most broadly condemned category, and, like the history of riot, approaches violence primarily in terms of violation. Far from being a universal, violence is not only culturally relative but also an unstable category within the context of any particular culture since whether acts of physical harm are deemed violent depends on who is doing them to whom, and where and when they occur.[11] Many of the actions that we would label 'violent' (with overtones of violation) were pervasive and readily sanctioned features of life in early modern England, and not just a product of exceptional circumstances. As a mundane feature of social relations, 'violence' was broadly condoned in a number of situations and settings in such a way that it was often not even recognized as such by the social actors themselves.

It is therefore important to be alert to the distinctions drawn by contemporaries themselves between violence and violation (or acceptable and unacceptable violence) in order to trace the many ways in which both were routinely connected with competing expressions of manhood. One of the most obvious forms of acceptable violence, with few overtones of violation, was disciplinary violence. It was an intrinsic part of the penal code, of the implementation of moral and social hierarchies, and of institutional and household discipline. Many forms of violent correction were designed to humiliate offenders with public shaming rituals and with symbolic gestures of debasement. Much of it was performed on behalf of the state, commissioned by various branches of the judiciary ranging from assize judges and magistrates to local constables, and it was almost entirely carried out by men, often in their capacity as governors of their

---

[10] Susan Amussen, ' "Being Stirred to Much Unquietness": Violence and Domestic Violence in Early Modern England', *Journal of Women's History*, 6 (1994); Elizabeth A. Foyster, *Manhood in Early Modern England: Honour, Sex and Marriage* (Harlow, 1999), 181–93.

[11] For an extremely useful discussion of this issue, see Philippa C. Maddern, *Violence and Social Order: East Anglia 1422–1442* (Oxford, 1992), ch. 1. See also David Riches, 'The Phenomenon of Violence', in id. (ed.), *The Anthropology of Violence*.

own 'little commonwealths'. Disciplinary violence therefore broadly served a patriarchal agenda for order, except when its implementation appeared excessive or inappropriate in such a way that it crossed the boundary into violation.[12]

Beyond its formal disciplinary role, violence was more generally a central inflection of status in interchanges between men, even if only threatened rather than actually carried out. The boundary between violence and violation in male interpersonal combat is much harder to probe, since routine (and acceptable) violence is less readily visible in the historical record than complaints of violation to the courts. Accounts of violence contained within judicial files, disciplinary records, civil actions for assault, and prosecutions for riot and affray are fraught with interpretative difficulties, not least because connotations of violation were intrinsic to the legal setting. The consequences of violent behaviour which was deemed excessive and/or illegitimate were frequently recorded without any indication of its causes or the initial intentions of its perpetrators. Often the only remains of violent encounters are laconic and opaque allegations which may have dwelt briefly on the weapons involved, the size of a bruise or depth of a wound, or the number of handkerchiefs required to mop up the blood, but which are tantalizingly silent about the circumstances of such injuries. Furthermore, litigants' and witnesses' statements were shaped by and for their audience at court, and offer no more than a set of partial and contrived narratives rather than a re-creation of the events themselves.

It is still possible, however, to gain some insight into the broader characteristics of male violence in early modern England. By looking at cases of injury, assault, and defamation (which was often accompanied by violence or the threat of violence) patterns of more routine violence can sometimes be glimpsed, albeit in mirror image. Rather than indexing the extremes of homicide, such cases at the petty end of the legal spectrum shed light on the boundaries between acceptable and unacceptable violence since they were often initiated not because an act of violence had taken place, but because it had somehow 'gone wrong', usually as a result of one party disregarding the tacit rules governing violent exchange between men. So, for example, it is likely that John Durant entered his suit against Henry Elwood (in the case which opened this chapter) not because he had been physically injured, but because he had been unduly humiliated by Elwood's behaviour. Many such cases were not a consequence of violence *per se*, therefore, but of violence that pushed beyond

---

[12] For an extreme case, see Cynthia B. Herrup, *A House in Gross Disorder: Sex, Law, and the 2nd Earl of Castlehaven* (Oxford, 1999).

acceptable limits or had unforeseen consequences. As a result, they are also suggestive of some of the situations in which violence was acceptable. Legal action was itself testimony to the fact that boundaries between acceptable and unacceptable forms of violent behaviour were blurred and contested. Violence and violation were linked in their turn not only to competing concepts of order, but also to the contradictions inherent in early modern notions of manhood itself.

This chapter addresses the meanings of manhood attached to violence in a range of contexts: from legally sanctioned corporal punishment and official forms of physical correction, to the more fluid patterns of male interaction evident in interpersonal combat. In particular, two related types of violence are discussed in order to probe its deep-rooted links with early modern masculinity. The first is the disciplinary violence that played a mundane role in policing the patriarchal order, functioning as an instrument of state and, by extension, household correction. Such regulatory violence nonetheless had its limits which, if crossed, conjured associations of violation attributed to the abuse of power. The second is the interpersonal violence that routinely contributed to the more informal regulation of hierarchies of male status, communicated through specific gestures and complex rules of interaction which were partly informed by the rituals of exemplary punishment. Similarly, if such exchanges crossed the boundary towards violation, they subverted these hierarchies, which in turn suggests the potential tension between patriarchal ideals and the widespread appropriation of violence in more disorderly assertions of manhood. Violence therefore conferred manhood in ways which both overlapped with and diverged from patriarchal concepts of order, often serving alternative masculinities according to the age, status, and context of its perpetrators.

JUDICIAL PUNISHMENT AND DISCIPLINARY VIOLENCE

The early modern judicial system entailed a harsh penal regime, founded upon 'the logic of exemplary punishment'.[13] At its most extreme, it achieved its impact by invoking terror through the drama of the death penalty.[14] More routinely its purpose was to inflict shame, and as a conse-

---

[13] P. G. Lawson, 'Lawless Juries? The Composition and Behavior of Hertfordshire Juries, 1573–1624', in J. S. Cockburn and Thomas A. Green (eds.), *Twelve Good Men and True: The Criminal Trial Jury in England, 1200–1800* (Princeton, 1988), 120.

[14] Douglas Hay, 'Property, Authority and the Criminal Law', in Douglas Hay et al., *Albion's Fatal Tree: Crime and Society in Eighteenth-Century England* (London, 1975). See also V. A. C. Gatrell, *The Hanging Tree: Execution and the English People, 1770–1868* (Oxford, 1994).

quence the public humiliation of the guilty party was a central feature of local regulatory measures. In an essentially face-to-face society, the power of such public correction lay in undermining the offender's reputation through belittling the guilty party with punishments primarily designed to revile and disgrace. Prostitutes were ritually carted out of town and literally shunned from the urban community, sometimes pelted with dirt and accompanied by a cacophony of rough music.[15] Another form of symbolic exclusion was excommunication, which barred offenders from the spiritual community of their parish. Other types of punishment placed the emphasis more firmly on physical debasement. Ducking stools, stocks, cages, and pillories all effected humiliation through public display. Likewise, whipping and, in more extreme cases, branding not only inflicted punitive pain, but also marked the bodies of offenders with disgrace.[16] In the case of branding, such marks were permanent, although the shame of public humiliation also had the power to inflict serious long-term damage on an individual's reputation, as suggested by defamation suits initiated to quash rumours of a personal history of such correction.[17] The debasement of offenders in these ways functioned symbolically to reassert moral hierarchies and to confirm patriarchal expectations that every person should perform the duties (and the degree of subordination) expected of his or her place.

Shaming punishments were widely administered in early modern England in ways which served to discredit deviations from, and alternatives to, patriarchal principles in both men and women. As prescribed by statute, stocks were routinely used both to confine and punish drunkards, and the cage as well as the ducking stool could be used to discipline scolds, often with a paper displayed above it detailing the nature of the offence. So, for example, a Southampton blacksmith was punished for abusing a constable and refusing to keep watch by being 'comitted to the Stocks with a paper over his head'; two Norwich men were stocked 'for drinkinge at Mawfries the Cooks'; and Prudence Wichingham was 'to be ducked and in the meane tyme . . . putt into the Cage' for her 'ill rule & beatinge & revylinge & threatnynge her neighbours'.[18] Whipping was

---

[15] Martin Ingram, 'Juridical Folklore in England Illustrated by Rough Music', in Christopher W. Brooks and Michael Lobban (eds.), *Communities and Courts in Britain 1150–1900* (London, 1997).

[16] J. A. Sharpe, *Judicial Punishment in England* (London, 1990), ch. 2. See also John Demos, 'Shame and Guilt in Early New England', in Carol Z. Stearns and Peter N. Stearns (eds.), *Emotion and Social Change: Toward a New Psychohistory* (New York, 1988).

[17] e.g. CUL, CUA, *William Gibbon* c. *William Bird*, Comm.Ct.II.4, fo. 42; WSRO, *Joan Wishlake* c. *John Colvell*, EpII/5/6, fo. 285ᵛ.

[18] *The Assembly Books of Southampton*, ii. *1609–10*, ed. J. W. Horrocks, Southampton Record

perhaps the most common form of corporal punishment, associated with such social outcasts as vagrants, petty thieves, and fornicators. Mothers of illegitimate children were particularly vulnerable, routinely stripped to the waist and whipped publicly until they bled. In 1613, the Somerset quarter sessions decreed that on a Saturday at noon, Elizabeth Stuckney should be 'whipped at Langport up and down the market until her back be bloody'.[19] Stripped of any shred of respectability, such women were paraded on market days 'for an example to others to avoid the like offence'. Sometimes suspected fathers were similarly punished, as when both parents of an illegitimate child were whipped in Glastonbury High Street, with 'two fiddlers playing before them in regard to make known their lewdness in begetting the said base child upon the Sabbath day coming from dancing'.[20] More often, though, the men involved escaped comparable disgrace, especially if convicted 'only on the confession of the mother', reflecting a double standard in cases of illicit sex which placed greater emphasis on female culpability and accorded lesser weight to women's words.[21]

Shaming punishments, particularly whipping and beating, were not exclusively dispensed by the magistrate, but were also staples of the institutional and household correction of young men (and, less frequently, young women) designed to reconfirm hierarchies of age. London livery companies often publicly whipped insubordinate apprentices in order ritually to put them in their place and in attempts to secure their conformity to the codes of behaviour expected of them. So in 1580, William

Society 21 (Southampton, 1920), 15; *Minutes of the Norwich Court of Mayoralty 1630–1631*, ed. William L. Sachse, Norfolk Record Society 15 (Norwich, 1942), 67; *Minutes of the Norwich Court of Mayoralty 1632–1635*, ed. William L. Sachse, Norfolk Record Society 36 (Norwich, 1967), 225. See also Steve Hindle, 'The Shaming of Margaret Knowsley: Gossip, Gender and the Experience of Authority in Early Modern England', *Continuity and Change*, 9 (1994); David Underdown, 'The Taming of the Scold: The Enforcement of Patriarchal Authority in Early Modern England', in Anthony Fletcher and John Stevenson (eds.), *Order and Disorder in Early Modern England* (Cambridge, 1985); Martin Ingram, ' "Scolding Women Cucked or Washed": A Crisis in Gender Relations in Early Modern England?', in Jenny Kermode and Garthine Walker (eds.), *Women, Crime and the Courts in Early Modern England* (London, 1994).

[19] *Quarter Sessions Records for the County of Somerset*, i. *1607–1625*, ed. E. H. Bates, Somerset Record Society 28 (London, 1907), 108. See also similar orders on pp. 132, 139, 154, 169, 170, 176. See also Ch. 4 n. 16 above.

[20] *Quarter Sessions Records for Somerset*, 131, 211. See also, e.g., *Records of the County of Wilts, Being Extracts from the Quarter Sessions Great Rolls of the Seventeenth Century*, ed. B. H. Cunnington (Devizes, 1932), 37. See also G. R. Quaife, *Wanton Wenches and Wayward Wives: Peasants and Illicit Sex in Early Seventeenth Century England* (London, 1979), 217–20.

[21] *Quarter Sessions Records for Somerset*, 322. See also Laura Gowing, *Domestic Dangers: Women, Words, and Sex in Early Modern London* (Oxford, 1996), 48–54; Keith Thomas, 'The Double Standard', *Journal of the History of Ideas*, 20 (1959); and p. 170 below.

Humfrey, an apprentice clothworker, was whipped before the court of assistants 'for divers & sundrie abuses towardes his Maister & Mistress, viz strikinge his Maister & Mistress, and callinge her barren scolde whore, and divers other undecent and uncomelie speeches not to be suffred in any Apprentice or servaunte'.[22] As an example to other apprentices of the disgrace of 'unthrifty' behaviour, an apprentice draper was similarly beaten in the company hall, stripped of his doublet and shirt, as punishment for fornicating with a maid.[23] Livery companies also made regular use of their own stocks. In 1561, Edward Shotbolte, an apprentice grocer, 'was openly punished in the hall syttynge in the stockes in the presence of the whole companye for pylfrynge & porloynynge sylver & money from... his late maister'. His humiliation was to be particularly acute because he had spent part of the stolen money on 'apparrell for a mayde that he was in love withall', which was to be 'hanged aboute him syttynge in the stockes to his greate shame'.[24]

Public beatings and ritual shamings were also a routine part of college life. In Trinity College, Cambridge, 'non-adultus' offenders (under 18 years) were thrashed before the entire student body, in a weekly ritual of chastisement which was written into their statutes.[25] Such beatings were not confined to the enclosed environment of the college. In 1583 a scholar of Pembroke was more openly disgraced when he was 'beaten with rods before all the youth of the University in the Public School street' because he had asked 'opprobrious questions' at the disputations and committed an assault at a college play.[26] In 1618, a scholar of Peterhouse, having attacked an official who was trying to break up a game of football, was stocked 'in the open hall at Peterhouse at dinner tyme', after which he had to make a speech 'in the acknowledgment of his faulte, & detesting the same thereby to restrayne others from doeing the like, & to incite them to a more civill, & discreete carriadge, & behavior'. Other offenders at the same footballing incident were whipped in the college hall at the same time.[27] Beyond reinforcing hierarchies of age, such punishments also sought to discredit alternative expressions of manhood

---

[22] Clothworkers' Hall, London, Court Orders 1558–81, fo. 245. See also fos. 80ᵛ, 207.
[23] William Herbert, *The History of the Twelve Great Livery Companies of London*, 2 vols. (London, 1834–6), ii. 424.
[24] Goldsmiths' Hall, London, Wardens Accounts and Court Minutes, viii. 161.
[25] Trinity College Statutes of 1560, trans. W. W. Rouse Ball, *Cambridge Notes, Chiefly Concerning Trinity College and the University*, 2nd edn. (Cambridge, 1921), 222.
[26] Cooper, *Annals*, v. 314. The vice-chancellor also prescribed whipping in the consistory for particularly unruly students. See, e.g., CUL, CUA, Comm.Ct.I.18, fo. 71; V.C.Ct.I.8, fo. 260ᵛ.
[27] CUL, CUA, *Proctors c. Rayement [Boothe]*, V.C.Ct.I.9, fos. 84ᵛ–85; *Proctors c. Rayement Boothe, George Withers, Broadbancke, Conyers, Key and Allot*, V.C.Ct.I.9, fo. 78ᵛ.

which clashed with patriarchal codes. Besides deliberate insubordination, these also included assertions of bravado rooted in the pursuit of illicit sex, excessive expenditure, and violence. By contrast, disciplinary correction claimed the legitimate use of violence in order to reinforce patriarchal principles.

Whipping and beating were also staples of household discipline. Household heads were accorded primary responsibility for disciplining their subordinates, seeking magisterial intervention only in cases of extreme unruliness. There was a risk that resorting to external mediation would be viewed in terms of a master's failure, as when a London fishmonger's complaints against his servant were deemed unworthy of consideration because they were symptomatic of his own error: 'for his want of governement over him, that was his owne faulte'.[28] Similarly, husbands who failed to control their wives could be the subject of scorn, the most extreme form of which was the 'riding', or charivari, in which husbands and wives were mocked and publicly shamed for upsetting the gender order.[29] In Cambridge in 1586, Cuthbert and Joan Johnson complained to the vice-chancellor that they had been humiliated in this way by James Jurdeine who had been hired 'by another' (allegedly for 8s.) to ride 'uppon a Cowlstaffe'. Jurdeine accused Joan Johnson of beating her husband, and parodied Cuthbert's response: 'Oh good wief... doe not beate me noe more aboute the shins nor face.' To leave the assembled crowd in no doubt of his meaning, Jurdeine continued as follows:

[He did] ryde aboute the Towne & streate or some parte thereof uppon a Cowlstaffe uppon the backes of Twoe men, and did by signes woordes tokens behaviors & gestures signifie declare & publishe that the sayd Johane had beaten the sayd Cuthbert hir husband. And that the sayd Cuthbert had behaved him selfe evell & unsemely towards his sayd wief, and the sayd Johanne towards her sayd husband.[30]

Both husband and wife were thus informally punished by their community for marital misdemeanours stemming from Cuthbert Johnson's loss of control with a reassertion of the gender hierarchy which he had failed to maintain.

A husband-beating wife inverted the normal course of disciplinary violence and automatically invoked connotations of violation. The vio-

---

[28] GL, Fishmongers' Company, Court Minutes, 1592–1610, MS 5570/1, 58.
[29] Martin Ingram, 'Ridings, Rough Music and the "Reform of Popular Culture" in Early Modern England', *Past and Present*, 105 (1984); id., 'Ridings, Rough Music and Mocking Rhymes in Early Modern England', in Barry Reay (ed.), *Popular Culture in Seventeenth-Century England* (London, 1985).
[30] CUL, CUA, *Cuthbert and Joan Johnson c. James Jurdeine*, V.C.Ct.I.2, fo. 93ᵛ.

lent wife was far more frequently deplored in popular literature than the abusive husband, even though the latter was more prevalent statistically.[31] Conversely, the beating of wives by their husbands, and, to a greater extent, children by parents and servants by masters and mistresses, was treated as a matter of course so long as it remained within 'moderate' bounds. These limits appear to have been quite flexible, determined by the reputation of the household involved and the vigilance of neighbours and kin, although there does seem to have been greater unease about the violent correction of wives than servants, since the latter's subordination was far less open to contest.[32] Husbands who violently mistreated their wives risked being subject to disciplinary violence themselves. So, in 1631, John Lane was committed to the Norwich bridewell 'for misusing his wife'. Although this punishment was 'respited', Lane consented that 'yf hee againe beate his wife hee is to be whipped at the post'.[33] Such cases suggest that interpretations of the patriarchal authority extended to household heads could vary considerably, and that there was considerable conflict over the degree to which it was deemed to involve the violent subordination of women. Disciplinary violence, therefore, could merge with more disorderly associations of violence with manhood, and, in such instances violent means served to undermine patriarchal ends by invoking connotations of violation. A householder's disciplinary authority might then be overridden by the intervention of a higher authority which rectified perceived abuses by exacting retributory subordination. Such intervention occasionally occurred on a broader scale, as when the justices of Kent bound over the borsholders, churchwardens, and overseers of Ightham to answer for their whipping and beating of a pregnant parishioner when she was 'very large with child, and within a fortnight of delivery'.[34]

The only legitimate purchase women had on disciplinary violence was when it was exercised by a mistress or mother against a servant or child. Prescriptive codes warned that mothers were more likely to mollycoddle than beat their children, and directed their advice about correction primarily to fathers.[35] In addition, moralists advised that mistresses should

[31] J. A. Sharpe, 'Domestic Homicide in Early Modern England', *Historical Journal*, 24 (1981); Frances E. Dolan, *Dangerous Familiars: Representations of Domestic Crime in England, 1550–1700* (London, 1994), ch. 1.
[32] Amussen, 'Being Stirred to Much Unquietness'; Foyster, *Manhood in Early Modern England*, 181–93.   [33] *Minutes of the Norwich Court of Mayoralty 1630–1631*, 187.
[34] Louis A. Knafla, *Kent at Law 1602: The County Jurisdiction: Assizes and Sessions of the Peace* (London, 1994), 190.
[35] e.g. William Gouge, *Of Domesticall Duties* (London, 1622), 556; John Dod and Robert Cleaver, *A Godly Form of Householde Government: For the Ordering of Private Families* (London, 1612),

exclude male servants from their disciplinary measures, since 'a manservant will much disdaine to be smitten by a woman'. While it was also considered a 'great reproach for a man to beat a maid-servant', in exceptional circumstances it was nonetheless permissible: 'if a maid should wax stout, and mannish, and turne against her mistresse, she being weake, sickly, with child, or otherwise unable to master her maid, the master may and must beate downe her stoutnesse and rebellion'.[36] That mistresses were more likely to be constrained from exercising disciplinary violence is suggested by the Clothworkers' Company's response to a complaint by an apprentice 'that his master and mistres dyd unlawfully beate hym' with an order that his mistress alone should 'not from hensforth beate hym'.[37] The scope for masters' physical correction of their servants appears to have been far greater, as indicated by some of the practices they were willing to defend in court. On being questioned about the disappearance of his 13-year-old apprentice, the Ely husbandman William Dey described the last time he had disciplined the boy in his barn: 'having hanged him up by the hands his feete tutching the grownde [Dey] did there whipp him with a shorte whipp like a dogg whipp & . . . he did give him not above iiij or v stripes. And the cause was for his runinge away.' He also assured justices that this was the first time he had whipped his apprentice in six months. A similar form of correction was used by Hugh Gardner, who 'tied a horse girth round his servant's neck and hung him up and he became insensible'.[38] While sometimes a particularly vigorous master's disciplinary powers were curtailed by a higher authority,[39] many cases of abuse seem to have come to light only *after* serious injury had been suffered by a servant, which suggests that masters enjoyed considerable

294. Levels of disciplinary violence against children by their parents are particularly difficult to discern. See Lawrence Stone, *The Family, Sex and Marriage in England 1500–1800*, abridged edn. (London, 1979), 115–27; Linda A. Pollock, *Forgotten Children: Parent–Child Relations from 1500–1900* (Cambridge, 1983), ch. 5.

[36] Gouge, *Of Domesticall Duties*, 665. The homily 'On the State of Matrimony' also declared that 'it is not to be borne with that an honest man should lay hands on his maidservant to beat her', *Certain Sermons or Homilies Appointed to be Read in Churches in the Time of Queen Elizabeth of Famous Memory* (London, 1890), 544. See also Laura Gowing, 'The Haunting of Susan Lay: Servants and Mistresses in Seventeenth-Century England', *Gender and History*, 14 (2002), 189.

[37] Clothworkers' Hall, London, Court Orders 1558–81, fo. 108ᵛ.

[38] CUL, EDR, examination of William Dey, E6/1; *Worcester County Records. The Quarter Sessions Rolls*, i: *1591–1643*, comp. J. W. W. Bund (Worcester, 1900), part I, 105. See also Peter Rushton, '"The Matter in Variance": Adolescents and Domestic Conflict in the Pre-industrial Economy of Northeast England, 1600–1800', *Journal of Social History*, 25 (1991).

[39] e.g. when the master of one Thomas Garthe was ordered not to correct him, 'nether for this or anie other his offence after but declare the same to this Companie upon the Committinge thereof, and they to judge of the ffautes & of his correction for the same', Clothworkers' Hall, London, Court Orders 1558–81, fo. 208.

autonomy in their use of disciplinary violence, since this kind of correction often went unchallenged until it was too late.

Disciplinary violence in all these contexts was used to humiliate and subordinate the guilty party, and its threat, and often its practice, was central to maintaining patriarchal principles of order. When used to uphold hierarchies of age, gender, and rank such disciplinary violence was deemed not only acceptable but necessary, with no connotations of violation unless it became excessive. Corporal punishment from earboxing to whipping reminded unruly subordinates of their place, through humiliating them and denying them autonomy over their bodies or the right of self-defence. The more elaborate shaming rituals of judicial punishment similarly sought to demean offenders either by symbolically marking them as outcasts, or by attacking their reputation and self-esteem through physical debasement. This is not to argue that the shaming intentions behind such punishments remained uncontested; authorities did not have complete control of the meanings of such processes for either offenders or spectators, and it is possible that the public display of an offence could be counterproductive, indirectly and unintentionally leading to its glorification.[40] This was particularly likely when apprentices and students were publicly corrected, since such events were often a product of a direct clash of codes of manhood, and offenders could be punished a second time for not taking their initial correction seriously enough.

While they were by no means a simple inscription of institutional authority, therefore, such punishments nevertheless informed, and were related to, a much broader language of violent gesture and interchange which took place far beyond the reaches of judicial control and the domestic setting. Violent behaviour was learned behaviour and magisterial and domestic discipline were prominent instructors. In devaluing the status of offenders through physical correction, regulatory officials and household heads also reiterated their own power and authority. As long as it was not excessive, disciplinary violence therefore accorded status as well as deprived others of it, and the beneficiaries in this equation were generally male—in their capacity either as householders or as stakeholders in the public maintenance of order. Such disciplinary rites also merged and sometimes clashed with broader links between violence and manhood, since violent forms of humiliation enjoyed widespread currency amongst men in ways which did not always serve an orderly or overtly patriarchal agenda.

[40] See, e.g., Peter Lake and Michael Questier, 'Agency, Appropriation and Rhetoric under the Gallows: Puritans, Romanists and the State in Early Modern England', *Past and Present*, 153 (1996).

THE GESTURES OF DISPUTED STATUS AND THE RULES OF FAIR PLAY

Male status and authority in early modern England were primarily gauged competitively. Competition between men was often expressed violently; such violence was not simply an untamed overspill of latent aggression, but contained precise meanings and was governed by elaborate rules of play, serving simultaneously to confer authority on its perpetrators and to degrade its victims. It was only perceived as violation when it breached accepted boundaries of propriety, determined by the status of opponents, the fairness of their match, and the location and cause of the dispute. Violence was therefore a vital tool in men's maintenance of hierarchy and reputation, routinely used to articulate subtle status distinctions between men. Yet it was also used as a critique of such hierarchies in forms akin to slanderous debasement. The gestures of disputed status were therefore as redolent as the language of insult, and need to be considered as well as the verbal abuse of the period which has received such extensive analysis by historians. Such gestures were in turn linked to varied codes of manhood—often far removed from strictly patriarchal formulations—which can occasionally be glimpsed beyond the immediate context of a dispute.

In certain situations male interpersonal violence was not just implicitly condoned or grudgingly suffered in early modern England, but, like disciplinary violence, broadly prescribed. This was clearly the case in gentlemanly codes of conduct, in which violence was centrally bound up with notions of honour and the articulation of privileged status. Although conduct writers emphasized the importance of restraint and self-control, even their prescriptive codes commonly assumed that the violent assertion of status was acceptable in certain situations. An example is provided by Simon Robson's *Courte of Civill Courtesie* (1577), which advised genteel young men how to 'frame their behaviour in all companies'.[41] Robson prescribed an intricate set of options for the young gentleman who found himself compromised by an insult. The two key issues which determined an appropriate response were the comparative status of opponents and the setting in which they found themselves. The status of an opponent was the primary consideration. If insulted by a superior, the gentleman was to avoid conflict at all costs. If abused by an equal, he must offer the first blow, or else issue a challenge to the field. An insult from an inferior

---

[41] Simon Robson, *A New Yeeres Gift. The Courte of Civill Courtesie: Assembled in the Behalfe of all Younge Gentlemen, to Frame their Behaviour in All Companies* (London, 1577).

warranted a simple diminutive 'rap on the face with a dagger'—a task which Robson also advised might be dispatched by one of a gentleman's serving men—suggesting that men of superior social standing assumed an automatic right to exact deference with violence, even when performed by a proxy.

Whenever possible, such actions should take place on neutral territory to avoid any suspicion of advantage, and therefore certain locations were deemed inappropriate for violent revenge. The court was the only place listed by Robson where no violence whatsoever could be countenanced, but fighting in another man's house, and particularly at another man's table, were also to be avoided. Other places also required restraint, although this varied according to whether a challenge or response was at issue. It was wrong to initiate blows in 'the house of mutch a mans better', but in requiting violence it was acceptable for the gentleman to respond in kind or 'at least shew his endevor theretoo'. Where restraint was required, it was nonetheless important to indicate readiness to fight in a more suitable location in order to avoid insinuations of cowardice, although young men were also warned not to make an issue of every minor slight.[42] Similar advice declared:

> hee which hath tried his manhoode, afterwards the world will judge and say, that he is a man of his hands, and that he dare fight upon a good occasion; but if he make a common occupation of fighting, hee will then bee accounted for a common quarreller, and his friends will refuse his company many times for doubt of his quarrelling, and yet hee shall never bee accounted, more then a man againe.

Here, according to Joseph Swetnam (who was perhaps better known for his verbal sparring with women), manhood itself was contingent upon the successful management of violent exchange.[43]

There are plentiful examples of violent assertions of manhood along such lines adopted by gentlemen students in Cambridge. Imputations of cowardice and concerns about status were central to the dispute which provoked a lengthy legal battle between three university members in 1604. The conflict was between Samuel Woodley and his brother on one side, and Charles Garth and George Ward along with their company at the Sun Inn on the other. Garth and Ward were disgruntled that Woodley, while acting in his capacity as deputy proctor, had confiscated their rapiers and daggers in an encounter on the previous night, ignoring their protestations that 'they weare gentle men' and therefore entitled to be armed.

---

[42] Ibid. 24–6.
[43] Joseph Swetnam, *The Schoole of the Noble and Worthy Science of Defence* (London, 1617), 41. Cf. id., *The Arraignment of Lewde, Idle, Froward and Unconstant Women* (London, 1615).

Determined to avenge the insult, Garth and Ward pursued Woodley and his brother on the following day, telling various townsmen that Samuel Woodley 'was but some cowardly fellow & not the mann that he was reported or taken to be', and calling Roger Woodley a cowardly boy and ass, further claiming that 'neyther he mr Woodye nor never a brother he had durst meete a man in the fielde'. With the reiteration of accusations of cowardice, the conflict erupted into a heated sword fight at the Sun Inn when Garth met Woodley's approach (allegedly in order to shake hands) with a drawn dagger and the words, 'Gods wounds keepe backe or I will let out yor gutts.' The ensuing fight, resulting in several minor injuries, did not satisfy the dispute, which was then transferred to the legal arena where each party estimated his damages at £200.[44]

That this sort of aggressive assertion of position was routinely maintained by gentlemen students can be glimpsed from the reaction of several scholars in 1600 to a stable boy who had inadvertently obstructed their path with a horse. Their response was to box the boy's ears and beat the horse, asking why 'he ledde out the horse when gentlemen came bye'.[45] When the boy dared to question his treatment by throwing a bone after them before running away, one of the scholars returned and stabbed the horse. The only reason the case came to court was because the horse's owner sought damages; the boy's treatment was incidental to the proceedings, yet it was an integral part of the scholars' superior stance. What is most interesting about this case is the boy's subtle critique (by throwing the bone) of their claims to rank, since it alerts us to the fact that calculated articulations of the 'latent violence' produced by competitive honour were by no means the sole prerogative of gentlemen.[46]

Such exchanges, both highly formalized and more fleeting, informed men's personal combat and related meanings of manhood throughout the social scale. Formal challenges were not exclusive to gentlemen, as we have already seen in the case above with the waterman Elwood's invitation to the field. Similarly, after quarrelling over a drink one Saturday night, a sherman (a shearer of woollen cloth) and a mariner in Newcastle appointed a time the next day for a fight to settle their differences, and the London clothworker Francis Leeche was challenged to the field by his

[44] CUL, CUA, *Samuel Woodley* c. *Charles Garth and George Ward*, V.C.Ct.II.8, fos. 57ᵛ, 71ᵛ–76; V.C.Ct.III.11, no. 24; *Charles Garth* c. *Samuel Woodley*, V.C.Ct.III.11, nos. 23, 25; Comm.Ct.II.12, fo. 1; V.C.Ct.II.8, fo. 85; Comm.Ct.II.12, fo. 5.
[45] CUL, CUA, *Roger Gostwick* c. *Phillip Ford, John Simpson, Humphrey Royden and Edwards*, V.C.Ct.II.3, fo. 26ᵛ.
[46] Mervyn James, 'English Politics and the Concept of Honour', in id., *Society, Politics and Culture: Studies in Early Modern England* (Cambridge, 1986), 313.

late servant who claimed that 'he wold have his harte[s] blood'.⁴⁷ The 'termes of comparison' blamed by James I for inciting duels—such as that begun by Theodore Kelly's assertion to Sir Arthur George that 'he was as good a gentleman as himselfe'—resonated just as potently in exchanges between men far beyond the gentry.⁴⁸ On being called a thief by Mr Anthony Ratcliffe, Roger Doon of Hunstanworth replied that 'he was as trewe for a poore man as he the said Anthony was for a gentleman', and when a Wakefield trooper questioned the worth of his company sergeant, the sergeant's response that 'he may be as good a man as any is here' sparked a fatal brawl.⁴⁹ A fight between two Cambridge cordwainers William Maphew and John Trott was similarly incited by Trott's mocking of the newly crafted boots Maphew proudly displayed to his friends in an alehouse. When Trott threw one of the boots on the ground, Maphew retorted that it was 'as good worke as you make', which provoked attempts to box each other's ears before they finally 'went to cuffs'.⁵⁰

Besides physical injury, lost honour and debased status were the central concerns of the majority of men who sought legal action for assault. Belittling gibes and taunts were often cited as both the accompaniment to and the provocation for blows. Nearly one-third of the assault cases heard by the Cambridge university courts cited insults as provocation, and defendants frequently justified violent responses as understandable if not appropriate reactions. Having been called a liar in the course of a mortgage dispute in 1631, the gentleman Henry Beston told the cordwainer John Dod that 'he Beston did come of a better stock & kynn, then [Dod] or any of his kynn did' and slapped him on the face to emphasize the point, symbolically asserting his right of disciplinary violence over Dod.⁵¹ Similarly, on being called a saucy and bankrupt knave, and being diminutively addressed as 'thou' (instead of the more respectful 'you')⁵²

---

⁴⁷ *Depositions and Other Ecclesiastical Proceedings from the Courts of Durham, Extending from 1311 to the Reign of Elizabeth,* Publications of the Surtees Society 21 (London, 1845), 73–4; Clothworkers' Hall, London, Court Orders 1581–1605, fo. 2. See also *Worcester County Records,* vol. i, part I, 23; DRO, *Wills* c. *Marshall,* Chanter 864, fo. 28.

⁴⁸ James I, *A Publication of his Maᵗⁱᵉˢ Edict and Severe Censure against Private Combats* (London, 1613), reproduced in Albert Forbes Sieveking (ed.), *Worke for Cutlers; or, A Merry Dialogue betweene Sword, Rapier and Dagger. Acted in a Shew in the Famous Universitie of Cambridge A.D. 1615* (London, 1904), 83–5; *Reports of Cases in the Courts of Star Chamber and High Commission,* ed. Samuel Rawson Gardiner (Camden Soc., London, 1886), 112.

⁴⁹ *Depositions from the Courts of Durham,* 63; PRO, ASSI 45/1/3/9.

⁵⁰ CUL, CUA, *William Maphew* c. *John Humbletoft (alias Trott),* V.C.Ct.III.8, fo. 157. See also V.C.Ct.III.16, no. 69; *John Humbletoft* c. *William Maphew,* Comm.Ct.II.17, fos. 51ᵛ, 59ᵛ.

⁵¹ CUL, CUA, V.C.Ct.II.29, fo. 24ᵛ. See also fo. 20; V.C.Ct.III.32, no. 10.

⁵² Jonathan Hope, 'The Use of *thou* and *you* in Early Modern Spoken English: Evidence from Depositions in the Durham Ecclesiastical Court Records', in Dieter Kastovsky (ed.), *Studies in Early Modern English* (Berlin, 1994).

by the baker and alderman Thomas Smart during an argument over a deceased man's goods, the launderer Toby Wood responded with both physical and verbal abuse. According to allegations, Wood not only called Smart 'goodman shit breeche', a fool, and a 'pillerly knave millerly knave', he also pulled off his cloak, shoved him in the chest, and threatened to box his ears.[53] In such instances violent gestures were used to restore honour which had been plundered by verbal abuse, and to humiliate an opponent by either emphasizing or achieving a disparity in status through blows.

That violence was intended to humiliate, or at least to level, is obvious from the gestures alleged in assault cases which functioned as a dramaturgical extension of the language of insult. Men drew upon a well-known repertoire of violent stances and postures to assert their status. It was particularly offensive, for example, to box the ears of an opponent. The Leicester tailor William Bate was imprisoned for two days because he abused one of the Mayor's brethren with 'evill and badd wordes [and] did also give hym a boxe of the eare', resorting to a staple of household discipline more appropriate for chastising subordinates by masters or parents.[54] Degradation of a different kind was at issue in a dispute of 1638 between William Fuller and John Phillips. Having accused each other of being drunk 'Phillips had draune his sword upon will Fuller . . . and his brother, and made them goe downe [on] their knees to him'— a blatant enforcement of subservience.[55] Spitting was a common gesture of defiance or derogation, such as when John Cooper of Felpham (West Sussex) abused a sidesman of his parish, 'calling him rogue and rascall, knave, villayne and divell, and in a beastly manner [did] spitt in his face'.[56] Brawls frequently involved striking up an opponent's heels, an action that automatically engendered degradation (and often serious injury) by swiping a man's feet from under him and landing him flat on his back. Joseph Swetnam recommended tripping up heels as a means of finishing off an enemy 'if you be cunning in wrestling', and it appears to have been frequently threatened and attempted, if not always carried

---

[53] CUL, CUA, *Thomas Smart* c. *Toby Wood*, V.C.Ct.II.22, fo. 50B. See also *Toby Wood* c. *Thomas Smart*, V.C.Ct.III.25, nos. 93–6; V.C.Ct.II.22, fo. 44ᵛ.

[54] *Records of the Borough of Leicester. Being a Series of Extracts from the Archives of the Corporation of Leicester*, iii: *1509–1603*, ed. Mary Bateson (Cambridge, 1905), 408. See also *York Civic Records*, vol. ix, ed. Deborah Sutton, Yorkshire Archaeological Society, 138 (York, 1978), 28.

[55] CUL, CUA, *William Fuller* c. *John Phillips*, V.C.Ct.II.32, fo. 121ᵛ.

[56] *Churchwarden's Presentments (17th Century). Part 1. Archdeaconry of Chichester*, ed. Hilda Johnstone, Sussex Record Society 49 (Lewes, 1948), 33. See also GL, Fishmongers' Court Minutes, MS 5570/1, 9; CUL, CUA, *John Rutterford* c. *Edward Hall*, Comm.Ct.II.13, fo. 103; *Kellam and Mary Manwaring* c. *Jeremy Chase*, V.C.Ct.III.27, no. 131.

off.[57] Richard Bowyer, a senior constable, reported failing to 'ley [a] druknen [sic] fellow by the heales' before being intercepted and 'affrontted and assallted' by several men who instead struck up his heels and stood on his chest.[58]

Another standard attack was to strike off an opponent's hat to compel the due respect evoked by hat-doffing. Charles Fotherby, a fellow of Trinity College, Cambridge, on witnessing a slanderous incident was so outraged by the 'unmannerly' behaviour of the defendant that he 'did strike [his] hatt of his head'. Charged with a similar assault, John Willington (a university proctor) justified his actions by claiming that despite his own bare head, the plaintiff had stood talking to him 'very saucely with his hatt one & never moveing it'.[59] Clothing more generally was a target of abuse. Clothes were often an important indicator of a man's status, and their damage or removal from a man in authority served as a literal dressing-down. University officials seem to have been particularly vulnerable to this kind of attack. In 1619, an examinant claimed that Robert Cooke, when resisting being detained by a university proctor, had not only punched the proctor on the face, but also 'did tare his bande from his neck & did aske the proctor for his Capp & booke & mr Proctor to his . . . disgrace was compelled to walke through the fayer without a bande & with a bloudye face'. In a similar case the defendant was accused of pulling off 'the liverie cloake from the shoulders of Roberte Bell', a servant to the proctor, which he 'did rent . . . in peeces'.[60] Clergymen also appear to have been vulnerable to defrocking by unsatisfied parishioners, such as the vicar of Coldwaltham (Sussex) who presented Richard Eager 'for laying violent hands on mee, in violently plucking and tearing my coate off from my backe'.[61] Cloaks, gowns, neck-bands, and ruffs were all vulnerable to attack, since their absence or dishevelment were marks of disgrace.

---

[57] Swetnam, *The Schoole of Defence*, 143.

[58] ESRO, QR/E 51, 24. See also, e.g., *York Civic Records*, 130; *The Case Book of Sir Francis Ashley J.P., Recorder of Dorchester, 1614–1635*, ed. J. H. Bettey, Dorset Record Society 7 (Dorchester, 1981), 51–2; CUL, CUA, *William Ellery* c. *Edmund Wenham*, V.C.Ct.III.23, no. 163; *Robert Man* c. *Edward Littlebury*, V.C.Ct.III.26, no. 178.

[59] CUL, CUA, *John Pomfret* c. *Edward Aynsworth*, V.C.Ct.II.28, fo. 14; *Riley* c. *John Willington*, V.C.Ct.II.25, fo. 87ᵛ. See also *Barnaby Gooch* c. *William Coote*, V.C.Ct.III.24, no. 26; *Office* c. *Mr Sheringham*, Comm.Ct.I.18, fo. *33ᵛ. For a discussion of the social significance of hat-doffing, see Penelope J. Corfield, 'Dress for Deference and Dissent: Hats and the Decline of Hat Honour', *Costume*, 23 (1989).

[60] CUL, CUA, *Proctor* c. *Robert Cooke*, V.C.Ct.III.23, fo. 213; *Arthur Johnson and Richard Anguish* c. *Joseph Ramson*, V.C.Ct.III.19, no. 49. See also *Thomas Woolly, MA* c. *Robert Orton*, V.C.Ct.III.25, nos. 81–2; Bodl., OUA, *Office* c. *Maurice Price*, Hyp/B/4, fo. 103.

[61] *Churchwarden's Presentments*, 40. See also *Depositions from the Courts of Durham*, 298–300.

Men's beards were also prominent targets. A Cambridge innkeeper, for example, complained that certain scholars had 'misused & injured [him] by pulling him by the beard & kicking & offering to strike upp [his] heles'.[62] Beard-pulling was sometimes accompanied by nose-tweaking, as in a case of 1584 brought by Thomas Crowforth (a baker) against Edward Wardall (a barber), who allegedly 'did in greate dispitefull & envious manner take the said Thomas Crowforthe ... by the bearde & pulled & shaked him by yt & plaied with his ... nose'.[63] The sting of such actions lay in their abuse of a recognized symbol of manhood, since the beard marked a man from a boy.[64] It was a badge of virility, authority, and maturity, implied by the use of the word 'beard' as a verb, meaning to affront. In many of the brawls on the streets and in the alehouses of early modern England, men were literally 'bearded', and thereby severely ridiculed and emasculated. Such ridicule was considered sufficiently serious by the Clothworkers' Company that in 1562 they imprisoned a journeyman for three days for pulling his master by the beard, and subsequently fined him 6s. 8d.[65] Another invasive form of emasculation was to grab a man by his genitals; thus Mary Randall of Norwich complained against Richard Streeke for 'takeinge her husband by the privie members'.[66] Perhaps the most vivid symbolic gesture of this kind, however, was that adopted by Humfry Smyth of Norwich who, having beaten his wife and struck the constable, 'in the presence of xl[tie] people or therabouts turned downe his hose & did his busynes'.[67] These were the gestures of disregard, if not blatant contempt. Bearding, nose-tweaking, ear-boxing, gown-pulling, spitting, and striking up heels were like the stock phrases of defamation suits. All such gestures sought to degrade their victims, and were calculated to inflict their greatest harm in the form of humiliation.

Such actions were therefore far more damaging as acts of defiance or humiliation than as physical abuse. In such instances violation was achieved through gestures designed to belittle, disgrace, and affront their victims. Litigation seems to have been initiated not simply because a violent exchange had taken place, but more specifically because of its nature and context, and the central concern of many litigants (when it

---

[62] CUL, CUA, *Thomas Redditt* c. *Alexander Ingland*, V.C.Ct.II.14, fo. 53ᵛ. See also *Godfrey Twelves* c. *Cantrell Legge*, V.C.Ct.III.15, no. 83; *Mr Clarke* c. *Thomas Tomson*, CUR 13, no. 4.

[63] CUL, CUA, *Thomas Crowforth* c. *Edward Wardall*, Comm.Ct.II.2, fo. 62. For a similar complaint, see also *William Elsden* c. *Robert Wing*, Comm.Ct.II.16, fo. 129.

[64] Will Fisher, 'The Renaissance Beard: Masculinity in Early Modern England', *Renaissance Quarterly*, 54 (2001).

[65] Clothworkers' Hall, London, Court Orders 1558–81, fo. 30.

[66] *Minutes of the Norwich Court of Mayoralty 1632–1635*, 75.

[67] *Minutes of the Norwich Court of Mayoralty 1630–1631*, 86.

can be detected) seems to have been the restoration of debased status. It is significant that very few litigants sought to condemn acts of violence as unseemly, brutish, or contradictory to normative codes of manhood which emphasized control and restraint. Instead, many cases were argued on the grounds of foul play: the offence lay not merely in resorting to blows, but primarily in disregarding the implicit codes of conduct expected to regulate physical confrontation.

From the pleading strategies adopted in such cases (complaining of foul play rather than of violence *per se*) it is possible to speculate upon some of the general rules governing informal combat between men, which bear a striking resemblance to those prescribed for gentlemen by Simon Robson, although they served a range of different agendas. Humiliating gestures which disregarded, or indeed inverted, hierarchies of age and status, such as a journeyman bearding his master, caused considerable offence. Unfair competition in terms of ability, weaponry, or numbers was also frequently emphasized by plaintiffs and witnesses of assaults. Having seen the schoolmaster Christopher Lawson knee a 14-year-old boy in the face, the yeoman Reginald Stowte reprimanded him with, 'Fye upon the, Lawson, doith thou evon thy wyll with a childe?'[68] Violence against the elderly was similarly offensive, such as an attack by the nailer William Harrisons against Edward Perry, described as a 'lame man of the age of threescore & xvj yeres' whom Harrisons had struck and beaten with his dagger before 'pull[ing] away parte of his bearde from his face'.[69] Nor was it considered fair to pursue a quarrel with men incapacitated by drink. So Angela Stedman deposed for Thomas Wolley of Peterhouse, Cambridge, claiming that he and his brother were attacked by Robert Orton out of malice rather than self-defence, 'because . . . mr Thomas Wolley seemed to be very weake, & his brother John Wolley was very weake because he was distempered with drinking as she conceyved, & therefore neyther of them were able to do him Robert Orton any great wrong'.[70]

Weapons could also create unfair advantage, as emphasized by William Westfield when he complained that his attacker had been armed with a dagger while he remained a 'naked man'—in other words unarmed and defenceless.[71] Unfair competition in terms of mismatched numbers also

---

[68] *Depositions from the Courts of Durham*, 306.
[69] *The Staffordshire Quarter Sessions Rolls*, v: *1603–1606*, ed. S. A. H. Burne (Kendal, 1940), 103. See also CUL, CUA, *James Hartley* c. *John Pecke*, Comm.Ct.II.6, fos. 149–153ᵛ.
[70] CUL, CUA, *Thomas Wolley, MA* c. *Robert Orton*, V.C.Ct.II.22, fo. 43ᵛ. See also Bodl., OUA, *Roger Acton* c. *John Wariner*, Hyp/B/4, fos. 22–5.
[71] CUL, EDR, Examination of William Westfield, E6/1/4.

breached rules of play, as suggested by Henry Allaby's response to his aggressors in 1594: 'my masters doe not plucke me by the heare, doe not pun me aboute the head: nor punche me, for I am a lone man, yf you were but one: I durst deale with eny one of you'. Similarly the Ely labourer John Johnson reported that he had objected to his attack by Richard and Henry Palfreman on the grounds that 'two weere two maney to sett upon one'.[72] It was wrong to hit a man when he was down, according to a witness of a dispute over grazing rights who intervened when he saw the plaintiff being held to the ground, intreating him to 'lett Pie ryse for he was a man & they ought not to hurt him [when] downe'.[73]

Broken promises of reconciliation could also intensify the gravity of a dispute, tipping the balance between violence and violation. Having been called a 'base fellow' by Thomas Foster at a wedding party in Eastbourne, Thomas Alfry automatically struck back with his fist. He and Foster then 'fell together by the eares', before Alfry pinioned Foster against two stools. On being entreated to relent, Alfry 'lett him rise', thinking that would be the end of the matter. He claimed his subsequent attack on Foster was justified, since Foster had broken the truce by returning to the chamber with his cane to hit Alfry. Counter-attacks that took an opponent unawares were not considered fair play, and were often deemed far more offensive than any initial, and by implication mutually agreed, aggression.[74]

Finally, the seriousness of an assault was also judged by its location. Cases involving male interpersonal combat suggest that in certain locations the use of violence to dispute status was fair game, or at least more acceptable than in others, in recognition of its common centrality to assertions of manhood. These locations were the more fluid spaces of the streets and the fields, where the potential for anonymity was greater and where, consequently, social hierarchies perhaps needed greater assertion and defence. Alternative codes of manhood were more clearly visible in such arenas, not least because they also offered greater opportunities to contest and appropriate the sources of patriarchal power held by men in authority. These spaces stand in stark contrast to the household or the church, the court or the council chamber, where hierarchies of status were more clearly expressed (for example in the form of seating plans) and more rigidly maintained. It is in these latter spaces that violent breaches of

[72] CUL, CUA, *Henry Allaby* c. *John Wilkinson*, Comm.Ct.II.6, fo. 9; EDR, Information of John Johnson, E/44, QS files 1637.
[73] CUL, CUA, *John Drake* c. *Thomas Pie*, Comm.Ct.II.17, fo. 64ᵛ.
[74] ESRO, QR/E 59, 45. See also, e.g., CUL, CUA, *John Cutchey* c. *Christopher Rudstone, MA*, V.C.Ct.III.22, no. 63; PRO, ASSI 45 1/3/57A. See also Amussen, 'Punishment, Discipline and Power', 24.

hierarchy automatically took on connotations of violation, and where, as a result, patriarchal masculinity was most clearly maintained. It was a particular insult, therefore, to abuse a man in his own house. This sentiment was vividly expressed by Grace Spencer, a labourer's wife, who having witnessed an assault in 1624 claimed that the aggressor 'might be ashamed to abuse an honest mann in his owne howse', adding that if the defendant had broken his assailant's head 'he had served him well enough for yor house is yor castell'.[75]

The emphasis on foul play, as opposed to mere physical harm, was partly attributable to pleading strategies adopted by litigants. Defendants sought mitigation for their actions, while plaintiffs and complainants sought to enhance their cases and to stress the extent of an injury in court without loss of face. Yet the gestures alleged and objections to certain forms of violence rather than violence *per se* are nonetheless indicative of the deep-rooted link between violence and manhood. Many cases appear to have been initiated because the victim of an assault had been literally unmanned, through either gestural abuse or contravention of the complex rules of engagement. The contingency of the boundary between acceptable and unacceptable violence suggests that violence was a regular, widely recognized, and often accepted feature of male interaction, routinely functioning to assert as well as contest claims for status and authority in connection with a range of male identities. This aspect of men's interchange was tacitly acknowledged and readily accommodated within patriarchal codes of manhood as a means by which men maintained and articulated the social order, as long as the boundaries of propriety were not inverted and the rules of play were not disregarded. Yet precisely because the links between violence and manhood were so strong, the boundary between violence and violation was readily crossed and could easily become blurred, and, as a result, patriarchal imperatives restricting the use of violence to certain contexts and social actors along contours of age and social status were both themselves contradictory and also frequently contested. Violence was intrinsic to the expression of a range of male identities encompassing attributes of fairness, honesty, order, control, autonomy, strength, forcefulness, bravado, resilience, and defiance.

The centrality of violence to assertions of male identity and authority was just as conspicuous in cases of group combat. When performed by

---

[75] CUL, CUA, *Thomas Witton* c. *William Ewsden*, Comm.Ct.II.20, fo. 104. See also a master's complaint against his journeyman for 'striking hym and breakinge his head in his owne howse', Clothworkers' Hall, London, Court Orders 1558–81, fo. 221ᵛ.

larger groups, the ritualized language of violent challenge and response conveyed and amplified male claims to status and authority, both legitimate and illegitimate. Group combat often involved defending territory through competitive tests of strength ranging in scale from football matches to international warfare. Male honour was closely bound up with such assertions of territorial authority and dominance; violence was as intrinsic to the policing of territorial boundaries as it was central to maintaining social hierarchies. Similarly, violence was used to challenge boundaries (for example in enclosure disputes) and the regulative violence of men in authority was widely misappropriated, particularly, but not exclusively, by groups of young or outcast men seeking status as suggested by the evidence of youthful misrule. Although there is some incidental evidence that unauthorized regulation was also carried out by women (who, for example, threw pails of water over, or broke the windows of, 'offenders' in their community), such activities lacked the overtones of male aggressive regulation which functioned as a declaration of collective masculine prowess.[76] When in the wrong hands such uses of violence were perceived in terms of violation. That the boundary between violence and violation was so fraught suggests the potency of violence in male assertions of authority, some of which upheld and some of which challenged the patriarchal order, but many of which ignored its imperatives altogether.

Violence was a deeply ingrained part of men's competitive interaction serving a broad range of interests, in association with varied meanings of manhood. At its extremes it could function to demarcate territory, to regulate and chastise, and to confer authority on its perpetrators, either legitimately with state sanction, illegitimately through appropriation, or in connection with alternative codes of manhood. On a more mundane level, violence was a vivid thread flamboyantly woven into the fabric of men's daily lives, often simply as the implicit threat suggested by bodily gestures and taunts, but nonetheless displayed as proof of strength and status in connection with a range of male identities. In this light, the rhetorical emphasis on control and restraint in conduct literature, as well as concerns for order contained in broader social commentary, need to be contextualized and reassessed. Violence clearly underpinned patriarchal authority itself, and its use as a disciplinary tool was widely diffused beyond the state and the magistrate to every household head. As a result,

[76] e.g. CUL, CUA, *John Westly* c. *Dorothy Dugresse*, V.C.Ct.II.32, fo. 141ᵛ; *Benjamin Prime* c. *Mary Muser*, Comm.Ct.II.16, fo. 128; *Minutes of the Norwich Court of Mayoralty 1632–1635*, 131, 173; *Case Book of Sir Francis Ashley*, 66.

it was open to extensive abuse, often as it merged with other codes of manhood rooted in toughness, strength, and physical prowess.

Patriarchal expectations of orderly comportment in men were therefore directly contravened by codes of conduct which seem to have governed men's interaction in the streets and fields of early modern England. Besides upholding the patriarchal order, violence also informed alternative meanings of manhood, and was in addition widely appropriated by men otherwise excluded from positions of authority in deliberately antipatriarchal stances. Ideals of men's controlled self-government exerted a frail, or at least a highly selective, hegemony, both in terms of their limited impact as well as in terms of the contradictions contained in official attitudes to violence. Just as rhetorical emphasis on restraint and control functioned at times to justify male superiority, so violence in other contexts served, arguably more powerfully, to reinforce men's claims to dominance and worth, often in ways which bore no relation to a patriarchal agenda. Although violence was one of the most powerful patriarchal resources, it was impossible to control, both because it was so diffuse and because it served a range of male identities beyond the patriarchal agenda for order. As a result it was held in check only by the shifting boundaries between violence and violation which were easily crossed and—like meanings of manhood itself—highly contested.

6
Respectability, Sex, and Status

IN 1603, the Cambridge haberdasher Ralph Hyde reprimanded his neighbour Margaret Cotton for spreading rumours that he had been cuckolded whilst away on business. He also insinuated that Cotton had stolen a book from his house. Her response suggested that she was deeply offended by his accusations:

> wooe worthe the, woe worth the that ever I knewe thee, thowe comest nowe to me as Judas did come to Christe to betraye him, thowe haste brought my name in question, and searched my house . . . thowe hast taken awaye mye good name[.] And he that takethe awaye his neighbors good name by the word of god is a blode sucker, and a man slayer, And thowe arte a greate churche goer, but by thy doeinges thowe shewest thye selfe to be an hipocrite.

Interestingly, it was on account of this speech (rather than her imputation of his wife's adultery) that Hyde entered a defamation suit against Margaret Cotton. She in turn justified her outburst by saying to the judge, 'Sir, I remember that mr Nelson sayd in a sermon which he made that he that takethe awaye his neighbors good name ys a robber and he that robbeth his neighbor of his goods maye restore them againe, but he that takethe away his neighbors good name canne never restore yt againe.'[1]

Cotton's diatribe vividly invoked the potentially damaging impact of slanderous words in early modern England, which is also suggested by comparatively high levels of defamation litigation between 1560 and 1640. The language of insult revealed by such cases has proved an extremely rich source for exploring the boundaries of honour and reputation in early modern England.[2] Slander suits provide direct evidence of

---

[1] CUL, CUA, *Ralph Hyde* c. *Margaret Cotton*, Comm.Ct.II.11, fo. 27ʳ⁻ᵛ.
[2] C. A. Haigh, 'Slander and the Church Courts in the Sixteenth Century', *Transactions of the Lancashire and Cheshire Antiquarian Society*, 78 (1975); J. A. Sharpe, *Defamation and Sexual Slander in Early Modern England: The Church Courts at York*, Borthwick Papers 58 (York, 1980); Martin Ingram, *Church Courts, Sex and Marriage in England, 1570–1640* (Cambridge, 1987), ch. 10; Peter Rushton, 'The Church Courts in North-East England in the Sixteenth and Seventeenth Centuries: An Historical Gossip Column?', *Sunderland's History*, 5 (1989); Laura Gowing, *Domestic Dangers: Women, Words, and Sex in Early Modern London* (Oxford, 1996), chs. 3–4. See also Peter Burke, 'The Art of Insult in Early Modern Italy', *Culture and History*, 2 (1987).

the ways in which men and women's honour could be undermined and are therefore an indirect guide to some of the components of early modern status and reputation. Legal action was one means both to restore a good name and to discredit those who had questioned it. Defamation litigation functioned like verbal tests of strength, with litigants putting their reputations on trial in order to prove their good character—as one Cambridge plaintiff put it, 'toe trye my selfe either an honest woman, or otherwise'.[3] The terms in which slander was both couched and rebuffed were clearly related to the prescriptive programme contained within the conduct literature, and defamation litigation sheds light on the ways in which men and women competed for respectability in patriarchal terms.

Historians have been particularly preoccupied with an apparent divergence along gendered lines of the terms in which reputation was disputed. It has been frequently argued that cases brought by women predominantly concerned their sexual morality, whereas cases brought by men were more likely to have involved issues of trustworthiness relating to economic matters.[4] Slander litigation seems to confirm the impression of a double standard which founded women's honour almost exclusively on chastity, making women more vulnerable to sexual slander and more concerned with their sexual reputations than men. By contrast, definitions of honesty for men appear to have been far more broadly conceived, and the impact of insinuations of sexual impropriety less grave. Laura Gowing's conclusion that 'women's reputation was always at heart about sexual honour, and . . . male honour covered a whole range of different fields' echoes Dod and Cleaver's tenet that a woman's primary duty was solely 'shamefastnes', whereas '[a] man needeth many things . . . too long to rehearse'.[5] According to Gowing, this polarity was so great in early modern England that there prevailed 'a vision in which the honour of women and men were wholly incommensurable'.[6]

Gowing's work contributes a sophisticated analysis of the cultural significance that there was no male equivalent for the word 'whore'. Her conclusions have not remained unchallenged, however, particularly

[3] CUL, CUA, *Mary Bland* c. *Nicholas Algate*, Comm.Ct.II.2, fo. 86.
[4] Sharpe, *Defamation and Sexual Slander*, 28–9; Susan Dwyer Amussen, *An Ordered Society: Gender and Class in Early Modern England* (Oxford, 1988), 98–104; Laura Gowing, 'Gender and the Language of Insult in Early Modern London', *History Workshop Journal*, 35 (1993). See also Peter N. Moogk, ' "Thieving Buggers" and "Stupid Sluts": Insults and Popular Culture in New France', *William and Mary Quarterly*, 3rd ser. 36 (1979); Mary Beth Norton, 'Gender and Defamation in Seventeenth-Century Maryland', *William and Mary Quarterly*, 3rd ser. 44 (1987).
[5] Gowing, *Domestic Dangers*, 107; John Dod and Robert Cleaver, *A Godly Form of Householde Government: For the Ordering of Private Families* (London, 1612), 350–1. See above, pp. 72, 76–7.
[6] Gowing, 'Gender and the Language of Insult', 19.

regarding reputations of early modern men. Bernard Capp has argued that men were also vulnerable to accusations of sexual laxity that could potentially inflict severe damage on their reputations and livelihoods.[7] It is also likely that husbands felt deeply implicated in and disgraced by accusations of sexual misconduct against their wives, and were often the sponsors of legal action to clear their names.[8] In addition, it has been suggested that women's reputations were more broadly conceived than is evident in slander litigation, encompassing economic and social as well as sexual dimensions.[9] This chapter suggests ways in which the model of gender polarity should be further qualified and considerably revised, with evidence of the broader foundations of reputation for women and examples of men's concern with accusations of sexual dishonour. Evidence that men were anxious about their sexual reputations does not, however, mean that they cared about them in the same way as women, or even in the same way as each other, and it will be argued that the impact of sexual insults against men was highly contingent and that notions of male respectability in these terms were very selectively applied. In addition, the full range of insults against men are examined beyond those imputing sexual impropriety in order to explore the degree to which respectability was contested in patriarchal terms and the ways in which patriarchal privilege was implicated in the processes of social differentiation.

It is important to be aware that defamation litigation is by no means a foolproof guide to early modern definitions of honesty. Negatively framed allegations of dishonesty do not provide a mirror image of positively defined concepts of honesty. This problem has been compounded by historians' reliance on church court records as evidence. While the high proportion of women amongst litigants (supplying roughly three-quarters of plaintiffs in some samples) allows considerable insight into the ways in which women disputed and defended reputation, the ecclesiastical setting nonetheless offered a comparatively narrow forum for their concerns.[10] Strict rules governed the admission of slander litigation in the

---

[7] Bernard Capp, 'The Double Standard Revisited: Plebeian Women and Male Sexual Reputation in Early Modern England', *Past and Present*, 162 (1999).

[8] Elizabeth A. Foyster, *Manhood in Early Modern England: Honour, Sex and Marriage* (Harlow, 1999), 148–64.

[9] Garthine Walker, 'Expanding the Boundaries of Female Honour in Early Modern England', and Faramerz Dabhoiwala, 'The Construction of Honour, Reputation and Status in Late Seventeenth- and Early Eighteenth-Century England', both in *Transactions of the Royal Historical Society*, 6th ser. 6 (1996).

[10] Sharpe, *Defamation and Sexual Slander*, 10, 27–8; Ingram, *Church Courts, Sex and Marriage*, 302; Gowing, *Domestic Dangers*, 35. For the continuation of this trend see also Tim Meldrum, 'A Woman's Court in London: Defamation at the Bishop of London's Consistory Court, 1700–1745', *London Journal*, 19 (1994).

church courts which were increasingly monitored by common lawyers in the seventeenth century.[11] Verbal abuse was actionable in church courts only if it maliciously imputed a spiritual crime that fell under ecclesiastical jurisdiction, which overwhelmingly concerned sexual morality.[12] Cases alleging temporal crimes, or which could be demonstrated to have resulted in actual loss or damage, fell under the common law. This distinction, although somewhat blurred during the sixteenth and seventeenth centuries, was highly instrumental in restricting the substance of slander litigation in the church courts to accusations of sexual incontinence (fornication, adultery, bearing an illegitimate child), drunkenness, and witchcraft. It is therefore important to remember that the terms in which reputation was contested in court were primarily dictated by this legal context, rather than being straightforwardly indicative of general preoccupations.

The legal context provided by the Cambridge university courts is advantageous in this regard, since it escaped the jurisdictional boundaries increasingly enclosing the church courts in the seventeenth century. Since admission of a case was contingent upon one of the litigants being associated with the university as a member, retainer, or employee rather than the precise substance of a suit, the university courts routinely heard cases imputing spiritual *and* temporal crimes. The slander litigation entered in this forum was therefore more representative of the broader foundations of reputation in early modern England than that heard separately in either the ecclesiastical or the common law courts. Although women were involved in far smaller proportions than in ecclesiastical forums, they nonetheless accounted for over a third of all litigants in defamation suits brought before the commissary for which depositions survive. The Cambridge evidence therefore affords a more detailed investigation of the types of defamation suit pursued by men, while still allowing sufficient scope for comparison with women's concerns in slander litigation. In addition, it is also possible to trace the

---

[11] For the extent of common law prohibitions suffered by the ecclesiastical courts during this period, see Ronald A. Marchant, *The Church under the Law: Justice, Administration and Discipline in the Diocese of York, 1560–1640* (Cambridge, 1969); Ralph A. Houlbrooke, *Church Courts and the People during the English Reformation, 1520–1570* (Oxford, 1979); Brian P. Levack, *The Civil Lawyers in England, 1603–1641: A Political Study* (Oxford, 1973); R. H. Helmholz, *Roman Canon Law in Reformation England* (Cambridge, 1990).

[12] R. H. Helmholz, 'Canonical Defamation in Medieval England', *American Journal of Legal History*, 15 (1971); W. S. Holdsworth, *A History of English Law*, 7th edn., revised, 16 vols. (London, 1956–72), viii. 333–78. See also Clara Ann Bowler, 'Carted Whores and White Shrouded Apologies: Slander in the County Courts of Seventeenth-Century Virginia', *Virginia Magazine of History and Biography*, 85 (1977).

different issues pursued by men from the town and university members, since the latter were as active as litigants in the vice-chancellor's court as women in the commissary's court (Table 1). Comparisons suggest that differences between men appear to have been as influential as differences between men and women in dictating the subject of defamation litigation, particularly in relation to issues of sexual morality.

Table 1. Defamation litigants in the Cambridge university courts, 1581–1640, by sex and town/gown status

	Vice-chancellor's court			Commissary's court		
	Total litigants (%)	Plaintiffs (%)	Defendants (%)	Total litigants (%)	Plaintiffs (%)	Defendants (%)
Men: town	55.5	50	61.1	59.9	60.6	59.2
Men: gown	26.4	33.3	19.4	5.1	7.3	2.9
Men: total	81.9	83.3	80.5	65.0	67.9	62.1
Women	13.2	11.1	15.3	33.2	29.2	37.2
Joint (husband and wife)	4.9	5.6	4.2	1.8	2.9	0.7

Given the unique utility of the Cambridge evidence, this chapter is primarily based on a close analysis of 307 injury cases alleging slander heard by the Cambridge university courts between 1581 and 1640 for which allegations or depositions survive. While gender-related patterns are a feature of this sample, it confirms recent impressions that there was nonetheless a degree of overlap between men and women's concerns in slander litigation: men pursued significant numbers of suits relating to their sexual morality, and in this legal forum women also sought redress in significant numbers against other kinds of accusations, particularly of theft and dealing in stolen goods. The insults refuted by university members also varied in emphasis from those alleged by townsmen, suggesting that the components of male reputation were related to age and marital status as well as gender. It appears from the Cambridge material that there was greater fluidity and contingency to the components of identity and reputation than is suggested by evidence from the church courts. A broad spectrum of honesty in which sexual and economic integrity was interwoven was selectively applied to both men and women with different emphases not only according to gender, but also age, rank, and context. This becomes even clearer in evidence suggestive of the positive construction of concepts of honesty (rather than the negative assertions of dishonesty contained within defamation litigation) which will be examined more closely in the next chapter.

More importantly, most of the insults against men alleged in the university courts and in many other jurisdictions appear to have concerned far more than narrowly defined issues of economic credit or sexual morality, but were articulated in terms of broader notions of honesty related to perceptions of social status. What is arguably most interesting about defamation litigation therefore is not only the terms in which slander was couched and refuted, but also the way in which such suits featured in men's competitive assertions of status. One of the most resonant refrains accompanying early modern insults was 'I'm as good a man as you'. Male preoccupations in slanderous exchanges were often a direct product of contests over rank and status, to which patriarchal concepts of manhood were firmly harnessed. By invoking normative concepts of honesty men drew on patriarchal notions of respectability to place themselves in relation to others, and by invoking the language of insult—as with the violent gestures of disputed status—they contested the social pretensions of opponents. It was this competitive assertion of position that fuelled not only much of men's invective against each other, but also their subsequent pursuit of slander litigation.

THE GENDERED COMPONENTS OF HONESTY AND REPUTATION

Although the university courts heard a far broader range of business than ecclesiastical courts, the defamation litigation heard by the vice-chancellor and the commissary is also by no means a transparent index to the components of honesty and reputation in early modern England. The defamatory language alleged in court often bore little relation to the actual circumstances of a dispute. Labels such as 'whore', 'rogue', or 'knave' were often used indiscriminately, sometimes serving merely to mark the seriousness of a quarrel or to raise the stakes of a conflict. An example is a dispute of 1582 between Ann Williamson, the wife of a barber, and Rose Tiffen who was married to a shearman. The slander occurred during a quarrel over Tiffen's refusal to allow Williamson's boy over her wall in order to enter her house. Locked out, and being denied the only possible access by Tiffen, Ann Williamson called her a 'spiteful drabbe'. In all likelihood growing out of a long history of tension between neighbours, the ensuing case seems to have been concerned less with a serious defence of Rose Tiffen's sexual reputation than with shifting the dispute onto more favourable ground in order to avenge the insult—since, as one witness remarked, 'the good name & fame of the sayd Tiffens wief is not herebye enye thinge at all hindred or impayred'. Williamson's use of the term 'drab' was not a comment on Tiffen's sexual behaviour; it merely demonstrated her desire to insult Tiffen, and thereby provided an actionable offence with which Tiffen chose to instigate legal action as a rebuke.[13]

Cases like these alert us to the complex circumstances which could produce actions for slander that often remained hidden behind nominal charges of defamatory insults. Disputes over straying animals, dirt-sweeping, rent payments, outstanding debts, and non-payment of wages were all extended into court through defamation litigation.[14] As far as they are discernible, vexatious overtones feature in much of the defamation litigation heard by the university courts. Nearly half (49 per cent) of the 307 cases involving slander for which depositions or allegations survive were linked in some way to other litigation, either through counter-suits or previous or subsequent actions. Many defamation suits were entered alongside cases for debt, with which they seem to have been connected. For example, when William Spicer entered an action for injury against John Scott in 1613 for being called 'a foole and a knave, and a base Rascall and a Roage and the vilest and dishonestest man living' he was in the process of being sued by Scott over an outstanding debt for work that Scott had done for him.[15] Some actions for slander were begun as a direct result of proceedings in the consistory, such as when one Piper and the draper Thomas Gill were 'wrangling' in court about a debt cause pending between them. According to one witness in a subsequent case over Gill's legal fees, 'Gill did take advantage of some wordes Piper then spake agaynst him Gill & thereupon did Gill then enter an action of Injury agaynst him the sayd Piper.'[16] The court's registrar even went to

[13] CUL, CUA, *John Tiffen* c. *Ann Williamson*, Comm.Ct.II.1, fos. 35–6. See also *Ann Moore* c. *Robert Slegge*, V.C.C.t.II.8, fos. 61, 62ᵛ.

[14] e.g. CUL, CUA, *Robert Wing* c. *William Elsden*, Comm.Ct.II.16, fos. 84, 86–94; *John Paske* c. *Grace and Michael Watson*, Comm.Ct.II.13, fos. 40–9; *John Paske* c. *Michael Watson*, Comm.Ct.II.13, fo. 24ʳ⁻ᵛ; *Thomas Oliver* c. *Richard Shelley*, V.C.Ct.II.22, fo. 117; *Cantrell Legge* c. *Thomasina Corbett*, Comm.Ct.II.13, fo. 95ʳ⁻ᵛ. See also Ingram, *Church Courts, Sex and Marriage*, 314–16; Christine Churches, 'False Friends, Spiteful Enemies: A Community at Law in Early Modern England', *Historical Research*, 71 (1998).

[15] CUL, CUA, *William Spicer, LLB* c. *John Scott*, V.C.Ct.III.18, fo. 44. See also Comm.Ct.II.17, fo. 94 and *John Scott* c. *William Spicer, LLB*, Comm.Ct.II.17, fo. 94ᵛ. For other examples of simultaneous debt and injury cases, see *Thomas Wickliffe* c. *Edward King* [injury], V.C.Ct.III.13, fo. 14, and *Edward King* c. *Thomas Wickliffe* [debt], V.C.Ct.III.13, fo. 17; *John Pickering* c. *William Gray* [injury], V.C.Ct.III.12, fo. 10, *John Pickering* c. *William Gray* [debt], V.C.Ct.III.12, fo. 11, and *William Gray* c. *John Pickering* [injury], V.C.Ct.III.12, fo. 14.

[16] CUL, CUA, *Martin Bery* c. *Thomas Gill*, V.C.Ct.II.7, fo. 6ᵛ.

the trouble of keeping a note 'in a private paper' of any actionable words spoken in court in order to give evidence of proceedings if necessary and 'to avoyd controversy about words uttered in Courte'.[17] Although vexatious litigation provoked widespread disapproval (often as part of defence strategies questioning the plaintiff's motives in bringing a suit), it is evident that it was a frequent occurrence.

This raises the issue of how useful an analysis of the insults alleged in slander suits can be as gauges of the components of honesty and reputation, given that sometimes they were simply the fuel to perpetuate quite separate tensions, and cannot always be taken at face value. Actionable words elicited selective responses, and often provoked litigation only when connected with other matters in dispute, or after prolonged wrangling. Yet even when only nominally connected to the real issues between parties, such cases are nonetheless suggestive of the seriousness with which defamatory language could be taken. Indeed, the fact that slander was not always related precisely to the behaviour of the victims of abuse is further suggestive of its potency, since it appears to have provided more powerful forms of critique than simple expressions of annoyance or other forms of complaint. The resonance of slanderous language was also related to its very real potential to inflict damage, and there were many cases in which the insult obviously was the central issue of the dispute as well as the resulting legal action. In these instances, the primary concern of plaintiffs was to clear their names of the alleged offence in order to reassert their respectability and restore their credit.

The power of certain words to injure and discredit others was widely recognized by litigants and witnesses, as suggested by the agonized cries of Margaret Cotton which opened this chapter. Witnesses often recounted their attempts to warn defendants of the dangers of slanderous language both as the provocation of litigation and the source of harm to others. When Robert Bales burst into Dr Clayton's rooms in St John's College, claiming that Hugh Baguley (a fellow of the college) had run away with his wife, one of the witnesses urged him 'to be well advised what he sayd, for that otherwise Mr Bagulye mighte undoe him Bales for useinge of suche speaches of him, yf he ... could not prove them'.[18] Witnesses and defendants attempted actively to dissociate themselves from injurious words, once again in recognition of their danger. This strategy was part of Robert Lawrence's defence in a defamation suit, claiming that having delivered his message from a woman in St Andrew's parish to John Cragge, he

[17] CUL, CUA, *John Symons* c. *John Paske*, Comm.Ct.II.13, fos. 13^v, 14^v.
[18] CUL, CUA, *Hugh Baguley, MA* c. *Robert Bales*, V.C.Ct.II.2*, fo. 5^v.

refused to repeat the conversation to Cragge's friends about Cragge's alleged paternity of a recently born child, saying to Cragge, 'tell yt to them yorselfe, for yt is a naughtye matter, & I will not deale with yt'.[19]

Allegations in injury cases in the Cambridge university courts included an estimate of damages, which also suggest that plaintiffs could be severely affected by slander. In defamation suits estimates of damages ranged from a few shillings to £1,000. These estimates implied that extensive financial damage could result from lost reputation. In another case involving the Cotton household, a witness for the pewterer Henry Cotton (Margaret Cotton's husband), who was suing the apothecary John Swetson for calling his family thieves, deposed that 'Cotton had better have spent a hundred pounds then to be soe wronged'. Similarly, a witness for Sir Hanger of St John's College in his suit against a fellow of Trinity College who had accused him of being drunk claimed that 'if his Sir Hangers father should take any deepe displeasure agaynst him Sir Hanger for the said wordes . . . Sir Hanger had beine better lost C^{li}'.[20] While such estimates were subjective, serving to emphasize the plaintiff's worth and consequent status, rather than products of an objective evaluative scheme attached to various insults, they nonetheless indicate that the university courts were willing at least to countenance claims of extensive harm caused by slander.[21] Occasionally, incidental evidence can be glimpsed of the tangible impact of defamation. For example, when Laurence Chaderton's retainer Thomas Reddit complained that he had been accused by Alexander Ingland of keeping a bawdy house, a scholar of Emmanuel College (of which Chaderton was master) deposed that he believed Reddit's 'good name and creditt' had been severely wronged, 'for that his . . . wyfe hath lost her washing [from] divers schollers by reason of the sayd Englands words'.[22] The reputation of this household had been sullied, with considerable impact on its domestic economy. Slander also destroyed trust and jeopardized inclusion in credit networks. After the tailor James Huitson had been denounced by the lawyer William Cotton (who was also suing him for debt) as 'a craftye cosenynge knave' and a cheat, one witness claimed that he 'did not soe well lyke of him . . .

---

[19] CUL, CUA, *John Cragge, MA* c. *Robert Lawrence*, V.C.Ct.II.2, fo. 43ᵛ.

[20] *Henry Cotton* c. *John Swetson*, Comm.Ct.II.11, fo. 40; *Richard Hanger, BA* c. *Paul Tompson, BD*, V.C.Ct.II.12, fo. 2.

[21] It was extremely rare for either the vice-chancellor or the commissary to award the full damages estimated by the plaintiff, and the monetary damages awarded in the small proportion of cases which proceeded as far as a formal judgment were usually no more than a third of the plaintiff's estimate, and often considerably lower.

[22] CUL, CUA, *Thomas Reddit* c. *Alexander Ingland*, V.C.Ct.II.14, fo. 50.

nor made the lyke accompte of him', adding that he 'would not neither did credit the sayd James Huitson with enye more monye'.[23]

Actionable words therefore held considerable power to threaten both the reputations and the livelihoods of early modern men and women, which is often why people went to such lengths to refute them in court. An analysis of defamatory language and the contexts of its usage, which at least partly determined when it was taken seriously, reveals some of the norms to which people resorted or clung on to when their status was threatened. Even, or perhaps especially, in vexatious cases, litigants invoked ideals of respectability in order to restore their comparative social standing which provide clues to the positive components of reputation. Although sometimes merely rhetorical, and at least partly determined by the legal context, the formal language of insult nonetheless suggests a lexicon of disgrace which could be employed to violate a person's claims to respectability, often, but not always, effectively. Defamation litigation therefore provides considerable evidence of the ways in which reputation might be undermined through allegations of dishonesty, and how this varied according not only to gender but also other determinants of status.

Although the clearest variation in the substance of defamation suits was along gendered lines, in the university courts this was not nearly as stark as suggested by evidence from the church courts, and the implicit concepts of honesty for men and women were far from incommensurable. Figs. 4 and 5 show the range and number of insults alleged by men and women in the 307 suits for which allegations or depositions survive between 1581 and 1640. The most obvious difference is the greater range of insults levelled against men. In addition, by far the greatest category of abuse against women was sexual—'whore', 'drab', 'queen', or 'jade'— while the most common terms of abuse against men were social: 'rogue', 'knave', 'jack', or 'rascal'. The second biggest category of insult against men was that of 'cozening' or false dealing, whereas accusations of untrustworthiness against women in these terms were comparatively rare in contrast to accusations of theft and dealing in stolen goods which comprised the second biggest category of insult against women. This general pattern of gender-related facets to reputation is evident in imputations of household disorder concerning both husband and wife. So, for example, in a joint action brought by the tailor John Simons and his wife Joan against the yeoman John Scott, they complained that Scott had called Joan Simons 'old Gill, old flurtes, and old Geny', and cast John Simons as

[23] CUL, CUA, *James Huitson* c. *William Cotton*, Comm.Ct.II.3, fos. 154, 159ᵛ.

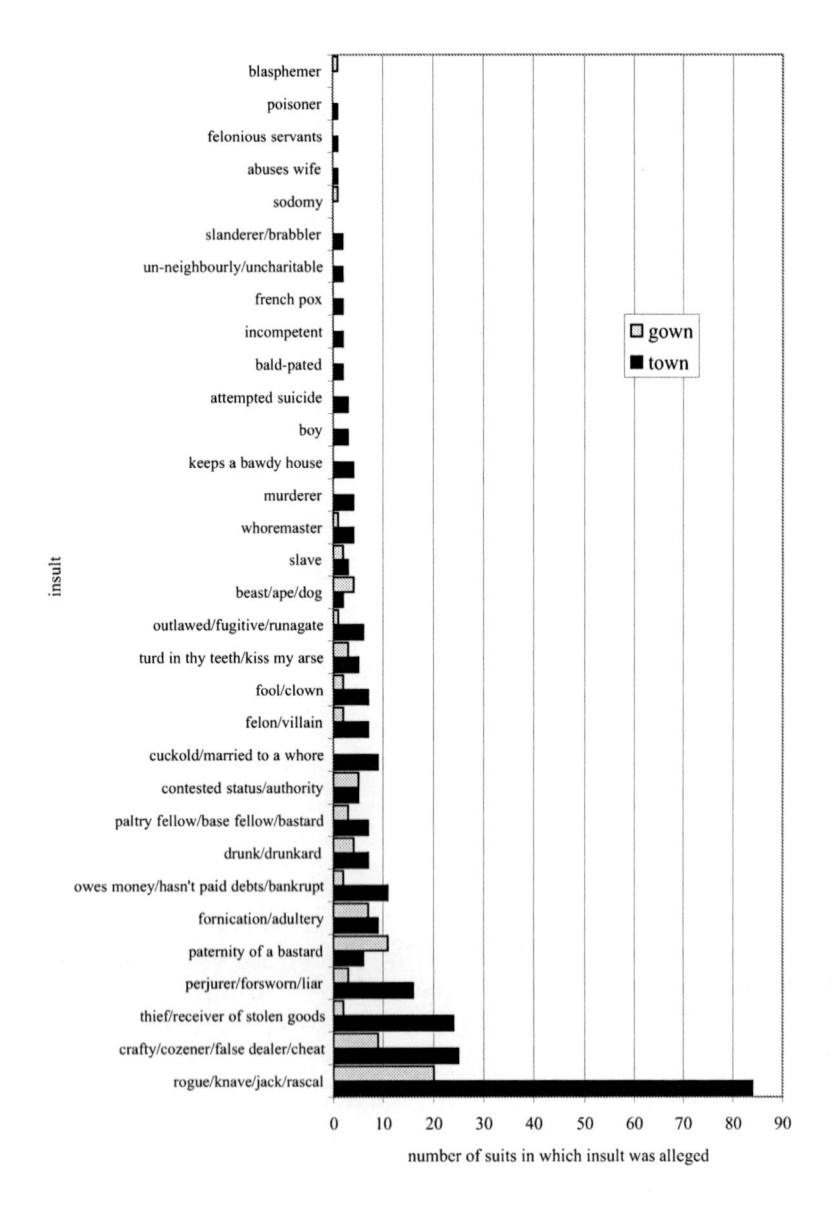

Fig. 4. Language of insult against men in Cambridge, 1581–1640

Respectability, Sex, and Status 163

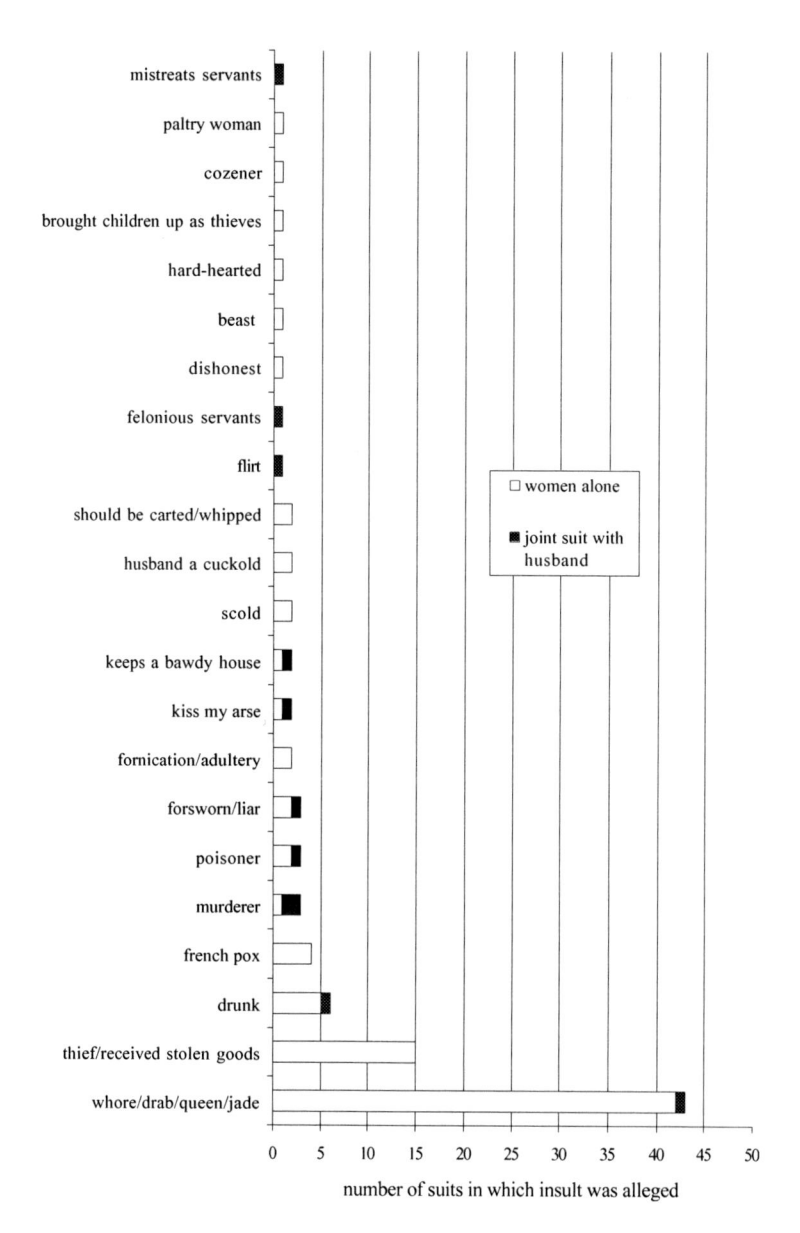

Insult	
mistreats servants	▮
paltry woman	☐
cozener	☐
brought children up as thieves	☐
hard-hearted	☐
beast	☐
dishonest	☐
felonious servants	▮
flirt	▮
should be carted/whipped	☐
husband a cuckold	☐
scold	☐
keeps a bawdy house	▮
kiss my arse	▮
fornication/adultery	☐
forsworn/liar	▮
poisoner	▮
murderer	▮
french pox	☐
drunk	▬▮
thief/received stolen goods	☐☐☐
whore/drab/queen/jade	☐☐☐☐☐☐☐☐▮

Legend: ☐ women alone; ▮ joint suit with husband

number of suits in which insult was alleged

Fig. 5. Language of insult against women in Cambridge, 1581–1640

an 'olde baldpated knave' who 'kepte a shusling with other mens monye'. Similarly, Thomas and Ann Boston complained that Margaret Wilson had called Thomas a 'theivish rogue' and Ann a 'queen' who poisoned the scholars she laundered for, which injury was estimated at £20.[24]

Men's reputations were most frequently attacked through questioning their economic integrity in terms of plain dealing, reliability, and personal worth. Thus in 1636 the innkeeper Thomas Smith complained that his credit had been undermined not only by Owen Saintpeere's accusation that he had stolen Saintpeere's horse, but also because of suggestions of his worthlessness which were couched as follows: 'you Smith goe paye yor debts, all the goods you have are made over to yor landlord for debt, you owe him, yf he be payd you are not worth a penny'. Similarly, Benjamin Prime (a stationer) sought legal action against Thomas Crowfoot (a baker) for calling him 'an ould Cosening knave, a roge, a bankrupt knave', which likewise suggested that he could not be trusted.[25] Men also sought to protect their professional identities from slanderous accusations. Francis Dalton sued Ann Moore for calling him a 'dumb priest' and a thief 'who comes in by the windowe', implying that:

[he] was on[e] which cam by his orders or some ecclesiasticall livinge or both, unlawfully and unhonestly and that the said ffrancis dalton did neglect his dutie in preachinge the word to such as he ought to have done beinge contented to take any profitt without any paynes performing, intendinge wholy his play at Cardes or such other unlawfull exercise rather than his dutie function and calinge and that he was a theefe and a man of noe reputacion.

As a consequence, he estimated his injury at £100, although at the time of the exchange he had also responded in kind by calling Ann Moore a 'queen'.[26] The lawyer John Blomfield was similarly concerned to protect his professional reputation from Elizabeth Twelves's assertion that he was 'a scurvy Cosening fellowe [who] keeps our monye & our wrightings from us & if it had not beine for him we had had our porcions payd over'. According to one of his witnesses 'the discredit that he maye have by the sayd words... spoken agaynst him is greate'.[27] Such examples conform to

---

[24] CUL, CUA, *John and Joan Simons* c. *John Scott*, V.C.Ct.II.8, fo. 104, V.C.Ct.III.11, no. 95; *Thomas and Ann Boston* c. *Margaret Wilson*, V.C.Ct.II.32, fos. 33ᵛ–34ᵛ. See also *James Hartlye* c. *Owen Wright*, V.C.Ct.III.4, no. 132.
[25] CUL, CUA, *Thomas Smith* c. *Owen Saintpeere*, V.C.Ct.II.32, fo. 57ʳ⁻ᵛ; *Benjamin Prime* c. *Thomas Crowfoot*, V.C.Ct.III.8, no. 8. See also *John Paske* c. *Grace Watson*, Comm.Ct.II.13, fo. 40ᵛ, and below pp. 192–3.
[26] CUL, CUA, *Francis Dalton, BD* c. *Ann Moore*, V.C.Ct.III.11, no. 88. See also *Ann Moore* c. *Robert Slegge*, V.C.Ct.II.8, fo. 57.
[27] CUL, CUA, *John Blomfield, LLB* c. *Elizabeth Twelves*, Comm.Ct.II.13, fos. 81ᵛ–82ᵛ.

a gendered pattern of reputation with which early modern historians are familiar: men's honesty was gauged through their interaction with both men and women, and more often in terms of their economic and social renown than their sexual propriety. The evaluation of women's honesty was more contingent on their interaction with men alone, and the sexual overtones of that contact. There are parallels here with Dod and Cleaver's advice that 'the dutie of the Husband is to deale with many men: and of the Wives to talke with few'.[28]

There were sufficient deviations from this general model, however, to suggest that it was only loosely applied and much more mutable than is often assumed. When the sample of insults against men and women is divided into broad categories, considerable variations become apparent (Figs. 6–8). Perhaps the most surprising feature of all is that only half of the alleged insults against women involved accusations of unchastity or some other kind of sexual shame. In addition, almost a third of insults complained about by university men and a fifth of all insults reported by townsmen also involved allegations of sexual misconduct. Although the assertion of sexual honesty was women's predominant concern in

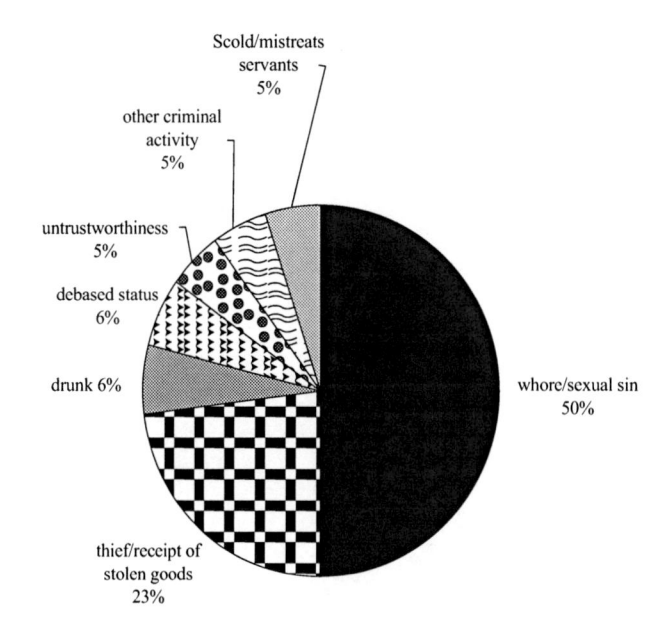

Fig. 6. Categories of insult against Cambridge women, 1581–1640

[28] Dod and Cleaver, *A Godly Form of Householde Government*, 168.

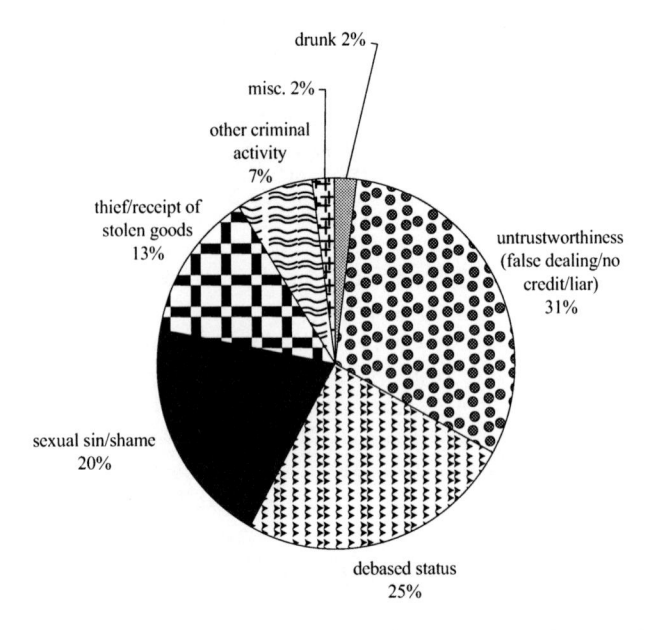

Fig. 7. Categories of insult against Cambridge townsmen, 1581–1640

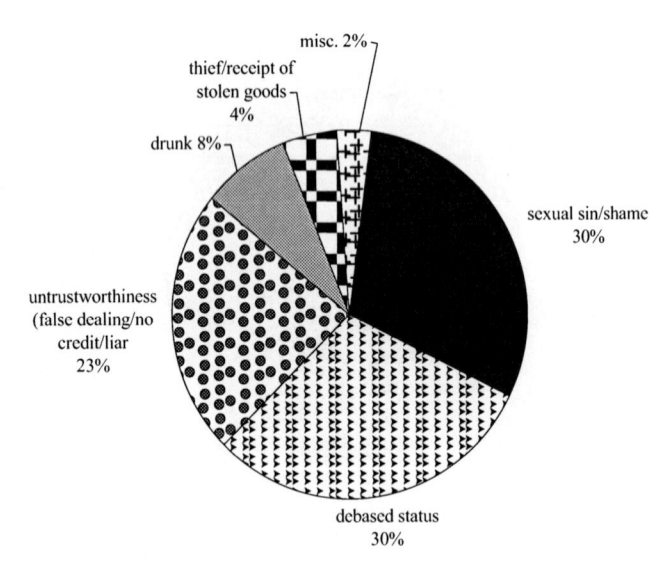

Fig. 8. Categories of insult against Cambridge university members, 1581–1640

the university courts, it was by no means their only preoccupation, and it was also shared by large numbers of men along other axes of difference besides gender.

Nearly a quarter of cases brought by women concerned allegations of theft or dealing in stolen goods, which accounted for a far greater percentage of insults against women than of insults against men. In relative terms, women were not only twice as likely as men to pursue cases alleging sexual misconduct, therefore, but also twice as likely to enter suits involving accusations of theft or the receipt of stolen goods. In contrast, by far the greatest disparity along gendered lines was the predominance of insults involving either untrustworthiness (in terms of false dealing, lying, and dubious credit) or debased status in complaints brought by men, and their comparative absence in cases brought by women. Relatively, men brought just over five times as many cases as women involving untrustworthiness and just under five times as many regarding debased status. Accordingly, the model of gender divergence in defamation litigation can be revised in three key ways. First, there was considerable overlap between men and women's concerns about sexual honesty, and a degree of divergence between different categories of men over the importance of such issues. Secondly, women's reputations were also vulnerable to accusations of 'economic' dishonesty, but this was much more likely to be linked with theft than with cheating or lying. Thirdly, associations of honesty with social status were far stronger for men than for women, and as a result gender divergence was at its most extreme in relation to issues of untrustworthiness and debased social status rather than sexual morality.

The degree of overlap between men and women's concerns for their sexual reputations is suggested by cases in which the honour of an entire household, or at least both partners in a marriage, was in jeopardy. Husbands clearly felt implicated in accusations of unchastity against their wives, and sometimes initiated legal action on their behalf.[29] Similarly, wives (rather than their husbands) occasionally responded to accusations of cuckoldry, as Agnes Harvie did when she sued John Scorye for calling her husband a 'Cookouldly knave meaning... that the sayd Agnes Harvye was a whore'.[30] Many joint suits naming both husband and wife as plaintiffs were also pursued. The reputation and economy of a whole household could be at risk from imputations of sexual shame, such as when John Wratham stood at the back gate of the Falcon Inn and 'did diswade . . .

[29] e.g. CUL, CUA, *Jeremy Biffen* c. *Richard Cholmley*, Comm.Ct.II.2, fo. 43; *John Tiffen* c. *Ann Williamson*, Comm.Ct.II.1, fos. 35–6. See also Foyster, *Manhood in Early Modern England*, 148–64.

[30] CUL, CUA, *Agnes Harvie* c. *John Scorye*, BA, V.C.Ct.III.4, no. 86. See also DRO, *Bickford* c. *Blackaller*, Chanter 866, unfoliated, 9 Feb. 1635/6.

divers companies of straungers and guests whoe were then readie to enter . . . and to lodge and diet there . . . from going into or lodging at the said Inn', telling them that 'there were none dwelt in that house or Inne but whores Baudes Cheaters and cutpurses meaning John Payne . . . his wife and the rest of his familie and housholde'.[31]

Many men were also solely exercised by accusations of sexual impropriety, which had the potential to cause considerable damage to them as individuals. As the suspected father of his maid's illegitimate child, it was reported that the brewer 'goodman Hardinge . . . ys lyke to loose one of his offices, because he . . . loved yonge fleshe' and that he 'was hardlye thought on for the same matter'. The servant William Benrose was similarly concerned to clear his name from the imputation that he had attempted the chastity of Mary Browne, estimating his injury at £40, and stressing in his allegations that he was 'a Batchelor & one whose preferment lyeth upon his honest life & behaviour & Conversacion'.[32] It is possible that unmarried men like Benrose were more vulnerable to accusations of sexual dishonour, and in different ways, than married men like Harding. This becomes clearer when the categories of defamation pursued by townsmen and university members are compared (Figs. 7–8). While allegations of sexual dishonesty supplied the third largest category of insult against townsmen, they comprised the largest category of insult against university men. Scholars brought actions against imputations of sexual impropriety in almost identical proportions to townsmen's litigation over untrustworthiness. This suggests that university men were disproportionately concerned with their sexual reputations in contrast to townsmen who were principally concerned with slurs on their trustworthiness and economic integrity. In relative terms they entered more than one and a half times as many cases relating to sexual insults as townsmen and only a third fewer than women.

Even if only in the context of the court, issues of chastity were therefore of considerable importance to university men as well as women. Excepting heads of colleges, the university's regulations required all of its members, young and old, to be celibate, and both students and fellows went to considerable lengths to stamp out rumours of sexual activity. The majority of suits brought by university men concerning sexual misconduct were for slander that had come to their attention indirectly, rather than from direct confrontation, whereas townsmen were more likely to

---

[31] CUL, CUA, *John Payne c. John Wratham*, V.C.Ct.III.27, no. 59. See also *Toby Taylor c. John Halliwell*, Comm.Ct.II.12, fo. 142, and *Thomas Reddit c. Alexander Ingland*, p. 160 above.

[32] CUL, CUA, *Robert Harding c. Margaret Millam*, Comm.Ct.II.9, fo. 3^{r-v}; *William Benrose c. Matthew Browne*, V.C.Ct.III.32, no. 117.

sue when sexual insults had been directed to their person. Paternity suits were a particular source of anxiety, and extensive time and money was spent in the university courts pursuing rumours of fornication, especially when it was claimed that it had led to an illegitimate birth. In July 1598, for example, Roger Andrews filed allegations against both Joan Linsey and Margaret Smith for claiming that he had fathered the child recently borne by widow Linsey's daughter. According to Andrews, insinuations were spreading throughout the town, from 'the high way betweene the spittle house of Cambridge and Trumpington foord' to 'the shopp of John Iverie in Sct Botulphes parish', and when his servant and one of his pupils from Pembroke Hall went to collect his laundry from widow Linsey, she asked 'what shall his child have then to lye in' and suggested that 'thou shalt see thy Tutors nowne boye'. Estimating his damages at over £300, this was a tide of scandal Andrews was keen to refute.[33]

The waves of damaged reputation resulting from sexual scandal rippled much further than the individual fellow or scholar concerned. Involving more than liability to support an illegitimate child, paternity suits touched the honour of the university itself. Colleges were well aware that their reputations could be severely tarnished by the illicit sexual activities of their members. As one case alleged, when reporting the adultery of one of their fellowship, certain members of Christ's College complained that 'there is a fame very scandalous concerninge his incontinency, which fame is soe spredd abroade, both in the towne and Colledge that itt redoundeth to the greate disgrace of our Socyetye'.[34] As this case suggests, accusations of improper behaviour were generated from within the university's own ranks as well as from the town. Although some were the result of humorous pranks, such as the libellous verses circulated against the young fellow Elias Travers, which implied that 'he had bene dishonest of his bodie & had dishonestlie & to some lewd & dishonest purpose brought to his bedde some wench or woman', some of the slanderous abuses suffered by university men at the hands of their colleagues were the product of genuine moral policing.[35] In attempting to clear his name from such imputations, a university man therefore also implicitly defended the reputation of both his college and the university in the same way that a married man might have pursued legal action to protect the reputation of his household.

[33] CUL, CUA, *Roger Andrews, MA* c. *Joan Linsey*, V.C.Ct.III.7, no. 170.
[34] CUL, CUA, *Thomas Bainbridge, MA* c. *Daniel Rogers, William Ames* et al., V.C.Ct.III.10, no. 14.
[35] CUL, CUA, *Elias Travers, MA* c. *Thomas Goodwin, BA*, V.C.Ct.III.19, no. 39. Cf. *Theophilus Field, DD* c. *Alexander Reade*, V.C.Ct.III.16, no. 75; V.C.Ct.III.17, no. 2, discussed on pp. 116–18 above.

The university courts were predisposed to protecting students and fellows from such accusations, employing legal formulae designed to submit any townswoman's claim of paternity to rigorous scrutiny.[36] The examination of Joan Yonger, described as 'a Roagish and vagrant person', was indicative of the ordeal a woman could undergo in court if she were suspected of lying. Three weeks after the birth of her illegitimate child Yonger was brought before the vice-chancellor to confess its paternity, which initially she refused to do, before relenting when threatened with a whip. Rather than naming John Gibson of Trinity Hall as its father— whom she had allegedly accused on many former occasions—she instead attributed the child to one Richard Bryse who had recently died. Gibson immediately stepped forward 'intreating Justice' from the vice-chancellor, claiming that 'the sayd Yonger being a very lewd woman had injured & defamed him by layeing the sayd Chylde to him'. At this point, James Tabor, registrar and scribe in the case, took over the narrative and recorded his own intervention:

I . . . did acquaynt the said vicechancellor that of my owne knowledge who had diverse tymes hard her confidently reporte Mr Gibson to be the father & had used many foule and slanderous speeches agaynst him & that she was such an impudent Queane that though she heare before him did denye it yet for feare of punishment yet soe sone as she was out of his sight she would be in the same noate agayne wherefore I desyred him to decree she might be well whipped for her lewd words used agaynst mr Gibson.

This provoked a further confession from Joan, who falling to her knees and weeping told the vice-chancellor that she had been put up to naming Gibson by Elizabeth Kempton, 'who had at least 12 sundry tymes spoken to her to that effect & bidden her to say Gibson was the father [and] he was able to keepe it & would give her monye rather than be discredited . . . for that . . . Mr Gibson had wronged her by puttinge her out her howse & distrayning her houshould stuff, for rent'.[37] The registrar's intervention (and its record in the first person singular) was highly unusual and is illustrative of the university's attempts to distance itself from the issue of illicit sex by working with the assumption that scholars were the vulnerable parties rather than the women alleging relationships with them. Although such an approach was seemingly vindicated by Yonger's confession in this case, it also worked against women's genuine claims to have been burdened with an illegitimate child.

---

[36] e.g. James Tabor's 'Commonplace of Practice in Curia Ecclesiastica', CUL, CUA, Collect.Admin. 38, fo. 43.

[37] CUL, CUA, V.C.Ct.III.14, no. 79.

While university men may have been more vulnerable to false accusations of paternity than their single counterparts in the town, they were also far better protected, and were therefore comparatively well placed to emerge unharmed from allegations of sexual impropriety. This is illustrated by two cases involving accusations of adultery against single men, with vastly different outcomes for each. In 1596, William Coville, a young fellow of Queens' College, and Bridget Edmunds, the wife of a prominent Cambridge citizen and former mayor, were charged with adultery. Although both were given the opportunity by the vice-chancellor to prove their innocence, Bridget Edmunds informed the next hearing that 'she myndes nor neither can she fynde in her harte to be sworne to cleare herselfe in this matter'.[38] She was duly condemned to perform public penance while Coville continued his quest for purgation despite considerable evidence against him, including reports of his own bragging of the affair.[39] Even though Bridget Edmunds had informed the court that 'Mr Covyll hath had carnall knowledge of hir bodye, and hath committed the fact of Adulterye with her'—a confession which provoked her husband to enter a suit of separation—Coville was nonetheless ultimately cleared of the offence, aided by six compurgators drawn (conveniently) from the ranks of the university.[40]

The fate of the apprentice Robert Simpson in the same year could not have been more different. He entered a defamation suit in response to Agnes Shawe's reports that he had committed adultery with her daughter-in-law, but he was unsuccessful in deflecting the accusation. Referred to by Agnes Shawe as 'the longe blacke knave' and her daughter-in-law's 'champion', Robert Simpson was portrayed by many witnesses as being prepared to go to any lengths to court Elizabeth Vepen. He was even reported to have dressed up in women's clothing to gain entrance into her house late one night, with one witness deposing that he had helped Simpson deck a 'womans wast coate & a kertle' for that purpose.[41] Simpson, like Coville, had made no secret of his activities and had boasted of his conquest to one witness claiming that 'he could have yt, when he would'.[42] His defamation suit backfired, however, and instead of winning redress he was himself bound to good behaviour. After disobeying his master by staying out all night he was then imprisoned, and after nine weeks of this punishment he wrote in desperation to the vice-

[38] CUL, CUA, *Office* c. *Bridget Edmunds*, V.C.Ct.I.3, fo. 111.
[39] CUL, CUA, *Office* c. *Bridget Edmunds and William Coville*, V.C.Ct.III.5, no. 69.
[40] CUL, CUA, *Office* c. *William Coville*, V.C.Ct.I.3, fo. 118.
[41] CUL, CUA, 'Examinations concerninge Vipens wife & Simpson', V.C.Ct.III.2, no. 261.
[42] CUL, CUA, V.C.Ct.III.2, no. 262.

chancellor begging for his release, claiming that he had 'loste the favor of my parentes and freindes, whoe by reason of these troubles hathe quite caste me off and forsaken me'.[43]

Despite conclusive evidence against both men, therefore, the university man was acquitted, and went on to pursue a successful career in the Church, while the servant from the town was imprisoned, to his 'greate impoverishemente and discreditt and . . . utter undoeinge'.[44] The consequences for the other parties involved also differed considerably. Bridget Edmunds's husband maintained his respectability, successfully dissociating himself both from his wife, and from Coville's counter-accusation that he had been 'taken with a whoare in the Corne at a midsomer fayre tyme', and was reappointed as Cambridge's mayor a few years later.[45] Bridget Edmunds, on the other hand, was disowned by her husband, and is unlikely ever to have recovered her former status. The impact of the Simpson case on Elizabeth Vepen and her husband John is less clear, although they remained together, and it did not prevent Elizabeth remarrying after John's death. Although it appears that single men could be more vulnerable to accusations of sexual misdemeanours than their married counterparts, men of privileged social status with access to institutional backing such as Coville were better able to avoid the consequences than subordinates like Simpson, whose harsh penalty was provoked as much by his disruptive disregard of hierarchy as by his sexual pursuits.[46]

Concepts of dishonesty were therefore neither monolithic nor rigidly gendered, but contingent, selectively invoked, and selectively applied. Women's reputations were attacked through accusations of theft and other crimes as well as unchastity, and, as will become evident in the next chapter, were also positively constructed in broader terms which encompassed attributes of thrift and industry as well as sexual propriety. Sexual honesty was a potent issue for men as well as women, and although most men were better placed than women to recover their respectability when challenged, those men privileged by social status and marital status were often better placed in this regard than others. Similarly, official constraints on the sexual activity of men varied according to their age and social position, and in some contexts their chastity could become as much of a public concern as that of women.

Several codes of sexual conduct appear to have operated simulta-

[43] CUL, CUA, Robert Simpson to Dr Goade, 11 Aug. 1596, V.C.Ct.III.2, no. 274. See also nos. 272, 275.

[44] Ibid.

[45] CUL, CUA, Letter to the minister of St Botolph's, 28 Aug. 1596, V.C.Ct.III.5, no. 65.

[46] Cf. G. R. Quaife, *Wanton Wenches and Wayward Wives: Peasants and Illicit Sex in Early Seventeenth Century England* (London, 1979), ch. 4.

neously amongst early modern men and women, therefore. In some instances accusations of illicit sex functioned as expressions of anger that bore little relationship to the behaviour of the accused. In others, they served as genuine critiques with potentially grave consequences for the accused, although sometimes they could be brushed off as irrelevant or little more than annoyances. Finally, in contexts far removed from the courtroom, illicit sex was often claimed by men as an accomplishment, rather than a disgrace, as is evident in reports of Coville and Simpson's boastfulness in this regard.[47] Although defamation litigation provides evidence of the potential potency of associations of sexual impropriety with dishonesty for many women and some men, it also attests to their limits and uneven application. Relatively, women were as disproportionately concerned with accusations of theft as they were with sexual slander. The seriousness with which accusations of sexual misconduct were taken by men was contingent upon the extent to which the originator of the slander as well as the plaintiff who sought to refute it had a purchase on respectability, and therefore men's involvement with sexual slander was connected as much with the differences between them as with the gender divide.

SLANDEROUS DEBASEMENT

The most striking point of gender divergence in slander litigation was the predominance of cases brought by men involving insinuations of debased status. These accounted for the largest category of defamation pursued by men (town and gown combined) and involved forms of abuse that were mostly absent from the slanderous exchanges reported by women. Insults such as 'rogue', 'jack', 'knave', 'rascal', and 'boy' had no female equivalent, and the terms 'fugitive', 'fool', 'clown', 'ape', 'dog', and 'slave' did not appear in the verbal abuse reported by Cambridge women. Nearly a third of all men's actions for defamation alleged the devaluation of their status in these and comparable terms, and the predominant goal of such litigation appears to have been the restoration of respectability in terms of comparative social standing, in ways which reiterated many of the attributes of patriarchal manhood detailed by conduct writers. Such concerns were by no means exclusive to Cambridge, and were a common characteristic of men's abusive exchanges reported in many different petty jurisdictions elsewhere in early modern England. They suggest that concepts of honesty and reputation for men were closely associated with

[47] See also above, pp. 120–1.

perceptions of the social order in ways which not only endorsed the patriarchal model of manhood but also harnessed it to the social demarcation of the 'better sort'.

Terms such as 'ape', 'beast', and 'dog' suggested a total absence of the reason expected of manhood by deploying the same extreme terms of deviation as conduct writers who equated unmanliness with beastliness. To call a man a 'fool' insinuated incompetence and questioned his claims to authority. The designation of a London cooper as a knave and a 'dwarfe' by one of his fellow guild members (subsequently fined 12*d*.) presumably achieved the same effect.[48] The term 'clown' appears to have implied an absence of sophistication, as is suggested by a dictionary definition of 'Rusticitie' as 'Rudenesse: clownish behaviour'.[49] Carrying an even greater sting was the label 'boy' which implied that a man had no claim to competence or authority in the first place. So, in an injurious comparison of their status, the Cambridge barber Edward Wardall told Thomas Crawforthe that he 'was an honest man & did kepe howse, when as he Crawforthe was but a scalde boye'. Similarly provoked, two Cambridge saddlers 'fell togither by the eares' because one had scoffed at the other as he was closing his shop, saying, 'what Boykin: art thou shuttinge upp thy windows', to whom he responded by asking him 'whoe he called boy' before retaliating with blows.[50] Such insults reiterated the importance of age and household status in conferring manhood along patriarchal lines.

Degrading subordination was, however, primarily inferred through references to a man's social position. The insult 'jack', for example, was a term of condescension commonly addressed to servingmen or labourers. To call a man a 'slave' implied that he was perpetually bound to serve another man, without any shred of autonomy, and permanently excluded from the citizenship of the commonwealth enjoyed by freemen. According to Sir Thomas Smith, the servility of such bondsmen was no less than 'beastlike'.[51] The label slave was often associated with other terms of abject status, such as when William Bateman of Tutbury (Staffordshire) reviled Richard Greaves as a 'Roge, Rascall, and beggerlye slave'.[52] The term 'rascal', often prefaced by the adjective 'base', insinu-

---

[48] GL, Coopers' Company, Court Minutes, 1567–96, MS 5602/1, 19 Sept. 1588.

[49] John Bullokar, *An English Expositor: Teaching the Interpretation of the Hardest Words Used in our Language* (London, 1616), sig. N4.

[50] CUL, CUA, *Thomas Crawforthe c. Edward Wardall*, Comm.Ct.II.2, fo. 52; *Mungye Withers c. Edward Kinge*, V.C.Ct.I.5, fo. 146ᵛ. See also Paul Griffiths, *Youth and Authority: Formative Experiences in England, 1560–1640* (Oxford, 1996), 101–3.

[51] Sir Thomas Smith, *De Republica Anglorum*, ed. Mary Dewar (Cambridge, 1982), 138.

[52] *The Staffordshire Quarter Sessions Rolls*, iv: *1598–1602*, ed. S. A. H. Burne (Kendal, 1935), 119.

ated low birth and a suspect character, and the labels 'runagate' or 'fugitive' involved similar deprecation. One Cambridge witness described the potential impact of such abuse when he recounted his warning to the tailor Thomas Tillett on hearing him call Thomas Wickliffe (a yeoman) a fugitive:

> theyse be hard words, thowe doest him great wronge, his credit in Cambridge ys worthe CC^{li} especiallye he beinge put in that trust by mr Gravener [his employer] as he ys . . . and yf yt were knowne that he were reported & taken for a fugitive or soe baselye accompted of: mr Gravener would not put him in suche trust, nor soe well esteeme of him: as nowe he dothe.[53]

Such insults denied men's claims to the autonomy and political maturity associated with adulthood, the agency afforded by credit, and the merits of respectable social standing. In other words, they stripped men of many of the attributes of patriarchal manhood.

The most common terms of abuse employed against men—'knave' and 'rogue'—held similarly debasing connotations. The term 'knave' originated as a mock title in opposition to 'knight' to describe menial servants. 'Rogue' possibly evolved from *roger*, a medieval term applied to a begging vagabond pretending to be a poor scholar. Over the sixteenth and seventeenth centuries the term 'rogue' accrued particularly potent associations with rootlessness and lawlessness as numbers of vagrants rapidly increased and the able-bodied, masterless poor became criminalized.[54] Early modern associations of these terms with deviance, low status, and dishonesty were clear in one Cambridge defendant's definition: 'these words Rogue, knave, & base knave doe signifie a man of dishonest lyfe & conversacion & one that is a vagabonde'.[55] Sometimes the two insults were combined, as when Augustine King called his minister a 'roguish knave'.[56] That the term 'knave' was firmly linked to concepts of honesty was evident in John Hammons's abuse of a Steyning (Sussex) churchwarden when he declared he was a 'knave and . . . no honest man'.[57] In such instances, the 'honesty' being disputed was not only related to behaviour

---

[53] CUL, CUA, *Thomas Wickliffe* c. *Thomas Tillett*, Comm.Ct.II.10, fo. 13.

[54] A. L. Beier, *Masterless Men: The Vagrancy Problem in England 1560–1640* (London, 1985); Paul Griffiths, 'Masterless Young People in Norwich, 1560–1645', in Paul Griffiths, Adam Fox, and Steve Hindle (eds.), *The Experience of Authority in Early Modern England* (Basingstoke, 1996). See also Paul Slack, *Poverty and Policy in Tudor and Stuart England* (London, 1988); Steve Hindle, *The State and Social Change in Early Modern England, c.1550–1640* (Basingstoke, 2000), ch. 6.

[55] CUL, CUA, *Robert Grime* c. *Anne Semar*, V.C.Ct.II.25, fo. 84^v.

[56] Louis A. Knafla, *Kent at Law 1602: The County Jurisdiction: Assizes and Sessions of the Peace* (London, 1994), 167–8.

[57] *Churchwarden's Presentments (17th Century). Part 1. Archdeaconry of Chichester*, ed. Hilda Johnstone, Sussex Record Society 49 (Lewes, 1948), 10.

but also to social pretension. The many other terms that were coupled with 'knave' are further indications of the types of dishonesty with which this insult—and by implication menial status—was linked. An excessive drinker might be dubbed an 'alehouse knave' or 'drunken knave' and illicit sex was condemned as the act of a 'base, whoremasterly knave'.[58] The frequent use of terms such as 'crafty knave', 'false knave', 'perjured knave', and 'forsworn knave' suggest that false dealing, theft, and deceit were also the expected attributes of this class of men.[59] So Miles Chambers was 'much troubled' when his master was called a knave and a cheater and 'did thinke that his friends had not placed [him] as a servant unto an honest man'.[60] When the London clothworker Edward Fleete called one of the company's assistants a 'Coseninge knave, and a pocky knave . . . and a Cutt throte knave' he added that he was 'one unmeete to live in a comon wealth'.[61] Knaves and rogues were outcasts and marginals, excluded access to the 'honesty' associated with the civic arena and, in these instances, with patriarchal manhood. Like the prescriptive codes of conduct literature, the language of insult denied the existence of any alternative sources of manhood associated with such behaviour.

The manner in which insults were exchanged is just as revealing as the terms of abuse themselves, often involving comparisons of status which directly equated men's honesty with their social standing. Debasing insults, or 'slightings', have been described as 'a kind of verbal theft . . . that enriched their speaker by stealing the reputation of their target', involving both the denial of reputation and the inversion of expected chains of deference.[62] The resolution of such disputes was therefore often concerned with restoring the social order as well as amicable relations between men. This was evident in a case between two London pewterers

---

[58] *Books of Examinations and Depositions, 1570–1594*, ed. G. H. Hamilton, Southampton Record Society 16 (Southampton, 1914), 8; NRO, *Paman* c. *Mathewe Gooch*, DN/DEP/32, fo. 85ᵛ; *Richardson* c. *Harman*, DN/DEP/41, fo. 122. See also *The Assembly Books of Southampton*, i: *1602–08*, ed. J. W. Horrocks, Southampton Record Society 19 (Southampton, 1917), 75, 77; WSRO, *Thomas Lulham* c. *Mr William Hilman*, EpII/5/6, fo. 43ᵛ; *Gregory Hills* c. *Mr Thomas Pearse*, EpII/5/6, fo. 94ᵛ; CUL, CUA, *Mary Kiswicke* c. *Robert Backhouse*, Comm.Ct.II.16, fo. 52ᵛ.

[59] e.g. NRO, *Maysters* c. *John Raven*, DN/DEP/32, fo. 70; GL, Pewterers' Company, Court Minutes, 1561–89, MS 7090/2, fo. 62ᵛ; CUL, CUA, *John Alcocke* c. *John Dawson*, Comm.Ct.II.6, fo. 174ᵛ; *Depositions and Other Ecclesiastical Proceedings from the Courts of Durham, Extending from 1311 to the Reign of Elizabeth*, Publications of the Surtees Society 21 (London, 1845), 88; Clothworkers' Hall, London, Court Orders 1558–81, fo. 245.

[60] CUL, CUA, *Thomas Russell* c. *Christopher Grey*, V.C.Ct.II.36, fo. 83.

[61] Clothworkers' Hall, London, Court Orders 1558–1581, fo. 127ᵛ. See also *Depositions from the Courts of Durham*, 106.

[62] Jane Kamensky, 'Talk Like a Man: Speech, Power, and Masculinity in Early New England', *Gender and History*, 8 (1996), 32.

of 1565. After an initial complaint by John Bowlting against Thomas Curtes 'for striking hym mysorderly in the open streate', Thomas Curtes reported that Bowlting had 'called hym openly in the Streate Prating Jack and lying Jack and did strike him to his dishonestie' and requested the master and wardens 'to take order therin'. Although both men were fined for their misdeeds, the dispute escalated as further insults were exchanged between them in open court, for which they were again fined. In addition, Bowlting insulted Thomas Curtes's brother (Mr William Curtes) who was standing for election as the company's master, claiming that he was biased in the case and that he misruled company business. The dispute ended only when Bowlting apologized to William Curtes and agreed 'from hensforth [to] take the saide Mr Curtes for his better'.[63] A dispute between two members of Christ's College, Cambridge, was also an attempt to restore deference, with one witness endorsing the plaintiff's estimate of his injury at £120 by claiming that, 'in regard of the disparitie of the persons of mr Rodgers and Mr Catlyn he [Rogers] hath reasons ... soe to esteme his said Injury'.[64] In this case, according to several witnesses, Catlyn's offence lay not only in comparing Rogers to a dog (and an oversexed one at that) but also in his utter disregard of Rogers's superior position as elder, fellow, and minister. The consequent litigation served to reassert his status as a man of worth, and Catlyn's as his inferior.

Many slanderous exchanges, like violent encounters, included variations on the theme of 'I'm as good a man as you'.[65] In Leicester in 1595, one Thomas Ward was bound over for saying to Mr Belgrave, 'setting your birth aside, I am as good as you'.[66] Similarly, in the course of an altercation between the Cambridge cordwainer Edward Yate and a fellow of King's College, Yate declared he was 'as good a man and as reverent a man as he the sayd Arthure Johnson', also calling him a 'pawltry fellowe' and tugging off his gown 'in very unsemely and disorderly manner'.[67] Such exchanges were frequently used to counteract assertions of authority. In response to Griffin Powell's attempt to dictate the price of salmon in his capacity as clerk of the market, John Pearse objected, 'what are you? peradventure I am as good a man as your selfe' and then 'put offe his hatt turning himselfe about, and holding uppe one of his legges in a scornefull manner, saieing nowe I knowe my dutie, and put his hatt one againe'. Another witness in the case claimed 'it hadde bin fitter for John

---

[63] GL, Pewterers' Company, Court Minutes, MS 7090/2, fos. 35, 37^v, 38^v–39^v.
[64] CUL, CUA, *Daniel Rogers, MA* c. *Francis Catlyn, MA*, V.C.Ct.II.8, fo. 25.
[65] See p. 143 above.
[66] *Records of the Borough of Leicester. Being a Series of Extracts from the Archives of the Corporation of Leicester*, iii: *1509–1603*, ed. Mary Bateson (Cambridge, 1905), 328.
[67] CUL, CUA, *Arthur Johnson, MA* c. *Edward Yate*, V.C.Ct.III.12, no. 98.

Pearse to have given better speechese then he did to mr Powell being an officer'.[68] A Surrey justice of the peace entered an action in the Court of Common Pleas when slandered as 'a knave and a villein' and in response to the claim that 'as honest a man as he ... was carried to Tyburn to be hanged'. He was awarded £20 in costs and damages.[69] The impact of this kind of insult depended on the degree to which such claims contravened hierarchies of status and authority. Thus when Robert Willows called the butcher Robert Smith a 'base knave & scurvie knave', Smith responded that Willows 'was a knave, & base bredd knave, in regarde of the birth of this Respondent, soe to miscall this Respondent & abuse him'.[70]

Men cited other indicators besides direct references to birth and authority in comparisons of their status, which could involve complex reckonings. Thus, in response to the question whether the gentleman John Carowe was 'as good a man at the least in Common estimacion within this town of Cambridg' as his opponent, one witness replied that 'he thinckethe the same Carowe to be the richer man, but Prance to be the better borne, better broughte upp & the wiser man of them twayne'.[71] Some assessments were made primarily on the basis of means. An exchange between Andrew Goodwin, a Cambridge innholder, and James Atkinson, acting as constable, culminated as Atkinson declared he 'was as honest a man as him Goodwin', to which Goodwin replied that he was as honest as Atkinson. Offended by Goodwin's objection that he was being over-officious in his duties as constable, Atkinson reiterated, 'I am honester then thou for I never lost my hare as thou didst'—a remark which implied that Goodwin's baldness was a result of excessive lewdness. The insults quickly turned to issues besides sexual propriety, however, when Atkinson insinuated Goodwin's relative poverty with the comment, 'I knowe the gather upp old shoes about the Colledge in a basket.' Goodwin replied in kind, claiming that Atkinson had many times fallen upon his charity: 'I gave the Breade and beere out of the Colledge gate.'[72] Both men sought to diminish the other and assert their relative superiority by inferring each other's dependence and limited means.

[68] Bodl., OUA, *Griffin Powell* c. *John Pearse*, Hyp/B/4, fo. 144ʳ⁻ᵛ. See also *Office* c. *Richard Paineter and John Smith*, in which it was declared that the 'reprochfull and unsemelie wordes' spoken by the bailiff Paineter were 'not fitt to be spoken by a better man then mr Paineter to ... mr doctor Kinge being vicechauncellar', Hyp/B/4, fo. 125.

[69] *Harris* v. *Scott*, *Select Cases on Defamation to 1600*, ed. R. H. Helmholz, Selden Society 101 (London, 1985), 78.

[70] CUL, CUA, *Robert Willows* c. *Robert Smith*, V.C.Ct.II.25, fo. 57.

[71] CUL, CUA, *Robert Prance, MA* c. *John Carowe*, V.C.Ct.III.4, no. 46a; V.C.Ct.II.1, fo. 23. The deponent making this assessment was John Slegge, also a gentleman.

[72] CUL, CUA, *Andrew Goodwin* c. *James Atkinson and Richard Griffin*, V.C.Ct.II.8, fos. 45ᵛ–47. See also V.C.Ct.III.10, no. 59.

Conducted along similar lines was a dispute between the bailiff Francis Clarke and the constable Hugh Jones over their comparative authority to regulate the Cambridge market. Having been called a 'busye fellowe', Jones 'was very sawsye in speeches' to Clarke, replying that he was 'as good a man as he mr Clarcke was', further bidding Clarke to 'goe hange him selfe'. According to the gentleman Francis Slegge who witnessed the event, Jones continued to disparage Clarke as follows:

> Jones said ... that Mr Clarcke was but an In mate, & dwellt in mr Chaces kitchen & sytts uppon ii*d* a yere, & will come & comptroll, And that then this deponent sayd to Jones that mr Clarcke sat at as greate a rent as he Jones did, and that then Jones sayd thus: viz: noe not by ii*d* a yere.

In this instance Clarke and Jones, and their witnesses, disputed their relative position as men using rents and householding status as a gauge, referring to apparently well-known local knowledge to inform their assessment of each other's social status.[73] That rents could be an important marker of respectability is suggested by their use to determine eligibility for office, as in Mytton (Yorkshire) where 'none shall be churchwarden but that payeth above a mark rent'.[74] Insults such as these reiterated patriarchal imperatives that linked manhood with self-sufficient mastery, and implied that they were the preserve of the better sort.

Occupation and spending power were also cited as indicators of position in such disputes, in ways which similarly emphasized associations of manhood with economic autonomy. Needing a servant for his kitchen, Edward Wenham (a cook) asked John Stooks if he would serve Wenham for 20*s.* a year, offering an initial payment of 12*d.* in earnest. Stooks was offended by the suggestion, and told Wenham that he kept 'as good a man to wash my dishes as you ... are', implying that menial status was more fitting for Wenham than himself. Stooks compounded the insult by throwing the money back at Wenham, saying 'have thy 12*d* for it is to buy thy schollers Commons', which (according to another deponent) implied to Wenham's discredit that 'the 12*d* was none of his owne'. In other words, it was suggested that Wenham did not wield any of his own purchasing power, but was merely a proxy for scholars. With his worth

---

[73] CUL, CUA, *Mr Clarke* c. *Hugh Jones*, V.C.Ct.III.5, no. 12.

[74] Quoted in J. S. Craig, 'Co-operation and Initiatives: Elizabethan Churchwardens and the Parish Accounts of Mildenhall', *Social History*, 18 (1993), 364. For criteria determining patterns of office-holding and pew allocation, see also Nick Alldridge, 'Loyalty and Identity in Chester Parishes 1540–1640', in S. J. Wright (ed.), *Parish, Church and People: Local Studies in Lay Religion, 1350–1750* (London, 1988), 94–7, 103–8, and Kevin B. Dillow, 'The Social and Ecclesiastical Significance of Church Seating Arrangements and Pew Disputes, 1500–1740', D.Phil. thesis (Oxford, 1990), chs. 4–5.

thus in question, Wenham retaliated in kind, saying, 'I shall have 12*d* in my purse to spende when such an one as you . . . will hange your selfe for 3*d*.' Another witness considered Wenham's anger to have been justified, since as he put it, 'Wenham hath ben allwayes accompted a man of better state place & Condicion in Cambridge then he Stooks.'[75] These men competed for credit in terms of spending power and its associations of independence and self-sufficient mastery. Stooks adamantly rejected a deferential role, asserting instead superior status over Wenham by claiming greater worth in terms of the resources available to him and his own capacity as a master over subordinates.

The inference of lowly occupational status was a potent way of abusing another man's authority. The Merchant Taylor Edward Aley was imprisoned for insulting the Company's warden in these terms, claiming that he was 'but a shifter, and lived only by making of shifts, and . . . was not worth a grote'.[76] Similarly, George Horsley, objecting to his appearance in the sheriffs' court in York, insolently declared 'that my lord mayor, his bredren and shyrryffs were more mete to dryve pyggs to the feyld than to be Justics of Peace', and a Devonshire vicar was likewise abused by one of his parishioners who declared, 'thou art worthye to kepe a stable for horses rather then to be of the minstery'.[77] Just as patriarchal codes of manhood denied the existence of alternative sources of male prowess, so such insults derived their impact from refusing to acknowledge the superiority of men in positions of authority, who were instead likened to journeymen, agricultural labourers, and stable boys.

Clothing also featured as an index of social standing in direct comparisons of status, often by subordinate men who sought to subvert the authority of their superiors. The apprentice Robert Simpson responded to Agnes Shawe's accusation that he did 'beshite the windowe' and ruin his hose (when escaping from her daughter-in-law's chamber after an adulterous liaison), with the retort, 'I weare as good hoase as thye husband doethe.'[78] The offence here stemmed from Simpson's blatant disregard of the disparity between himself and John Shawe, a prominent Cambridge citizen at least twice his age. Similarly insulting were refusals to accept the authority designated by a livery. Besides calling the servant John Symcocke a drunken rascal and a 'scurvy jack', Josiah Archer also

---

[75] CUL, CUA, *John Stooks* c. *Edward Wenham*, Comm.Ct.II.18, fos. 38ᵛ–42ᵛ.
[76] Charles Mathew Clode, *Memorials of the Guild of Merchant Taylors of the Fraternity of St John the Baptist* (London, 1875), 213.
[77] Quoted in D. M. Palliser, 'Civic Mentality and the Environment in Tudor York', in Jonathan Barry (ed.), *The Tudor and Stuart Town: A Reader in English Urban History 1530–1688* (Harlow, 1990), 228; DRO, *Hamish* c. *Saunders*, Chanter 864, fo. 18.
[78] CUL, CUA, *Robert Simpson* c. *Agnes Shawe*, Comm.Ct.II.6, fo. 93ᵛ.

goaded, 'for all thy sylver buttons thy cloathes on thy backe ar non of thy owne'. And when William Spicer (lawyer, and fellow of Trinity Hall) claimed that 'he did ware a better cloth' than John Thriplow (who was sporting the livery of the Lord Chamberlain) Thriplow retaliated by calling Spicer a 'base slave, A Jacke an apes and a Jacke' who had forsworn himself 'by twentye times'. In justifying his comments, Thriplow complained he had been provoked by Spicer's assertion that he 'did neither care for [Thriplow] nor his Lorde'.[79]

Perhaps the most blatant denial of status and authority were the related challenges 'a turd in your teeth' and 'kiss my arse'—terms of abuse which were sometimes cited by complainants as the sole provocation for litigation. So the Cambridge Master of Arts Francis Dighton sued his college butler for his remarks to Dighton's servant about payment for some beer. According to Dighton's allegations, Francis Saville had said 'yf thy master will not pay for it a turde in his teeth . . . let him kisse mine arse, & repeated those words a turd in his teeth twise or thrise'. Dighton estimated his injury at 1,000 marks (£666) and went to considerable lengths to pursue Saville in court in order to restore their hierarchical relationship which had been flagrantly inverted to its most extreme opposite.[80] Petty officials seem to have been frequently regaled with such degrading suggestions. When John Browning of York bade the constable William Huton to 'kisse his tale', Huton replied that 'none wold bid him kiss his tale but a knave'. The curate of Ford (Sussex) complained that one of his churchwardens 'required me to put my nose in his tayle and in a maydes bum standing by'. Similarly demeaning was Roger Eccleston's resistance to the Norwich clerk of the market, 'Callinge him knave & sayinge a turd in your teeth'.[81] General abuse in these terms was also sometimes levelled against women. For example, as the Cambridge draper Barnaby Claydon was beating a boy who had hit his dog, he responded to Elizabeth Parris's objections by saying, 'if it offend you I will hould up . . . the doggs tayle whylst you kisse his arse'. Similarly John Humbletoft told Elizabeth

[79] CUL, CUA, *John Symcocke* c. *Josiah Archer*, V.C.Ct.III.12, no. 101; *William Spicer, LLB* c. *John Thriplow*, V.C.Ct.III.19, nos. 67, 81.

[80] CUL, CUA, *Francis Dighton* c. *Francis Saville*, V.C.Ct.III.10, no. 38. See also nos. 41–2, 93, and V.C.Ct.II.8, fos. 4ᵛ, 31, 34, 38. For a similar case, see *John Cragge, MA* c. *John Cronfoot*, V.C.Ct.III.3, no. 24.

[81] *York Civic Records*, vol. ix, ed. Deborah Sutton, Yorkshire Archaeological Society 138 (York, 1978), 29; *Churchwarden's Presentments*, 6; *Minutes of the Norwich Court of Mayoralty 1632–1635*, ed. William L. Sachse, Norfolk Record Society 36 (Norwich, 1967), 99. See also *The Case Book of Sir Francis Ashley J.P., Recorder of Dorchester, 1614–1635*, ed. J. H. Bettey, Dorset Record Society 7 (Dorchester, 1981), 87; *Depositions from the Courts of Durham*, 94; F. G. Emmison, *Elizabethan Life: Morals and the Church Courts* (Chelmsford, 1973), 63; Christopher Marsh, 'Sacred Space in England, 1560–1640: The View from the Pew', *Journal of Ecclesiastical History*, 53 (2002), 305.

Newman to 'come kisse my arse & goe shyte thou art good for nothinge els'.[82] By breaking taboos surrounding human excrement, and suggesting the inversion of rituals of neighbourly exchange, as well as disregarding the hierarchies that were supposed to operate between men, such insults were utterly debasing.[83]

In her survey of slander litigation in the Bishop of London's consistory, Laura Gowing noted that men's honesty 'seems to lack the potential of competition that is so fruitful a ground for women's insults'.[84] However, as is evident from cases from other jurisdictions, men did not simply gauge their honesty competitively, but their entire social standing. This was carried out in almost entirely gender-specific ways, with reference to birth, means, occupation, and authority. The terms in which men disputed each other's honesty, and by implication their social position, thus paid considerable lip-service to the patriarchal attributes of householding status, financial autonomy, plain dealing, and political participation (particularly in terms of office-holding). They also coincided with the self-styling of the 'better sort' or the 'able and sufficient men' of early modern England.[85] That 'knave', 'jack', 'rogue', 'slave', 'rascal', 'fugitive', and 'boy' held such potent meanings as insults reinforced expectations that youths and lower-ranking men were not to be trusted. Slanderous debasement in these terms therefore achieved its impact either by denying men's claims to patriarchal dividends or by positing competing conceptions of the social scale in ways which disregarded hierarchies of patriarchal privilege. In disputes between men of different rank, the abuse lay in attempts to level social distinctions or to invert the social order. In cases between men of comparative status, litigation was often provoked by the attempts of one party to claim hierarchical precedence over the other. The mediation of a superior authority was often necessary to resolve such competing claims, and to repair the social order as well as social harmony, and to reiterate its patriarchal basis, both in terms of the subordination of women and of certain men.

---

[82] CUL, CUA, *Barnaby Claydon* c. *Elizabeth Parris*, Comm.Ct.II.10, fo. 69; *Thomas and Elizabeth Newman* c. *John Humbletoft*, V.C.Ct.III.28, no. 21.

[83] Edmund Leach, 'Anthropological Aspects of Language: Animal Categories and Verbal Abuse', in Eric H. Lenneberg (ed.), *New Directions in the Study of Language* (Cambridge, Mass., 1964).

[84] Gowing, *Domestic Dangers*, 77.

[85] Keith Wrightson, 'Estates, Degrees and Sorts: Changing Perceptions of Society in Tudor and Stuart England', in Penelope J. Corfield (ed.), *Language, History and Class* (Oxford, 1991), 44–8; id., ' "Sorts of People" in Tudor and Stuart England', in Jonathan Barry and Christopher Brooks (eds.), *The Middling Sort of People: Culture, Society and Politics in England, 1550–1800* (Basingstoke, 1994); H. R. French, 'Social Status, Localism and the "Middle Sort of People" in England 1620–1750', *Past and Present*, 166 (2000).

That men seem to have been constantly competing for status is suggestive both of the fragility of conceptions of the social scale and of individual men's claims to position in early modern England, and of the competition between different meanings of manhood. Honesty and reputation in patriarchal terms appear to have been hard won and easily lost by early modern men, many of whom clung to the cusp of respectability in a period of acute economic fluctuation and instability.[86] The boundaries between honesty and dishonesty were more blurred than those claiming respectability would have liked, which is perhaps why slanderous debasement was taken so seriously.[87] What is also clear is the particular resonance of slander in these terms for men rather than women. The insults voiced by men and women followed a clearly gendered pattern. While women were active in policing moral hierarchies, men appear to have borne primary responsibility for the policing of social hierarchies, albeit sometimes expressed in moral terms, and in ways which implicated competing codes of manhood. In the rare instances when women did voice critiques of each other in social terms, it was usually with reference to the status of their fathers or husbands, such as when Mary Robbes said 'she was as good a woman as Mrs. Morgan, and that the said Mrs. Morgan was but a pedler's daughter, and that her father went about with a footepack', or when Rachel Humbletoft told Elizabeth Newman that her husband was 'but a base buttler [who] lives by the baskett & the tapp to[o]'.[88] According to R. E. Pahl, by the nineteenth century, women (through their imposition of standards of domestic honour) had became 'the most skilled guardians and gatekeepers of social status hierarchies'.[89] In the early modern period it appears that this was a role primarily performed by men, through the adoption of competitive defences of their position in terms of birth, rank, age, means, occupation, authority, character, and patriarchal prestige.

---

[86] See, e.g., Michael Mascuch, 'Social Mobility and Middling Self-Identity: The Ethos of British Autobiographers, 1600–1750', *Social History*, 20 (1995); Craig Muldrew, *The Economy of Obligation: The Culture of Credit and Social Relations in Early Modern England* (Basingstoke, 1998), ch. 9.

[87] Paul Griffiths, 'Overlapping Circles: Imagining Criminal Communities in London, 1545–1645', in Alexandra Shepard and Phil Withington (eds.), *Communities in Early Modern England: Networks, Place, Rhetoric* (Manchester, 2000). See also Joseph P. Ward, *Metropolitan Communities: Trade Guilds, Identity, and Change in Early Modern London* (Stanford, Calif., 1997), ch. 3.

[88] *Quarter Sessions Records for the County of Somerset*, i: *1607–1625*, ed. E. H. Bates, Somerset Record Society 28 (London, 1907), 69–70; CUL, CUA, *Thomas Newman* c. *Rachel Humbletoft*, V.C.Ct.II.22, fo. 195.

[89] R. E. Pahl, *Divisions of Labour* (Oxford, 1984), 112.

While concepts of honesty and reputation were more multifaceted than suggested by the defamation litigation heard in the church courts, with a greater element of gender convergence than has often been allowed, they were nonetheless also clearly gender related. The most striking difference between the insults reported by men and women is the relative frequency and potency of socially degrading abuse against men. Such slightings suggest that reputation for men was far more directly linked to their social and patriarchal standing, whereas for women it was more likely to be a product of their marital and moral status (primarily undermined through accusations of unchastity and theft). The terms and manner of slanderous debasement are indicative of the competitive edge to male interaction and the fragility of the resource for which they competed, which, in these instances, was the respectability associated with patriarchal position. Defamation litigation also suggests that such terms were not universally respected or acknowledged by early modern men and women. The courtroom offered a forum where men could refute abuse and reassert claims to status in terms of rank, authority, autonomy, sufficiency, and trustworthiness in bids to rectify, if not rewrite, the social order and to reassert hierarchies of manhood. As the previous chapter has clearly shown, however, litigation was not the sole means of redress, and many men chose the violent gestures of rebuke instead of, and sometimes as well as, a defamation suit. Violence as well as litigation could put a man in his place, in ways which also often functioned to assert alternative codes of male prowess.

Litigation was therefore only one of at least two possible responses to allegations of dishonesty, and seems to have been favoured by men seeking restoration of their status in patriarchal terms. A third response was to be unmoved by such insults, especially if the evaluative scheme they suggested was irrelevant, either owing to the context the victim of abuse was in, or to the existence of alternative strategies of assessment. So, for example, some defendants and witnesses claimed that the insults cited in court had been spoken 'in merryment', which suggests that terms of abuse could sometimes feature in friendly exchange as well as hostile disputes.[90] Other men did not have the resources to dispute their reputation in court, even if they had encountered insults that they deemed damaging; defamation litigation itself was therefore primarily a resource for the respectable. Although poorer plaintiffs whose goods were valued at below 40*s.* could request to be admitted as a litigant *in forma pauperis*,

---

[90] DRO, *Bancks* c. *Mooreton*, Chanter 866, unfoliated, 10 Apr. 1635. See also, e.g., CUL, CUA, *James Borowes* c. *William Meys*, Comm.Ct.II.2, fo. 79; EDR, *John Eaton* c. *John Buskyn*, D/2/11, fos. 29ᵛ, 30ᵛ.

which effectively waived their court fees, this occurred only very occasionally. In a series of sample years from the act books of the university courts only one such instance occurred in a case of injury, in which the plaintiff was more concerned with the assault that had left him unable 'to follow his daylie labour', than with the verbal abuse that had accompanied it.[91] The language of insult therefore only provides selective and indirect evidence of concepts of honesty, and the degree to which they were generally internalized or invoked in other contexts is unclear. It is therefore necessary to investigate, as far as it is possible, the extent to which positive assertions of credit, as opposed to negative, context-related forms of discredit, coincided with the patriarchal tenets of reputation, honesty, and status as disputed in slander litigation.

[91] CUL, CUA, *William Mortimer* c. *Edmund Wenham*, V.C.Ct.I.9, fo. 135ᵛ.

7
Credit, Provision, and Worth

In 1591, John Stodderd, a Cambridge schoolmaster, was discredited as a witness in the following terms as:

suche a person as neyther had nor hath any care to provide for himself or his wiffe and familye in suche sorte and in such manner as every honest person hath and doth[,] but carelessely and negligentlye neglectinge his function and vocation doth unthriftelye haunt alehouses and tipplinge houses and other unseemely and unhonest places spendinge unthriftely such commoditye as he getteth, growinge and runninge into other mens debte and daunger.[1]

According to this assessment, it was a man's 'function and vocation' to maintain his family. Conversely, a man who diverted resources from the household economy was labelled as dishonest, negligent, and unseemly. Such neglect was dangerous, not only for the man's wife and family but also for other men whose credit might also be jeopardized by such unthriftiness.

That householders and married men should be providers was as important a tenet of patriarchal ideology as the expectation of chastity in women. As we have seen, according to Dod and Cleaver the husband's duty was 'to get money and provision' through 'entermedling' with other men, while the wife was to 'keepe the house', to be 'solitary and withdrawne', and above all to safeguard her honour.[2] According to Susan Amussen, the association of female honour and reputation with chastity was probably the least contested principle of social evaluation in early modern England.[3] The links between early modern concepts of manhood and provision have, on the other hand, received far less scrutiny by historians than the association of femininity with chastity, even though they were as central to the normative gender roles prescribed by early

---

[1] CUL, CUA, *William Nicholson* c. *George Newman*, V.C.Ct.III.2, no. 95.

[2] John Dod and Robert Cleaver, *A Godly Form of Householde Government: For the Ordering of Private Families* (London, 1612), 168. See also above, pp. 76–7.

[3] Susan Dwyer Amussen, 'The Gendering of Popular Culture in Early Modern England', in Tim Harris (ed.), *Popular Culture in England, c.1500–1850* (Basingstoke, 1995). Although cf. G. R. Quaife, *Wanton Wenches and Wayward Wives: Peasants and Illicit Sex in Early Seventeenth Century England* (London, 1979), ch. 7.

modern moralists. The defamation litigation pursued by men indirectly linked notions of male credit and respectability to patriarchal attributes of self-sufficiency, plain dealing, trustworthiness, and the provision and command of varied resources. This chapter investigates the ways in which credit was positively constructed and claimed by men and women during the course of routine social practice, and the degree to which this diverged from patriarchal prescriptions for male provision and primacy in the world of exchange.

There is no doubt that patriarchal notions of manhood in terms of self-sufficient mastery exerted a powerful influence over contemporary estimates of men's status in the streets, market places, workshops, and households of early modern England. Specific meanings of manhood were attached to men's economic agency, echoing aspects of the conduct literature's patriarchal vision of order and corroborating certain character traits of the ideal-type householder. The language of social description clearly linked male status to patriarchal notions of credit and worth in similar terms to slander disputes. However, the practical realities of men and women's strategies for survival belied, or at least did not always live up to, the expectations suggested by normative evaluative schemes. First, most wives and many children were vital contributors to the family economy, and were sometimes the principal and occasionally the sole providers in their households. While this was often the necessary outcome of an unstable economy of makeshifts, many married women appear not only to have performed the role of provision, but also to have derived credit from their labour and commercial activities in some of the same terms as men. Secondly, many men were excluded from claiming credit in these terms, either because of their inability to provision the households they headed or on account of their age and marital status which excluded them from householding altogether.

The most difficult question raised by such evidence concerns the degree to which such deviations from the patriarchal model of male provision were judged according to this evaluative scheme by the social actors themselves. The varied ways in which men and women eked a living are suggestive of alternative household strategies which gave short shrift to patriarchal norms. Although such strategies were criticized in patriarchal terms, particularly by those of the 'better' sort, they were most likely a product of alternative evaluative schemes as well as of necessity. At the very least, they suggest that patriarchal ideals were often an irrelevance for many men and women, or at most of only secondary importance to the challenges of subsistence. Credit and the honesty associated with it were therefore class-related as well as gender-related concepts. While poorer men who displayed the attributes of thrift and 'painful' industry were designated honest, they had little purchase on the credit associated with worth and the command of resources. The unrelenting drudgery of honest hardship, particularly considering its derisory rewards, appears to have seemed emasculating rather than empowering to the many men in early modern England who were denied access to the more exclusive attributes of honesty such as worth, esteem, and authority. Increasing numbers therefore sought status in other ways, and according to contrary evaluative systems. The potency of such alternatives is difficult to assess, particularly as they can only be glimpsed through disciplinary records which were themselves the product of a patriarchal critique. It nonetheless seems that alternative sources of male status as well as a growing exclusivity to concepts of honesty informed divergent meanings of manhood which increasingly existed in tension with each other along class-related lines. As a result, access to the patriarchal dividend began to be subtly reshaped.

CREDIT, WORTH, AND THE LANGUAGE OF SOCIAL DESCRIPTION

When John Peckett pledged himself to Anne Singleton at the gate of his master's house in 1598, he not only undertook to forsake all others but also 'promised that by godes grace she should never want as longe as he had wherewithall to relyve her'.[4] It was a commonplace that married or householding men in early modern England would diligently provide for their dependants, and that their 'honesty' was contingent upon fulfilling this obligation. Precursors of the 'breadwinning' male are apparent in such expectations, although the household's collective credit remained of paramount importance and dependent on the actions and reputations of all its members. The economic success of a household required the thrift and labour of all, but the gendered division of this labour was judged according to principles of 'husbandry' or 'oeconomy' (in terms of household management) which particularly emphasized male provision. More broadly, male credit was evaluated in terms of honest dealing and access to and command of resources, with the result that many men seem to have had a far stronger sense than women of their worth in economic terms. For men, worth was a central and quantifiable aspect of their identity which needed constant defence and assertion in competitive bids for status.

[4] NRO, *John Peckett* c. *Anne Singleton*, DN/DEP/32, fo. 9.

Male provision was an important component of normative concepts of honesty as articulated in the course of routine social practice. So Katherine Tancock remarked to one of her neighbours in Plymouth, 'Thow hast an honest man to thy husband and taketh great paynes for his livinge.'[5] On being reprimanded for his neglect, the London clothworker Richard Hall 'promised to use his servantes honestly as an honest man ought to do' and to give them 'three meales a daie as other mens prenties have'. John Deye also 'promysed to kepe the companye of his wyffe as a honest man ought to doo, And to make of her as shall become an honest man'.[6] Richard Blanket of Rye was likewise bound in £10 so that he 'do well and honestly use and inttreate his wiff, which he nowe hath and se the childe kepte nurrished and brought upe, of which his wiff was lately deliverid... And farther that he do not frequent the tiplinge or victualing houses... there to sitt drinkinge typlinge or Idely to spend his tyme.'[7] As this last example suggests, the expectation of male provision informed a powerful line of critique. Thus Mary Knight complained to a Sussex justice of the peace that 'about a fortnight since her husband went from her and leaft her only eighteene pence and noe other provision there being a daughter of his and a daughter of this examinants to live with it'.[8] Similarly, James Yxforth was described by the Norwich census of the poor as an 'evell husbond', being a worsted weaver 'not in work' and unable to support his three children.[9]

Dissolute husbands provoked disapproval on the grounds that they abnegated their responsibilities to provide for their families. Thus the Leicester authorities were concerned to punish the 'many unthriftie persons being poore men & havying wyfe & children [who] use commonlye to sytt & typple in alehowses & typlinghowses... to the impoveryssyng of them that so abuse their tyme, whylst their poore wyfes, chyldren, and famele almost starve at home for lacke of that that the said evyll disposed people superflewusley spend'.[10] Derisive labelling in these terms carried sufficient import that men were prepared to enter actions for injury in response to charges of neglect. The Cambridge cobbler John Newman

[5] DRO, *Trenne* c. *Hancock*, Chanter 866, unfoliated, 8 Apr. 1635.
[6] Clothworkers' Hall, London, Court Orders 1558–81, fos. 146, 116ᵛ.
[7] ESRO, Rye 1/5, fo. 37ᵛ. See also *Depositions and Other Ecclesiastical Proceedings from the Courts of Durham, Extending from 1311 to the Reign of Elizabeth*, Publications of the Surtees Society 21 (London, 1845), 97–8.
[8] ESRO, QR/E 21, 107. See also 106.
[9] *The Norwich Census of the Poor 1570*, ed. John F. Pound, Norfolk Record Society 40 (Norwich, 1971), 73. See also the descriptions of John Fyn and William Bushe, 80.
[10] *Records of the Borough of Leicester. Being a Series of Extracts from the Archives of the Corporation of Leicester*, iii: *1509–1603*, ed. Mary Bateson (Cambridge, 1905), 108–9. See also 128.

sued Agnes Wilson in 1587 for claiming, as one witness reported, that he 'did starve his wife'. Another witness in the case gave a fuller account of Agnes Wilson's accusations, couched as follows: 'Goodman Newman: you goe abroade to the Bowles & at yor pleasure, but you had more nede to tarye at hom & to bestowe that: uppon yor wyef whoe is sickley, and weake, for she is lost for wante of good kepeinge & for lacke of good attendaunce & good lokeing toe.'[11]

Negligent husbands also risked forfeiting their credit to their wives, as in the case of a Cambridge maltster, Robert Oliver, who was characterized in 1625 as 'a drunkard and a bad husband'. Consequently, as many witnesses reported, the bargaining for barley required for his business was done by his wife, 'who only was trusted with buyeing & selling of malte (the sayd Robert being an idle dissolut fellowe & one that spent whatsoever he could gett into his hande)'.[12] Such acknowledged dependency could be regarded pejoratively, and sometimes provided the substance of insults. On answering an action for injury in 1592, the waterman William Parry claimed that he had been provoked by Frances Tompson's accusation that 'he was glad of a cantell of bredd that his wyef brought hoame with hir'.[13] Reproofs such as these undermined a man's status by questioning either his ability or his will to provide for his family, and derived their impact from expectations that a married man should not be dependent on his wife for his livelihood and should not neglect his duty to provide.

Such concerns were more generally related to an emphasis on thrift and industry as an essential part of a man's vocation. While labour was by no means deemed to be a male preserve, as women's work was a crucial component of a household's ability to survive and profit, it was nonetheless repeatedly invoked in connection with notions of a man's credit. Robert Sheppard was endorsed by his neighbours in Westfield (Sussex) as 'verie painfull honest, industryous' despite being 'verie poore', and the blacksmith Gabriel Fuller, a 'poor man', was recommended to the Kent justices as 'a purposeful, industrious and honest man'.[14] Men deemed to be not only poor but also idle were cast in quite a different light. So Edmund Beeston attempted to discredit the Cambridge draper William Browne (who had entered an injury suit against him) by asking witnesses to comment on whether Browne was 'a verie poore beggarlie fellowe and

---

[11] CUL, CUA, *John Newman* c. *Agnes Wilson*, Comm.Ct.II.3, fos. 107ᵛ–108.
[12] CUL, CUA, *Robert Oliver* c. *John Sherman*, Comm.Ct.II.2, fos. 2, 4.
[13] CUL, CUA, *Frances Tompson* c. *William Parry*, Comm.Ct.II.4, fo. 197.
[14] ESRO, QR/E 20; Louis A. Knafla, *Kent at Law 1602: The County Jurisdiction: Assizes and Sessions of the Peace* (London, 1994), 213–14.

not worth a groat if his debts were payde[.] And [whether] he doth live verie dissolutie and idly not following his trade nor taking anie honest course of life to mainteyne himself his wife and Children.'[15] Imputations of idleness automatically carried associations of disrepute, and brought a man's worth into question. Deponents in a case of 1626, for example, were doubtful about a fellow witness's estimation of his own worth at £10. Neighbours of the tailor James Browning declared him to be 'an idle & lose fellowe ... that haunteth alehowses, & in them mispendeth his tyme', and claimed that since his only means of income was his 'trade & hand labor', he must be worth considerably less than £10 because 'he never followed that but was allwayes goeing & running upp & downe the street'. Similarly, in a petition against him, John Whistons of Areley (Staffordshire) was characterized as 'one that laboreth not to get his livinge by truth so that his neighbours knowe not howe he liveth except it be uppon the spoile of the Countrey'.[16]

This sort of social and economic assessment of men was a central, and gendered, part of the 'culture of credit' recently elucidated by Craig Muldrew. The 'competitive piety' with which households sought to establish and maintain credit within their communities involved a language of social description that had different emphases for men and women.[17] Patriarchal imperatives of male provision could become caught up in the processes of social evaluation and differentiation that were connected to assessments of male worth more generally. To question a man's ability to provide also disputed his worth, which was often articulated as a central component of male identity. This was partially conveyed by men's responses to the question often posed in civil law procedure which asked how much a witness was worth, all debts paid. So, Robert Hilliard of Wotton Rivers (Wiltshire) declared that 'he liveth upon a tenement of the Earle of Hartfords worth yeerely nyne ponds at the least and maintaineth a familie in honest sort', and that he was worth £20.[18] The notary Thomas Sherd answered that he was worth 40s., adding that 'he livethe by his trade honestlye as becommeth an honest man to do'. This point was stressed more defensively by the cordwainer Robert Wood, who said that 'he getteth his lyveinge honestlye & truelye, & that yf enye man will chardge him to the contrarye he is redye to answer him'. Similarly,

[15] CUL, CUA, *William Browne* c. *Edmund Beeston*, V.C.Ct.III.24, no. 35.
[16] CUL, CUA, *Thomas and Elizabeth Newman* c. *John Humbletoft*, V.C.Ct.II.23, fos. 23, 24ᵛ; *The Staffordshire Quarter Sessions Rolls*, iv: *1598–1602*, ed. S. A. H. Burne (Kendal, 1935), 457.
[17] Craig Muldrew, *The Economy of Obligation: The Culture of Credit and Social Relations in Early Modern England* (Basingstoke, 1998), part II. See also id., 'Interpreting the Market: The Ethics of Credit and Community Relations in Early Modern England', *Social History*, 18 (1993).
[18] Bodl., OUA, *William Farr* c. *John Ringe*, Hyp/B/4, fo. 87.

the brewer John Shawe claimed that although he did not know what he was worth 'he lyveth honestlye of that which he hathe as an honest man oughte to do'.[19] The shoemaker Bartholomew Chipney declared he was worth £10, and likewise claimed that he 'liveth honestly out of dept and liveth by his labor & trade'.[20] Others emphasized their hard work in lieu of any concrete worth. The shoemaker Daniel Haymer claimed that he was worth nothing, but got 'his lyvinge by his ffingers endes according to his trade'. Similarly, a labourer from Lewes replied that he was 'worth litle or nothing at all, & liveth by all kinde of labor, which anie will sett him at worke about'.[21] These men appealed to expectations of provision, vocation, and, at the very least, industry to demonstrate their credit, worth, and honesty not only as witnesses, but more generally as men.

Such statements were indicative of the importance of 'worth' in these terms to the evaluation of male credit and even manhood itself. It was suggested that to be worth nothing was to be economically impotent, untrustworthy, and by implication less than a man. One man sought to undermine an action for debt against him by attacking his opponent's credit in these terms, provoking a witness to comment that the plaintiff was 'nought worth his debts beinge paid and that soe the common fame goeth of him in Cambridge', and the husbandman Thomas Barnes (a witness in another suit) was described as being 'very poore' and discredited as 'a man of noe accompte where he dwells, & of little estimation & so accompted of'.[22] Such worthlessness deprived men of claims to esteem and account, and could bring about their exclusion from credit networks. Men of no worth were not dependable in a developing market economy which was founded upon myriad bonds of trust.[23] A worthless man could not pay his debts, and was therefore a danger to others to whom he was linked by chains of credit, as well as to his own family for whom he was expected to provide. Having no credit, therefore, was easily elided with poverty and dishonesty, however hard a man worked. Thus a Cambridge innkeeper complained that the accusation that he was 'not worth a penny' implied he 'was a very poore man . . . & that he was not to be trusted, he was soe poore'.[24] Similarly, a London fishmonger complained against an

[19] CUL, CUA, *Robert Prance* c. *John Carowe*, V.C.Ct.II.1, fos. 25, 39ᵛ; *Gregory Dawson* c. *Leonard Glascocke*, Comm.Ct.II.6, fo. 207.

[20] Bodl., OUA, Hyp/B/4, fo. 75ᵛ.

[21] ESRO, EpII/5/6, fo. 285ᵛ; EpII/5/8, fo. 28ᵛ.

[22] CUL, CUA, *John Borne* c. *Hugh Williams*, Comm.Ct.II.4, fo. 94ᵛ; *John Prance* c. *Thomas Hodilowe*, Comm.Ct.II.1, fo. 52ᵛ.

[23] Muldrew, 'Interpreting the Market'.

[24] CUL, CUA, *Thomas Smith* c. *Owen Saintpeere*, V.C.Ct.II.32, fo. 57ʳ⁻ᵛ. See also *Ralph Parris* c. *Nathaniel Masters*, Comm.Ct.II.18, fo. 78ᵛ.

apprentice 'for givinge him very vile & lewde words & speeches seeking utterly to discredit & overthrowe him, saying that hee was not able to paye his debtes and if every man were paide hee was not worthe a groate'.[25] If a man's worth was doubted, he lost his credit and was excluded from the relations of trust which both bound communities and accorded status and agency.

A man's worth was the index by which his ability to pay his debts was gauged. As such, it was often referred to by litigants as synonymous with his word. John Patson of London was condemned to pay 6*s.* 8*d.* in damages and a further 11*s.* 4*d.* in costs for calling John Scolye 'a rascall, a beggerlie knave, a drunken knave' and claiming at Sturbridge Fair that 'I can have of credit uppon my worde one Hundrethe Powndes as soone as you can be credited for a groate.' Edward Wenham was similarly exercised by Christopher Greene's accusation 'that noe mann would take [his] worde for fowerpence or a groate'.[26] To question a man's word was a serious insult, which provided the substance of many slander suits and was often cited as provocation for violent retaliation.[27] A man suspected of betraying his word lost his worth, as he was no longer deemed trustworthy. Yet worth could be difficult to assess, as regretted by John Jeepe who was duped when a poverty-stricken inmate of the Cambridge gaol was transformed with a cloak and a sword to look like 'an able and sufficient man', in order to pose as a surety.[28] In addition, given the extent of credit relations in early modern England, a man's worth was neither fixed nor secure, but spread over a series of unpredictable networks beyond his control. Hence the significance of the clause in the interrogatory questioning a deponent's worth, which required the estimate to take into account all outstanding debts. A man's worth was dependent on a complex set of reckonings, and was therefore constantly being re-balanced and assessed. The degree to which witnesses' statements of their worth were accurate in monetary terms is impossible to judge. Formal accounting in this period was at best rudimentary and generally non-existent, and, if the journal of the London turner Nehemiah Wallington is any guide, artisans such as he had very little idea of the value of their assets.[29] Yet many such men

[25] GL, Fishmongers' Company, Court Minutes, 1592–1610, MS 5570/1, 9.
[26] CUL, CUA, *John Scolye* c. *John Patson*, Comm.Ct.V.7, fo. 110; *Christopher Greene* c. *Edward Wenham*, V.C.Ct.II.36, fo. 73A^v.
[27] e.g. CUL, CUA, *Mr Sherbrocke* c. *John Robinson*, V.C.Ct.I.24, fo. 65^v; *Benjamin Prime* c. *Margaret Cronfoot*, V.C.Ct.III.8, no. 4; *Henry Wolfe* c. *Andrew Goodwin*, Comm.Ct.II.13, fo. 98. For violent responses, see Ch. 5 above.
[28] CUL, CUA, *James Eversden* c. *John Jeepe*, Comm.Ct.II.20, fo. 49^v.
[29] Paul S. Seaver, *Wallington's World: A Puritan Artisan in Seventeenth-Century London* (Stanford, Calif., 1985), ch. 5.

did articulate a precise sense of their worth in ethical terms of honesty and credit, invoking as many as possible of the patriarchal expectations pertaining to the ideal-type householder. For some men this involved claims of considerable worth and the authority associated with being 'able and sufficient'. For others it was more narrowly and more precariously rooted in the values of thrift and industry. The honest hardship of a poor labouring man was far less encompassing than the honesty appealed to, for example, by the petitioners against John Whistons for his misdemeanours, who styled themselves 'his sufficient and honest neighbours'. Similarly, it was 'certen . . . honest and substantiall men' of St Martin within Ludgate who addressed a petition for the relief of orphan children. Concepts of honesty for lower-ranking men were more more selectively applied, and differently configured, than those claimed by the 'honeste and credit[able] persons' of another London parish who sought to exclude the 'inferior and meaner sorte of the multitude' from their vestry meetings.[30] Claims to honesty in terms of authority, worth, and the command of resources were therefore related to social position as well as appropriate behaviour. So it was emphasized that a Wiltshire couple 'lived honestly and peaceably amongst their neighbours . . . *albeit* their estate in wealth be none of the richest'. In contrast, the Cambridge brewer John Sherman was more automatically endorsed as 'an honest and able mann'.[31] The impression of ability and sufficiency marked men off not only from their dependants, but also from their social inferiors, by conferring a degree of authority. While the patriarchal tenets of plain dealing, diligent application to a calling, and the ability to provide for one's family were expected of all householding men, the worth, account, and honesty associated with financial 'ability' and self-sufficient mastery also correlated with social privilege.

Notions of manhood rooted in economic independence and heading and provisioning a household were therefore not always an asset to all householding men. For some, they featured more as a potent critique

[30] *Staffordshire Quarter Sessions Rolls*, iv. 456; Goldsmiths' Hall, London, Wardens Accounts and Court Minutes, viii. 72; GL, St Dunstan in the West, Vestry Minutes, 1588–1663, MS 3016/1, 43. See also Steve Hindle, 'Exclusion Crises: Poverty, Migration and Parochial Responsibility in English Rural Communities, *c*.1560–1660', *Rural History*, 7 (1996); id., 'A Sense of Place? Becoming and Belonging in the Rural Parish, 1550–1650', in Alexandra Shepard and Phil Withington (eds.), *Communities in Early Modern England: Networks, Place, Rhetoric* (Manchester, 2000); id., 'Extortion and Entitlement: Negotiating Inequality in English Rural Communities, 1550–1650', in Michael J. Braddick and John Walter (eds.), *Negotiating Power in Early Modern Society: Order, Hierarchy and Subordination in Britain and Ireland* (Cambridge, 2001).

[31] *Records of the County of Wilts, Being Extracts from the Quarter Sessions Great Rolls of the Seventeenth Century*, ed. B. H. Cunnington (Devizes, 1932), 69, my emphasis; CUL, CUA, Thomas Hobson c. John Sherman, snr, V.C.Ct.II.22, fo. 216.

than a positive identity. Patriarchal prescriptions of male self-sufficiency, economic independence, and responsibility towards others informed the ethics of evaluation by which subtle status distinctions as well as broader hierarchies were established. Within this evaluative framework, economic impotence was undermining because it brought about exclusion from credit networks. Worthlessness deprived men of their word, since they had no means to vouch for, and therefore could not be trusted. By implication, men of no worth were of no consequence and of no account. Such men were also a danger. They were dangerous not only because they could not be trusted, but also because they threatened others with their consequent dependence. Furthermore if they were unable to provide for others they would require provision themselves, thus jeopardizing the social order as well as parish coffers. Patriarchal expectations of economic autonomy and self-sufficiency were therefore part of the common conceptual currency in early modern England, although by no means an unqualified benefit to all householding men.

WOMEN'S PROVISION AND ALTERNATIVE HOUSEHOLD STRATEGIES

Although the patriarchal imperatives of self-sufficiency linking male worth with economic agency exerted a powerful influence, they certainly did not go unchallenged—by both women and men. Expectations of male provision may have informed the language of social description, but they did not always underpin the practical realities of household economies or even the evaluative schemes associated with divisions of labour. One obvious area of contradiction was the many varied ways in which married women performed the roles of provision and exchange nominally expected of their husbands, often deriving credit from them in comparable terms. In addition, some households resorted to strategies for survival which involved even greater deviation from the patriarchal model by rejecting the primacy of the nuclear family unit altogether.

Married women made many varied contributions to their households' commercial life which often remain hidden in the formal records of transactions and debt litigation. In the Cambridge university courts over 90 per cent of all litigants in debt cases for which depositions survive were men. However, although debt litigation was undoubtedly male dominated, it was not a simple reflection of a male monopoly over commercial activity itself. The records of the university courts are particularly useful in highlighting this point, because they include depositions in debt cases— material that was not produced by borough courts where the vast bulk of disputes over debt were ordinarily resolved.[32] Many debt cases heard in the university courts were only nominally brought by men, involving transactions apparently conducted independently by their wives. Such cases, alongside incidental detail from depositions, suggest a considerable degree of overlap in the economic activities of householding couples. Women's commercial pursuits were not just craftily connived exceptions which proved a patriarchal rule, but were indicative of women's central and *expected* contributions to a broad range of 'household work strategies'.[33]

In 1588 Richard Newmarsh sued John Borne for debts resulting from exchanges in which neither had been directly involved. Borne responded to Newmarsh's allegations, by claiming that no more than 22s. was in question: 'viz: xiiijs. of yt is for monye which his this respondents wyef did borowe of the sayd Richard Newmarshe his wyef at certeyne tymes, and thother viijs. of yt ys for victuall whiche this sayde respondents wyef had... from the sayd Richard Newmarsh and his wyef or one of them'.[34] In the same year, the cook Edward Parker was exercised by a suit which seems to have exclusively concerned debts owing to his wife by the executor for a deceased fellow of St John's College for numerous services she had provided before his death. The debts included 12d. 'for twoe racks of mutton which . . . the sayd Agnes with hir owne monye did bye and dresse for the sayd John Johnson', and several other unspecified sums for napkins, socks, and nightcaps which Agnes Parker had delivered to his college room. In this, and in many other cases, it appears that the women involved were independently running service businesses, which only became their husbands' concern when litigation was necessary.[35] Just as men became responsible for widows' economic affairs on remarriage, so it appears they could be liable for their wives' commercial activities which transpired *within* marriage, but which generally remained hidden behind men's nominal responsibility in debt litigation. Cases such as these suggest that in terms of their practical economic dealings, the distinction between widows and wives was a little less clear cut than the legal fiction

---

[32] Craig Muldrew, 'Rural Credit, Market Areas and Legal Institutions in the Countryside in England, 1550–1700', in Christopher W. Brooks and Michael Lobban (eds.), *Communities and Courts in Britain 1150–1900* (London, 1997); id., *The Economy of Obligation*, ch. 8.

[33] R. E. Pahl, *Divisions of Labour* (Oxford, 1984), 20. See also Michael Roberts, '"To Bridle the Falsehood of Unconscionable Workmen, and for her own Satisfaction": What the Jacobean Housewife Needed to Know about Men's Work, and Why', *Labour History Review*, 63 (1998).

[34] CUL, CUA, *Richard Newmarsh c. John Borne*, Comm.Ct.II.3, fo. 181.

[35] CUL, CUA, *Edward Parker c. Laurence Johnson*, Comm.Ct.II.3, fos. 46–47ᵛ. See also, e.g., *John Odell c. Thomas Redditt*, V.C.Ct.II.28, fo. 13, over laundry services provided by Odell's wife; *Ann Lockwood c. Thomas Gillam*, Comm.Ct.II.1, fo. 1ʳ⁻ᵛ, involving 10s. owed by Gillam's wife.

of coverture admitted. This was formally acknowledged by the borough court in Cambridge, which granted 'where a woman covert havinge an husband useth any craft within the sayd Burroughe by her sole with the which the husband medleth not that woman shalbe charged as a woman sole of all that which toucheth her craft'.[36]

This impression of married women being extensively, and at times independently, involved in credit networks is indirectly corroborated over the course of many debt cases ostensibly involving men alone. Women contracted debts in their own right with both men and other women, often as a result of independent business concerns. In a tenancy agreement of 1628 between Thomas Birch and the chandler Richard Briggs, it was agreed that 'Thomas Birch his wyfe was to have one parte in the shopp of the sayd howse', presumably for her own trade.[37] In a different suit, the maltster John Shawe attested to his wife's credit as follows:

Agnes Shawe for manie yeares past (but not of late) hathe bene accompted reputed & taken within the towne of Cambridge & other places, to have bene a greatt dealler bargayner byer & seller of and for divers things & speciallye fissh, and to have gayned well therby in tymes past but not of late[.] And that she hathe bene . . . verie provident and carefull in former tymes in such her bargaines, for to make profitt and Commoditie by the same.[38]

Women such as Agnes Shawe appear to have held a positive sense of vocation and occupational identity from being involved in bargaining, profit, and provision. This was articulated by Agnes Beeton (a butcher's wife) during a heated exchange with Lucy Wenham (a servant) in 1618 over a piece of meat Wenham had tried to return. Beeton adamantly refused to accept the meat, saying, 'you shall not change it I wilbe *master* my selfe', and subsequently sued Wenham for damaging her credit by suggesting that she was an 'unjust dealing woman in hir trade and profession'.[39] Married women were not only involved in trade; they also claimed credit in terms of honest dealing, 'professional' status, and the authority derived from conducting business.

Married women seem to have been involved in extensive buying and selling, particularly of clothes and household wares. In 1581 Helen Arante described George Ingram's request to her husband that she 'sell his wiefs cassocke for him', and Parnell Morrill refused to return a cloak which she had bought in 1618 from a student, claiming 'she had never had

---

[36] Downing College, Cambridge, Metcalfe's Thesaurus, Bowtell MS 11, fo. 157^v.
[37] CUL, CUA, *Thomas Birch* c. *Richard Briggs*, V.C.Ct.II.25, fo. 6.
[38] CUL, CUA, *John Atkin* c. *John and Agnes Shawe*, Comm.Ct.II.8, fo. 30^{r-v}.
[39] CUL, CUA, *Agnes Beeton* c. *Lucy Wenham*, V.C.Ct.III.23, nos. 32, 30, my emphasis.

or bought it to be for her owne use, but only payd downe the money for a Londoner'.[40] Women were widely involved in pawn networks, and seem to have been accorded particular skill in evaluating household goods.[41] Isabel York deposed in 1616 that in lieu of rent she had sold goods 'out of the house . . . namely bedd steeds & such like things' which she had been 'driven to sell to myntyen her husband & familye . . . by her husbands commande, & consente', and she confirmed that they had been worth 40s. 'which she knoweth to be soe because she had them her selfe & sould most of them'.[42] That this was a skill requiring training and considerable expertise is suggested by the deposition of Agnes Goodwin, aged 20. When asked the value of some distrained goods, she replied, 'as towcheinge the valors prices or estimations of the sayd goods parcells houshould stuffe & ymplements of houshould in the sayd Schedule mentioned: she saythe that she can saye notheinge att all, for that she is a younge women, & as yet hathe no skyll that waye'.[43]

Married women were commonly involved in handling money. Reckonings, tallying, and exchange were an unquestioned and intrinsic part of both men and women's daily lives. Responding to the brewer Michael Homes's allegations against him in an action for debt, the maltster John Culpy reported that 'the wyef of the sayd micheall Homes did paye to this respondent the Summe of ix^{li} . . . in parte payment of a greater Summe dwe'.[44] Everyday trading and bartering were conducted both jointly and independently by husbands and wives. William Taylor recounted his reckonings with Gilbert Magnolls and his wife in a way which suggested their joint enterprise, confessing that he 'was indebted unto the sayd Gilbert Magnolls & magnolls his wief in xxxvijs. viijd. & not above for certeyne things [he] . . . had of theirs & soulde for them which . . . he saythe he paid

---

[40] CUL, CUA, *George Ingram* c. *Henry Mase*, Comm.Ct.II.1, fo. 8; *Adrian Scroope, BA* c. *John and Parnell Morrill*, Comm.Ct.II.18, fo. 27. See also Sara Mendelson and Patricia Crawford, *Women in Early Modern England* (Oxford, 1998), ch. 6; Jeremy Boulton, *Neighbourhood and Society: A London Suburb in the Seventeenth Century* (Cambridge, 1997), ch. 3.

[41] Garthine Walker, 'Women, Theft and the World of Stolen Goods', in Jenny Kermode and Garthine Walker (eds.), *Women, Crime and the Courts in Early Modern England* (London, 1994), 92; Michael Roberts, 'Women and Work in Sixteenth-Century English Towns', in Penelope J. Corfield and Derek Keene (eds.), *Work in Towns 850–1850* (Leicester, 1990), 95; Boulton, *Neighbourhood and Society*, 89.

[42] CUL, CUA, *John Scott* c. *Benjamin Prime*, Comm.Ct.II.16, fo. 96. When estimating his worth in the course of a marriage settlement, the Cambridge yeoman Thomas Hodylowe was dependent on his daughters for an assessment of the quantity and value of the featherbeds in his possession, *John Prance* c. *Thomas Hodylowe*, Comm.Ct.II.2, fo. 0^{v}.

[43] CUL, CUA, *Kenelme Picking* c. *William Warborton*, Comm.Ct.II.3, fo. 132^{v}.

[44] CUL, CUA, *Michael Homes* c. *John Culpy*, Comm.Ct.II.4, fo. 41^{v}. See also, e.g., *John Waller* c. *Amos Iverson* (for evidence of rent payments by Iverson's wife), Comm.Ct.II.4, fo. 162; *Thomas Brigham* c. *John Payne* (for reckoning conducted by Payne's wife), V.C.Ct.II.24, fo. 4.

over to Hugh Garthesyde gent for & to the use of . . . Gilberte magnolls & his wief'. Conversely, in an injury cause initiated by Ann Bradley, the deposition of John Halliwell (a tailor) suggested that his wife's economic affairs were unknown to him. Responding to an interrogatory questioning his indebtedness to the plaintiff, Halliwell said that although he owed Richard Bradley 7*s.*, 'whether there be enye recknings betwene this deponents wief & the sayd Richard Bradley & Agnes his wief . . . he sayeth that he knoweth not'.[45]

Married women were also involved in the widespread processes of informal arbitration and reconciliation when reckonings were disputed.[46] So a witness in a debt case between Richard Ellwood and the weaver Henry Mase concerning a delivery of sea coals recounted that he had 'often tymes hard the sayd Elwoods wief saye since this sute beganne, that if maise woulde paye the one halfe of the monie due for the coales . . . she woulde paye the other halfe for a quietnes sake'. Similarly, in attempting to avoid litigation with John Harvey, James Morley 'did agree with the sayd John Harveys wief in the sayd John Harveys house . . . for the sayd debt', which they arranged was to be paid in weekly instalments of 6*d.*[47] Married women also acted as informal arbitrators in other people's disputes, as in a case of 1604, when a servant requested Joan Filoe 'to talk with his master Cotton to paye him that wages was behind'.[48] Married women therefore frequently 'intermeddled' with other men and women as mediators as well as producers, buyers, and sellers.

The extent to which married women acted either independently of, jointly with, or as subordinates to their husbands is impossible to assess, and levels of independence and interdependence must have varied considerably within the context of particular marriages and different economic settings. There is certainly plentiful evidence of women acting as 'deputies' for their husbands, such as Ann Iverson, who in 1590 returned a lease to Francis Yearle and demanded £9 11*s.* from him 'at the appointment of the sayd Amos hir husband', and such as Thomas Lapith's wife, who in 1594 'had bene at Cambridge aboute his . . . busines'.[49] There is also occasional evidence of women arranging contracts on their husbands'

[45] CUL, CUA, *Thomas Gill* c. *William Taylor*, Comm.Ct.II.1, fo. 2; *Ann Bradley* c. *Thomas Barker*, Comm.Ct.II.2, fos. 89ᵛ–90.

[46] Craig Muldrew, 'The Culture of Reconciliation: Community and the Settlement of Economic Disputes in Early Modern England', *Historical Journal*, 39 (1996).

[47] CUL, CUA, *Richard Ellwood* c. *Henry Mase*, Comm.Ct.II.2, fo. 54; *John Harvey* c. *James Morley*, Comm.Ct.II.3, fo. 12ᵛ.

[48] CUL, CUA, *Henry Cotton* c. *John Swetson*, V.C.Ct.II.8, fo. 109Aᵛ.

[49] CUL, CUA, *Amos Iverson* c. *Francis Yearle*, Comm.Ct.II.3, fo. 228ᵛ; *Henry Allaby* c. *John Wilkinson*, Comm.Ct.II.6, fo. 11.

behalf, and women were often present when the initial bargains under dispute were made.[50] Conversely, perhaps the most obvious evidence of husbands acting on their wives' behalf is their appearances in court to sue over their debts. Similarly, although wives were often answerable to their husbands, there is also incidental evidence that husbands felt accountable to their wives. When the tailor Thomas Woods sued the gentleman Edward Overton for horse hire, with a written bill as evidence, Overton complained that he had only signed the bill 'at the earnest request of the sayd woods as he protested not to take advantage of the sayd bill but only to shew his wyfe & give her satisfaction'.[51]

Varying levels of independence and interdependence are suggested by married women's responses in the university courts and in ecclesiastical jurisdictions elsewhere to the question asking how much they were worth. Many women simply confirmed their legal dependency dictated by the common law concept of coverture, which denied independent property rights to married women.[52] In 1597, for example, Katherine Bins (a cobbler's wife) deposed that she was 'under covert baron, and therefore is worthe notheinge of her self, and that [which] she hathe is her husbandes'.[53] Similarly Jane Woodcock declared that 'she is a marryed woman and all that she hath is her husbandes'.[54] Some women merely informed the court of their husband's occupation and worth rather than making any reference to their own, such as Grace Spencer who responded that her husband was a poor labourer worth little or nothing.[55] Some wives seem to have had no idea of their husband's worth. Helena Hull, the wife of a London skinner, claimed that, 'she lyveth of her husband who payeth money to the Queene but whether it be for subsidy or no she canot tell'.[56] Similarly Ursula Troye, the wife of a Norfolk husbandman, declared that 'her husband is a subsidy man but what he is worth every man payd she knoweth not'.[57] In the same case, Margery Smith (married

---

[50] e.g. CUL, CUA, *Thomas Walton* c. *William Rayne*, V.C.Ct.II.25, fo. 70ᵛ; *Robert Lee* c. *John Tennant*, V.C.Ct.II.27, fo. 1; *Thomas Shilborne* c. *Richard Fairchild*, Comm.Ct.II.20, fo. 140ᵛ.

[51] CUL, CUA, *Thomas Woods* c. *Edward Overton*, V.C.Ct.II.30, fo. 36. See also *Peter Atkinson* c. *Stephen Smith*, Comm.Ct.II.4, fo. 235.

[52] Amy Louise Erickson, *Women and Property in Early Modern England* (London, 1993), 24–6.

[53] CUL, CUA, *Mary Campion* c. *John Carowe*, Comm.Ct.II.6, fo. 180. For similar responses by married women see also the depositions of Agnes Burffe, fo. 88ᵛ; Mary Rust, fo. 92ᵛ; Thomasina Cockley, fo. 102; Margaret Wilkinson, fo. 104ᵛ.

[54] NRO, *Thomas Moore* c. *Peter Woodcock*, DN/DEP/32, fo. 63.

[55] CUL, CUA, *Thomas Witton* c. *William Ewsden*, Comm.Ct.II.20, fo. 104ᵛ. See also the deposition of Alice Walker, fo. 105.

[56] GL, London Commissary Court, *Teeler als Anson* c. *Roger Tysdale*, MS 9065A, fo. 19ᵛ.

[57] NRO, *Joanne Smith* c. *Elizabeth Sharpe*, DN/DEP/32, fo. 81ᵛ. See also the deposition of Elizabeth Clerke, fo. 10ᵛ.

to a labourer) claimed that she did not know 'her husbands substance', but also claimed that she herself had 'certaine freeland', which suggests that both partners in this marriage had an independent sense of their worth.[58] A more extreme situation was portrayed by Mary Parnby who declared that her husband was worth nothing, adding 'but for herselfe because her husband hath delt unkindely with her she hath xx noables a yeere alowed her by her ... brother in lawes'.[59] A few women spoke of their own considerable independent worth in blatant contradiction of the terms of coverture. Ann Prime incongruously maintained that she was 'under covert baron, & sayeth she is worth 40s. her debts payed', while Margaret Swetson simply informed the court that she was worth £10 with no reference to her husband whatsoever.[60]

The dictates of coverture appear to have seemed irrelevant to women in situations of poverty, as suggested by Barbara Neyborough's response that 'her husband is a very poore man, & ... she is worth the Cloaths of her backe her debts payed'.[61] Many such women spoke of their worth in terms of the joint labours they performed with their husbands, often laying claim to the attribute of honest hardship in the same way as men. Although Margaret Dodding declared that she was 'worthe nothinge but that she hathe of hir husband', she also added that 'she livethe honestlie and trulie by hir labor'. Similarly, Ann Heathers replied that 'her hosband is a jorneyman tayler and he and she live by their labour and have not any thinge els to live uppon'.[62] Beatrice Swynney in 1600 deposed that she and her husband had 'lyved well & honestlye ever since they first came to this Towne to dwell, & have gotten & doe gett theire lyveinges by bothe theire labors, And ... as they owe lytle: soe they ar worth lytle.'[63] In a similar vein, Margaret Bray was described as having been one who 'go[es] abroade to worke, from howse to howse as many honeste women use to do', and thus of comparable worth to her 'honeste poore labouring man' of a husband.[64]

In practice, therefore, the patriarchal dictates of male provision and

[58] NRO, *Joanne Smith* c. *Elizabeth Sharpe*, DN/DEP/32, fo. 82.
[59] CUL, CUA, *Daniel Rogers, MA* c. *Francis Catlyn, MA*, Comm.Ct.II.12, fo. 102ᵛ.
[60] CUL, CUA, *Ralph Parris* c. *Nathaniel Masters*, Comm.Ct.II.18, fo. 80ᵛ; *Nathaniel Jackson, BA* c. *Anthony Swetson*, Comm.Ct.II.20, fo. 25ᵛ.
[61] CUL, CUA, *William Ellery* c. *Edward Wenham*, V.C.Ct.II.20, fo. 10.
[62] CUL, CUA, *Nicholas Parnbye* c. *John Wilkinson*, Comm.Ct.II.6, fo. 133ᵛ; Bodl., OUA, *Office* c. *Francis Freeman*, fo. 99ᵛ. Her husband, however, merely referred to his own labour in his answer to the same question: 'he is a pore man and liveth uppon his trade being a Jorneyman tayler', fo. 100ᵛ. See also the depositions of Mary Vachan, fo. 98, and Jane Ward, fo. 99.
[63] CUL, CUA, *Walter House* c. *John Fidling*, Comm.Ct.II.9, fo. 2. See also the deposition of Alice Waigate in the same case, V.C.Ct.II.2*, fos. 48ᵛ–49.
[64] GL, London Commissary Court, *Taylor* c. *Foster*, MS 9065A/2, fo. 44.

exchange were countered by the commercial pursuits of many married women, and the language of social description which could be used negatively to stigmatize men by reminding them of their responsibilities to labour and provide was also at times positively extended to endorse women. This suggests a routine acceptance of a household ideology far less differentiated by gender than that proposed by Dod and Cleaver. Credit, in terms of plain dealing, vocational diligence, and provision, was a gender-related, rather than gender-specific, concept, and for the majority of folk confronted with the demands of subsistence its patriarchal configuration was irrelevant. Despite the prevalent rhetoric of male provision and worth, which could function as a particularly acute critique, men did not—indeed could not—monopolize commercial activity and credit networks. It is unlikely that most husbands and wives routinely perceived their commercial activities in the strictly gendered terms which preoccupied contemporary moralists, and it is unlikely that women's business dealings were viewed as a threat to the social order. For the majority of married men and women, the maintenance and survival of their household was their predominant and, most importantly, their *mutual* concern which required adaptability and the best possible use of resources rather than adherence to a patriarchal blueprint.

For many, survival precluded patriarchal pride and instead fostered a broad ethic of independence shared by the many men and women whose primary goal was to avoid becoming dependent on the parish. Agnes Reynolds, for example, complained in a case of assault that she was no longer able to 'work for hir living', adding that before being injured 'she gott the chiefest parte of hir owne, hir husbandes, and ther childrens mayntenance by hir sewinge and workinge needleworke'.[65] Sometimes wives were the sole providers for their families, particularly, it seems, in situations of extreme poverty. The Norwich census of the poor listed many such cases. Jone Saye, aged 37, spun white warp together with her younger sister Elizabeth to support not only themselves but also Jone's 30-year-old husband, a woollen weaver 'in no worke', who it was noted instead 'help[ed] his wyf in hir wolle'. Jone Browne, aged 40 years, was described as 'a womans taylor'. Still nursing two suckling children, she supported her 'vagrant' husband with the aid of a fifteen-year-old son who made buttons. In a similar situation was 'Katherin, the wyf of Thomas Attkyns, of 50 yeres, a cervingman that helpeth hir nott at al, & hathe 6 childerne, the eldest 10 yer that make buttons'.[66]

[65] CUL, CUA, *Agnes Reynolds* c. *Thomas Pie*, V.C.Ct.III.14, no. 2.
[66] *Norwich Census of the Poor*, 34, 25, 31. For other men similarly supported, see, e.g., William Grene, 26, Richard Galiston, John Brother, John Coulson, 31, Edmund Pendelton, 33.

Besides many instances of divergence from the gender roles prescribed by patriarchal models which emphasized male provision, there is also evidence of divergence from the patriarchal structure of the nuclear household. Some families were forced to pool resources and sacrifice a degree of economic independence in the interests of survival and, possibly, in relation to a positive sense of collectivism in active contrast to patriarchal imperatives. Hence the churchwardens of Chilcompton (Somerset) complained of Mathias Griffin 'who hath no certain place of abode or dwellinge to their knowledge but is a wanderer from place to place' who had married 'a lewd woman the daughter of a very poor man named Robins dwelling in a house built upon the lord's waste for the poor there, wherein there are two or three coopells besides the said Griffin'.[67] In 1617 the spinster Frances Horner complained to the Worcestershire justices that she was denied access to the fire and sometimes to indoor lodging in her dwelling in the parish of Newland because it also contained 'two more households', who obviously did not wish to accommodate a lone woman.[68] A. Hassell Smith has identified such survival techniques in operation in the 1590s in the north Norfolk village of Stiffkey, where more than 50 per cent of the families lived in some sort of shared or divided property.[69]

Other couples resorted to the expedient of separation as one or other (although usually the husband) went in search of work. Such subsistence migration often became blurred with vagrancy, and urban authorities in particular seem to have expended considerable punitive efforts in attempts to reunite spouses, many of whom had been separated for extensive periods.[70] So Walter Wright, lodging in Norwich with widow Holdord and working for one Richard Thurlowe while his wife and two children remained in Aylsham, was 'Comitted to Bridwell till he consent

[67] *Quarter Sessions Records for the County of Somerset*, i: *1607–1625*, ed. E. H. Bates, Somerset Record Society 28 (London, 1907), 122.
[68] *Worcester County Records: The Quarter Sessions Rolls*, i: *1591–1643*, comp. J. W. W. Bund (Worcester, 1900), part I, 247.
[69] A. Hassell Smith, 'Labourers in Late Sixteenth-Century England: A Case Study from North Norfolk [Part II]', *Continuity and Change*, 4 (1989), 373. For later examples of complex (and often non-nuclear) household arrangements of the poor see Thomas Sokoll, 'Old Age in Poverty: The Record of Essex Pauper Letters, 1780–1834', in Tim Hitchcock, Peter King, and Pamela Sharpe (eds.), *Chronicling Poverty: The Voices and Strategies of the English Poor, 1640–1840* (Basingstoke, 1997). For examples of single women establishing 'alternative family structures' in this period and beyond, see Pamela Sharpe, 'Literally Spinsters: A New Interpretation of Local Economy and Demography in Colyton in the Seventeenth and Eighteenth Centuries', *Economic History Review*, 44 (1991), 56.
[70] A. L. Beier, *Masterless Men: The Vagrancy Problem in England 1560–1640* (London, 1985), chs. 3–4; Paul Slack, 'Vagrants and Vagrancy in England, 1598–1664', *Economic History Review*, 2nd ser. 27 (1974).

to depart & live with his wife'.[71] John Flaxmer, who had been working as a tapster at the Bull for a year and a quarter, was similarly ordered to return to his wife and two children in Drayton, or else be rated at 12d. a week.[72] In Southampton Edward Batchiller, a sievemaker, 'cominge to this Towne verie suspiciouslue as a vagraunt or wanderinge person [was] ordered to retorne to his wife or ellse to be whipped'. Christian Burnell was similarly ordered to leave 'and repayre to her husband now working in Andover'.[73] Other lone wives risked being apprehended as vagrants, such as Margaret Vynsent, wife of John, who was punished and then issued with a passport to Dorchester 'where she says her husband lives'.[74]

Given such risks, it is difficult to discern the extent to which such separations involved mutual consent. In many instances it appears that wives and children had simply been abandoned, and it was again feared that they would become dependent on parish support. Thus Alice Reade was left in Norwich with 'a sukyng child' and three other children 'without help' by her husband who 'is run awaye', and the churchwardens of Bignor (Sussex) presented John Batchellor and Robert Wilson 'for that they have not kept company with theire wives almost for the space of half a years, the former leaving her without necessary mayntenance, the la[t]ter lefte his with iij small children upon the parrishe'.[75] Occasionally spouses were actually forced apart at the insistence of parish authorities who were reluctant to condone marriages between those of limited means. Thus Anthony Addames complained that despite having been born and bred in Stockton where he 'took great pains for his living all the time he was able', its parishioners refused to admit his new wife 'saying that they would breed a charge among them'. Addames was forced to keep his wife in the neighbouring parish of Bewdley while he continued to work in Stockton, sending her the 'the best relief he can'. His wife and child's subsequent eviction from Bewdley prompted his petition to the Worcestershire jus-

---

[71] *Minutes of the Norwich Court of Mayoralty 1630–1631*, ed. William L. Sachse, Norfolk Record Society 15 (Norwich, 1942), 154. See also orders relating to Robert Betts, 138; John Colson, 203.

[72] *Minutes of the Norwich Court of Mayoralty 1632–1635*, ed. William L. Sachse, Norfolk Record Society 36 (Norwich, 1967), 156–7. See also orders relating to John Smyth, 90; William Caister, 102; Robert Streeke, 127.

[73] *The Assembly Books of Southampton*, ii: *1609–10*, ed. J. W. Horrocks, Southampton Record Society 21 (Southampton, 1920), 74; *The Assembly Books of Southampton*, iii: *1611–1614*, ed. J. W. Horrocks, Southampton Record Society 24 (Southampton, 1924), 14–15. See also the order relating to Margarett Morlie, 28.

[74] *Poverty in Early-Stuart Salisbury*, ed. Paul Slack, Wiltshire Record Society 31 (Devizes, 1975), 33. See also the measures taken against Anne Mathewe, 26; Dorothy Lyminge, 35; Eleanor Vaughan, 40.

[75] *Norwich Census of the Poor*, 25; *Churchwarden's Presentments (17th Century). Part 1. Archdeaconry of Chichester*, ed. Hilda Johnstone, Sussex Record Society 49 (Lewes, 1948), 62.

tices in which he appealed for a house in Stockton 'or else his poore wife and child are like to perish without the door'.[76] The patriarchal imperative of the nuclear household was not always upheld even by parish authorities, therefore, whose decision-making (either to reunite married couples or enforce their separation) appears to have been driven by economic expedience, although in ways which often clashed with both the needs and desires of the couples involved.

Not all separations were viewed with regret. Martha Howlings seemed less concerned to be reunited with her husband William who had 'gone from her' than to retrieve 'diverse goods which were hers when she was sole [that] are... in the Custody of Howlyngs Inkeeper father of the said William'. At her request for 'some helpe of her said Father in lawe' and her promise 'never to trouble him more', the Norwich mayor's court persuaded him to give her 10s.[77] It is also possible that some separations were the product of alternative attitudes to marriage which viewed it as a more fleeting arrangement than the conduct writers for whom it was the foundation of the social order. This is also suggested by the temporary coupling of vagrants who travelled together, such as William Wilcockes and Jane 'his alleged wife' who were punished by the Salisbury authorities for having a counterfeit passport.[78] While such couples briefly adopting the guise of marriage were considered 'lewd' by the authorities, in all likelihood their alliances at the very least served a logic of pragmatism, if not an alternative set of principles favouring the autonomy peculiar to an itinerant existence, or the independence associated with fleeting liaisons.[79] Whether through choice, expediency, or desperation, and whether enforced, or the product of betrayal or a joint decision, such separations were indicative of the extent to which the patriarchal model was unworkable, unappealing, or simply irrelevant for many men and women in early modern England.

LONE MEN

While many wives performed the function of provision, and some couples deviated dramatically from the nuclear family model, increasing numbers of men were entirely excluded from assuming the patriarchal

---

[76] *Worcester County Records*, vol. i, part I, 267. See also Steve Hindle, 'The Problem of Pauper Marriage in Seventeenth-Century England', *Transactions of the Royal Historical Society*, 6th ser. 8 (1998).

[77] *Minutes of the Norwich Court of Mayoralty 1632–1635*, 214.

[78] *Poverty in Early-Stuart Salisbury*, 31. See also 29, 41, 59, 61–2.

[79] Beier, *Masterless Men*, chs. 4–5.

status associated with marriage and becoming a householder. In a period witnessing rapid demographic expansion from the mid-sixteenth century, unmatched by sufficient economic growth, fears concerning economic dependency were ubiquitous, with important implications for early modern concepts of manhood.[80] In the patriarchal framework of evaluation, to be of worth as a man presupposed a degree of economic independence that was becoming beyond the reach of many. The construction of credit in these terms was contingent upon hierarchies of age, and, increasingly, social status, involving the subordination of growing numbers of men as well as women. For these men, the patriarchal language of social description was primarily a critique rather than a resource to which they aspired, which they appear to have countered with alternative codes of manhood. Such a situation intensified the pressure on patriarchal definitions of manhood which attempted to stigmatize subordinate men as unmanly, as men excluded from a householding position pursued many of the avenues traditionally associated with youthful misrule in asserting their status as men.

Clearly, one of the preconditions of male credit in its patriarchal sense was householding status. Echoing the sentiments of Francis Bacon that equated unmarried men with fugitives, a court official explained to a Cambridge journeyman who objected to being bound over that, 'a jorney man ys as it were a fugitive persone, excepte he be a townsman or a marryed man'. In other words, he was not to be trusted, and, as his opponent put it, as such he was 'here to daye and gon to morrowe, & yf his master should put him oute of service: he hathe noe place to abide in'.[81] To have the freedom of the town, or to be married, implied the independent status which was the social and economic basis of patriarchal manhood. This was, however, a position held by a decreasing minority of males at any one time. It had to be striven for by the majority of men, it did not arrive automatically, and for many men it did not ever fully transpire. As a consequence, many men sought alternative sources of male status in response to their subordination by patriarchal evaluative schemes.

When asked their worth in court, male servants and apprentices responded in very different terms from their householding counterparts such as the 36-year-old Suffolk gentleman William Soone who declared

---

[80] For a detailed case study of the social and economic impact of, and the cultural responses to, demographic change, see Keith Wrightson and David Levine, *Poverty and Piety in an English Village: Terling, 1525–1700*, rev. edn. (Oxford, 1995). See also Keith Wrightson, *English Society, 1580–1680* (London, 1982), ch. 2.

[81] CUL, CUA, *Thomas Wickliffe c. Thomas Tillett*, Comm.Ct.II.10, fos. 10*ᵛ, 11ᵛ. See also above, pp. 74–5.

that 'being a maried man he lyveth of him self'.[82] William Hornsey, aged 18, told the court that 'as he is an apprentice, & under age he is worth nothing'. Another 18-year-old, who described himself as a cooper, declared that he was 'mayntayned by his father & hath nothing of his owne', and according to the 17-year-old John Andrewes, he was 'under his ffathers government, and litle worth in his owne goods'.[83] These young men were still in a state of dependency, and consequently lacked economic autonomy. They may have been involved in credit networks, but they were expected to act only as subordinates and deputies. So, for example, in assessing Thomas Cotton's age and consequent liability for horse-hire charges, one witness deposed that Cotton 'hath bought, & sould wares in his ffathers shopp but for his father only & under him, & to his use only'. In other words, Cotton was not yet accounted an autonomous economic agent. Thomas Russell's status as an independent creditor was similarly questioned in a debt case by a witness who claimed that Russell 'did still dwell with his mother who did keepe the shopps of her husbande after his death & sould such wares as her husband did in her lyfe tyme, & for about fower yeeres after ... the sayed Thomas Russell then dwelling with his mother, & servinge her as her servant did buye & sell such wares for her'.[84]

Such young men had far less economic agency than married women since they were more restricted by their dependent status from trading in their own names. Authorities actively prevented both single men and women from living 'at their own hand'.[85] Many trading privileges were restricted to householders. So Thomas Page from Suffolk was prosecuted at Sturbridge Fair for selling butter and cheese 'beinge a man unmaried'.[86] In Wiltshire in 1611, Anthony Spering was presented 'for Keping Shope ... not being of adge nether maried', and John Pile was presented 'for that he liveth at libertie and worketh by the daye, being a singell man being out of covenant [service] one yeare and a quarter'.[87] In Southampton the enforced subordination of young men was expected when several tailors complained against John Shering and Oliver Smith

---

[82] GL, London Commissary Court, *Teeler als Awson* c. *Roger Tysdale*, MS 9065A, fo. 24ᵛ.
[83] CUL, CUA, *John Paske* c. *Michael Watson*, V.C.Ct.II.19, fo. 5; *Thomas and Elizabeth Newman* c. *John Humbletoft*, V.C.Ct.II.22, fo. 204ᵛ; NRO, DN/DEP/32, fo. 27.
[84] CUL, CUA, *Andrew Goodwin* c. *Thomas Cotton*, Comm.Ct.II.18, fo. 37ᵛ; *Thomas Russell* c. *Thomas Punsaby*, V.C.Ct.II.27, fo. 8.
[85] Paul Griffiths, *Youth and Authority: Formative Experiences in England, 1560–1640* (Oxford, 1996), ch. 7.
[86] CUL, CUA, *Proctors* c. *Thomas Page*, Comm.Ct.V.7, fo. 30.
[87] *Records of the County of Wilts*, 33.

'being younge men and latelie gonn from their mrs for worcking privatlie in their chambers'.[88]

A few young men nonetheless confidently anticipated their future economic autonomy in answers to questions of their worth. Thus Peter Woodcock, the son of a clergyman, declared when aged 23 that, 'he serveth his father and is not worth much *as yet*'.[89] Giles Duckington at 30 declared that 'his estate at this present is very small but after his mothers decease it wilbe worth C^{li} & better'. Much younger, yet just as confidently assured of a smooth transition from his minority to a situation of substantial worth, was the scrivener Nathaniel Chadwick. At 16 he responded that 'he now kepeth with mr Johnsone of litcham and is litle worthe in his owne goods, but after his mothers decease he is to have so mutche lands as he estemeth to be worth about two hundred pounds which was left to him by his father'.[90] He assumed that his phase of dependency at the margins of economic agency would be limited, and confidently claimed status as a 'master-in-waiting'.[91]

Not all young men, however, viewed their future so positively. In a period of abundant labour and few resources, many men were denied an easy maturation process into an economically autonomous manhood. In Cambridge, for instance, where regulation by craft guilds was absent, an influx of migrant labour meant that the 'classic' transition from apprentice to journeyman to master was no longer the norm—a situation that was compounded by contracting numbers admitted to the freedom of the town.[92] Cambridge was not unusual in this respect, as many towns in the late sixteenth and early seventeenth centuries attempted to accommodate and regulate an ever-increasing floating population of migrant workers and craftsmen. In Chester, for example, of 240 journeymen joiners working between 1600 and 1640, fewer than 10 per cent were recruited to the ranks of master craftsmen.[93] John Bye, a migrant with his wife and child to

---

[88] *Assembly Books of Southampton*, iii. 13.

[89] NRO, *Thomas Moore* c. *Peter Woodcock*, DN/DEP/32, fo. 54^v, my emphasis. See also the answer of Stephen Woodcock, fo. 61^v. Similar answers were given, e.g., in CUL, CUA, *Ralph Parris* c. *William Colbey*, V.C.Ct.II.22, fo. 96; *John Atkinson* c. *William Gregory*, V.C.Ct.II.32, fo. 162^v.

[90] CUL, CUA, *Godfrey Twleves* c. *Edward Goodwin and Cantrell Legge*, Comm.Ct.II.17, fo. 8; NRO, DN/DEP/32, fo. 28^v.

[91] Peter Rushton, ' "The Matter in Variance": Adolescents and Domestic Conflict in the Pre-Industrial Economy of Northeast England, 1600–1800', *Journal of Social History*, 25 (1991), 101.

[92] Nigel Goose, 'Household Size and Structure in Early-Stuart Cambridge', *Social History*, 5 (1980), 375.

[93] Donald Woodward, *Men at Work: Labourers and Building Craftsmen in the Towns of Northern England, 1450–1750* (Cambridge, 1995), 69. For his more general comments on journeymen see pp. 64–72. For other examples of high numbers of urban migrants, see Peter Clark, 'The Migrant in

Southampton in 1608, was suffered to stay if he promised only to take on journey work and 'not to open anie windowes'.[94] The acceptance of newcomers became rarer, and increasingly conditional upon their sufficient means. So the turner Richard Bushnell and his wife were allowed to stay in 1608, since 'he is thought to be a man of good behaviour and estate', and the sergeweaver Abraham Norries was tolerated in 1609, because he was 'a man of good sufficiencye to live and dwelleth in a howse by himselfe'. The vast majority, however, were turned away.[95] By the 1630s the Norwich authorities were forbidding the employment of journeymen from the surrounding countryside 'because the City is so filled with them their wives & Children'.[96] Such findings quickly dispel the assumption that urban craftsmen would become masters in their turn.

The system of transitional, life-cycle service (as opposed to a perpetually subordinated proletariat) was beginning to splinter by the late sixteenth century. Increasing numbers of men were becoming primarily and permanently dependent on wage labour without yet holding a positive sense of class identity. Wage labourers were faced with pretty bleak prospects at the turn of the seventeenth century. Due to the bulging population and high levels of inflation, employment was scarce, irregular, and not particularly fruitful.[97] In addition, according to patriarchal concepts of male worth, wage labourers were men of little or no credit, held in low esteem.[98] The adaptation required in such a situation often necessitated deviation from the standard life-cycle pattern centred around the patriarchal nuclear family. The 'privilege' of marriage itself was not an option for a significant proportion of men and women who could not muster

Kentish Towns 1580–1640', and Paul Slack, 'Poverty and Politics in Salisbury 1597–1666', both in Peter Clark and Paul Slack (eds.), *Crisis and Order in English Towns, 1500–1700: Essays in Urban History* (London, 1972). See also Beier, *Masterless Men*, ch. 2; Boulton, *Neighbourhood and Society*, 158; Paul Griffiths, 'Masterless Young People in Norwich, 1560–1645', in Paul Griffiths, Adam Fox, and Steve Hindle (eds.), *The Experience of Authority in Early Modern England* (Basingstoke, 1996). Cf. Ilana Krausman Ben-Amos, 'Failure to Become Freemen: Urban Apprentices in Early Modern England', *Social History*, 16 (1991).

[94] *The Assembly Books of Southampton*, i: *1602–08*, ed. J. W. Horrocks, Southampton Record Society 19 (Southampton, 1917), 95. See also *The Assembly Books of Southampton*, iv: *1615–1616*, ed. J. W. Horrocks, Southampton Record Society 25 (Southampton, 1925), 53–9, 68–72, 74–84, for regulations against the employment of foreigners.

[95] *Assembly Books of Southampton*, i. 64; ii. 18. For orders sending newcomers away, see, e.g., ii. 18–19.

[96] *Minutes of the Norwich Court of Mayoralty 1632–1635*, 131.

[97] A. Hassell Smith, 'Labourers in Late Sixteenth-Century England: A Case Study from North Norfolk [Part I]', *Continuity and Change*, 4 (1989); Beier, *Masterless Men*, 22–8.

[98] Christopher Hill, 'Pottage for Freeborn Englishmen: Attitudes to Wage-Labour', in id., *Change and Continuity in Seventeenth-Century England* (London, 1974); Woodward, *Men at Work*, ch. 4.

sufficient resources to support an independent household.[99] It has been estimated that well over a fifth of those born in England between 1604 and 1628 never married.[100] It is difficult to know what became of such men and women in their adulthood, since, just as it is frustratingly impossible to know the full extent of women's occupational identities owing to their designation as spinsters, wives, or widows, so our picture of early modern social relations is hampered by a lack of information about the age and marital status of the many men listed in administrative records. However, they were most likely expected to remain subordinate to householders for their entire lives, rather than just their youth, and were excluded from escaping the ties of dependency which marked the servant or journeyman's lot. As a result they were subjected to the same kind of social evaluation applied to young men or men deemed to be of no worth.

According to the patriarchal model of manhood which subordinated men on the grounds of age and socio-economic status, such dependent males were not fully men, even though they lived in a social and demographic setting which increasingly did not correspond to the patriarchal ideal of the nuclear family. While patriarchal ideology may well have appealed to the self-styled 'better sorts' both as a central component of their respectability and as a form of critique serving a regulative agenda, it is unlikely that its consequent language of social description was universally espoused, particularly by those men and women who were increasingly excluded from its benefits. It would be wrong, therefore, to collude with dominant discourses which located manhood exclusively in the values of thrift, provision, worth, and vocation. Some lone men, as well as some married men, sought alternative sources of positive male identity, competing for male status and asserting their manhood in ways which contradicted and existed in tension with patriarchal ideology. Dependency did not stop males from being men; it meant they had to seek alternative forms of manhood which functioned as a form of male resistance to patriarchal norms, or at the very least served to undermine them. Patriarchal ethics of social evaluation did not go unchallenged, therefore, especially by many men themselves. In her work on journeymen in early modern Germany, Merry Wiesner has identified what she has called a 'class-specific' ideology of male status rooted in quite different forms of self-assertion from those of their masters: 'Transience, prodi-

---

[99] Wrightson, *English Society*, 70.
[100] E. A. Wrigley and R. S. Schofield, *The Population History of England, 1541–1871: A Reconstruction* (Cambridge, 1993), 260; J. A. Goldstone, 'The Demographic Revolution in England: A Reexamination', *Population Studies*, 40 (1986), 17. See also Hindle, 'The Problem of Pauper Marriage'.

gality, physical bravery, and comradliness made one a true man among journeymen, in sharp contrast to the master's virtues of thrift, reliability, and stability.'[101] It is clear that similar alternatives were asserted by men in early modern England, increasingly along the fault lines of social status as many of the excesses traditionally associated with youth culture began to take on class-related as well as age-related connotations.

Although counter-codes of conduct were not formulated as coherently as patriarchal ideals, not least because of their threat to those in authority, they can nonetheless be glimpsed indirectly when they collided with disciplinary and regulative initiatives. One example is the bravura and 'good fellowship' associated with drinking rituals, which were by no means exclusive to the immoderation of youth. Despite attempts to label such behaviour as 'dishonest' and 'disorderly', it is clear that excessive drinking held considerable appeal for men of all ages.[102] Contrary to the value of thrift, men who spent much time and money in the alehouse asserted their independence from the cares and labours of honest hardship. So John Pope, Nichollas Laurance, and Peter Hibberd were punished for their 'inordinatt drinkinge' together with Thomas Williams, 'a verie poore man who pawned his cloake there and spent... xviij*d.*'. One Canton was presented in 1632 as 'a person that hath noe setled aboade nor a house houlder' who had lodged in Cambridge for three nights and 'carried & demeaned himselfe loosely & uncivilly . . . suspected of being a dishonest man, & a frequenter & haunter of alehouses, & naughty places'. In Somerset, objections were raised against John Maryne who was 'by profession a hooper, but lyveth very Idelly from place to place... comonly... in an Alehows'. In Newick (Sussex) William Pearse was doubted as a witness because he 'hath byne & ys geeven muche to drinkinge and hathe Consumed most parte of his stocke and goods and ys litle worthe as the Common voyce & fame goethe'.[103] From the later sixteenth-century the alehouse became associated with riot, excess, sedition, and the disruption of family life in the minds of the respectable, who themselves increasingly withdrew from its ambit. Yet for the participants themselves, most of whom were labouring men, the alehouse was a place of respite from patriarchal evaluative schemes, if not the locus of an alternative society.[104]

---

[101] Merry Wiesner, '*Wandervögels* and Women: Journeymen's Concepts of Masculinity in Early Modern Germany', *Journal of Social History*, 24 (1991), 776. See also her 'Guilds, Male Bonding and Women's Work in Early Modern Germany', *Gender and History*, 1 (1989).
[102] e.g. *Assembly Books of Southampton*, ii. 102; Bodl., OUA, Hyp/B/4, fo. 62ᵛ.
[103] *Assembly Books of Southampton*, ii. 46; CUL, CUA, Comm.Ct.I.18, fo. 57ᵛ; *Quarter Sessions Records for the County of Somerset*, 80; WSRO, Butler c. *Doppe and Colman*, EpII/5/5, fo. 287ᵛ. See also fo. 293ᵛ.
[104] Peter Clark, *The English Alehouse: A Social History 1200–1830* (London, 1983), chs. 6–7; id.,

Other forms of 'ill rule' considered against 'good conversations and honest condicions' were gambling and disorderly conduct. The Merchant Taylors' Company, for example, decreed that its livery men and freemen should retain their dignity by being 'no comon ryoter, comon dice player comon night walker ... nor customablie haunt uncovenable places'. Similarly the Pewterers' Company ordered that 'if any of the clothing doo happen to mysuse them selves ... otherwise then lyke honest and Syvell men, or become dronkerdes, Brawlers or such unsemely demeanors' they would be expelled from the livery.[105] Local officials in Wiltshire were exercised by the weavers Thomas Bullman, who was presented for 'common playing at bowles having nothing to maintain it', and Nicholas Turner, 'for betting 6*d*. a game at bowles [with] noe abilitie to maintaine it'.[106] Such actions stood in stark contrast to ideals of thrift and vocation. Used here as a derogatory term, the label 'common' also suggested that they held widespread appeal, in contravention of the values espoused by the 'able and sufficient' sort. The London pewterer John Bowlting similarly transgressed when he 'mysue[d] hym self to playe at unlawfull games called shove grote for money', although his offence seems to have related less to his expenditure than to his 'having no Respect with whom he playeth'.[107] Violent and often socially disruptive articulations of male status were also routinely claimed by labouring men in rejection of the meek demeanour expected of them by their social superiors. So, for example, Humphrey Grove, Richard Grove, and John Grove the younger of Haghley (Worcestershire), armed with bills, pikestaffs, and daggers, challenged various inhabitants of Old Swinford to fight, before going to 'the top of a hill there adjoining and hooted and shouted and called for the cowardly boys of Old Swinford to come forth to them'.[108]

It is difficult to assess whether such codes of behaviour were simply compensatory measures, with the implication that the men concerned were merely aspiring, yet frustrated, patriarchs, rather than consciously creating and participating in conflicting, and increasingly class-based, codes of manhood. Obviously, pursuing forms of manliness in terms of

'The Alehouse and the Alternative Society', in Donald Pennington and Keith Thomas (eds.), *Puritans and Revolutionaries: Essays in Seventeenth-Century History Presented to Christopher Hill* (Oxford, 1978); Keith Wrightson, 'Alehouses, Order and Reformation in Rural England, 1590–1660', in Eileen and Stephen Yeo (eds.), *Popular Culture and Class Conflict, 1590–1914: Explorations in the History of Labour and Leisure* (Brighton, 1981).

[105] William Herbert, *The History of the Twelve Great Livery Companies of London*, 2 vols. (London, 1834–6), 418; GL, Pewterers' Company, Court Minutes, 1561–89, MS 7090/2, fo. 47ᵛ.
[106] *Records of the County of Wilts*, 57. See also *Worcester County Records*, vol. i, part I, 31–2.
[107] GL, Pewterers' Company, Court Minutes, MS 7090/2, fo. 70.
[108] *Worcester County Records*, vol. i, part I, 23. See also Ch. 5 above.

prodigality and physical bravado protected men neither from financial hardship nor from the critiques of patriarchal discourse, since notions of manhood overlapped as well as clashed, and did not exist in discrete separation. Furthermore, the articulation of male status in terms of excess, prodigality, and violence was not restricted to those excluded from householding status on the grounds either of age or of poverty. Rather, it was also indicative of the many contradictions inherent in concepts of manhood in early modern England. Men occupying patriarchal positions sought status at times from violent conduct or participation in drinking culture, although imperatives of honesty and respectability had an increasingly inhibiting effect for many who wished to dissociate themselves from the perceived excesses of their social inferiors.

While the culture of credit helped to reinforce the ethic of male honesty rooted in provision, worth, and plain dealing, it also served to establish loose hierarchies of masculinity which produced conflict. As a result, some of the attributes of patriarchal manhood in terms of credit and worth were subtly remapped onto contours of social status, and became the preserve of the 'honest' or 'better' sorts—the 'able and sufficient' men. While labouring men who married still derived a degree of patriarchal authority from their relationship with their wives (i.e. patriarchal in the feminist sense), their kinship with the householders of the middling sort became more distant. Increasing numbers of unmarried adult males were denied full patriarchal authority, and the manhood associated with them and the 'poorer sort' became more readily associated with disruption, informing stereotypes of dissolute, spendthrift deviants requiring external sources of discipline in the absence of the ability to discipline themselves. Limited access to the patriarchal model of manhood did not result in the emasculation of those who were excluded, however, who instead drew upon other sources of male prestige that had traditionally either been associated with young men or had been more easily and more generally incorporated within a broader repertoire of adult male identity. Although it was a powerful ideology, positive constructions of manliness were not defined purely in relation to patriarchy by many men, but were also a product of the varied ethics of violence, excess, bravado, prodigality, collectivism, and contrary assertions of independence. Like ideals of chastity, silence, and obedience for women, notions of male credit based on provision and honest dealing were a central aspect of social description in early modern England. Yet similarly, they were contested, or simply ignored, both by the large numbers of women who were involved in provision and commercial pursuits, and by the many men who, excluded from the patriarchal dividend, turned instead to potent alternatives.

8
The 'Ancienter Sort'

IN 1614, Walter Howard sent a petition to the king pleading for aid on account of his infirmity after several years' military service in Ireland and the Low Countries:

> Yor Maties poore peticoner being aged doth now feele and fynd his body to be much debilitated & much diffected of his sight wch hath happened unto hym by the hurts bruses colde & sickness with many other Calamities the wch he hath indured & receaved in ye warrs, he having in charge a wyfe & fyve Children & small meanes or none at all to releeve there wants is now constrayned to deplore his mysery and want unto yor Royal Matie to redresse ye same, or otherwise both yor peticoner his wyfe and children are likely to perishe.

Granted an annual pension of 4 marks by the Wiltshire justices, Howard was able to maintain himself and provide for his family in a position of at least semi-retirement, which was a relatively fortunate situation in early modern England.[1] Yet, physically debilitated, and dependent upon the state for a large part of his living, it is questionable whether he retained much of a claim to patriarchal manhood. As we have already seen, age, as well as social status, determined the distribution of patriarchal dividends, and its impact was as profound for the old as for the young. This final chapter focuses on the closing stages of the life course in order to investigate the extent to which old men had access to patriarchal privilege, and the degree to which they also might have been associated with alternative meanings of manhood.

The history of old age is a relatively neglected field by contrast with histories of birth, childhood, youth, marriage, and death. Demographers have long since dispelled assumptions that old age was a rarity in pre-industrial society; the proportion of the population over 60 in England between 1560 and 1640 has been estimated at around 8 per cent.[2] While

---

[1] *Records of the County of Wilts, Being Extracts from the Quarter Sessions Great Rolls of the Seventeenth Century*, ed. B. H. Cunnington (Devizes, 1932), 310. See also the petitions of John Ducketts, 46; George Inges, 68; John Allen, 101.

[2] E. A. Wrigley and R. S. Schofield, *The Population History of England, 1541–1871: A Reconstruction* (Cambridge, 1993), 216, 528. For local variations, see Peter Laslett, *Family Life and Illicit Love*

scholars have also rejected the myth of a pre-modern golden age for the elderly, comparatively little detail has been recovered relating to the experiences of the aged in the early modern period.[3] In addition, in the even rarer instances when questions of gender have been explicitly raised in relation to ageing, they have almost exclusively addressed the lives of elderly women.[4] With the exception of important recent work by Margaret Pelling, the relationship between old age and masculinity remains unexplored.[5] Given the extent to which age influenced meanings of manhood and dominated the distribution of patriarchal resources it is essential to study its role in later life as well as in the contested territory between youth and 'man's age'.

Such a task is more easily called for than executed. One of the reasons why old age has been so 'shockingly untended' as a field is the difficulty of locating the elderly in a largely age-blind historical record.[6] Before the search for the aged can even be attempted, a working definition of what constituted old age in early modern England is required, which itself is no simple business. The more recently introduced chronological markers of 60 or 65 were arbitrarily selected and bear little relation to early modern understandings of ageing.[7] Theoretical schemes of the ages of man varied considerably over the chronological onset of old age. The

in *Earlier Generations: Essays in Historical Sociology* (Cambridge, 1977), 188; Lynn Ann Botelho, 'Provisions for the Elderly in Two Early Modern Suffolk Communities', Ph.D. thesis (Cambridge, 1996), 129.

[3] Laslett, *Family Life and Illicit Love*, ch. 5; Peter N. Stearns, 'Introduction', to id. (ed.), *Old Age in Preindustrial Society* (New York, 1982); Margaret Pelling and Richard M. Smith (eds.), *Life, Death and the Elderly: Historical Perspectives* (London, 1991); Pat Thane, *Old Age in English History: Past Experiences, Present Issues* (Oxford, 2000).

[4] Peter N. Stearns, 'Old Women: Some Historical Observations', *Journal of Family History*, 5 (1980); Margaret Pelling, 'Older Women: Household, Caring and Other Occupations in the Late Sixteenth-Century Town', in ead., *The Common Lot: Sickness, Medical Occupations and the Urban Poor in Early Modern England* (London, 1998); Lynn Botelho and Pat Thane (eds.), *Women and Ageing in British Society since 1500* (Harlow, 2001); Alison Rowlands, 'Witchcraft and Old Women in Early Modern Germany', *Past and Present*, 173 (2001).

[5] Margaret Pelling, 'Finding Widowers: Men without Women in English Towns before 1700', in Sandra Cavallo and Lyndan Warner (eds.), *Widowhood in Medieval and Early Modern Europe* (Harlow, 1999); ead., 'Who Most Needs to Marry? Ageing and Inequality among Women and Men in Early Modern Norwich', in Botelho and Thane (eds.), *Women and Ageing*. See also ead., 'Old Age, Poverty, and Disability in Early Modern Norwich: Work, Remarriage, and Other Expedients', in Pelling and Smith (eds.), *Life, Death and the Elderly*.

[6] Stearns (ed.), *Old Age in Preindustrial Society*, 1.

[7] Janet Roebuck, 'When does "Old Age" Begin? The Evolution of the English Definition', *Journal of Social History*, 12 (1979). See also Lloyd Bonfield, 'Was there a "Third Age" in the Preindustrial English Past? Some Evidence from the Law', in John M. Eekelaar and David Pearl (eds.), *An Aging World: Dilemmas and Challenges for Law and Social Policy* (Oxford, 1989).

most pessimistic of medical tracts placed the beginning of old age at 35, while the most optimistic delayed it until 60.[8] In many schemes, however, and particularly those allowing for a period of 'green' or 'flourishing' old age, ageing began at around 50 and had fully set in by 60 or 65.[9] Similar assumptions can be discerned in rare snippets of incidental commentary which explicitly referred to ageing in numerical terms. When William Popley (himself aged 80 years 'and upwardes') was questioned about a survey he had conducted of the manor of Barton (Gloucestershire) he recalled that most of the tenants who had been sworn to give evidence were 'very old men', by which he meant 'some above threscore and some fyftie and some above at the tyme of the making of the same Survey'.[10] Such evidence supports the use of 50 as the milestone from which to approach ageing in the early modern past, rather than the preference of historical demographers for 60 or even 65.[11]

Chronological markers such as these were often only approximations, since many men and women did not have a precise numerical sense of their age.[12] Most of the witnesses in the dispute involving the manor of Barton, for example, only gave estimates of their age. William Warde, a yeoman, and Robert Edwards, a husbandman, were both listed as being 60 years 'and above', while the innholder John Warren was 50 years 'or there abouts'.[13] Some witnesses who made multiple appearances in court gave varying accounts of their years. A Cambridge carpenter Francis Harvey declared his age as 56 in May 1625 and as 60 just four months later, and a Sussex husbandman William Rucke was recorded as being both 60 and 65 in 1606.[14] Literate and highly educated men could be similarly imprecise about their age. John Cragge, a fellow of St Catharine's College, Cambridge, stated that he was 72 in 1601, yet claimed the venerable age of 80 just four years later.[15] Conversely, the Cambridge tailor William Tomson remained 63 for well over thirteen months, and a husbandman from Ditchling (Sussex) judged his age to be 60 on three different occa-

[8] William Bullein, *The Government of Health* (London, 1595), fo. 12; William Vaughan, *Directions for Health, both Naturall and Artificiall* (London, 1617), 214. See also Fig. 3 and p. 41 above.
[9] e.g. James Hart, *KAINIKH; or, The Diet of the Diseased* (London, 1633), 12; Simon Goulart, *The Wise Vieillard, or Old Man* (London, 1621), 24–5.
[10] PRO, E133/1/87, fos. 9–10.
[11] Pelling, 'Old Age, Poverty, and Disability'; Botelho, 'Provisions for the Elderly', 19.
[12] Keith Thomas, 'Numeracy in Early Modern England', *Transactions of the Royal Historical Society*, 5th ser. 37 (1987), 126.
[13] PRO, E133/1/87, fos. 1–7ᵛ.
[14] CUL, CUA, V.C.Ct.II.22, fos. 179ᵛ, 194; WSRO, EpII/5/7, fos. 54, 142.
[15] CUL, CUA, V.C.Ct.II.3, fo. 44; Comm.Ct.II.12, fo. 55.

sions over the course of five years.[16] Vague estimates such as these were at odds with the precision occasionally claimed by younger people such as the carpenter Richard Soundy who declared himself to be 20½.[17]

The extreme over-representation of men and women aged 50 and 60 'or thereabouts' amongst deponents over 50 in the Cambridge university courts and the Lewes archdeaconry court suggest that these were convenient general markers of age either for older witnesses themselves or for the scribes who took their depositions (Figs. 9–10). Of 593 witnesses in the Lewes archdeaconry court claiming to be in their fifties, over half (55 per cent) said they were 50, and of 401 witnesses in their sixties, almost three-quarters (70 per cent) cited their age as 60 'or thereabouts'. Even more stark is the predominance of witnesses aged 60 and over in equity proceedings regarding customary rights in Cambridgeshire, heard by the Court of Exchequer (Fig. 11). The high percentage of those between 60 and 69 claiming to be 60 suggests that in this forum 60 was a more important marker than 50. Although this was at least partly attributable to diminishing life expectancy and a narrowing age structure, it is significant that the percentage of those in their sixties referring to their age in round numbers was much higher than those in their seventies as well as their fifties. While witnesses may well have claimed the authority associated with age from 50 and above, therefore, it appears that 60 was more definitively symbolic of old age.

Men seeking to excuse themselves from office on account of their age occasionally referred to their longevity numerically. Again, 60 was a common reference point. Adrian Barton sought exemption from serving as constable for the precinct next Temple Bar in London 'in respect of his yeres beinge neere Threescore', and was also subsequently discharged from serving on the wardmoot inquest 'in respect of his age and weaknes'. Similarly, the Sussex physician Obadiah Bexhill sought exemption from being an overseer of the poor 'by reason of his great age and other infirmityes being in his threescore & sixt yeare'.[18] As these cases suggest, old age was as much a product of incapacity as accumulated years, and it was more often judged in functional rather than chronological terms.[19] The numerical ages of the men and women admitted to the

---

[16] CUL, CUA, V.C.Ct.II.1, fo. 146; Comm.Ct.II.6, fo. 114; WSRO, EpII/5/6, fos. 5, 143, 190, 196.

[17] WSRO, EpII/5/13, fo. 104. See also the description of Mary Higham, who claimed to be 19½, EpII/5/12, fo. 55.

[18] GL, St Dunstan in the West, Vestry Minutes, 1588–1663, MS 3016/1, 126, 158; ESRO, QR/EW 53, no. 18.

[19] Botelho and Thane (eds.), *Women and Ageing*, introduction. See also Keith Thomas, 'Age and Authority in Early Modern England', *Proceedings of the British Academy*, 62 (1976).

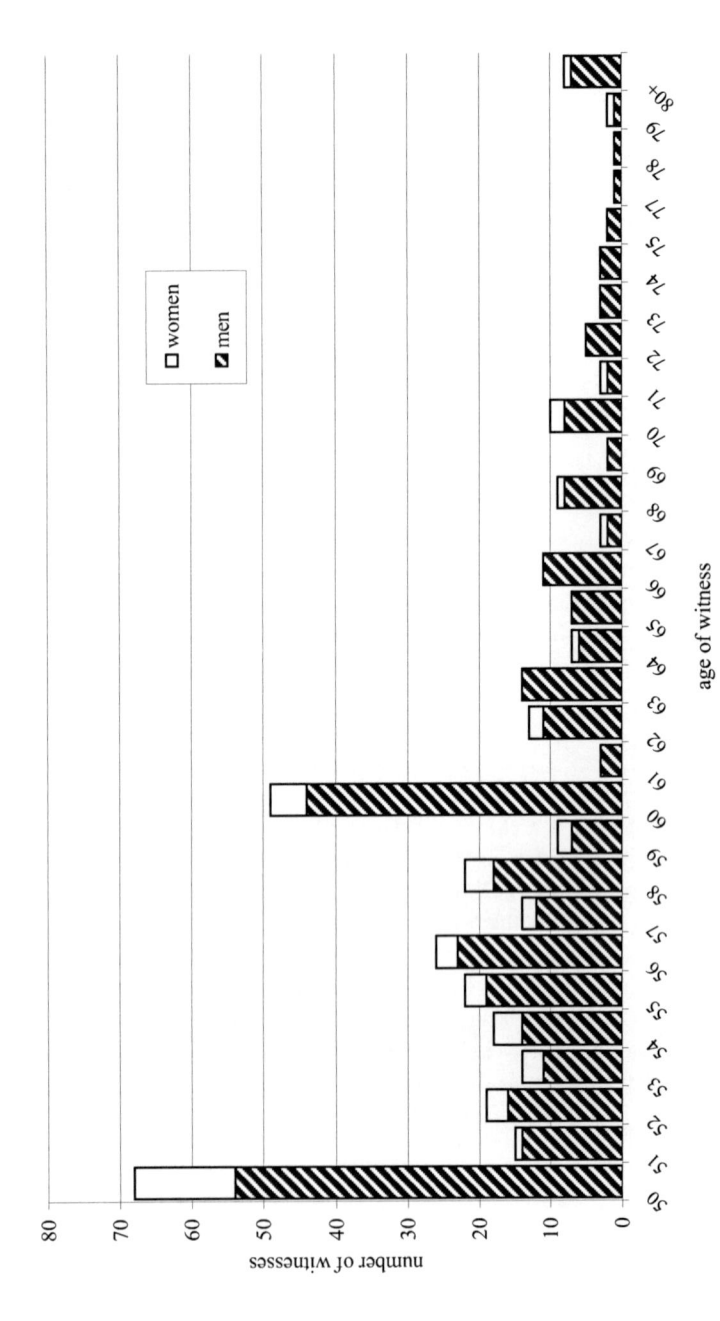

Fig. 9. Ages of witnesses over 50 in the Cambridge university courts, 1581–1640

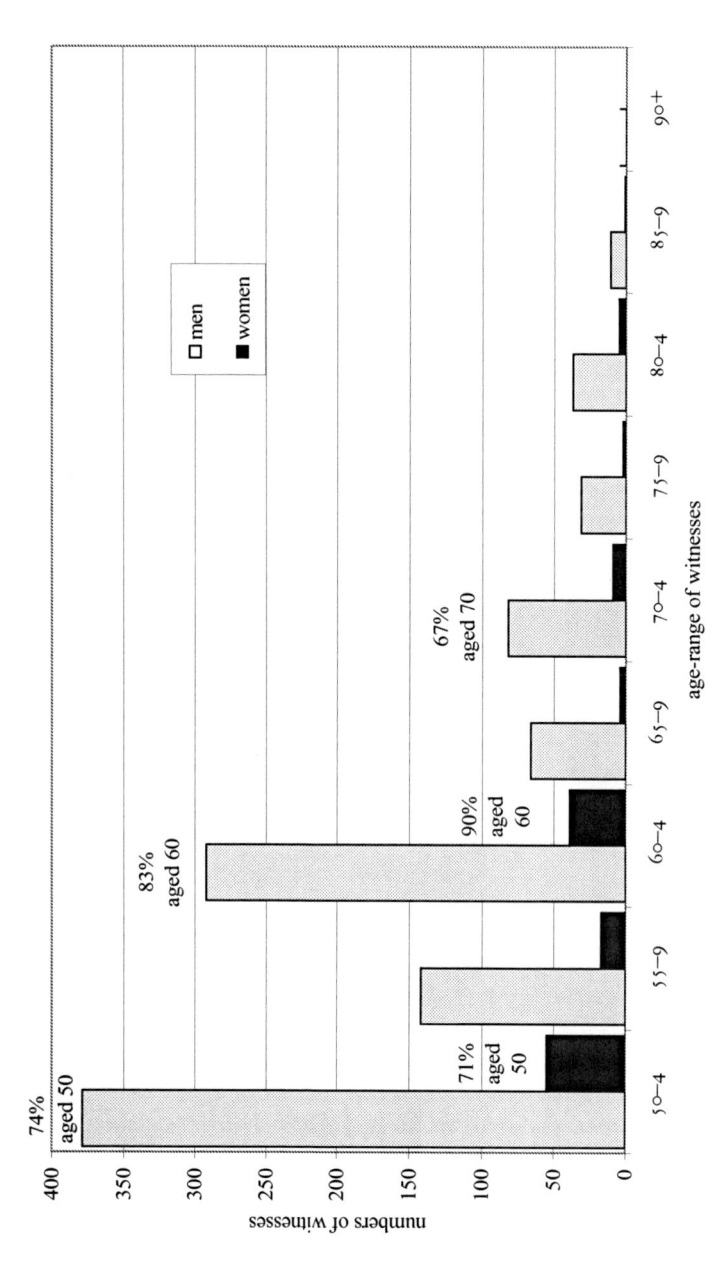

Fig. 10. Ages of witnesses over 50 in the Lewes archdeaconry court, 1581–1640

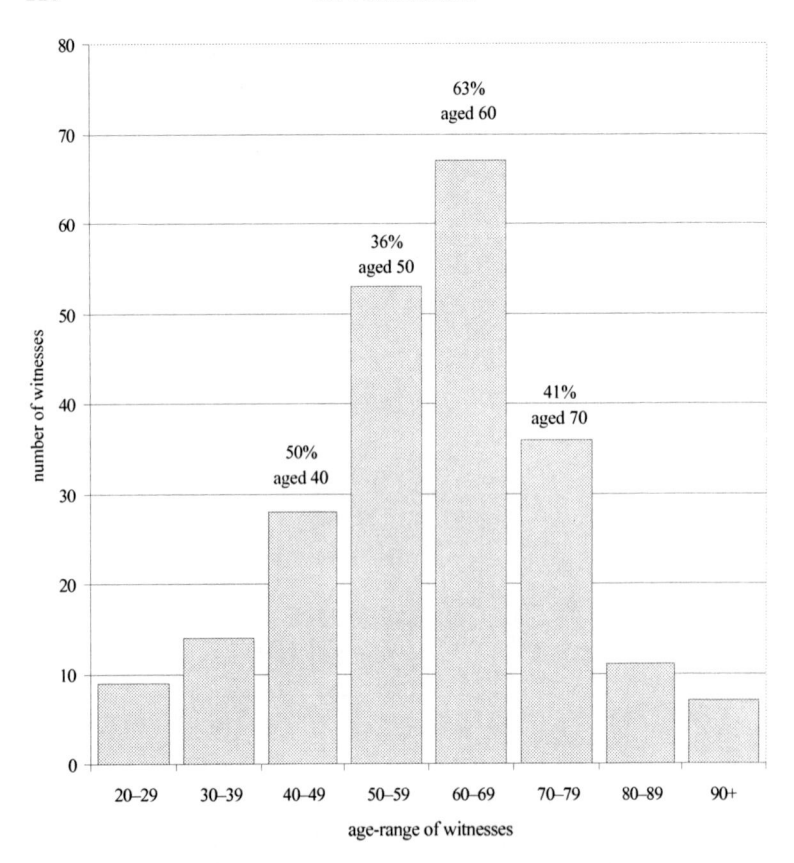

Fig. 11. Age of Cambridgeshire witnesses in the Court of Exchequer, 1587–1638

Tooley Foundation in Ipswich, for example, were considered irrelevant. Instead, old age was signified by 'lamenes', 'ympotency', and 'infirmitie', and the extreme need it generated in those who were of 'poore estate'.[20]

The primacy of cultural and functional definitions of age meant that there were significant differences between concepts of age for men and women in early modern England. Recent research by Lynn Botelho suggests that the onset of old age was both earlier in the life cycle and faster for women than for men, whose ageing was more gradual and piecemeal. Women's entry into old age was biologically triggered by the menopause and more obviously related to its visible effects, whereas men's ageing was

[20] *Poor Relief in Elizabethan Ipswich*, ed. John Webb, Suffolk Records Society 9 (Ipswich, 1966), 24, 26, 29, 27.

more closely linked to their ability to sustain themselves and their households economically.[21] Yet despite the earlier onset of old age in women it is possible that ageing was less of a handicap for them than has been traditionally asserted, and that women were actually better equipped than many men to adapt to the challenges of old age.[22] In addition it is likely that they enjoyed a greater degree of continuity with their earlier lives. Indeed, it has been suggested that some older women experienced greater independence and autonomy in their later years than in their youth, and that for them old age could be comparatively liberating.[23] Men, on the other hand, had more to lose than to gain in later life; their access to patriarchal dividends diminished as they became physically debilitated with age, and they had less recourse to the potent alternative sources of manhood rooted in excess, strength, and bravado adopted by many of their younger counterparts.

Although men and women's experiences of old age in relation to their earlier lives may have diverged considerably, it is possible that there was also a degree of gender convergence between men and women in old age—particularly amongst those of more limited means—which may have been positive for women but was negative for men. Ultimately, this was as dependent on socio-economic status and physical capacity as gender, and one of the most striking features of evidence relating to ageing in early modern England is the diversity of experience it represents. The 'ancient men' who recounted local custom at least temporarily enjoyed a form of authority expressly derived from both age and gender. Older men with adequate resources and/or good health could claim prolonged access to aspects of patriarchal manhood associated with self-sufficiency and provision. However, those blighted by incapacity, particularly if they could no longer support themselves, saw their status as men eclipsed as the negative aspects of ageing became the primary determinants of their identity.

THE REPORT OF ANCIENT MEN

Some of the most positive available evidence relating to the treatment and experiences of old men in early modern England is contained within the files of customary disputes. As guardians of the details of local

---

[21] Lynn Botelho, 'Old Age and Menopause in Rural Women of Early Modern Suffolk', in Botelho and Thane (eds.), *Women and Ageing*.
[22] Pelling, 'Finding Widowers'; ead., 'Who Most Needs to Marry?'
[23] Amy M. Froide, 'Old Maids: The Lifecycle of Single Women in Early Modern England', in Botelho and Thane (eds.), *Women and Ageing*. Cf. Shulamith Shahar, *Growing Old in the Middle Ages*, trans. Yael Lotan (London, 1997).

tradition relating to property rights, access to land, tithe payments, and other customary dues and obligations, older men were automatically privileged on account of their age as well as their gender. In the formal appointment of old men as repositories of local knowledge, age could sometimes overcome social status as a designator of authority. The aged witnesses were not exclusively drawn from the 'able' or 'sufficient' men who governed parish affairs, but also included men of little or no worth, primarily respected for their accumulated years, particularly if they had been long-term residents of a place. Such respect, however, was not unfailingly extended to old men; it constituted a specific and exceptional application of gerontocratic principles which in other contexts held less sway. Nonetheless, it was one important and largely gender-specific way in which older men could lay claim to political importance, ritual authority, and intellectual capital.[24]

Witnesses in customary disputes were overwhelmingly male. Of a sample of 225 Exchequer depositions by commission to Cambridgeshire between 1587 and 1638, only four were given by women, and of a sample of 204 witnesses in disputes over tithes or custom relating to church repairs in the archdeaconry of Lewes between 1587 and 1624, only one was female. Older women were also particularly under-represented in the Cambridge university courts. Whereas 21 per cent of witnesses under 50 were women, they accounted for only 14 per cent of those over 50 and only 10 per cent of those over 60. The authority associated with longevity, at least in the formal setting of the courtroom, was almost entirely gender specific; it was the testimony of old men rather than old women that legitimized customary knowledge as deriving from 'tymes long before the memory of man'.[25]

This was not because women were ignorant about customary rights. Very occasionally, particular customs appear to have been the preserve of women. Unusually, nearly half the witnesses in a dispute over the custom of making cheese in Gislingham (Norfolk) were older women. This was probably because they were responsible for producing the cheese due in place of tithe milk which was made according to an age-old method using the morning and evening milk on nine specific days of the year. Maria Swayne (aged 64) recalled in her widowhood that when she had come

---

[24] Andy Wood, 'Custom and the Social Organization of Writing in Early Modern England'; Adam Fox, 'Remembering the Past in Early Modern England: Oral and Written Tradition', both in *Transactions of the Royal Historical Society*, 6th ser. 9 (1999). See also Adam Fox, *Oral and Literate Culture in England 1500–1700* (Oxford, 2000), ch. 5.

[25] WSRO, *Michael Start c. Robert Alse*, EpII/5/7, fo. 90. See also Andy Wood, *The Politics of Social Conflict: The Peak Country 1520–1770* (Cambridge, 1999), 171–3.

newly wed to a farm in Gislingham which had 'a great dayrie of Cowes', there was 'some debate' between the parson and his parishioners about the payment of tithes. As a newcomer seeking confirmation of local practice she 'by the advise & consent of her ... husband did repaire to divers of the antientest & better sorte of women of the said parish to enquire of them concerning the payment of their tithes'. The women she consulted (many of whom she accorded the honorific title of 'old goodwife') informed her that 'thoughe there were some differences betwixt some of their husbands & other men of their towne concerning the payment of tithes yett they did and would pay their tithes as formerly they had done'. This was in the form of nine 'unflett' cheeses—a custom which Maria Swayne herself subsequently observed. In this instance it was the older women of the parish who established customary practice, not just as witnesses in this dispute of 1633, but by having persisted in their dairying habits for more than forty years regardless of their husbands' objections.[26] This case is exceptional, and primarily attributable to women's responsibility for dairying in early modern England, but it does suggest that women could be instrumental both in the determination of customary duties and rights through their own practices and in preserving their memory.

More often, however, women's knowledge of custom is barely discernible in legal records, and was usually only solicited as a result of their association with particular men. Margaret Watson, a yeoman's wife aged 70, gave evidence regarding entitlement to the profits from the 'vicar's meadow' in Chesterton (Cambridgeshire) that was as precise and as detailed as the testimony of her co-witnesses who were all men in their sixties. Her residency in the parish for fifty-nine years was the basis of her assertion that the rights to the land in question had belonged to the vicars of Chesterton since 'tyme oute of mynde'. Interestingly, her husband Thomas was not amongst the other witnesses, and it is possible that she was a deponent in lieu of him.[27] The rare instances when Cambridgeshire women gave evidence to the Court of Exchequer tended to involve references to the actions of their late husbands who, obviously, could no longer supply important evidence themselves. So Alice Harrison (aged 50) appeared in 1595 as the 'somtimes wife of Thomas Randle', and gave evidence about his seizure of four acres of land in the manor of Wittlesey in his capacity as deputy bailiff twenty years previously. Likewise, answering questions about an area of pasture called the Pingle in Haddenham, Agnes Govy, aged 58, deposed she knew that it had been enclosed for twenty-six years because her husband had occupied it for one year before

[26] NRO, *Johannes Symonds* c. *Christopher Smeare*, DN/DEP/41, fos. 107ᵛ–108.
[27] CUL, CUA, *Thomas Parrishe* c. *William Osse*, Comm.Ct.II.2, fo. 115ᵛ.

his death. Her additional statement that 'after her husbands decease then this deponent herself had it for one yeare also' is another reminder that women as well as men had interests in many customary disputes.[28] Yet despite their understanding of and interest in customary rights, women were seldom approached to contribute their knowledge to the formal record.

By contrast, this was a role for which men were groomed from their youth. Old men giving evidence in tithe disputes, for instance, often recalled their first inclusion in Rogationtide perambulations of the parish, which traditionally included the instruction of boys by the older and substantial male inhabitants on the details of parish boundaries.[29] The octogenarian Thomas Amore of Ditchling (Sussex) referred to his participation when both old and young: 'hee hathe oftentimes gone the perambulacion aboute the Boundes with other the antientt parishioners asweell of late as lx yeares agoe & upwardes'. William Feldwicke, a 63-year-old yeoman of West Hoathly (Sussex), recalled that 'about three or foure & forty yeares agon [he] together with the then old men & others ... did first walke the Bouns & lymitts of the sayd parrishe ... according to the directions of the ... old men'. Other early memories suggest that boys began to be included in perambulations when in their teens. John Gatland, a lifelong inhabitant of the same parish, began walking the bounds at the age of 16 with 'the then oldest men & others', and John Freeman, a 65-year-old yeoman of Brightling (Susssex), had been 'goinge a procession in and about the saide parishe for these fifty yeares'.[30] Such events accorded a ritual authority to the old men directing the proceedings and initiated teenage boys into the duties of remembrance. The young and the old were thus linked as the furthest points of a potential memory span in a way that temporarily sidelined the middle-aged and 'substantial' men of the parish.

While the rituals of perambulations often involved feasting and festivities, harsher measures were also employed to aid remembrance. The Sussex husbandman John Clarke linked his knowledge of the parish borders of Worth spanning some forty-seven or forty-eight years to the parson's violent actions as they were walking the bounds when Clarke had been a boy of 12 or 13:

---

[28] PRO, E134/37Eliz/Hil20; E134/42Eliz/Trin 10. See also the deposition of Anna Body, WSRO, EpII/5/9, fos. 37ᵛ–38.

[29] Ronald Hutton, *The Rise and Fall of Merry England: The Ritual Year 1400–1700* (Oxford, 1994), 35, 176, 217. See also id., *The Stations of the Sun: A History of the Ritual Year in Britain* (Oxford, 1997), ch. 26; Keith Thomas, *Religion and the Decline of Magic* (London, 1978), 71–4.

[30] WSRO, *Thomas Rawood c. Thomas Lucas and Francis More*, EpII/5/6, fo. 10ᵛ; *Churchwardens of West Hoathly c. John Ridley*, EpII/5/11, fo. 135ᵛ; *Richard Instead c. Michael Whiston*, EpII/5/10, fo. 14ᵛ; *Mr Thomas Pye c. Edmund Hawes*, EpII/5/6, fo. 179.

hee shall never forget that when they came in theire sayd perambulacion, unto the sayd grounds called Stroodgate in question . . . his sayd master Parson of Worth aforesaid did pull & hold this deponent so hard by the eares that thereby hee might remember where the parrishe of Worth & West Hothely aforesaid parted in that place, that they were sore a good while after, by which token hee alwaies Calleth to mynde as hee passeth that way the same severing of the said parrishes & the grounds aforesaid.[31]

Boys may well have ended such days not only with full stomachs, but also with bruises and sore heads as local knowledge was physically inscribed and preserved.

Witnesses in disputes over custom were distinguished as much by their age as by their gender. It is clear that authority in such matters was not simply the preserve of men but of *old* men.[32] Robert Sekyn, a 76-year-old husbandman of Swavesey (Cambridgeshire), could confirm very little of the allegations in a tithes dispute beyond what he had heard 'diverse oulde & ancient men saye'. When asked why he had been called as a witness he answered that he had no idea, 'except yt was for that he is an olde man of greate age, & there remayninge from his youthe', which suggests that at times the weight of old age was deemed more important in the selection of witnesses than their detailed knowledge of the issues in dispute.[33] More often, however, old men did prove to be the living caches of information they were expected to be, and weighty reliance was placed upon their knowledge. The churchwardens of Brightling, 'desirous to have Certen notice or knowledge of their Boundiers', hired 'an olde man whoe was borne in the saide parishe (and knewe the boundes therof very well) to goe with them from place to place & from Boundier to Boundier' in order to show them 'how farre their parishe wentte' and to 'point out the Boundes unto them'.[34] In such situations of doubt, it appears that parish officials turned to the memories of old men more often than the written record to confirm local knowledge. Only one case involving disputed custom within a thirty-five-year period in the Lewes archdeaconry court included a reference to written records—in this instance a register of responsibility for repairing enclosures within the churchyard. This 'ancient booke' was regularly consulted by the minister, churchwardens, and 'other ancient men of the parrishe', yet repairs were assessed not only according to the book but also as dictated by the 'reporte of old men'.[35]

[31] WSRO, *Richard Instead* c. *Michael Whiston*, EpII/5/10, fos. 14ᵛ, 15ᵛ–16.
[32] Thomas, 'Age and Authority', 233–4.
[33] CUL, EDR, *Thomas Manyngham* c. *Thomas Chapman*, D/2/11, fos. 76ᵛ–77.
[34] WSRO, *Mr Thomas Pye* c. *Edmund Hawes*, EpII/5/6, fo. 179ʳ⁻ᵛ.
[35] WSRO, *Goodman and Jenner* c. *Luxford*, EpII/5/9, fos. 26ᵛ–27.

Old men's authority in such matters was derived from two main sources. The first was their own lived experience, stretching back over several decades. The customs they recounted were authenticated in terms of their own knowledge over a considerable period of time. Often deponents' experience of local practices was uninterrupted since their youth, suggesting that they had earned a position of seniority in their parishes through long-term residence. Bartholomew Cooke, a Cambridgeshire labourer 'of thage of threscore yeares or therabouts', recounted the rights of copyholders in the manor of Caventry 'duringe the time of his remembraunce which is aboute fforty yeares'.[36] The beginning of a man's 'remembrance' often dated back to his late teens or early twenties, suggesting this was an age of nascent political consciousness for young men. Others cited memories from early boyhood, which may well have pre-dated their formal inclusion in perambulations, where they occurred. The 60-year-old yeoman William Curdy, having lived in Wilby (Suffolk) since the age of 5, verified the manner of paying tithes for chickens there with which he had 'ben acquainted... these fyfty yeres last past'. The labourer Matthew Parker, aged 66, confirmed that Cambridge Castle was in the parish of Chesterton 'for that he dwelt and hath been brought upp nere the said Castell ever since he was eight yeares of age'. Similarly, a 70-year-old husbandman was certain that particular land in West Firle (Sussex) was exempt from paying tithes because he had 'dwelt all his life tyme in the said parrishe, & hath knowne the peeces of ground before mencioned ever since hee was a boy & had any understanding'.[37]

Some witnesses simply provided snapshots of customary practice with memories of particular incidents that had happened in their youth before they had settled elsewhere. The octogenarian yeoman John Farmer, for instance, recalled the process of collecting tithes for his brother fifty years previously in the parish of Warbleton, although he had not lived there for nearly twenty years. Richard Jenner, a bellows-maker and long-term resident of Keymer (Sussex), remembered how as a boy in nearby Cuckfield (his birthplace) he had had a conversation about repairs to an enclosure with 'one Richard Blaker an olde man', which warranted his inclusion as a witness in a dispute about church repairs even though he had not been a parishioner for thirty years.[38] Others asserted their authority in terms of their former status as householders or occupants of land in a place. The shoemaker Benjamin Cole could give evidence

---

[36] PRO, E134/39&40Eliz/Mich3.
[37] NRO, *Mr Osiandus David* c. *Borret*, DN/DEP/32, fo. 17ᵛ; PRO, E134/2&3Chas1/Hil5; WSRO, *Michael Start* c. *Robert Alse*, EpII/5/7, fo. 91.
[38] WSRO, *Thomas Stolyon* c. *Thomas Lord*, EpII/5/8, fo. 19; *Gard* c. *Mr Ward*, EpII/5/5, fo. 146.

about tithes in Alfriston (Sussex) both because he had been an inhabitant for forty years and because he had 'kept house' there for at least twenty-eight years. Similarly, although Thomas Head's memory of custom in Salehurst (Sussex) stretched back for forty years, it was confirmed and strengthened by his statement that he had formerly occupied lands there for over twenty years.[39] Several witnesses claimed authority in matters of custom as former office-holders. The 65-year-old husbandman John Arcoll could verify the customary manner of collecting contributions for church repairs in West Minston (Sussex) because he had served as churchwarden some twelve or thirteen years previously, and William Feldwicke (a yeoman) corroborated the same for his parish having been 'diverse tymes Churchwarden of the sayd parrishe'.[40] Many witnesses were, however, comparatively humble and principally derived authority from their age. The 77-year-old weaver John Marten, giving evidence about tithing customs in Woodmancote (Sussex), declared that he was worth little in his own goods, being parish clerk and living merely 'by his wages'. In the same case a tanner, Edward Ansty, aged 60, deposed that he was 'little worth and liveth by his labour'.[41] The testimony of both was nonetheless considered important.

Beyond recollecting their own experience of customary practices either as incidental onlookers or as influential or long-term participants, old men also chronicled episodes of local history relevant to disputes. Richard Crabb, a 70-year-old husbandman from Littleport, was able to cite as precedents several former breaches of grazing rights dating back over a forty-year period which had not been tolerated by officers of the bishops of Ely. The 80-year-old yeoman Robert Cooper listed all the incumbents of Salehurst for a period of over fifty years.[42] Others remembered the enclosure of land, the construction of new tenements, and the successive occupancy of buildings and land as well as offices.[43] Old men also recalled local landmarks that had long since disappeared. In 1588, for example, John Ellyott, a blacksmith aged around 60, could 'very well remember' a pear tree that had 'stoode upon nomans acre' which had

---

[39] WSRO, *George Vernon* c. *William Varlet*, EpII/5/8, fo. 48ᵛ; *Thomas Lord* c. *John Wildegos*, EpII/5/11, fo. 59ᵛ.
[40] WSRO, *John Lawrence and Thomas Alcocke* c. *Nicholas Chaloner*, EpII/5/10, fo. 89ᵛ; *Churchwardens of West Hoathly* c. *John Ridley*, EpII/5/11, fo. 135.
[41] WSRO, *Mr Holney* c. *Thomas Beard*, EpII/5/12, fo. 44ʳ⁻ᵛ.
[42] PRO, E134/31&32Eliz/Mich31; WSRO, *Thomas Lord* c. *John Wildegos*, EpII/5/11, fos. 57ᵛ–58.
[43] e.g. CUL, CUA, *Thomas Parishe* c. *William Osse*, fo. 111ʳ⁻ᵛ; PRO, E134/22Jas1/Hil10; E134/4Chas1/Mich37; E134/13Chas1/Mich22; E133/1/61.

once marked the parish boundary 'in the time of procession in Queene Maries time'.[44]

As this last example suggests, knowledge of custom was sometimes authenticated with reference to national as well as local events. The dissolution of the monasteries was a common reference point. In 1603 an 80-year-old Cambridgeshire labourer summoned to mind a tithe barn that had once been part of the nunnery of Swaffham Bulbeck, but that was beyond the recall of his fellow witnesses. His story of 'the last prioresse of the Priorie ... at the tyme of the dissolutione thereof', whom, he claimed, 'he well knewe', lent further credence to his account. He recalled that 'her Christian name was Joane but she desyred to be called dame Jane and ... shee remained in a Cave in the ground at the viccaredge for the most parte by the space of one yeare or there abouts after the dessolucione'.[45] The reigns of former monarchs were also sometimes mentioned. So, in 1591 the shoemaker Robert Harrison, claiming to be 100 years old, recalled that before the enclosure of a particular yard, the inhabitants of Ely had customarily processed through it 'as he well remembereth in the tyme of kinge Henrye the Eight', and various men of the manor of Wittlesey claimed memory of courts leet and baron held 'before the desolution' and 'in the tyme of kynge Henry the Eight' some forty years subsequently.[46] Personal experience of custom was therefore verified through a variety of historical milestones which, in the context of the courtroom, substantiated the authority of old men.

The second main source of old men's authority in such matters was their knowledge of the memories of *former* old men. Besides old men's direct experience of the long term, the weightiest authentication of custom lay in their recollection of long-deceased forebears. Many witnesses pre-dated their own experiences with reference to the practices of their fathers. The weaver Thomas Daniell's own testimony about the manner of paying tithes in East Hoathly (Sussex) was further substantiated by his statement that he 'hathe knowen his father to paye in lyke maner'. A yeoman in the same case also declared that he had known the custom of paying tithes for sixty years and had 'knowen his father pay before him'.[47] Similarly, Thomas Avery (aged 80) was an authority on paying tithe corn in Warbleton (Sussex) because he 'was bred in the said parrishe ... with Edward Avery his father whoe dwelt & occupied lands within the said parrishe about threeskore yeares agon & so by the space of forty

---

[44] WSRO, *Wheler* c. *Kenisley*, EpII/5/5, fo. 63ᵛ.
[45] PRO, E134/44&45Eliz/Mich7.
[46] PRO, E134/33Eliz/East4; E134/38&39Eliz/Mich16.
[47] WSRO, *Durrantt* c. *Springett*, EpII/5/5, fos. 232ᵛ, 240.

yeares following from theme together'. As a young man he had gained his knowledge of tithe payments while working for his father 'in his businesses of husbandry' before subsequently occupying his own lands in the parish from around the time of his father's death.[48] References to the practices of fathers, and occasionally grandfathers or 'Ancestores', coupled custom with notions of lineage and hereditary right and invested old men with ancestral authority.[49]

It was not just memories of fathers which corroborated oral tradition, however, but of old men in general. The 'report of old men' was given priority because it was linked in a series of chains to the memories of bygone old men. According to the 60-year-old yeoman Edward Payne, the cost of church repairs had been borne by the parishioners of West Hoathly for forty years of his own knowledge and 'tyme out of mynd as [he] hath heard of his Auntients'. Stephen Baker, aged 66, declared that divine service had been read by the parsons of Hamsey (Sussex) in a chapel that had been accounted part of that parish 'tyme out of minde, as hee hathe heard his father & other antyentt parishioners there saye'. Garrett Funell, a 64-year-old yeoman, referred to the 'Common reporte of antientt men' to confirm that the manor of Alciston (Sussex) had belonged to Battle Abbey which had been 'suppressed before [he] came to any rype knowledge'. The Sussex fisherman John Conny at the venerable age of 86 declared that 'hee hath many Tymes heard elder men then himself Inhabiters of Meeching report & say that the sayd Greenbrooke is wthin the parrishe of Meeching', thus infusing his own seniority with that of others.[50] Disputes over custom were littered with references to the memories of 'the then old men', former 'elders', 'ancients', or the 'ancienter sort'. Old men referring back to the knowledge of their predecessors laid claim to memories stretching far across the generations: they had word from their elders who had testified in turn of the authority of their ancients, and so on—beyond the memory of man.

This was not a role for the men who, perhaps paradoxically, displayed one of the classic signs of ageing: failing memory. The discomfort of Luke Dallocke as he was being questioned about a bargain he had witnessed some nine months previously is implicit in his frequent interjections of 'as he nowe remembrethe' and 'justlye he cannot tell'. By the end of the

---

[48] *Thomas Lord* c. *John Jeffry and William Hemsley*, EpII/5/8, fo. 65. See also PRO, E134/3Jas1/East18.
[49] WSRO, *Thomas Everiste* c. *Robert Holland*, EpII/5/7, fo. 9.
[50] WSRO, *Churchwardens of West Hoathly* c. *John Ridley*, EpII/5/11, fo. 136ᵛ; *Thomas Cowlstock and Thomas Sharman* c. *Samuel Norden*, EpII/5/5, fo. 364; *John Butcher* c. *Mr Knighte*, EpII/5/6, fo. 65; *Parishioners of Meeching* c. *Colvyll and Colvyll*, EpII/5/7, fo. 76ᵛ.

third interrogatory (having responded to the allegations) he confessed that he could not remember the 'formall words' of the bargain, since it had occurred 'longe since' and 'alsoe for that he beinge aboute the age of lx. yeres [he] can not so well carrye things in his mynde and memorye as he did when he was of yonger yeres, or as others doe which ar of yonger yeres then he'. In a different case, the octogenarian blacksmith John Loader declared that 'he cannot depose [any]thing of his certayne knowledge or remembrance . . . because he is an aged mann & [his mem]orye is naught & fayleth him'.[51] That memory failure held associations of discredit is suggested by the response of one witness to questions about the 69-year-old defendant's credibility: 'he truely in his conscience doeth beleive that mr Sherman . . . is an honest and able mann but sayeth that he beleiveth that mr Shermans memorye might fayle him'.[52] The implication was that although unwittingly so, such men were not trustworthy.

When taken seriously as the appointed guardians of the oral tradition, however, old men played a pivotal role between past, present, and future. Formally charged with preserving the memories of their ancestors and passing them on to future generations, they were the official repositories of customary tenets that informed local identity, influenced people's livelihoods, and often provided the substance of local politics. This does not mean that they went unchallenged, which is evident alone from the number of legal disputes over customary rights. Yet it does suggest their particular authority on account of their age and their gender. It was the one arena in which old men were positively privileged above their middle-aged counterparts in a way that could also sometimes level status distinctions between the aged themselves. In relation to matters of custom, the 'ancienter sort' rivalled—and indeed trumped—the 'able and sufficient' men of the parish according to gerontocratic principles. However, it would be wrong to assume that such principles were extended to all old men without any discrimination, or that they suffused all aspects of elderly men's lives. Long-term residents were favoured over the peripatetic, and men with failing memories were overlooked. In addition, their authority as arbiters of custom did not generate universal respect or privilege for old men, whose access to other marks of status was more likely to have been diminished rather than heightened by age.

---

[51] CUL, CUA, *Francis Phillips* alias *Saunders* c. *Thomas Emons*, Comm.Ct.II.8, fos. 35–6; *William Williams* c. *William Empson*, V.C.Ct.II.29, fo. 1.
[52] CUL, CUA, *Thomas Hobson* c. *John Sherman, snr*, V.C.Ct.II.22, fo. 216.

AGEING, WORK, AND IMPOTENCE

Although in many instances men's authority as founts of tradition was heightened with age, their grip on other aspects of male status loosened. This was not necessarily linked to chronological markers of age: there was no concept of an age for retirement, for example. Instead, it was often a function of the physical, social, and economic impact of ageing which was experienced in various ways and at different points by individual men according to their own life histories, their means, and their state of health. Incidental detail from depositions of over 1,000 witnesses over 50 affords fleeting insights into the varied experiences of older men in early modern England. While some sought to be excused from office on the grounds of age, others continued to perform parish duties well into their sixties and occasionally beyond. Many men of considerable age can be glimpsed supporting themselves and others with a variety of occupations, and several remained self-sufficient until death. Many more, however, became increasingly debilitated, unemployable, and dependent upon others. Provisioned by younger wives, children, or charity, such men relinquished claims to patriarchal manhood in terms of self-sufficient mastery and resumed a subordinate social role on the grounds of their age. While they may have shared some of the same alternative household strategies of men struggling to maintain themselves on account of their economic status, they had less recourse to the alternative sources of manhood rooted in violence, bravado, and excess pursued by many of their younger counterparts.

Although 'essentially it was men in their forties and fifties who ruled', old age did not exclude men from holding office where they were able and willing to serve.[53] Most of the key roles in the Tudor administration were performed by men in their fifties, sixties, and seventies.[54] Incidental evidence suggests that older men also staffed local offices, such as John Hide, a London merchant who had served as deputy of his ward for four years from the age of 67, and Richard Frenche who was mayor of Hastings when 70.[55] In late sixteenth-century Oxford, the average age of councillors was 50 and aldermen 61.[56] Several Cambridge aldermen whose ages

---

[53] Thomas, 'Age and Authority', 211.
[54] Georges Minois, *History of Old Age: From Antiquity to the Renaissance*, trans. Sarah Hanbury Tenison (Cambridge, 1989), 296–7.
[55] GL, London Commissary Court, MS 9065A/2, fo. 177^{r-v}; WSRO, EpII/5/6, fo. 232^v.
[56] Carl I. Hammer, Jr., 'Anatomy of an Oligarchy: The Oxford Town Council in the Fifteenth and Sixteenth Century', *Journal of British Studies*, 18 (1978). See also Steven R. Smith, 'Growing Old in an Age of Transition', in Stearns (ed.), *Old Age in Preindustrial Society*.

can be ascertained through record linkage were in their sixties, and at least one, Edward Potto, remained an alderman into his seventies, having served as mayor for the third time at the age of 68.[57]

Some Cambridge deponents in their sixties had witnessed disputes while serving as constable. A tailor, William Tomson, testified to serving warrants for arrest and putting offenders in the stocks while acting as constable in his early sixties, and one Thomas Mott was instrumental in calming a drunken brawl in Jesus Lane on a Saturday night while performing his duties as constable at the age of 69 or 70.[58] Others held parish appointments. The 66-year-old grocer Edward Dodson was out collecting money for the poor of Great St Mary's when he witnessed a defamatory exchange at Henry Cotton's stall.[59] Churchwardens were also drawn from amongst older men; several male witnesses in their sixties in the archdeaconry court of Lewes, for example, gave evidence while acting in this capacity.[60] Age, therefore, by no means automatically disqualified men from office. It may even have made some candidates more attractive on account of their experience, and for some older men office-holding remained a source of authority and prestige, particularly if they had a history of participation in local affairs.[61]

Older men fitting this profile of long-term residence and with a history of office-holding also appear to have been instrumental in the informal processes of mediation and arbitration that were such an essential part of community relations in early modern England.[62] So, for example, two Cambridge alderman, Henry Clarke (aged 63) and Nicholas Graunte (aged 57), acted as arbitrators in a dispute over the title to the Half Moon Inn between two men they had both known for over twenty years.[63] Similarly,

[57] Downing College, Cambridge, Metcalfe's Thesaurus, Bowtell MS 11, fo. 200ᵛ.

[58] CUL, CUA, *William Jackson* c. *John Hall*, Comm.Ct.II.6, fo. 114ᵛ; *Margaret Corbett and Thomas Taylor* c. *Richard Fallowes*, V.C.Ct.II.1, fo. 146ʳ⁻ᵛ; *John Pomfrett* c. *Edmund Aynsworth*, V.C.Ct.II.32, fo. 1ᵛ.

[59] CUL, CUA, *Ralph Hyde* c. *Margaret Cotton*, Comm.Ct.II.11, fo. 53ʳ⁻ᵛ.

[60] e.g. WSRO, Thomas Newmann, EpII/5/5, fo. 415ᵛ; George Partridge, EpII/5/6, fo. 79ᵛ; Nicholas Lucas, EpII/5/12, fo. 9ᵛ.

[61] For the extent and significance of popular participation in a range of local offices, see Mark Goldie, 'The Unacknowledged Republic: Officeholding in Early Modern England', in Tim Harris (ed.), *The Politics of the Excluded, c.1500–1850* (Basingstoke, 2001). See also Eric Carlson, 'The Origins, Function, and Status of the Office of Churchwarden, with Particular Reference to the Diocese of Ely', in Margaret Spufford (ed.), *The World of Rural Dissenters, 1520–1725* (Cambridge, 1995).

[62] Craig Muldrew, 'The Culture of Reconciliation: Community and the Settlement of Economic Disputes in Early Modern England', *Historical Journal*, 39 (1996). See also above, p. 199.

[63] CUL, CUA, *John Towers* c. *John Cuthbert*, Comm.Ct.II.4, fos. 143–145ᵛ. See also *John Baxter* c. *Henry Ellwood*, V.C.Ct.II.3, fo. 78ʳ⁻ᵛ; *Thomas Barker* c. *Robert Heylocke*, Comm.Ct.II.6, fo. 74.

the three parishioners selected to approve a disputed churchwarden's account in the parish of Winkleigh (Devon) were aged 50, 60, and 70, two of whom had lived there since birth.[64] The aged were also included amongst those called upon to assess damaged property and to determine the cost of repairs in cases of trespass and disputed responsibility.[65]

Older men were sought as mediators in their capacity as parents, masters, mentors, and patrons. Because of the comparatively late age of marriage in early modern England, surviving parents were often agents in their children's marriage negotiations at relatively advanced ages. William Hunne, for example, a Brighton fisherman in his late sixties, warned his future son-in-law against seeking 'some greater wealthe & substance with my daughter then I shalbe willing or able to spare & disburse with her'. Only once he was assured that Robert Baker sought his 'good will' rather than his goods, did Hunne relent, giving him a half share in a new boat with certain nets 'in token of my good will & meaninge towards yor preferment & livinge with my daughter', further promising that after his decease he would 'make her better worthe, and leave her as good parte of my goods as to any of my daughters or children except my heire'.[66] Older men and women were also instrumental as marriage brokers for younger people other than their own children. Of eighty-four witnesses in matrimonial causes within the diocese of Canterbury who had acted as intermediaries between suitors, over a fifth were aged 50 and above.[67] In addition, older men were approached for guidance and support in their capacity as grandparents, such as John Hooke whose grandson sought him out in preference to his guardian for help when he wished to leave his master's service after 'some difference' between them, and such as John Robinson 'the elder' whose grandson was bound as his apprentice.[68]

Many other patronage networks also seem to have linked old and young. The rector of Hooe (Sussex) turned to a 60-year-old yeoman, Robert Daniel, to intercede with one Mr Levett 'to helpe him to bee farmer unto the parsonadge', who accordingly 'did deale with the said mr Levett for him in that behalf, & was present when the said Mr Levett did let unto the said John ffowler the Rectory by word of mouth'.[69] The Cambridge

[64] DRO, Chanter 866, unfoliated, 14 Jan. 1635/6.
[65] e.g. CUL, CUA, *Nicholas Driver, LLB* c. *Francis Batisforde*, Comm.Ct.II.16, fos. 71–72ᵛ; *Robert Gascye alias Wing* c. *William Elsden*, Comm.Ct.II.16, fo. 88.
[66] WSRO, *Joan Hunne* c. *Robert Baker*, EpII/5/5, fo. 133ʳ⁻ᵛ.
[67] Diana O'Hara, *Courtship and Constraint: Rethinking the Making of Marriage in Tudor England* (Manchester, 2000), 109.
[68] ESRO, Information of John Hooke, QR/E 22, no. 121; *Durham Civic Memorials*, ed. C. E. Whiting, Publications of the Surtees Society 160 (Durham, 1952), 105.
[69] WSRO, *John Fowler* c. *Colman, Wooddall and Newin*, EpII/5/9, fo. 10.

gentleman Mathew Stokys was 73 when he went to the Dolphin Inn on behalf of his former servant, Helen Bemont, to 'intreate' one William Hedley for remittance of part of an obligation she owed.[70] An 80-year-old labourer, Lawrence Harrowe, was asked to supply a character reference for Mary Walker, an alleged bastard-bearer, whom he had known 'by the space of many yeares', and whom he insisted was a 'mayd of honest life & Conversacion'.[71] Similarly, Edward Tutt, defamed by the accusation that he had 'deflowered' Elyn Avis, sought help from John Rede, a 75-year-old yeoman of Marefield (Sussex), whose house he often visited. Tutt asked Rede 'to goe to Turners hill where she dwelt and enquire of her behavioure there how she had used and behaved herselfe there before she came unto the said Tutt', in order to discredit her testimony. Rede went to Turner's Hill, where he instead attempted to smooth things over with Avis herself, adopting a somewhat more pragmatic approach:

[he] told her that it was ill done of her to slander him and saide yt was a waye to shame herselfe to make that exclamation and wished her (yf any suche matter weare) rather to take some peece of monie or a Bullocke or somthinge naming and offeringe her for his freinds sake foure nobles of monie which she was contented to have taken and to make noe more a doe therof.

Tutt was, however, unimpressed by his mentor's intervention, insisting that 'he would not geve her any thinge sayeinge she had more neede to geve him somthinge havinge soe slandered and abused him'.[72] Although Rede's efforts failed in this instance, it is clear that many older men were considered useful go-betweens and peace-makers whose services were called upon to resolve a range of conflicts. While this may not have been a function of their age *per se*, their long-term knowledge of the parties or issues involved contributed to the trust placed in them, and, at the very least, such evidence is suggestive of the continued involvement of men in a range of familial and community concerns well beyond middle age, often despite their failing powers. Older men appear not to have been hindered in such roles by the blindness associated with age, for example. John Fitzherbert, aged 72, witnessed his sister's will aurally 'being old & his sight something dimme' since he was sure he could 'well call [it] to mynde'. Similarly, John Baxter oversaw the arrangements for his stepdaughter's widowhood in his sixties, apparently unhampered by his lack of sight.[73]

[70] CUL, CUA, *John Benson* c. *William and Helen Bemont*, Comm.Ct.II.3, fo. 197.
[71] WSRO, *Mary Walker* c. *Simon Frend*, EpII/5/9, fo. 46.
[72] WSRO, *Elyn Avis* c. *Edward Tutt*, EpII/5/5, fos. 154ᵛ–155.
[73] WSRO, EpII/5/7, fo. 58; CUL, CUA, *Elizabeth Mathewe* c. *Edward Lucas*, V.C.Ct.II.1, fos. 103–4.

Old age in chronological terms was clearly not a bar to participation in local affairs, nor even when functionally manifested in blindness. However, the process of ageing nonetheless often presaged a gradual repositioning of many men within the community as they withdrew from positions of influence. Age was often cited in requests for dispensation from office by men who were no longer able or willing to serve. Henry Adams and Humfry Hooper sought exemption from serving as constables in the London parish of St Dunstan in the West on account of 'theire ages & the infirmities of theire bodies'. Adams was 64 and 'muche troubled with the disease of the stone' and Hooper was 61 and 'often troubled with swellinge in his leggs'.[74] In the parish of St Andrew, Holborn, assistants were regularly replaced as a result of 'infirmities growinge by age'. In 1599, for example, the vestry were concerned that one of the assistants, William Bradly, was 'aged & impotent in body [and] was for that cause unable to come amongest us & perfourme the service belonging to his place'. As a result they 'thought good to supply his roume, with a more able & sufficient person'. Such men, 'enfebled with age', were excluded from the ranks of the chief inhabitants and were no longer counted amongst the able and sufficient men of the parish.[75]

In these instances, the ill effects of ageing cited as an excuse from office-holding appear to have been genuinely debilitating. In others, complaints of old age may well have been primarily used to avoid the burdens of office, for which men were willing to pay considerable fines. In a few cases, however, dispensation was more positively associated with notions of reward for long-term service. In 1629 Mr Humfrey Seale was 'freed of all insueinge offices' by the vestry of St Bartholomew by the Exchange not only 'in regard of his old age' but also in recognition of his 'obliged services and imployments abroade and his good services donne for this parishe in the Visitacion'.[76] In St Dunstan in the West, John Stutfield was granted dispensation from the office of scavenger 'in due consideration of [his] antiquitie, that he had dwelt in the parishe as a shopp keeper & houwsholder xx yeres at the least'. In this case, antiquity, or being an 'ancient' man of the parish, was linked to concepts of seniority which allowed for a dignified retirement from office, which was less directly a product of need or incapacity than a reward for duty.[77] Such examples are comparatively rare, however, suggesting that the beneficent dispensation of those 'in yeres' was highly selective, associated with long-

---

[74] GL, St Dunstan in the West, Vestry Minutes, MS 3016/1, p. 51.
[75] GL, St Andrew Holborn, Vestry Minutes, MS 4249, fos. 18ᵛ, 20ᵛ, 21.
[76] GL, St Bartholomew by the Exchange, Vestry Minutes, 1567–1643, MS 4384/1, 381.
[77] GL, St Dunstan in the West, Vestry Minutes, MS 3016/1, 74. See also 21, 54.

term residence and service, and a man's ability to pay the accompanying fine for dispensation as well as the availability of other candidates for office.[78]

Even in its most positive light, therefore, retirement from office-holding did not stem from a more general concept of retirement, particularly in relation to work. Indeed, many men sought exemption in order that their working lives were not jeopardized by the demands of local duty. Obadiah Bexhill, for example, requested dispensation not only because of his age and ill health—'much afflicted with the Stone and other diseases'—but also because of 'his profession of Phisicke'. Similarly, Adrian Barton wished to be excused from serving as constable both on account of his years and 'in respectt of his early and late attendance on sicke persons in his profession beinge an Apothecary' that would interfere with his adequate performance of the office.[79] Incidental details of men's continued efforts to eke a living in old age are far more prevalent than evidence relating to their participation as office-holders. For those unable to work, the scope for positive alternatives was extremely limited unless they were of considerable means. Even the comparatively wealthy may have found themselves in a precarious position owing to the demands of subsequent generations and the mutable economic conditions of early modern England. While these circumstances overshadowed the experiences of the majority in early modern England, regardless of age, the elderly were less likely to recover from positions of poverty than their younger counterparts, and less likely to have found a positive sense of male identity in such situations.

Older men can be glimpsed performing a variety of tasks which suggest either that retirement was not sought or, more likely, that it was not an option for those able to continue working. Many men persevered in their occupations until advanced years. George Sander, a Cambridge butcher, witnessed a slanderous exchange from his own stall in the butchery at the age of 71. A barber-surgeon, Ralph Browne, was still practising at the age of 79, according to his account of preparing a cure for John Standishe's leg which had been injured in an archery accident, for which he received the hefty sum of 40*s*. At 72, the locksmith Richard Brachier identified an iron crowbar he had made a decade previously, and the yeoman Andrew Foster was still bargaining for and delivering barley in and around Cambridge at the age of 70.[80] Henry Parnell ploughed several acres for

---

[78] GL, St Dunstan in the West, Vestry Minutes, MS 3016/1, 32.
[79] ESRO, QR/EW 53, no. 18; GL, St Dunstan in the West, Vestry Minutes, MS 3016/1, 126.
[80] CUL, CUA, *John Paske* c. *Grace and Michael Watson*, Comm.Ct.II.13, fo. 48; *John Standishe*

Thomas Oliver at the age of 60, and another yeoman, Henry Benden, was waiting at his master's table (where he overheard defamatory speeches) at the age of 62. A 70-year-old weaver, William Barkshire, declared that he was worth £10 and that he lived 'by his trade and his lands', and the tailor Thomas Hother, although worth little, nonetheless eked a living from his trade at 60.[81] Similarly, despite his poverty, Nicholas Crystcrosse was able to keep his two children in school while working as a cobbler at the age of 68.[82]

Despite Thomas Tusser's adage that 'youth bids us labour, to get what wee can, for age is a burthen to labouring man', numerous older men remained dependent on their labour for their livelihood.[83] Many an old man declared that he lived 'by his labour' in statements of worth. One Edward Osburne, for example, claimed at 70 that he was worth £4 in his own goods, adding that he 'getteth his living by his labour ymployed in husbandry', and Christopher Barnarde, aged 60, likewise declared that he was worth £5 and that he lived by his labour as a husbandman.[84] Such men were set to a variety of tasks. Edmund Powell, a husbandman nearing 60, witnessed a slanderous exchange while at work 'in hedging' for the defendant. Another husbandman, William Colbrooke, described cutting down 30 cords of wood cited in a tithes dispute, for which labour he was paid by the defendant's clerk. If his estimate of his age is to be believed, he had been 77 at the time. Henry Grime, a labourer, mentioned his employment as 'one of the workmen ... about the making upp of a mudd wall' (as it turned out, on a disputed boundary) when getting on for 70.[85]

Some older men appear to have modified their working practices to accommodate the constraints of age, such as the London butcher William Pecke who bought meat to sell in his shop in St Nicholas shambles from a butcher nearby in Smithfield, 'because he was an old man and not able to travaile into the Contrey himself to buy his ware'. Others abandoned

c. *William Barley*, Comm.Ct.II.3, fos. 40ᵛ–41ᵛ; *Thomas Barker* c. *Robert Heylocke*, Comm.Ct.II.6, fo. 65ᵛ; *John and Agnes Shaw* c. *Edward Upcher*, Comm.Ct.II.4, fo. 229.

[81] CUL, CUA, *Thomas Oliver* c. *Thomas Hobson*, V.C.Ct.II.22, fo. 112; WSRO, *Gregory Hills* c. *Mr Thomas Pearse*, EpII/5/6, fo. 96; *Churchwardens of Seaford* c. *Gratwicke*, EpII/5/11, fo. 184ᵛ; *Elizabeth Butcher* c. *John Butcher*, EpII/5/8, fo. 82.

[82] *The Norwich Census of the Poor, 1570*, ed. John F. Pound, Norfolk Record Society 40 (Norwich, 1971), 82.

[83] Thomas Tusser, *Five Hundred Points of Good Husbandry* (London, 1614), 16.

[84] WSRO, *Thomasine Page* c. *William Rowne*, EpII/5/11, fo. 70ᵛ; *Agnes Giles* c. *Ro: Wooddye*, EpII/5/7, fo. 18. See also the depositions of John Cheale, EpII/5/8, fo. 122ᵛ; John Beane, EpII/5/11, fo. 153ᵛ.

[85] WSRO, *Mr John Saddler* c *Thomas Rawkins*, EpII/5/11, fo. 118; *Mr Bathhurst* c. *Edmund Hawes*, EpII/5/6, fo. 243ᵛ; CUL, CUA, *William Williams* c. *William Empson*, V.C.Ct.II.29, fo. 15ᵛ.

their trades altogether, such as James Huitson, who at 60 declared that he got his living 'honestly' by victualling and letting horses, despite his occupational designation as a tailor.[86] The Norwich census of the poor suggests that several older men struggling to make ends meet turned to other sources of income when they could not find or were unable to perform the work for which they had been trained. This often involved a shift towards more minor employments or domestic work. John Robardes, despite being a cordwainer, was 'at work for thospital pore' at the age of 60, and Wylliam Pynchin (aged 56) was listed as a 'laborer that kepeth prisoners'. Many worsted weavers were also forced to find alternatives: John Cok and Quyntyn Russell, both aged 60, instead 'use[d] labor'; Jamys Wodehouse wove lace; Richard Kedge filled pipes; and William Cocker sold aqua vitae.[87] Older men also supported themselves through work as journeymen, such as William Tollye who at the age of 80 had maintained himself and his family as a journeyman weaver in the Worcestershire parish of Hanbury for the previous fourteen years until his recent sickness.[88] Others were forced to turn to subsistence migration.[89] Such expedients were by no means the preserve of older men who adopted many of the same strategies for survival as their younger counterparts who were unable to find a secure economic footing.[90] However, their services may have been more often considered surplus to requirement in a saturated labour market and in the context of a youth-heavy population.[91] Petitioners from the manor of Hartlebury (Worcestershire), for example, were prepared to guarantee the good conduct of William Glasse, a blacksmith, in order that he remain in their parish because, 'They have no other Smith ... but an old man who is decayed in his work by age' whom they were hoping Glasse might supplant.[92]

The testimony of older men in work is in stark contrast to the bleaker experiences of those men no longer able to get their living and listed amongst the indigent. The Norwich census of the poor included several

---

[86] GL, London Commissary Court, *Simon Neale* c. *Margaret Pecke alias Spatchurste*, MS 9065A, fo. 152ᵛ; CUL, CUA, *Gregory Dawson* c. *Leonard Glascocke*, Comm.Ct.II.6, fo. 206.

[87] *Norwich Census of the Poor*, 30, 56, 70, 93, 74, 90, 30. See also Pelling, 'Old Age, Poverty, and Disability', 82–3.

[88] *Worcester County Records. The Quarter Sessions Rolls*, i: *1591–1643*, comp. J. W. W. Bund (Worcester, 1900), 213.

[89] Pelling, 'Old Age, Poverty, and Disability', 82.

[90] For examples of younger men employed outside their occupations, see *Norwich Census of the Poor*, 30 (John Yonges), 35 (Wylliam Richeson, Francis Waymer, John Both), 50 (Thomas Wylliam), 70 (Launcelot Sybole).

[91] Wrigley and Schofield, *The Population History of England*, 216.

[92] *Worcester County Records*, 54.

older men who had been designated 'past work', such as 'Andrew Reynoldes of 60 yere, laborer [who] work[s] not for age', Walter Holles, aged 77, 'al croked & not hable to work', Edward Brasonet, aged 60, 'a diseased man of both leges', and Thomas Damet, a 67-year-old cobbler 'that work not for that he se not'.[93] That others were simply unable to find employment is suggested by the frequent refrains 'not in work', 'with no work', 'that work not', 'out of worke', and 'that occupy not'.[94] How well placed such men were in relation to younger men seeking employment is difficult to assess. It does appear, however, that they were less adaptable in the face of hardship than their elderly female counterparts who were far more rarely unemployed, and whose public role as carers gave them 'a positive value in society which men over 50 would have lacked'.[95] As a consequence, as Margaret Pelling has argued, older widowers—much more so than older widows—appear to have viewed marriage as one 'expedient' in the face of unemployment, incapacity, and poverty.[96] Many such older men depended upon the labour of considerably younger wives and children for their maintenance. John Davi, for example, aged 77 and 'past work', was married to a 40-year-old woman who spun white warp for their living, generating sufficient income that they were not candidates for alms. Similarly, the 95-year-old Edward Stokes, 'nott hable to worke', was supported by the lace-weaving of his 40-year-old wife and the eldest of their three children (aged 9), which left them 'indifferently' poor and, according to the census-takers, in no urgent need of relief.[97] Such men were unlikely to have been merely weathering temporary periods of unemployment like many younger men similarly reliant on the contributions of wives and children to the household economy, but had instead become permanently dependent on maintenance by their families.

Despite the existence of attitudes which either denied or ridiculed the sexuality of older men, several continued to father children well into their advanced years. One of the facts gleefully reported about Thomas Parr, who, according to legend, lived until he was 152, was that he had

---

[93] *Norwich Census of the Poor*, 61, 37, 54, 76, 34.

[94] Ibid. 29 (Jherom Rabi), 38 (Thomas Rushbrok, John Covi), 39 (Thomas Pallmer, John Love), 40 (Henry Cullyngton), 41 (William Bennett, Thomas Rogers), 43 (Robert Galiarde), 46 (Richard Cok).

[95] Pelling, 'Old Age, Poverty, and Disability', 84. See also ead., 'Older Women: Household, Caring and Other Occupations'; Diane Willen, 'Women in the Public Sphere in Early Modern England: The Case of the Urban Working Poor', *Sixteenth Century Journal*, 19 (1988); Claire S. Schen, 'Strategies of Poor Aged Women and Widows in Sixteenth-Century London', in Botelho and Thane (eds.), *Women and Ageing*; and cf. Botelho, 'Provisions for the Elderly', ch. 7.

[96] Pelling, 'Finding Widowers'; ead., 'Who Most Needs to Marry?'

[97] *Norwich Census of the Poor*, 61, 72.

performed penance for adultery at the age of 105.[98] That sexual incontinence was little tolerated in old men is suggested by the expulsion of Rychard Sexton from the Tooley Foundation in Ipswich at the age of 60 (four years after his admittance) for 'whoredome'—the only application of this term to a man encountered in the course of this research. Also derogatory was the labelling of an adulterous bailiff by his neighbours as 'the owld gowty legged Bayly'.[99] Disapproval of procreational sex by older men within marriage, however, is less evident, and many parented children in old age. The third child of John Wytherly, listed as just a quarter of a year old, was apparently fathered when Wytherly was 79 or 80. Valentine Leke, aged 70, and his 26-year-old wife also had a child described as 'veri yonge', and in addition to their five children (all under 13), Robert Poynter's wife was 'byg with another' when he was 64 and out of work.[100] Elsewhere in Ipswich, the youngest child of Petar Rowlande (aged 74) and his wife Anne (aged 48) was 2½ when they were admitted to Christ's Hospital before Rowlande's death less than two years later.[101] While it is possible that some of these infants and toddlers were the product of previous marriages, it seems not unreasonable to presume that at least a few were the biological offspring of their elderly fathers. At the very least, it demonstrates that older men performed parental roles to young children well into later life. Yet although such men of advanced years repeated the processes of household formation and continued to father children, their function appears not to have been as rigidly governed by imperatives of male provision since many were primarily or even permanently dependent on others for their maintenance. Older women continued to perform parenting roles to young children in their capacity as grandmothers, and their more frequent appearance than grandfathers in orders for the maintenance of illegitimate or orphaned children suggests that they were deemed better-suited than older men for this task.[102]

Many older men with adult children entered into relations of dependence of a different sort. According to pre-industrial census data, around

---

[98] John Taylor, *The Olde, Old, Very Olde Man; or, The Age and Long Life of Thomas Par* (London, 1635), sigs. C^v–C2.

[99] *Poor Relief in Elizabethan Ipswich*, 89; NRO, *Mathew alias Peter c. Adam Tarver*, DN/DEP/32, fo. 69^v.

[100] *Norwich Census of the Poor*, 66, 30, 68. See also 40 (Henry Cullyngton), 41 (William Bennett), 47 (Robert Kindersley), 48 (Robert Johnson).

[101] *Poor Relief in Elizabethan Ipswich*, 91.

[102] e.g., *The Assembly Books of Southampton*, iii: *1611–1614*, ed. J. W. Horrocks, Southampton Record Society 24 (Southampton, 1924), 21; *Worcester County Records*, 115; *Quarter Sessions Records for the County of Somerset*, i: *1607–1625*, ed. E. H. Bates, Somerset Record Society 28 (London, 1907), 356.

50 per cent of men and roughly a third of women over 65 co-resided with a child.[103] Some such men appear to have been entirely dependent on their adult offspring. John Bacon, for example, a 67-year-old widower, was listed in the Norwich census as 'allmost blynd, & doth nothinge & lyveth of his son that kepe a skole'.[104] Elderly women were more likely than men to be co-resident with their married children, which suggests that they were more easily or more readily absorbed into their children's families than older men. This was possibly because of their greater potential to contribute to the household economy, and in some instances it is likely that co-residence was more for the benefit of the child involved rather than their elderly mother.[105] Many more older women than men lived on their own, which also suggests that they had less need of some form of co-residence than their male counterparts and can be read as further evidence of their comparative adaptability with age.[106] Older men of limited means, on the other hand, may well have been deemed a greater burden to their married children, and were more likely to secure familial support through marriage to a younger woman than by co-residence with a child.[107]

Older men of greater sufficiency were better placed to devise contracts with their children for maintenance in later life in return for pre-mortem bequests. It is not possible to carry out the kind of statistical analysis of the incidence and changing nature of formal retirement agreements that has been accomplished using medieval manorial records.[108] While provisions for better-off women can often be discovered in their husband's wills, it is harder to find evidence of retirement arrangements for early modern men.[109] Occasionally, however, the details of settlements can be glimpsed in older men's statements of their worth in court. Thomas Bathurst, for

---

[103] Richard Wall, 'Elderly Persons and Members of their Households in England and Wales from Preindustrial Times to the Present', in David I. Kertzer and Peter Laslett (eds.), *Aging in the Past: Demography, Society and Old Age* (London, 1995), 88.

[104] *Norwich Census of the Poor*, 68.

[105] See, e.g., ibid. 33 (Cicely Male), 78 (Margaret Taylor), 84 (Cycely Love).

[106] Between 1599 and 1796, 2% of men over 65 lived alone compared with 16% of women. Richard Wall, 'Relations between the Generations in British Families Past and Present', in Catherine Marsh and Sara Arber (eds.), *Families and Households: Divisions and Change* (Basingstoke, 1992), 66.

[107] Pelling, 'Finding Widowers'; ead., 'Who Most Needs to Marry?' See also Laslett, *Family Life and Illicit Love*, 200–13.

[108] Richard M. Smith, 'The Manorial Court and the Elderly Tenant in Late Medieval England', in Pelling and Smith (eds.), *Life, Death and the Elderly*; Elaine Clark, 'The Quest for Security in Medieval England', in Michael M. Sheehan (ed.), *Aging and the Aged in Medieval Europe* (Toronto, 1990).

[109] See Botelho, 'Provisions for the Elderly', ch. 4.

example, a centenarian millwright, declared that he was worth nothing 'forasmutche as he hathe devided his goods to his iij sonnes & otherwhile dwelleth with one & sometime with an other as he seeth good at his pleasure because he is very olde'. The Norfolk yeoman William Edwards, acting as a witness for his son, similarly declared at the age of 65 that he had 'nothinge of his owne' but received his 'dyet and lodginge' from his son to whom he had 'turned over all his goods and substaunce'. John Chimery, a 70-year-old yeoman, similarly derived his 'bord & diet' from his son-in-law, although it is unclear whether he had given him anything in return.[110] Other men exchanged their goods in return for a cash pension rather than bed and board. The yeoman George Lindfild, for example, declared that 'hee hath xx^{li} per annum to live by, & hath disposed of a great part of his estate to & among his Children'.[111]

Not all arrangements involved offspring. Finding himself 'not well in health', Anthony Prior turned to one Thomas Lawnder for his maintenance, requesting an annual pension of 20s. in return for his house and his goods and the services customarily performed by children or other executors after death. His public declaration of this arrangement was as follows:

I have bargayned with this man ... for my howse and goods payinge xxs yerely and to kepe me with my goods so longe as I lyve and when I am deade to pay my debts and bury me honestly in a Coffyn and then all the reste of my goods that is lefte after my debtes be paid and my body buried I geve them holy unto him.

According to one witness he wished to support Lawnder and his wife-to-be and 'to do the yonge Cupple good' for the sake of 'olde goodman watson', whose relationship to Prior is unclear.[112]

Such arrangements may have bought older men a degree of security in later life, but they came at a considerable personal cost. Although it is possible that the transferral of wealth to the next generation was viewed as a fitting continuation of a man's estate, it nonetheless left him in a position of no worth or 'substance'. Men who exchanged their goods for bed and board, particularly when no pension was involved, consigned themselves to a situation of total dependence, not dissimilar to that of young children, and often in direct competition with their needs. Contemporary commentators were doubtful about the merits of such arrangements. John

---

[110] WSRO, *Thomas Large* c. *James Mitchell*, EpII/5/6, fo. 333; NRO, *Tytley & Rawlinges* c. *Edwards*, DN/DEP/32, fo. 41; CUL, CUA, *Nathaniel Sally* c. *William Hickes*, V.C.Ct.II.32, fo. 115^v.

[111] WSRO, *Mr Alan Car* c. *Richard Infeld*, EpII/5/9, fo. 60^v.

[112] GL, London Commissary Court, *Thomas Lawnder* c. *Thomas Watson*, MS 9065A, fos. 29–30.

Dod and Robert Cleaver's portrayal of the prospects for aged parents who surrendered all their assets to their children was pretty bleak:

so long as the parents have any thing to give, and something may be gotten by them, all that while they will be kinde and loving, and strive who shall shew most dutie, and well is he that can get the old parents to him: but when once he is drawne drie, and they have suckt all from him, then he is neglected of all, then every day is a yeare till he be dead, then he is a burthen and a clog; then they exclaime, that he doth nothing but spend, and troubleth the familie.[113]

Cautionary tales also detailed the abuse of such arrangements by selfish offspring and warned elderly parents against prematurely forfeiting all their bargaining power.[114] The petition of William Stonylandes, seeking redress against his daughter and son-in-law, suggests that such abuses were not just the stuff of fiction. Aged 76 when he made his complaint, he claimed that he had married his only daughter to Walter Hill 'in the hope they would be a comfort' to him 'in these his latter yeres', and had conveyed his entire estate to them and their heirs. Subsequently Hill had taken away his father-in-law's only cow, despite having 'three verye good kyne of his owne', thus leaving Stonylandes with 'none other beast in the world to releeve him and his poore old wyffe wthall'. In addition his daughter had assaulted her mother when she had attempted to enter Hill's grounds, and Hill had 'endangered' both his mother- and father-in-law 'manye tymes'. Thus, according to Stonylandes's petition, they were left sick and without any form of relief.[115] That children were unwilling and often unable to support elderly parents is further suggested by numerous orders issued by justices requesting performance of the filial duty of provision.[116]

For older men unable to maintain themselves and who had no recourse to familial support of any kind, the last resort was parish relief. Old age was clearly one of the most vulnerable stages in life-cycle patterns of poverty, and an elderly person's receipt of a parish pension usually marked the beginning of a final phase of permanent and deepening dependency on the parish until death.[117] That the elderly were treated as the accept-

---

[113] John Dod and Robert Cleaver, *A Plaine and Familiar Exposition of the Ten Commandements* (London, 1618), 195.

[114] e.g. Bartholomaeus Battus, *The Christian Mans Closet. Wherein is Conteined a Discourse of the Training of Children. Nowe Englished by W. Lowth* (London, 1581), fo. 73^{r-v}; William Averell, *A Dyall for Dainty Darlings, Rockt in the Cradle of Securitie* (London, 1584), sig. C3. See also Thomas, 'Age and Authority', 238–9. The classic portrayal of such ill-fated arrangements is, of course, Shakespeare's *King Lear*.

[115] *The Staffordshire Quarter Sessions Rolls*, v: *1603–1606*, ed. S. A. H. Burne (Kendal, 1940), 16–17.

[116] e.g. *Quarter Sessions Records for Somerset*, 73; Louis A. Knafla, *Kent at Law 1602. The County Jurisdiction: Assizes and Sessions of the Peace* (London, 1994), 185, 193.

able face of the 'deserving' poor is suggested by the Salisbury orders of 1626 which decreed that a poor box should be placed at the gate of every inn to receive alms from travellers to be attended by 'two aged impotent poor people . . . in a quiet and still manner'.[118] This did not mean that older people were automatically deemed candidates for relief, however, and provision differed widely from place to place.[119] Aged men, no longer 'able by their labour to relieve themselves in any sort', were amongst petitioners to justices of the peace seeking orders for relief which was not forthcoming from their parishes.[120] In addition, the elderly could find themselves shunted from parish to parish by overseers who sought to protect ratepayers from the burden of their relief, and the impotence associated with their advanced years was not always a safeguard against punishment for vagrancy—including whipping.[121] Elderly petitioners for relief were therefore as subject to a complex range of criteria assessing their desert as the many others in need of aid in early modern England. The male pensioners favoured by the Tooley Foundation in Ipswich, for example, were characterized by their long-term residence in Ipswich, their previous service to the town, their respectability, and their extreme infirmity. Recipients of relief were often credited as 'beynge of honeste fame and reporte' as well as characterized as being needy.[122] The fact that Richarde Kynge, 'an auncient inhabitant of this towne and somtyme one of the nomber of the aldermen . . . whom God now hathe visited', and Robert Sallowes, 'somtyme a hedboroughe and one of the nomber of the xxiiij^{ti}', were granted relief is suggestive of the potential levelling effect of old age, although it also indicates that their former position influenced perceptions of their entitlement to relief.[123]

[117] Tim Wales, 'Poverty, Poor Relief and the Life-Cycle: Some Evidence from Seventeenth-Century Norfolk', in Richard M. Smith (ed.), *Land, Kinship and Life-Cycle* (Cambridge, 1984). See also W. Newman Brown, 'The Receipt of Poor Relief and Family Situation: Aldenham, Hertfordshire, 1630–1690', in Smith (ed.), *Land, Kinship and Life-Cycle*; Marjorie K. McIntosh, 'Networks of Care in Elizabethan English Towns: The Example of Hadleigh, Suffolk', in Peregrine Horden and Richard Smith (eds.), *The Locus of Care: Families, Communities, Institutions, and the Provision of Welfare Since Antiquity* (London, 1998).

[118] *Poverty in Early-Stuart Salisbury*, ed. Paul Slack, Wiltshire Record Society, 31 (Devizes, 1975), 89.

[119] Lynn Botelho, 'Aged and Impotent: Parish Relief of the Aged Poor in Early Modern Suffolk', in Martin Daunton (ed.), *Charity, Self-Interest and Welfare in the English Past* (London, 1996).

[120] *Poverty in Early-Stuart Salisbury*, 101. See also Knafla, *Kent at Law*, 177.

[121] See, e.g., the treatment of Richard Fear and of William Porter, *Quarter Sessions Records for Somerset*, 4, 11, 13–14, 135–6.

[122] *Poor Relief in Elizabethan Ipswich*, 26. This was a label attached to both men and women. See, e.g., the descriptions of Elizabeth Blewe, 27; Jane Lumney, 28, Martyn Topcliffe, 31.

[123] Ibid. 31, 30.

Historians of old age have perhaps been over-preoccupied with the extent to which conditions for the aged have improved or diminished over time, as opposed to how their fortunes compared with the rest of society in which they lived. While it would be wrong to resurrect theories of a golden age for the pre-modern elderly, the absence of a chronological marker of old age did afford opportunities for men of advanced ages to remain instrumental in a range of social, political, and economic roles. Old age was no bar to office-holding, parenting, provisioning, and brokering in a range of situations, providing it was not accompanied by severe physical incapacity. Although this was a crucial proviso, it nonetheless meant that at least some older men retained access to aspects of patriarchal manhood well into their later lives. In addition, in the specific context of customary disputes, older men were privileged above their middle-aged counterparts as the guardians of local tradition and thereby acceded to an exclusive form of political participation both within and beyond their communities.

This did not shield many from diminished status, however. In a period in which economic autonomy was difficult to maintain even in the best of circumstances, older men were ill placed to preserve even the semblance of self-sufficient mastery. If the Norwich census of the poor is representative, many headed households in name alone, and were supported by the labour of younger wives and children. Others were dependent upon adult children for their maintenance, reversing roles with their offspring for whom they had once provided themselves. Although higher proportions of elderly women than men lived with married children, it is probable that older men were more economically vulnerable than women as they aged, and less able to adapt to a life of makeshifts. In situations of last resort, however, both men and women relied on their parish for support, and decrepitude—in terms of incapacity and need—became the primary determinant of their identity, often overriding distinctions of gender and even social status. For such men, the dividends of patriarchal manhood had long since expired and there was no alternative positive male identity with which to escape 'impotence'.

Conclusion: Manhood, Patriarchy, and Gender in Early Modern England

It seems entirely fitting that manhood was often referred to in early modern England as an 'estate'. Manhood was a positive category of status and a form of privilege associated with a complex range of attributes and myriad processes of inclusion and exclusion. One of the primary distinctions upon which it was founded was, evidently, gender difference. There was no comparable sense of womanhood as an 'estate', and, in prescriptive commentary at least, women who displayed some of the attributes reserved for manhood were reviled as monstrous rather than celebrated as manly. Yet concepts of manhood were not premised simply on a gender hierarchy. This was an estate that was neither equally shared, nor, as a consequence, uniformly defined by all men. In its dominant forms it was mapped along three other central axes of difference: age, householding status, and, often less explicitly, social status. The 'estate' of manhood was associated with adulthood, corresponding to a phase in the life course that was often deemed not to begin until 30 or 35 and was considered by many to be over at 50. It was also linked to householding status, which most men achieved through marriage. Finally, many of its attributes—such as 'honesty'—were more subtly and exclusively aligned with the self-styled respectability of the 'better sort', also informing a critique of those men who were by contrast designated 'mean', 'rude', or 'base'.

When configured within these parameters, concepts of manhood coincided with patriarchal principles that both privileged males over females, and favoured particular men above others. Patriarchal manhood endorsed a gender hierarchy that exalted maleness as a cultural category by ranking men generically above women. This was patriarchy in a feminist sense. In its early modern sense, however, it most frequently served the interests of middle-aged, householding men, and, increasingly, those considered of 'able and sufficient' means. Furthermore, it was a complex compound, associated with a range of attributes that were selectively invoked and applied, and not exclusively associated with manhood in its patriarchal formulations. Strength, thrift, industry, self-sufficiency, honesty, authority, autonomy, self-government, moderation, reason, wisdom, and wit were all claimed for patriarchal manhood, either as the duties expected of men occupying patriarchal positions or as the justification for their associated privileges. These qualities held a range of associations; access and aspirations to them varied; and different configurations served different men in different contexts. Autonomy, self-sufficiency, or honesty all might have meant something quite different to a gentleman than to a master craftsman, for example. And a genteel reader of Sir Thomas Elyot's *Castel of Helth* might have aspired to manhood primarily rooted in reason, wisdom, and moderation, whereas an 'able and sufficient' husbandman was more likely to have identified with the merits of strength, thrift, and industry. In addition, patriarchal manhood was selectively applied and invoked—for example by university authorities who condemned violent posturing by students yet sanctioned similar behaviour by their own regulatory body, the proctor's watch.

Patriarchal manhood was not only contingent and multifaceted, therefore, but also often contradictory in its different emphases. Contradictions arose within prescription and practice, and not just between them. So, for example, prescriptive literature on marriage warned men of the dangers love posed to manhood, while emphasizing its fundamental necessity as the foundation for marital relations. Husbands were instructed to be autonomous, yet also warned that they were mutually implicated in all their wives' doings. Conduct writers advised wives that husbands held absolute authority over them, to which they should submit without question, while counselling husbands that they would be foolish to exercise it and to exact this kind of obedience. Similar tensions seem to have existed between attitudes towards the violent correction of wives. Wife-beating was often represented as a vice exercised by 'the common sort of men', suggesting contradictions between commonly held expectations of male dominance in terms of men's power over women on the one hand, and more selectively applied associations of male authority with rational self-government and the moderate rule of a range of subordinates on the other.[1] Here patriarchy in a feminist sense had the potential to clash with patriarchy in its early modern sense, which, increasingly, conceived of male authority in socially related terms.

Such fissures within concepts of patriarchal manhood were minor in comparison with the friction generated by the explicitly *anti-patriarchal*

---

[1] *Certain Sermons or Homilies Appointed to be Read in Churches in the Time of Queen Elizabeth of Famous Memory* (London, 1890), 537.

stances adopted by some men. Nightwalking, violent disruption, immoderate drinking, and the rampant pursuit of illicit sex inverted the attributes of patriarchal manhood in celebration of counter-codes of manhood rooted in prodigality, transience, violence, bravado, and debauchery. While the excesses of youthful misrule offer the most vivid examples, these deliberately subversive actions were not exclusive to young men, but also included those disenfranchised on grounds other than age, as well as men occupying patriarchal positions who (temporarily or otherwise) flouted the codes of behaviour expected of them. Patriarchal discourse went to considerable lengths to condemn such excesses as forms of deviation in terms of puerility, effeminacy, bestiality, or degeneration. Yet, particularly when associated with and endorsed by the fraternal bonds of camaraderie, the perpetrators of such actions clearly derived a potent sense of manhood from them. This, in turn, illustrates not only the degree of explicitly anti-patriarchal resistance performed by men, but also the levels of conflict between different meanings of manhood.

Such conflict did not solely exist along patriarchal/anti-patriarchal lines. This is suggested by critiques of youthful misrule that, rather than condemning it in terms of unmanly degeneration, instead linked such excesses to other kinds of manhood. University authorities, for example, were concerned that students did not demean themselves by adopting codes of manhood that were beneath them, deemed 'light' or 'lewd', and contrary to injunctions for 'decent behaviour and polished manners'.[2] Similarly, concerns to discourage various types of male behaviour with the label 'common' conveyed an implicit recognition of alternative forms of manhood articulated along socially related lines.

The alternative meanings of manhood acknowledged by such critiques were not explicitly anti-patriarchal, and often incorporated attributes of patriarchal manhood as well as some of the values intrinsic to counter-codes. A wage labourer's concept of honesty in terms of 'painful' industry may have overlapped to a degree with the values of a ratepaying yeoman. The latter, however, would also have enjoyed more exclusive access to the respectability associated with the honesty claimed by 'able and sufficient' men. Respectability in these terms was also a far more gender-specific concept, since the narrower version associated with honest hardship was also claimed by many women who were as instrumental as men in provisioning their households. Conversely, a man consigned to perpetual journeywork may have adopted many of the same actions as rebellious youths—such as excessive drinking or macho postur-

---

[2] *Records of Early English Drama: Cambridge*, ed. Alan H. Nelson, 2 vols. (Toronto, 1989), ii. 1144.

ing—although as an expression of his independence from, rather than a direct critique of, patriarchal codes. Alternative meanings of manhood evolved as expedients, particularly amongst men excluded from patriarichal privileges, rather than as explicit counter-codes. Shared household strategies that deviated from the nuclear model by pooling resources, for example, may have led to a greater emphasis on collectivism than self-sufficient mastery. Similarly, alehouse culture enabled the expression of manhood in terms of robust fraternity, carefree consumption, and at least temporary independence from the values of thrift, moderation, and painful drudgery.

Men, therefore, as well as women, undermined, resisted, or simply ignored patriarchal imperatives. Meanings of manhood did not always coincide with patriarchal expectations, but often existed in tension with them. Despite the force of patriarchal ideology, it was not successful in fixing manhood exclusively on its terms, and, as a result, it would be mistaken to equate manhood with patriarchy, or to view manhood as wholly defined in relation to it. Patriarchy itself was riddled with contradictions, in both its conception and practice. Men occupying patriarchal positions did not always perform the duties expected of them, but also drew on meanings of manhood contrary to patriarchal imperatives. Many others were excluded from patriarchal dividends on the grounds of age, marital status, and social status. They were not, however, excluded from claiming manhood. However powerfully it was articulated by contemporaries, we should not push the patriarchal model of gender relations so far that we are forced to categorize subordinate males as 'pseudo women' any more than we should view commercially active widows as honorary men, or politically vocal wives as 'fictive widows'.[3] Subordinate or marginalized men asserted potent meanings of manhood either in explicit resistance or as independent alternatives to patriarchal codes.

By becoming aware of the complex gender differences that existed *between* men, it becomes possible to categorize what R. W. Connell has called the 'social organization of masculinity'. Attempting to chart the relations between different types of manhood, Connell has established a fourfold classification, at the pinnacle of which sits 'hegemonic' manhood. The three other categories over which hegemonic manhood dominates comprise complicity (through benefiting from the 'patriarchal dividend' without occupying a hegemonic position); subordination (often blurred with femininity); and marginalization through social

---

[3] Mary Prior, 'Women and the Urban Economy', in ead. (ed.), *Women in English Society 1500–1800* (London, 1985), 96; Mary Beth Norton, *Founding Mothers and Fathers: Gendered Power and the Forming of American Society* (New York, 1996), 162–4, 174, 316, 397–9.

and cultural exclusion.[4] While patriarchal manhood was undoubtedly hegemonic in early modern England, its dominance should not be overestimated by historians. A modified scheme is therefore necessary to account for the social organization of early modern masculinity, which does not over-prioritize hegemonic manhood, and which can accommodate anti-patriarchal and alternative concepts of manhood. Patriarchal notions of manhood were themselves undermined by internal inconsistencies and contradictions, and competing forms of manhood exerted a powerful influence. Conflicting meanings of manhood are not always easily categorized as subordinate, complicit, or marginalized in relation to patriarchy, since they were often articulated in terms of active resistance. In addition, alternative meanings of manhood exerted an autonomous authority, independent of patriarchal manhood, and not solely defined in its shadow.

The differences between men were as central to the practice of patriarchy as the differences between men and women—some of which were not always as stark as a dichotomous model of gender relations would have us believe. In defamation litigation there was a far greater degree of gender convergence in matters of sexual honour than in matters relating to debased status. There was also a considerable degree of overlap in the contributions that many men and women made to the household economy, which risks being masked by a literal reading of the prescriptive literature's insistence on a much stricter separation of men and women's duties. While it is clear that patriarchal manhood, particularly in its feminist sense, should not be underestimated, operating to the profound disadvantage of women and structurally reinforced at almost every turn, female subordination was also selective. Patriarchal principles were not always deemed relevant for women as well as men—for example when a household's subsistence was solely dependent on the labour of married women and children.

Besides an appreciation of gender convergence as well as divergence, a comprehension of the varied meanings of manhood and the complex links between them has far broader implications for approaches to gender relations in early modern England. Just as meanings of manhood were varied, unstable, and contradictory, and—most importantly—not wholly determined by their relation to patriarchal ideology, so the construction and experience of femininity occurred in ways which both countered and were independent of patriarchal prescriptions. Although the scope for deviation was possibly less broad for women than for men, they likewise either benefited from, were subordinated by, resisted, or ignored patri-

[4] R. W. Connell, *Masculinities* (Cambridge, 1995), 76–81.

archal dictates. A multirelational model of gender relations in early modern England is therefore necessary, in place of approaches that merely measure the degree to which either men's or women's behaviour lived up to patriarchal prescriptions, or that weigh up the extent of male domination and female subordination. Such a model also takes account of the variations in gender identity within each sex as well as between them. As a result, it becomes possible to assess levels of resistance to and independence from patriarchal imperatives, as well as the basis of their authority. It also enables a more subtle analysis of the processes of inclusion and exclusion relating to the distribution of patriarchal dividends over time.

While it is clear that men were the primary beneficiaries of patriarchy, they were by no means privileged equally, and many instead derived a positive sense of male identity from alternative codes of manhood. Although meanings of manhood were multiple, highly contingent, and selectively invoked by different men either over the span of a lifetime or even during the course of a single day, it is possible to identify broader patterns to such variations. As a result, a more complex narrative of changing gender relations can be contemplated which is not solely premised on the shifting dynamics between the sexes but which also takes into account the relations between different categories of men and of women. Tracing the ways in which different men either benefited from, resisted, ignored, or were subordinated by patriarchal codes sheds light on an important long-term shift in the gender history of early modern England. Recent discussions of long-term change have commonly involved narratives tracing a gradual transition from concepts of gender difference in terms of a hierarchy placing men above women to notions of incommensurability between the sexes.[5] However, such accounts are beginning to be questioned as a result of more critical scrutiny of the complexity of gender change.[6] A further corrective to arguments positing over-schematic patterns of change is provided by considering the shifting dynamics within each sex, as well as between them. This appears to have involved a transition from a situation in which patriarchal manhood was primarily conferred along the lines of age and marital status to a situation in which patriarchal manhood became increasingly class-related.

[5] See, e.g., Thomas Laqueur, *Making Sex: Body and Gender from the Greeks to Freud* (Cambridge, Mass., 1990); Anthony Fletcher, *Gender, Sex and Subordination in England 1500–1800* (London, 1995); Michael McKeon, 'Historicizing Patriarchy: The Emergence of Gender Difference in England, 1660–1760', *Eighteenth-Century Studies*, 28 (1995).

[6] Karen Harvey, 'The Substance of Sexual Difference: Change and Persistence in Representations of the Body in Eighteenth-Century England', *Gender and History*, 14 (2002); ead., 'The Century of Sex? Gender, Bodies, and Sexuality in the Long Eighteenth Century', *Historical Journal*, 45 (2002).

The decades between 1560 and 1640 were pivotal to this longer-term redistribution of the benefits of patriarchy. Two details of the period's socio-economic history crystallize this point. First is the startling demographic data which suggests that well over a fifth of those born in England between 1604 and 1628 never married.[7] These men and women were denied access to the normative roles of master and mistress, governing their own 'little commonwealth' of the household, and were, presumably, absorbed as subordinates into the households of the increasing minority of householders. Furthermore, as suggested by the evidence of broken households, increasing numbers seem to have been unable to maintain themselves as householders, even if they had once attained householding status. As marriage became a 'privilege, rather than a right', large numbers of men—and men of the 'poorer sort'—were denied this particular form of patriarchal authority.[8] Instead, alternative codes of manhood, rooted in values ranging across prodigality, excess, bravado, brawn, transience, and collectivism, were positively claimed by, and became increasingly associated (often negatively) with, the 'meaner' sorts of men.

The second, and related, issue is the permanent dependence of increasing numbers of men on wage labour, as the system of transitional, life-cycle service gradually broke down and an incipient labouring class emerged. As a result, some of the attributes of patriarchal manhood in terms of orderly, rational self-control, and, increasingly, in terms of civility, were realigned with distinctions of social status, and became more exclusively associated with the 'better' or 'middling' sorts. By contrast, the patriarchal authority of labouring men became more exclusively focused on their relationship with women, and the meanings of manhood espoused by different social groups began to diverge. Lower-ranking men were increasingly denied access to the full patriarchal dividend, and their basis for complicity with the 'hegemonic' model became ever more narrow. This was a further dimension of the social polarization of the period, and helps to situate late sixteenth- and early seventeenth-century anxieties about disorderly men.[9] It also helps to contextualize the emergent discourses of civility, and, subsequently, politeness that have preoccupied historians of eighteenth-century masculinity, which need to

---

[7] J. A. Goldstone, 'The Demographic Revolution in England: A Re-examination', *Population Studies*, 40 (1986), 17.

[8] Keith Wrightson, *English Society, 1580–1680* (London, 1982), 70.

[9] See also Susan Amussen,' "The Part of a Christian Man": The Cultural Politics of Manhood in Early Modern England', in Susan D. Amussen and Mark A. Kishlansky (eds.), *Political Culture and Cultural Politics in Seventeenth-Century England: Essays Presented to David Underdown* (Manchester, 1995).

be approached as class-based codes of conduct and therefore part of this longer-term shift in the distribution of patriarchal dividends.[10]

While age and marital status nonetheless remained integral to male identities, the gaps within each sex were therefore becoming more marked in terms of social status. Married men of the middling sorts had increasingly less in common with their labouring counterparts, and it is possible that similarities of age were less likely to override social status distinctions. The one exception to this was in old age, which followed the opposite trajectory. In the sixteenth and early seventeenth centuries, social status and health appear to have been primary determinants of the degree to which older men maintained a stake in the patriarchal dividend. It is likely that, as chronological markers of age became more important and more fixed from the later seventeenth century, the scope for autonomy amongst the aged became more limited, regardless of their means.[11]

The period between 1560 and 1640 was part of a long-term shift in the relationship between patriarchal, anti-patriarchal, and alternative concepts of manhood and the groups of men with which these conflicting codes were associated. Aspects of patriarchal manhood, such as honest respectability and, in the longer term, civility, became reserved for the 'able and sufficient', rather than being more evenly distributed amongst adult married men. Alternative meanings of manhood, such as those associated with the alehouse, gradually became linked with particular groups of men—along contours of class as well as age—rather than being more broadly accommodated within a shared repertoire of male identity. Differences of social status became as important as distinctions of age and marital status as sites of conflict between meanings of manhood. The inevitable corollary was that the articulation of alternative codes of manhood was becoming both more class related and arguably a great deal more potent. It has often been observed that one of the most notable features of patriarchy is its persistence through adaptability.[12] We should not forget that the same was true of its alternatives and the many forms of resistance adopted by men as well as women in early modern England.

---

[10] Tim Hitchcock and Michèle Cohen (eds.), *English Masculinities 1660–1800* (Harlow, 1999); Philip Carter, *Men and the Emergence of Polite Society: Britain 1660–1800* (Harlow, 2000).

[11] Keith Thomas, 'Age and Authority in Early Modern England', *Proceedings of the British Academy*, 62 (1976), 248.

[12] e.g. Judith M. Bennett, 'Feminism and History', *Gender and History*, 1 (1989); Fletcher, *Gender, Sex and Subordination*, ch. 20; Sylvia Walby, *Theorizing Patriarchy* (Oxford, 1990).

BIBLIOGRAPHY

UNPRINTED SOURCES

Bodleian Library, Oxford
Oxford University Archives:
   Depositions, 1604–19: Hyp/B/4.

Cambridge University Library
Cambridge University Archives:
   Commissary's Court Act Books, 1585–93, 1598–1605, 1618–23, 1632–7: Comm.Ct.I.2–3, 6–7, 12–14, 23–6.
   Commissary's Court Depositions, 1580–1640: Comm.Ct.II.1–7, 10–11, 13, 15–18, 20, V.C.Ct.II.22*, 32.
   'Commonplace of Practice in Curia Ecclesiastica': Collect.Admin 38.
   Monday Courts, 1619–37: V.C.Ct.I.47, 49, Comm.Ct.I.18.
   Sturbridge Fair Court, 1585–1602, 1604–14: Comm.Ct.V.7.
   Vice-Chancellor's Act Books, 1589–97, 1600–4, 1617–22, 1629–34: V.C.Ct.I.2–3, 5–6, 9, 26–8, 52–3.
   Vice-Chancellor's Court Depositions, 1593–1645: V.C.Ct.II.1, Comm.Ct.II.8, V.C.Ct.II.2, 2*, 3–4, 6–11, Comm.Ct.II.12, V.C.Ct.II.12–20, Comm.Ct.II.19, V.C.Ct.II.22–31, 33–6, Comm.Ct.II.21.
   Vice-Chancellor's Court *Exhibita*, 1579–1633: V.C.Ct.III.1–32.
Ely Diocesan Records:
   Assizes and Gaol Delivery Files, 1605–14, 1616–30: E/6, E/7.
   Quarter Sessions Files, 1607, 1632, 1637: E/44.

Clothworkers' Hall, London
Court Orders 1558–81, 1581–1605.

Devon Record Office, Exeter
Consistory Court Depositions, 1593–8, 1634–40: Chanter 864, 866.

Downing College, Cambridge
Metcalfe's Thesaurus: Bowtell MS 11.
Wickstede's Thesaurus: Bowtell MS 12.

East Sussex Record Office, Lewes
Rye Presentments, Summonses and Estreats, 1579–1817: Rye 7.

Rye Hundred, Sessions and Assembly Books, 1582–95: Rye 1/5.
Quarter Sessions Rolls, 1625–7: QR/E 20–5.

Emmanuel College, Cambridge
Emmanuel College Archives:
   Admonitions Book, 1586–1775: CHA1.4.A.

Goldsmiths' Hall, London
Wardens, Accounts and Court Minutes, vols. viii–ix, xii.

Guildhall Library, London
Armourers and Brasiers' Company, Court Minutes, 1559–1621: MS 12071/2.
Armourers and Brasiers' Company, Yeomanry Court Minutes, 1552–1604: MS 12073.
Carpenters' Company, Court Minutes, 1533–76: MS 4329/1.
Coopers' Company, Court Minutes, 1567–96: MS 5602/1.
Fishmongers' Company, Court Minutes, 1592–1610: MS 5570/1.
Grocers' Company, Court Minutes, 1556–91: MS 11588/1.
London Commissary Court, Deposition Books (testamentary causes), 1594–7, 1597–1603: MS 9065A/2, MS 9065A.
Pewterers' Company, Court Minutes, 1561–89: MS 7090/2.
St Andrew Holborn, Vestry Minutes: MS 4249.
St Bartholomew by the Exchange, Vestry Minutes, 1567–1643: MS 4384/1.
St Dunstan in the West, Vestry Minutes, 1588–1663: MS 3016/1.
St Martin Orgar, Vestry Minutes and Churchwardens' Accounts, 1471–1615: MS 959/1.

Norfolk Record Office, Norwich
Consistory Court Depositions, 1598, 1633: DN/DEP/32, DN/DEP/41.

Public Record Office, London
Assizes 45/1.
Court of Exchequer, Depositions taken by Commission: E134.
Court of Exchequer, Depositions before the Barons: E133.

St John's College, Cambridge
St John's College Archives:
   Orders and Admonitions, 1627–1780: C5.1.
   Correspondence: D5, D57, D94, D105.

Trinity College, Cambridge
Trinity College Archives:
   Admissions and Admonitions, 1566–1759.
   Muniment Conclusion Book, 1607–73.

West Sussex Record Office, Chichester
Archdeaconry of Lewes, Deposition Books, 1586–1626: Ep II/5/4–12.

PRINTED SOURCES

ABBOT, ROBERT, *A Wedding Sermon Preached at Bentley in Darby-Shire* (London, 1608).
ALLISON, K. J., 'An Elizabethan Village "Census"', *Bulletin of the Institute of Historical Research*, 36 (1963), 91–103.
The Assembly Books of Southampton, i: *1602–08*, ed. J. W. Horrocks, Southampton Record Society 19 (Southampton, 1917).
The Assembly Books of Southampton, ii: *1609–10*, ed. J. W. Horrocks, Southampton Record Society 21 (Southampton, 1920).
The Assembly Books of Southampton, iii: *1611–1614*, ed. J. W. Horrocks, Southampton Record Society 24 (Southampton, 1924).
The Assembly Books of Southampton, iv: *1615–1616*, ed. J. W. Horrocks, Southampton Record Society 25 (Southampton, 1925).
AUBREY, JOHN, *Brief Lives and Other Selected Writings*, ed. Anthony Powell (London, 1949).
The Autobiography and Correspondence of Sir Simonds D'Ewes, Bart., during the Reigns of James I and Charles I, ed. James Orchard Halliwell, 2 vols. (London, 1845).
AVERELL, WILLIAM, *A Dyall for Dainty Darlings, Rockt in the Cradle of Securitie* (London, 1584).
B., STE, *Counsel to the Husband: To the Wife Instruction* (London, 1608).
BACON, FRANCIS, *The Historie of Life and Death. With Observations Naturall and Experimentall for the Prolonging of Life* (London, 1638).
BACON, Sir FRANCIS, *The Essayes or Counsels, Civill and Morall*, ed. Michael Kiernan (Oxford, 1985).
BANISTER, JOHN, *The Historie of Man, Sucked from the Sappe of the Most Approved Anathomistes* (London, 1578).
BARROUGH, PHILIP, *The Methode of Phisicke, Conteyning the Causes, Signes, and Cures of Inward Diseases in Mans Body from the Head to the Foote* (London, 1583).
BATTUS, BARTHOLOMAEUS, *The Christian Mans Closet. Wherein is Conteined a Discourse of the Training of Children. Nowe Englished by W. Lowth* (London, 1581).
Books of Examinations and Depositions, 1570–1594, ed. G. H. Hamilton, Southampton Record Society 16 (Southampton, 1914).
BRATHWAIT, RICHARD, *The Prodigals Teares; or, His Fare-Well to Vanity* (London, 1614).
—— *The English Gentleman: Containing Sundry Excellent Rules how to Accommodate Himselfe in the Manage of Publike or Private Affaires* (London, 1630).
BRETON, NICHOLAS, *An Olde Mans Lesson and a Young Mans Love* (London, 1605).
BRUELE, GUALTERUS, *Praxis Medicinæ; or, The Physicians Practice: Wherein are Contained Inward Diseases from the Head to the Foote* (London, 1632).
BULLEIN, WILLIAM, *The Government of Health* (London, 1595).

BULLOKAR, JOHN, *An English Expositor: Teaching the Interpretation of the Hardest Words used in our Language* (London, 1616).
The Case Book of Sir Francis Ashley J.P., Recorder of Dorchester, 1614–1635, ed. J. H. Bettey, Dorset Record Society 7 (Dorchester, 1981).
CAWDREY, ROBERT, *A Table Alphabeticall of English Wordes*, 4th edn. (London, 1617).
CECIL, WILLIAM, *The Counsell of a Father to his Sonne, in Ten Severall Precepts* (London, 1611).
Certain Sermons or Homilies Appointed to be Read in Churches in the Time of Queen Elizabeth of Famous Memory (London, 1890).
CHILLESTER, HENRY, *Youthes Witte; or, The Witte of Grene Youth* (London, 1581).
Churchwarden's Presentments (17th Century). Part 1. Archdeaconry of Chichester, ed. Hilda Johnstone, Sussex Record Society 49 (Lewes, 1948).
CICERO, MARCUS TULLIUS, *The Worthye Booke of Old Age Otherwyse Entituled the Elder Cato, now Englished* (London, 1569).
CLELAND, JAMES, *The Instruction of a Young Noble-Man* (Oxford, 1612).
CLEVER, WILLIAM, *The Flower of Phisicke. Wherein is Comprehended a True Method for Mans Health: With Three Bookes of Philosophie for the Due Temperature of Mans Life* (London, 1590).
CLODE, CHARLES MATHEW, *Memorials of the Guild of Merchant Taylors of the Fraternity of St John the Baptist* (London, 1875).
COGAN, THOMAS, *The Haven of Health* (London, 1636).
Complaint and Reform in England, ed. William Huse Dunham, Jr., and Stanley Pargellis (New York, 1938).
COOPER, CHARLES HENRY, *Annals of Cambridge*, 5 vols., vol. v, ed. J. W. Cooper (Cambridge, 1842–1908).
The Court of Good Counsell. Wherein is Set Downe How a Man Should Choose a Good Wife and a Woman a Good Husband (London, 1607).
COWPER, WILLIAM, *A Mirrour of Mercie; or, The Prodigals Conversion, Full of Comfortable Consolations* (London, 1614).
CROMPTON, WILLIAM, *A Wedding-Ring, Fitted to the Finger of Every Paire that Have or Shall Meete in the Feare of God* (London, 1632).
CROOKE, HELKIAH, *Mikrokosmographia: A Description of the Body of Man*, 2nd edn. (London, 1631).
CROOKE, SAMUEL, *The Guide unto True Blessednesse; or, A Body of the Doctrine of the Scriptures, Directing Man to the Saving Knowledge of God*, 2nd edn. (London, 1614).
CROUCH, HUMFREY, *Loves Court of Conscience . . . Wherunto is Annexed a Kinde Husband's Advice to his Wife* (London, 1637).
CUFFE, HENRY, *The Differences of the Ages of Mans Life* (London, 1607).
D., E., *The Copy of a Letter. The Former Part Conteineth Rules for the Preservation of Health* (London, 1606).
DARIOT, CLAUDE, *A Breefe and Most Easie Introduction to the Astrologicall Iudgement of the Starres*, trans. Fabian Wither (London, 1598).
Depositions and Other Ecclesiastical Proceedings from the Courts of Durham, Extending from

1311 to the Reign of Elizabeth, Publications of the Surtees Society 21 (London, 1845).
The Diary of Sir Simonds D'Ewes (1622–1624): Journal d'un étudiant londinien sous le règne de Jacques 1er, ed. Élisabeth Bourcier (Paris, 1974).
A Discourse of the Married and Single Life. Wherein, by Discovering the Misery of the One, is Plainely Declared the Felicity of the Other (London, 1621).
DOD, JOHN, and CLEAVER, ROBERT, *A Godly Form of Householde Government: For the Ordering of Private Families* (London, 1612).
―― ――*A Plaine and Familiar Exposition of the Ten Commandements* (London, 1618).
DU LAURENS, ANDRÉ, *A Discourse of the Preservation of the Sight: Of Melancholike Diseases; of Rheumes, and of Old Age,* trans. R. Surphlet (London, 1599).
Durham Civic Memorials, ed. C. E. Whiting, Publications of the Surtees Society 160 (Durham, 1952).
EATON, RICHARD, *A Sermon Preached at the Funeralls of that Worthie and Worshipfull Gentleman, Master Thomas Dutton of Dutton, Esquire* (London, 1616).
ELYOT, Sir THOMAS, *The Castel of Helth* (London, 1561).
The Fathers Blessing; or, Second Councell to his Sonne. Appropriated to the Generall, from that Perticular Example his Majestie Composed for the Prince his Sonne (London, 1616).
FEREBE, GEORGE, *Lifes Farewell; or, A Funerall Sermon. At the Funerall of John Drew Gentleman* (London, 1615).
The Foure Ages of Man (London, 1635).
GARDINER, SAMUEL, *Portraitur of the Prodigal Sonne* (London, 1599).
GATAKER, THOMAS, *Marriage Duties Briefely Couched Togither* (London, 1620).
―― *Pauls Desire of Dissolution, and Deaths Advantage* (London, 1620).
―― *Abrahams Decease. A Meditation on Genesis 25.8. Delivered at the Funerall of Mr. Richard Stock* (London, 1627).
―― *The Decease of Lazarus Christ's Friend. A Funerall Sermon. At the Buriall of John Parker Merchant* (London, 1640).
GOEUROT, JEHAN, *The Regiment of Life,* trans. Thomas Phayer (London, 1546).
GOUGE, WILLIAM, *Of Domesticall Duties* (London, 1622).
―― *The Dignity of Chivalry; Set Forth in a Sermon Preached before the Artillery Company of London* (London, 1626).
GOULART, SIMON, *The Wise Vieillard, or Old Man* (London, 1621).
GUILD, WILLIAM, *A Yong Mans Inquisition, or Triall. Whereby All Young Men (as of All Ages) may Know how to Redresse and Direct their Waies, According to Gods Word* (London, 1608).
H., B., *The Glasse of Mans Folly, and Meanes to Amendment, for the Health and Wealth of Soule and Body,* 2nd edn. (London, 1615).
HAKEWILL, GEORGE, *An Apologie or Declaration of the Power and Providence of God in the Government of the World* (Oxford, 1630).
HALL, JOSEPH, *Characters of Vertues and Vices,* in *A Recollection of Such Treatises as have bene Heretofore Severally Published, and are now Revised, Corrected, Augmented* (London, 1615).
HANNAY, PATRICK, *A Happy Husband; or, Directions for a Maide to Choose her Mate. As Also, a Wives Behaviour towards her Husband after Marriage* (London, 1619).

HART, JAMES, *KAINIKH; or, The Diet of the Diseased* (London, 1633).
HIERON, SAMUEL, *The Bridegroome* (London, 1613).
HUNNIS, WILLIAM, *Hunnies Recreations: Conteining Foure Godlie and Compendious Discourses, Intituled Adams Banishment: Christ his Crib. The Lost Sheepe. The Complaint of Old Age* (London, 1595).
JAMES I, *Basilikon Doron; or, His Majesties Instructions to his Dearest Sonne, Henry the Prince* (London, 1603).
——*A Publication of his ma*^{ties} *Edict and Severe Censure against Private Combats* (London, 1613), reproduced in Albert Forbes Sieveking (ed.), *Worke for Cutlers; or, A Merry Dialogue betweene Sword, Rapier and Dagger. Acted in a Shew in the Famous Universitie of Cambridge A.D. 1615* (London, 1904), 83–5.
Keepe within Compasse; or, The Worthy Legacy of a Wise Father to his Beloved Sonne (London, 1619).
KNAFLA, LOUIS A., *Kent at Law 1602: The County Jurisdiction: Assizes and Sessions of the Peace* (London, 1994).
LA FRAMBOISIÈRE, NICOLAS ABRAHAM DE, *An Easy Method to Know the Causes and Signs of the Humour Most Ruleth in the Body* ([London?], 1640).
LEMNIUS, LEVINUS, *The Touchstone of Complexions Expedient and Profitable for All such as be Desirous and Carefull of their Bodily Health*, trans. Thomas Newton (London, 1633).
LENTON, FRANCIS, *The Young Gallants Whirligigg; or, Youths Reakes* (London, 1629).
——*Characterismi; or, Lentons Leasures* (London, 1631).
LESSIUS, LEONARDUS, *Hygiasticon; or, The Right Course of Preserving Life and Health unto Extream Old Age*, trans. N. Ferrar (Cambridge, 1634).
The Letters of John Paige, London Merchant, 1648–1658, ed. George F. Steckley, London Record Society Publications 21 (London, 1984).
MARTYN, WILLIAM, *Youths Instruction* (London, 1612).
Minutes of the Norwich Court of Mayoralty 1630–1631, ed. William L. Sachse, Norfolk Record Society 15 (Norwich, 1942).
Minutes of the Norwich Court of Mayoralty 1632–1635, ed. William L. Sachse, Norfolk Record Society 36 (Norwich, 1967).
The Mirrour of Friendship: Both How to Knowe a Perfect Friend, and How to Chose Him, trans. T. Breme (London, 1584).
MORRAY, WILLIAM, *A Short Treatise of Death in Sixe Chapters: Together with the Aenigmatic Description of Old Age and Death, Written Ecclesiastes 12* (Edinburgh, 1633).
MOULTON, THOMAS, *The Mirrour or Glasse of Health* (London, 1580).
Muld Sacke; or, The Apologie of Hic-Mulier (London, 1620).
NASH, THOMAS, *The Anatomie of Absurditie: Contayning a Breefe Confutation of the Slender Imputed Prayses to Feminine Perfection, with a Short Description of the Seuerall Practises of Youth, and Sundry Follies of our Licentious Times* (London, 1589).
NEWMAN, ARTHUR, *Pleasures Vision: With Deserts Complaint and a Short Dialogue of a Womans Properties, betweene an Olde Man and a Young* (London, 1619).
NICCHOLES, ALEXANDER, *A Discourse of Marriage and Wiving* (London, 1615).
NORDEN, JOHN, *The Fathers Legacie. With Precepts Morall, and Prayers Divine* (London, 1625).

The Norwich Census of the Poor, 1570, ed. John F. Pound, Norfolk Record Society 40 (Norwich, 1971).
The Office of Christian Parents: Shewing how Children are to be Governed throughout All Ages and Times of their Life (Cambridge, 1616).
P., W., *The Prentises Practise in Godlinesse, and his True Freedome* (London, 1613).
PARKER, MARTIN, *Hold your Hands Honest Men for here's a Good Wife hath a Husband that Likes her, in Every Respect, but Onely he Strikes her, then if you Desire to be Held Men Compleat, what ever you doe your Wives doe not Beat* (London, 1634).
PARTRIDGE, JOHN, *The Widowes Treasure, Plentifully Furnished with Secretes in Phisicke* (London, 1585).
PEACHAM, HENRY, *The Complete Gentleman*, ed. Virgil B. Heltzel (Ithaca, NY, 1962).
Peter Idley's Instructions to his Son, ed. Charlotte D'Evelyn (London, 1935).
PLUTARCH, *A President for Parentes, Teaching the Vertuous Training up of Children and Holesome Information of Yongmen* (London, 1571).
Poor Relief in Elizabethan Ipswich, ed. John Webb, Suffolk Records Society 9 (Ipswich, 1966).
Poverty in Early-Stuart Salisbury, ed. Paul Slack, Wiltshire Record Society 31 (Devizes, 1975).
PRESTON, JOHN, *The Patriarchs Portion; or, The Saints Best Day. Delivered in a Sermon at the Funeral of Sir Thomas Reynell* (London, 1619).
PRICE, SAMPSON, *The Two Twins of Birth and Death. A Sermon. Upon the Funeralls of Sir W. Byrde* (London, 1624).
The Problemes of Aristotle, with Other Philosophers and Phisitions (Edinburgh, 1595).
Quarter Sessions Records for the County of Somerset, i: *1607–1625*, ed. E. H. Bates, Somerset Record Society 28 (London, 1907).
R., M., *The Mothers Counsell; or, Live within Compasse. Being the Last Will and Testament to her Dearest Daughter* (London, 1630?).
RALEIGH, Sir WALTER, *Sir Walter Raleighs Instructions to his Sonne and to Posterity* (London, 1632).
READING, JOHN, *The Old Man's Staffe, Two Sermons Shewing the Onely Way to a Comfortable Old Age* (London, 1621).
Records of the Borough of Leicester. Being a Series of Extracts from the Archives of the Corporation of Leicester, iii: *1509–1603*, ed. Mary Bateson (Cambridge, 1905).
Records of the County of Wilts, Being Extracts from the Quarter Sessions Great Rolls of the Seventeenth Century, ed. B. H. Cunnington (Devizes, 1932).
Records of Early English Drama: Cambridge, ed. Alan H. Nelson, 2 vols. (Toronto, 1989).
Regimen Sanitatis Salerni, trans. Thomas Paynell (London, 1575).
Reports of Cases in the Courts of Star Chamber and High Commission, ed. Samuel Rawson Gardiner (London, 1886).
RICH, BARNABY, *My Ladies Looking Glasse. Wherein may be Discerned a Wise Man from a Foole, a Good Woman from a Bad* (London, 1616).
ROBSON, SIMON, *A New Yeeres Gift. The Courte of Civill Courtesie: Assembled in the Behalfe of All Younge Gentlemen, to Frame their Behaviour in All Companies* (London, 1577).

SCOT, PATRICK, *Omnibus & Singulis. Affording Matter Profitable for All Men, Alluding to a Fathers Advice or Last Will to his Sonne* (London, 1619).
Select Cases on Defamation to 1600, ed. R. H. Helmholz, Selden Society 101 (London, 1985).
SHEAFE, THOMAS, *Vindiciæ Senectutis; or, A Plea for Old-Age* (London, 1639).
SMITH, HENRY, *A Preparative to Mariage. The Summe Whereof was Spoken at a Contract, and Inlarged After* (London, 1591).
SMITH, Sir THOMAS, *De Republica Anglorum*, ed. Mary Dewar (Cambridge, 1982).
SOWERNAM, ESTER, *Ester hath Hang'd Haman; or, An Answere to a Lewde Pamphlet Entituled, the Arraignment of Women* (London, 1617).
The Staffordshire Quarter Sessions Rolls, iv: *1598–1602*, ed. S. A. H. Burne (Kendal, 1935).
The Staffordshire Quarter Sessions Rolls, v: *1603–1606*, ed. S. A. H. Burne (Kendal, 1940).
The Statutes of Sir Walter Mildmay Kt Chancellor of the Exchequer and One of her Majesty's Privy Councillors, Authorised by him for the Government of Emmanuel College Founded by him, trans. Frank Stubbings (Cambridge, 1983).
STUBBES, PHILIP, *The Anatomie of Abuses: Contayning a Discoverie, of Vices in a Verie Famous Ilande called Ailgna* (London, 1583).
SWETNAM, JOSEPH, *The Araignment of Lewde, Idle, Froward and Unconstant Women* (London, 1615).
——*The Schoole of the Noble and Worthy Science of Defence* (London, 1617).
TAYLOR, JOHN, *The Olde, Old, Very Olde Man; or, The Age and Long Life of Thomas Par* (London, 1635).
TAYLOR, THOMAS, *A Good Husband and a Good Wife: Layd Open in a Sermon* (London, 1625).
TILNEY, EDMUND, *A Brief and Pleasant Discourse of the Duties in Mariage, Called the Flower of Friendshippe* (London, 1568).
TURNER, RICHARD, *Youth Know thy Selfe* (London, 1624).
TUSSER, THOMAS, *Five Hundred Points of Good Husbandry* (London, 1614).
Two Elizabethan Puritan Diaries, ed. M. M. Knappen (Chicago, 1933).
A Two-fold Treatise, the One Decyphering the Worth of Speculation, and of a Retired Life. The Other Containing a Discoverie of Youth and Old Age (Oxford, 1612).
VAUGHAN, WILLIAM, *Directions for Health, both Naturall and Artificiall* (London, 1617).
VENNER, TOBIAS, *Via Recta ad Vitam Longam; or, A Plaine Philosophicall Demonstration of the Nature, Faculties, and Effects of All such Things as by Way of Nourishments Make for the Preservation of Health* (London, 1628).
VICARY, THOMAS, *The English-mans Treasure with the True Anatomie of Mans Body* (London, 1633).
WALKINGTON, THOMAS, *The Optick Glasse of Humors. Wherein the Foure Complections are Succinctly Painted Forth* (London, 1607).
WEVER, R., *An Enterlude Called Lusty Iuuentus* (London, 1565).
WHATELY, WILLIAM, *A Bride Bush; or, A Direction for Married Persons* (London, 1623).
——*A Care-Cloth; or, A Treatise of the Cumbers and Troubles of Marriage* (London, 1624).

WHITAKER, TOBIAS, *The Tree of Humane Life; or, The Bloud of the Grape. Proving the Possibilitie of Maintaining Humane Life by the Use of Wine* (London, 1638).
Wiltshire County Records: Minutes of Proceedings in Sessions, 1563 and 1574 to 1592, ed. H. C. Johnson, Wiltshire Archaeological and Natural History Society 4 (Devizes, 1949).
Worcester County Records: The Quarter Sessions Rolls, i: *1591–1643*, comp. J. W. W. Bund (Worcester, 1900).
Xenophons Treatise of Householde, trans. G. Heruet (London, 1573).
York Civic Records, vol. ix, ed. Deborah Sutton, Yorkshire Archaeological Society 138 (York, 1978).
YOUNG, THOMAS, *Englands Bane; or, The Description of Drunkennesse* (London, 1617).

SECONDARY WORKS

ALLDRIDGE, NICK, 'Loyalty and Identity in Chester Parishes 1540–1640', in S. J. Wright (ed.), *Parish, Church and People: Local Studies in Lay Religion, 1350–1750* (London, 1988).
ALLEN, JUDITH, ' "Mundane" Men: Historians, Masculinity and Masculinism', *Historical Studies*, 22 (1987), 617–28.
AMUSSEN, SUSAN DWYER, *An Ordered Society: Gender and Class in Early Modern England* (Oxford, 1988).
——' "Being Stirred to Much Unquietness": Violence and Domestic Violence in Early Modern England', *Journal of Women's History*, 6 (1994), 70–89.
——'The Gendering of Popular Culture in Early Modern England', in Tim Harris (ed.), *Popular Culture in England, c.1500–1850* (Basingstoke, 1995).
——'Punishment, Discipline and Power: The Social Meanings of Violence in Early Modern England', *Journal of British Studies*, 34 (1995), 1–34.
—— and KISHLANSKY, MARK A. (eds.), *Political Culture and Cultural Politics in Seventeenth-Century England: Essays Presented to David Underdown* (Manchester, 1995).
BALL, W. W. ROUSE, *Cambridge Notes, Chiefly Concerning Trinity College and the University*, 2nd edn. (Cambridge, 1921).
BARKAN, LEONARD, *Nature's Work of Art: The Human Body as Image of the World* (New Haven, 1975).
BARRY, JONATHAN (ed.), *The Tudor and Stuart Town: A Reader in English Urban History 1530–1688* (Harlow, 1990).
BEATTIE, J. M., 'Violence and Society in Early-Modern England', in Anthony N. Doob and Edward L. Greenspan (eds.), *Perspectives in Criminal Law: Essays in Honour of John Ll. J. Edwards* (Ontario, 1985).
——*Crime and the Courts in England, 1660–1800* (Oxford, 1986).
BEIER, A. L., *Masterless Men: The Vagrancy Problem in England 1560–1640* (London, 1985).
BEIER, LUCINDA MCCRAY, *Sufferers and Healers: The Experience of Illness in Seventeenth-Century England* (London, 1987).

BEN-AMOS, ILANA KRAUSMAN, 'Failure to Become Freemen: Urban Apprentices in Early Modern England', *Social History*, 16 (1991), 155–72.
—— 'Women Apprentices in the Trades and Crafts of Early Modern Bristol', *Continuity and Change*, 6 (1991), 227–52.
—— *Adolescence and Youth in Early Modern England* (New Haven, 1994).
BENDALL, SARAH, BROOKE, CHRISTOPHER, and COLLINSON, PATRICK, *A History of Emmanuel College, Cambridge* (Woodbridge, 1999).
BENNETT, JUDITH M., 'Feminism and History', *Gender and History*, 1 (1989), 251–72.
BOCK, GISELA, 'Women's History and Gender History: Aspects of an International Debate', *Gender and History*, 1 (1989), 7–30.
—— 'Challenging Dichotomies: Perspectives on Women's History', in Karen Offen, Ruth Roach Pierson, and Jane Rendall (eds.), *Writing Women's History: International Perspectives* (Basingstoke, 1991).
BONFIELD, LLOYD, 'Was there a "Third Age" in the Preindustrial English Past? Some Evidence from the Law', in John M. Eekelaar and David Pearl (eds.), *An Aging World: Dilemmas and Challenges for Law and Social Policy* (Oxford, 1989).
BOTELHO, LYNN, 'Aged and Impotent: Parish Relief of the Aged Poor in Early Modern Suffolk', in Martin Daunton (ed.), *Charity, Self-Interest and Welfare in the English Past* (London, 1996).
—— and THANE, PAT (eds.), *Women and Ageing in British Society since 1500* (Harlow, 2001).
BOULTON, JEREMY, *Neighbourhood and Society: A London Suburb in the Seventeenth Century* (Cambridge, 1997).
BOWLER, CLARA ANN, 'Carted Whores and White Shrouded Apologies: Slander in the County Courts of Seventeenth-Century Virginia', *Virginia Magazine of History and Biography*, 85 (1977), 411–26.
BRADDICK, MICHAEL J., and WALTER, JOHN (eds.), *Negotiating Power in Early Modern Society: Order, Hierarchy and Subordination in Britain and Ireland* (Cambridge, 2001).
BRAY, ALAN, *Homosexuality in Renaissance England* (London, 1982).
—— 'Homosexuality and the Signs of Male Friendship in Elizabethan England', *History Workshop Journal*, 29 (1990), 1–19.
—— 'To be a Man in Early Modern Society: The Curious Case of Michael Wigglesworth', *History Workshop Journal*, 41 (1996), 155–65.
BREITENBERG, MARK, *Anxious Masculinity in Early Modern England* (Cambridge, 1996).
BREWER, JOHN, and STYLES, JOHN (eds.), *An Ungovernable People: The English and their Law in the Seventeenth and Eighteenth Centuries* (New Brunswick, NJ, 1980).
BROD, HARRY (ed.), *The Making of Masculinities: The New Men's Studies* (London, 1987).
BROOKS, CHRISTOPHER W., and LOBBAN, MICHAEL (eds.), *Communities and Courts in Britain 1150–1900* (London, 1997).
BROWN, ELSA BARKLEY, 'Polyrhythms and Improvization: Lessons for Women's History', *History Workshop Journal*, 31 (1991), 85–90.

BRYSON, ANNA, 'The Rhetoric of Status: Gesture, Demeanour and the Image of the Gentleman in Sixteenth- and Seventeenth-Century England', in Lucy Gent and Nigel Llewellyn (eds.), *Renaissance Bodies: The Human Figure in English Culture c.1540–1660* (London, 1990).

BURKE, PETER, 'The Art of Insult in Early Modern Italy', *Culture and History*, 2 (1987), 68–79.

——, HARRISON, BRIAN, and SLACK, PAUL (eds.), *Civil Histories: Essays Presented to Sir Keith Thomas* (Oxford, 2000).

CADY, JOSEPH, '"Masculine Love," Renaissance Writing, and the "New Invention" of Homosexuality', in Claude J. Summers (ed.), *Homosexuality in Renaissance and Enlightenment England: Literary Representations in Historical Context* (New York, 1992).

CAPP, BERNARD, 'The Double Standard Revisited: Plebeian Women and Male Sexual Reputation in Early Modern England', *Past and Present*, 162 (1999), 70–100.

CARLSON, ERIC, 'The Origins, Function, and Status of the Office of Churchwarden, with Particular Reference to the Diocese of Ely', in Margaret Spufford (ed.), *The World of Rural Dissenters, 1520–1725* (Cambridge, 1995).

CARTER, PHILIP, *Men and the Emergence of Polite Society: Britain 1660–1800* (Harlow, 2000).

CHURCHES, CHRISTINE, 'False Friends, Spiteful Enemies: A Community at Law in Early Modern England', *Historical Research*, 71 (1998), 52–74.

CLARK, ELAINE, 'The Quest for Security in Medieval England', in Michael M. Sheehan (ed.), *Aging and the Aged in Medieval Europe* (Toronto, 1990).

CLARK, J. W., *The Riot at the Great Gate of Trinity College, February 1610–11*, Cambridge Antiquarian Society, Octavo Series 43 (Cambridge, 1906).

CLARK, PETER, 'The Alehouse and the Alternative Society', in Donald Pennington and Keith Thomas (eds.), *Puritans and Revolutionaries: Essays in Seventeenth-Century History Presented to Christopher Hill* (Oxford, 1978).

——*The English Alehouse: A Social History 1200–1830* (London, 1983).

—— and SLACK, PAUL (eds.), *Crisis and Order in English Towns, 1500–1700: Essays in Urban History* (London, 1972).

——*English Towns in Transition 1500–1700* (Oxford, 1976).

COCKBURN, J. S., 'Patterns of Violence in English Society: Homicide in Kent 1560–1985', *Past and Present*, 130 (1991), 70–106.

CONNELL, R. W., *Gender and Power: Society, the Person and Sexual Politics* (Cambridge, 1987).

——*Masculinities* (Cambridge, 1995).

CORFIELD, PENELOPE J., 'Dress for Deference and Dissent: Hats and the Decline of Hat Honour', *Costume*, 23 (1989), 64–79.

COWAN, BRIAN, 'What was Masculine about the Public Sphere? Gender and the Coffeehouse Milieu in Post-Restoration England', *History Workshop Journal*, 51 (2001), 127–57.

CRAIG, J. S., 'Co-operation and Initiatives: Elizabethan Churchwardens and the Parish Accounts of Mildenhall', *Social History*, 18 (1993), 357–80.

CRAWFORD, PATRICIA, 'Attitudes to Menstruation in Seventeenth-Century England', *Past and Present*, 91 (1981), 47–73.
——'Public Duty, Conscience, and Women in Early Modern England', in John Morrill, Paul Slack, and Daniel Woolf (eds.), *Public Duty and Private Conscience in Seventeenth-Century England: Essays Presented to G. E. Aylmer* (Oxford, 1993).
——' "The Poorest She": Women and Citizenship in Early Modern England', in Michael Mendle (ed.), *The Putney Debates of 1647: The Army, the Levellers, and the English State* (Cambridge, 2001).
CURTIS, MARK H., *Oxford and Cambridge in Transition, 1588–1642* (Oxford, 1959).
DABHOIWALA, FARAMERZ, 'The Construction of Honour, Reputation and Status in Late Seventeenth- and Early Eighteenth-Century England', *Transactions of the Royal Historical Society*, 6th ser. 6 (1996), 201–13.
DAVIES, KATHLEEN M., 'Continuity and Change in Literary Advice on Marriage', in R. B. Outhwaite (ed.), *Marriage and Society: Studies in the Social History of Marriage* (London, 1981).
DAVIS, NATALIE ZEMON, ' "Women's History" in Transition: The European Case', *Feminist Studies*, 3 (1976), 83–103.
——*Society and Culture in Early Modern France* (Cambridge, 1987).
——*Fiction in the Archives: Pardon Tales and their Tellers in Sixteenth-Century France* (Cambridge, 1988).
DAVIS, ROBERT C., *The War of the Fists: Popular Culture and Public Violence in Late Renaissance Venice* (Oxford, 1994).
DEBUS, ALLEN G., *The English Paracelsians* (London, 1965).
DEMOS, JOHN, 'Shame and Guilt in Early New England', in Carol Z. Stearns and Peter N. Stearns (eds.), *Emotion and Social Change: Toward a New Psychohistory* (New York, 1988).
DOLAN, FRANCES E., *Dangerous Familiars: Representations of Domestic Crime in England, 1550–1700* (London, 1994).
DRIESSEN, HENK, 'Gestured Masculinity: Body and Sociability in Rural Andalusia', in Jan Bremmer and Herman Roodenburg (eds.), *A Cultural History of Gesture: From Antiquity to the Present Day* (London, 1991).
EALES, JACQUELINE, 'Gender Construction in Early Modern England and the Conduct Books of William Whately (1583–1639)', in R. N. Swanson (ed.), *Gender and Christian Religion*, Studies in Church History 34 (Woodbridge, 1998).
ELIAS, NORBERT, *The Civilizing Process: The History of Manners and State Formation and Civilization*, trans. Edmund Jephcott (Oxford, 1994).
EMMISON, F. G., *Elizabethan Life: Morals and the Church Courts* (Chelmsford, 1973).
ERICKSON, AMY LOUISE, 'Common Law versus Common Practice: The Use of Marriage Settlements in Early Modern England', *Economic History Review*, 2nd ser. 43 (1990), 21–39.
——*Women and Property in Early Modern England* (London, 1993).
EZELL, MARGARET J. M., *The Patriarch's Wife: Literary Evidence and the History of the Family* (Chapel Hill, NC, 1987).

FISHER, WILL, 'The Renaissance Beard: Masculinity in Early Modern England', *Renaissance Quarterly*, 54 (2001), 155–87.

FLETCHER, ANTHONY, 'Men's Dilemma: The Future of Patriarchy in England, 1560–1660', *Transactions of the Royal Historical Society*, 6th ser. 4 (1994), 61–81.

——*Gender, Sex and Subordination in England 1500–1800* (London, 1995).

FOX, ADAM, 'Remembering the Past in Early Modern England: Oral and Written Tradition', *Transactions of the Royal Historical Society*, 6th ser. 9 (1999), 233–56.

——*Oral and Literate Culture in England 1500–1700* (Oxford, 2000).

FOYSTER, ELIZABETH A., *Manhood in Early Modern England: Honour, Sex and Marriage* (Harlow, 1999).

FRENCH, H. R., 'Social Status, Localism and the "Middle Sort of People" in England 1620–1750', *Past and Present*, 166 (2000), 66–99.

GASKILL, MALCOLM, *Crime and Mentalities in Early Modern England* (Cambridge, 2000).

GATENS, MOIRA, *Imaginary Bodies: Ethics, Power and Corporeality* (London, 1996).

GATRELL, V. A. C., *The Hanging Tree: Execution and the English People, 1770–1868* (Oxford, 1994).

GOLDIE, MARK, 'The Unacknowledged Republic: Officeholding in Early Modern England', in Tim Harris (ed.), *The Politics of the Excluded, c.1500–1850* (Basingstoke, 2001).

GOLDSTONE, J. A., 'The Demographic Revolution in England: A Re-examination', *Population Studies*, 40 (1986), 5–33.

GOOSE, NIGEL, 'Household Size and Structure in Early-Stuart Cambridge', *Social History*, 5 (1980), 347–85.

GORN, ELLIOTT J., '"Gouge and Bite, Pull Hair and Scratch": The Social Significance of Fighting in the Southern Back Country', *American Historical Review*, 90 (1985), 18–43.

GOWING, LAURA, 'Gender and the Language of Insult in Early Modern London', *History Workshop Journal*, 35 (1993), 1–21.

——*Domestic Dangers: Women, Words, and Sex in Early Modern London* (Oxford, 1996).

——'The Haunting of Susan Lay: Servants and Mistresses in Seventeenth-Century England', *Gender and History*, 14 (2002), 183–201.

GRIFFITHS, PAUL, *Youth and Authority: Formative Experiences in England, 1560–1640* (Oxford, 1996).

——'Meanings of Nightwalking in Early Modern England', *Seventeenth Century*, 13 (1998), 212–38.

—— Fox, ADAM, and HINDLE, STEVE (eds.), *The Experience of Authority in Early Modern England* (Basingstoke, 1996).

HADLEY, D. M. (ed.), *Masculinity in Medieval Europe* (Harlow, 1999).

HAIGH, C. A., 'Slander and the Church Courts in the Sixteenth Century', *Transactions of the Lancashire and Cheshire Antiquarian Society*, 78 (1975), 1–13.

HALE, DAVID GEORGE, *The Body Politic: A Political Metaphor in Renaissance English Literature* (The Hague, 1971).

HAMMER, CARL I., Jr., 'Anatomy of an Oligarchy: The Oxford Town Council in the Fifteenth and Sixteenth Century', *Journal of British Studies*, 18 (1978), 1–27.
HARVEY, KAREN, 'The Century of Sex? Gender, Bodies, and Sexuality in the Long Eighteenth Century', *Historical Journal*, 45 (2002), 899–916.
——'The Substance of Sexual Difference: Change and Persistence in Representations of the Body in Eighteenth-Century England', *Gender and History*, 14 (2002), 202–23.
HASSELL SMITH, A., 'Labourers in Late Sixteenth-Century England: A Case Study from North Norfolk [Part I]', *Continuity and Change*, 4 (1989), 11–52.
——'Labourers in Late Sixteenth-Century England: A Case Study from North Norfolk [Part II]', *Continuity and Change*, 4 (1989), 367–94.
HAY, DOUGLAS, 'Property, Authority and the Criminal Law', in Douglas Hay et al., *Albion's Fatal Tree: Crime and Society in Eighteenth-Century England* (London, 1975).
HEALY, MARGARET, *Fictions of Disease in Early Modern England: Bodies, Plagues and Politics* (Basingstoke, 2001).
HELMHOLZ, R. H., 'Canonical Defamation in Medieval England', *American Journal of Legal History*, 15 (1971), 255–68.
——*Roman Canon Law in Reformation England* (Cambridge, 1990).
HENDERSON, KATHERINE USHER, and MCMANUS, BARBARA F., *Half Humankind: Contexts and Texts of the Controversy about Women in England, 1540–1640* (Urbana, Ill., 1985).
HERBERT, WILLIAM, *The History of the Twelve Great Livery Companies of London*, 2 vols. (London, 1834–6).
HERRUP, CYNTHIA B., *A House in Gross Disorder: Sex, Law, and the 2nd Earl of Castlehaven* (Oxford, 1999).
HILL, CHRISTOPHER, *Change and Continuity in Seventeenth-Century England* (London, 1974).
——'Male Homosexuality in Seventeenth-Century England', in *The Collected Essays of Christopher Hill*, 3 vols. (London, 1986).
HINDLE, STEVE, 'The Shaming of Margaret Knowsley: Gossip, Gender and the Experience of Authority in Early Modern England', *Continuity and Change*, 9 (1994), 391–419.
——'Exclusion Crises: Poverty, Migration and Parochial Responsibility in English Rural Communities, c.1560–1660', *Rural History*, 7 (1996), 125–49.
——'The Problem of Pauper Marriage in Seventeenth-Century England', *Transactions of the Royal Historical Society*, 6th ser. 8 (1998), 71–89.
——*The State and Social Change in Early Modern England, c.1550–1640* (Basingstoke, 2000).
HITCHCOCK, TIM, and COHEN, MICHÈLE (eds.), *English Masculinities 1660–1800* (Harlow, 1999).
HODGKIN, KATHERINE, 'Thomas Wythorne and the Problem of Mastery', *History Workshop Journal*, 29 (1990), 20–41.
HOFF, JOAN, 'Gender as a Postmodern Category of Paralysis', *Women's History Review*, 3 (1994), 149–68.

HOLDSWORTH, W. S., *A History of English Law*, 7th edn., revised, 16 vols. (London, 1956–72).
HOPE, JONATHAN, 'The Use of *thou* and *you* in Early Modern Spoken English: Evidence from Depositions in the Durham Ecclesiastical Court Records', in Dieter Kastovsky (ed.), *Studies in Early Modern English* (Berlin, 1994).
HOULBROOKE, RALPH, *Church Courts and the People during the English Reformation, 1520–1570* (Oxford, 1979).
HUFTON, OLWEN, *The Prospect before Her: A History of Women in Western Europe*, i: *1500–1800* (London, 1995).
HULL, SUZANNE W., *Chaste, Silent and Obedient: English Books for Women, 1475–1640* (San Marino, Calif., 1982).
HUTSON, LORNA, *The Usurer's Daughter: Male Friendship and Fictions of Women in Sixteenth-Century England* (London, 1994).
HUTTON, RONALD, *The Rise and Fall of Merry England: The Ritual Year 1400–1700* (Oxford, 1994).
—— *The Stations of the Sun: A History of the Ritual Year in Britain* (Oxford, 1997).
INGRAM, MARTIN, 'Ridings, Rough Music and the "Reform of Popular Culture" in Early Modern England', *Past and Present*, 105 (1984), 79–113.
—— 'Ridings, Rough Music and Mocking Rhymes in Early Modern England', in Barry Reay (ed.), *Popular Culture in Seventeenth-Century England* (London, 1985).
—— *Church Courts, Sex and Marriage in England, 1570–1640* (Cambridge, 1987).
JAMES, MERVYN, *Society, Politics and Culture: Studies in Early Modern England* (Cambridge, 1986).
JAMES, SUSAN, 'Reason, the Passions, and the Good Life', in Daniel Garber and Michael Ayers (eds.), *The Cambridge History of Seventeenth-Century Philosophy*, 2 vols. (Cambridge, 1998).
JAY, NANCY, 'Gender and Dichotomy', *Feminist Studies*, 7 (1981), 38–56.
JENNER, MARK, 'The Politics of London Air: John Evelyn's *Fumifugium* and the Restoration', *Historical Journal*, 38 (1995), 535–51.
JONES, ANN ROSALIND, 'Nets and Bridles: Early Modern Conduct Books and Sixteenth-Century Women's Lyrics', in Nancy Armstrong and Leonard Tennenhouse (eds.), *The Ideology of Conduct: Essays on Literature and the History of Sexuality* (London, 1987).
JONES, JOHN WINTER, 'Observations on the Origin of the Division of Man's Life into Stages', *Archaeologia*, 35 (1853), 167–89.
KAHN, COPPÉLIA, *Man's Estate: Masculine Identity in Shakespeare* (Berkeley, 1981).
KAMENSKY, JANE, 'Talk Like a Man: Speech, Power, and Masculinity in Early New England', *Gender and History*, 8 (1996), 22–47.
KEARNEY, HUGH, *Scholars and Gentlemen: Universities and Society in Pre-industrial Britain, 1500–1700* (London, 1970).
KERMODE, JENNY, and WALKER, GARTHINE (eds.), *Women, Crime and the Courts in Early Modern England* (London, 1994).
KING, LESTER S., 'The Transformation of Galenism', in Allen G. Debus (ed.), *Medicine in Seventeenth-Century England* (Berkeley, 1974).
KUCHTA, DAVID, 'The Semiotics of Masculinity in Renaissance England', in

James Grantham Turner (ed.), *Sexuality and Gender in Early Modern Europe: Institutions, Texts, Images* (Cambridge, 1993).

KUEFLER, MATHEW, *The Manly Eunuch: Masculinity, Gender Ambiguity, and Christian Ideology in Late Antiquity* (Chicago, 2001).

LACOUR, EVA, 'Faces of Violence Revisited: A Typology of Violence in Early Modern Rural Germany', *Journal of Social History*, 34 (2001), 649–67.

LAKE, MARILYN, 'The Politics of Respectability: Identifying the Masculinist Context', *Historical Studies*, 22 (1986), 116–31.

LAKE, PETER, and QUESTIER, MICHAEL, 'Agency, Appropriation and Rhetoric under the Gallows: Puritans, Romanists and the State in Early Modern England', *Past and Present*, 153 (1996), 64–107.

LANE, JOAN, *Apprenticeship in England, 1600–1914* (London, 1996).

LAQUEUR, THOMAS, *Making Sex: Body and Gender from the Greeks to Freud* (Cambridge, Mass., 1990).

LASLETT, PETER, *Family Life and Illicit Love in Earlier Generations: Essays in Historical Sociology* (Cambridge, 1977).

LAWSON, P. G., 'Lawless Juries? The Composition and Behavior of Hertfordshire Juries, 1573–1624', in J. S. Cockburn and Thomas A. Green (eds.), *Twelve Good Men and True: The Criminal Trial Jury in England, 1200–1800* (Princeton, 1988).

LEACH, EDMUND, 'Anthropological Aspects of Language: Animal Categories and Verbal Abuse', in Eric H. Lenneberg (ed.), *New Directions in the Study of Language* (Cambridge, Mass., 1964).

LEVACK, BRIAN P., *The Civil Lawyers in England, 1603–1641: A Political Study* (Oxford, 1973).

LLOYD, GENEVIEVE, *The Man of Reason: 'Male' and 'Female' in Western Philosophy* (Minneapolis, 1984).

LOCKRIDGE, KENNETH A., *On the Sources of Patriarchal Rage: The Commonplace Books of William Byrd and Thomas Jefferson and the Gendering of Power in the Eighteenth Century* (New York, 1992).

LYMAN, PETER, 'The Fraternal Bond as a Joking Relationship: A Case Study of the Role of Sexist Jokes in Male Group Bonding', in Michael S. Kimmel (ed.), *Changing Men: New Directions in Research on Men and Masculinity* (Newbury Park, Calif., 1987).

MACAULAY, THOMAS BABINGTON, *History of England from the Accession of James II*, 5 vols. (London, 1849–61).

MACDONALD, MICHAEL, *Mystical Bedlam: Madness, Anxiety, and Healing in Seventeenth-Century England* (Cambridge, 1981).

MACFARLANE, ALAN, in collaboration with Sarah Harrison, *The Justice and the Mare's Ale: Law and Disorder in Seventeenth-Century England* (Oxford, 1981).

MCINTOSH, MARJORIE K., 'Networks of Care in Elizabethan English Towns: The Example of Hadleigh, Suffolk', in Peregrine Horden and Richard Smith (eds.), *The Locus of Care: Families, Communities, Institutions, and the Provision of Welfare Since Antiquity* (London, 1998).

MCKEON, MICHAEL, 'Historicizing Patriarchy: The Emergence of Gender Difference in England, 1660–1760', *Eighteenth-Century Studies*, 28 (1995), 295–322.

MACLEAN, IAN, *The Renaissance Notion of Woman: A Study in the Fortunes of Scholasticism and Medical Science in European Intellectual Life* (Cambridge, 1980).

MADDERN, PHILIPPA C., *Violence and Social Order: East Anglia 1422–1442* (Oxford, 1992).

MARCHAND, RONALD A., *The Church under the Law: Justice, Administration and Discipline in the Diocese of York, 1560–1640* (Cambridge, 1969).

MARSH, CHRISTOPHER, 'Sacred Space in England, 1560–1640: The View from the Pew', *Journal of Ecclesiastical History*, 53 (2002), 286–311.

MASCUCH, MICHAEL, 'Social Mobility and Middling Self-Identity: The Ethos of British Autobiographers, 1600–1750', *Social History*, 20 (1995), 45–61.

MAY, LARRY, and STRIKWERDA, ROBERT A., 'Male Friendship and Intimacy', in eid., *Rethinking Masculinity: Philosophical Explorations in Light of Feminism* (Baltimore, 1992).

MELDRUM, TIM, 'A Woman's Court in London: Defamation at the Bishop of London's Consistory Court, 1700–1745', *London Journal*, 19 (1994), 1–20.

MENDELSON, SARA, and CRAWFORD, PATRICIA, *Women in Early Modern England* (Oxford, 1998).

MINOIS, GEORGES, *History of Old Age: From Antiquity to the Renaissance*, trans. Sarah Hanbury Tenison (Cambridge, 1989).

MITTERAUER, MICHAEL, *A History of Youth*, trans. Graeme Dunphy (Cambridge, Mass., 1993).

MOOGK, PETER N., '"Thieving Buggers" and "Stupid Sluts": Insults and Popular Culture in New France', *William and Mary Quarterly*, 3rd ser. 36 (1979), 524–47.

MOSSE, GEORGE L., *The Image of Man: The Creation of Modern Masculinity* (Oxford, 1996).

MUIR, EDWARD, *Mad Blood Stirring: Vendetta and Factions in Friuli during the Renaissance* (Baltimore, 1993).

MULDREW, CRAIG, 'Interpreting the Market: The Ethics of Credit and Community Relations in Early Modern England', *Social History*, 18 (1993), 163–83.

——'The Culture of Reconciliation: Community and the Settlement of Economic Disputes in Early Modern England', *Historical Journal*, 39 (1996), 915–42.

——*The Economy of Obligation: The Culture of Credit and Social Relations in Early Modern England* (Basingstoke, 1998).

NELSON, ALAN H., *Early Cambridge Theatres: College, University and Town Stages, 1464–1720* (Cambridge, 1994).

NITECKI, ALICIA K., 'Figures of Old Age in Fourteenth-Century English Literature', in Michael M. Sheehan (ed.), *Aging and the Aged in Medieval Europe*, Papers in Medieval Studies 11 (Toronto, 1990).

NORTON, MARY BETH, 'Gender and Defamation in Seventeenth-Century Maryland', *William and Mary Quarterly*, 3rd ser. 44 (1987), 3–39.

——*Founding Mothers and Fathers: Gendered Power and the Forming of American Society* (New York, 1996).

O'HARA, DIANA, *Courtship and Constraint: Rethinking the Making of Marriage in Tudor England* (Manchester, 2000).

PAGEL, WALTER, *Paracelsus: An Introduction to Philosophical Medicine in the Era of the Renaissance* (Basel, 1958).
PAHL, R. E., *Divisions of Labour* (Oxford, 1984).
PARKER, ROWLAND, *Town and Gown: The 700 Years' War in Cambridge* (Cambridge, 1983).
PASTER, GAIL KERN, 'Nervous Tension: Networks of Blood and Spirit in the Early Modern Body', in David Hillman and Carla Mazzio (eds.), *The Body in Parts: Fantasies of Corporeality in Early Modern Europe* (London, 1997).
—— 'The Unbearable Coldness of Female Being: Women's Imperfection and the Humoral Economy', *English Literary Renaissance*, 28 (1998), 416–40.
PATEMAN, CAROLE, *The Sexual Contract* (Cambridge, 1988).
PELLING, MARGARET, *The Common Lot: Sickness, Medical Occupations and the Urban Poor in Early Modern England* (London, 1998).
—— 'Finding Widowers: Men without Women in English Towns before 1700', in Sandra Cavallo and Lyndan Warner (eds.), *Widowhood in Medieval and Early Modern Europe* (Harlow, 1999).
—— and SMITH, RICHARD M. (eds.), *Life, Death and the Elderly: Historical Perspectives* (London, 1991).
POLLOCK, LINDA A., *Forgotten Children: Parent–Child Relations from 1500–1900* (Cambridge, 1983).
—— ' "Teach Her to Live under Obedience": The Making of Women in the Upper Ranks of Early Modern England', *Continuity and Change*, 4 (1989), 231–58.
—— 'Living on the Stage of the World: The Concept of Privacy among the Elite of Early Modern England', in Adrian Wilson (ed.), *Rethinking Social History: English Society 1570–1920 and its Interpretation* (Manchester, 1993).
—— 'Childbearing and Female Bonding in Early Modern England', *Social History*, 22 (1997), 286–306.
—— 'Rethinking Patriarchy and the Family in Seventeenth-Century England', *Journal of Family History*, 23 (1998), 3–27.
POMEROY, SARAH B., *Xenophon, Oeconomicus: A Social and Historical Commentary, with a New English Translation* (Oxford, 1994).
POOVEY, MARY, 'Feminism and Deconstruction', *Feminist Studies*, 14 (1988), 51–65.
PRIOR, MARY (ed.), *Women in English Society 1500–1800* (London, 1985).
QUAIFE, G. R., *Wanton Wenches and Wayward Wives: Peasants and Illicit Sex in Early Seventeenth Century England* (London, 1979).
RICHES, DAVID (ed.), *The Anthropology of Violence* (Oxford, 1986).
ROBERTS, MICHAEL, 'Women and Work in Sixteenth-Century English Towns', in Penelope J. Corfield and Derek Keene (eds.), *Work in Towns 850–1850* (Leicester, 1990).
—— ' "To Bridle the Falsehood of Unconscionable Workmen, and for her own Satisfaction": What the Jacobean Housewife Needed to Know about Men's Work, and Why', *Labour History Review*, 63 (1998), 4–30.
ROEBUCK, JANET, 'When does "Old Age" Begin? The Evolution of the English Definition', *Journal of Social History*, 12 (1979), 416–28.

ROPER, LYNDAL, *Oedipus and the Devil: Witchcraft, Sexuality and Religion in Early Modern Europe* (London, 1994).
ROTUNDO, E. ANTHONY, *American Manhood: Transformations in Masculinity from the Revolution to the Modern Era* (New York, 1993).
ROWLANDS, ALISON, 'Witchcraft and Old Women in Early Modern Germany', *Past and Present*, 173 (2001), 50–89.
RUBLACK, ULINKA, 'The Public Body: Policing Abortion in Early Modern Germany', in Lynn Abrams and Elizabeth Harvey (eds.), *Gender Relations in German History: Power, Agency and Experience from the Sixteenth to the Twentieth Century* (London, 1996).
RUSHTON, PETER, 'The Church Courts in North-East England in the Sixteenth and Seventeenth Centuries: An Historical Gossip Column?', *Sunderland's History*, 5 (1989), 24–36.
—— ' "The Matter in Variance": Adolescents and Domestic Conflict in the Pre-industrial Economy of Northeast England, 1600–1800', *Journal of Social History*, 25 (1991), 89–107.
SAMUEL, RAPHAEL (ed.), *People's History and Socialist Theory* (London, 1981).
SCHIEBINGER, LONDA, *The Mind Has No Sex? Women in the Origins of Modern Science* (Cambridge, Mass., 1989).
SCHINDLER, NORBERT, *Rebellion, Community and Custom in Early Modern Germany*, trans. Pamela E. Selwyn (Cambridge, 2002).
SCHOCHET, GORDON J., *Patriarchalism in Political Thought: The Authoritarian Family and Political Speculation and Attitudes Especially in Seventeenth-Century England* (Oxford, 1975).
SCOTT, JOAN, 'Gender: A Useful Category of Historical Analysis', *American Historical Review*, 91 (1986), 1053–75.
SEARS, ELIZABETH, *The Ages of Man: Medieval Interpretations of the Life Cycle* (Princeton, 1986).
SEAVER, PAUL S., *Wallington's World: A Puritan Artisan in Seventeenth-Century London* (Stanford, Calif., 1985).
SEDGWICK, EVE KOSOFSKY, *Between Men: English Literature and Male Homosocial Desire* (New York, 1985).
SHAHAR, SHULAMITH, *Growing Old in the Middle Ages*, trans. Yael Lotan (London, 1997).
SHARPE, J. A., *Defamation and Sexual Slander in Early Modern England: The Church Courts at York*, Borthwick Papers 58 (York, 1980).
——'Domestic Homicide in Early Modern England', *Historical Journal*, 24 (1981), 29–48.
——*Crime in Seventeenth-Century England: A County Study* (Cambridge, 1983).
—— ' "Such Disagreement betwyx Neighbours": Litigation and Human Relations in Early Modern England', in John Bossy (ed.), *Disputes and Settlements: Law and Human Relations in the West* (Cambridge, 1983).
——'The History of Violence in England: Some Observations', *Past and Present*, 108 (1985), 206–15.
——'Plebeian Marriage in Stuart England: Some Evidence from Popular

Literature', *Transactions of the Royal Historical Society*, 5th ser. 36 (1986), 69–90.

——*Judicial Punishment in England* (London, 1990).

——*Instruments of Darkness: Witchcraft in England 1550–1750* (London, 1997).

SHARPE, PAMELA, 'Literally Spinsters: A New Interpretation of Local Economy and Demography in Colyton in the Seventeenth and Eighteenth Centuries', *Economic History Review*, 44 (1991), 46–65.

——'Dealing with Love: The Ambiguous Independence of the Single Woman in Early Modern England', *Gender and History*, 11 (1999), 209–32.

SHEPARD, ALEXANDRA, 'Legal Learning and the Cambridge University Courts, c.1560–1640', *Journal of Legal History*, 19 (1998), 62–74.

——'Manhood, Credit and Patriarchy in Early Modern England, c.1580–1640', *Past and Present*, 167 (2000), 75–106.

—— and WITHINGTON, PHIL (eds.), *Communities in Early Modern England: Networks, Place, Rhetoric* (Manchester, 2000).

SIMON, JOAN, 'The Social Origins of Cambridge Students, 1603–1640', *Past and Present*, 26 (1963), 58–67.

SLACK, PAUL, 'Vagrants and Vagrancy in England, 1598–1664', *Economic History Review*, 2nd ser. 27 (1974), 360–79.

——(ed.), *Rebellion, Popular Protest, and the Social Order in Early Modern England* (Cambridge, 1984).

——*Poverty and Policy in Tudor and Stuart England* (London, 1988).

SLOAN, A. W., *English Medicine in the Seventeenth Century* (Durham, 1996).

SMITH, BRUCE R., *Homosexual Desire in Shakespeare's England: A Cultural Poetics* (Chicago, 1991).

SMITH, HALLETT, 'Bare Ruined Choirs: Shakespearean Variations on the Theme of Old Age', *Huntington Library Quarterly*, 39 (1976), 233–49.

SMITH, HILDA L., *All Men and Both Sexes: Gender, Politics, and the False Universal in England 1640–1832* (Philadelphia, 2002).

SMITH, RICHARD M. (ed.), *Land, Kinship and Life-Cycle* (Cambridge, 1984).

SOKOLL, THOMAS, 'Old Age in Poverty: The Record of Essex Pauper Letters, 1780–1834', in Tim Hitchcock, Peter King, and Pamela Sharpe (eds.), *Chronicling Poverty: The Voices and Strategies of the English Poor, 1640–1840* (Basingstoke, 1997).

SOMMERVILLE, MARGARET R., *Sex and Subjection: Attitudes to Women in Early-Modern Society* (London, 1995).

SPIERENBURG, PIETER, 'Faces of Violence: Homicide Trends and Cultural Meanings: Amsterdam, 1431–1816', *Journal of Social History*, 27 (1994), 701–16.

STEARNS, PETER N., 'Old Women: Some Historical Observations', *Journal of Family History*, 5 (1980), 44–57.

——(ed.), *Old Age in Preindustrial Society* (New York, 1982).

STONE, LAWRENCE, 'The Educational Revolution in England, 1560–1640', *Past and Present*, 28 (1964), 41–80.

——(ed.), *The University in Society*, 2 vols. (Princeton, 1974).

——*The Family, Sex and Marriage in England 1500–1800*, abridged edn. (London, 1979).

STONE, LAWRENCE, 'Interpersonal Violence in English Society 1300–1980', *Past and Present*, 101 (1983), 22–33.
—— 'A Rejoinder', *Past and Present*, 108 (1985), 216–24.
TADMOR, NAOMI, ' "Family" and "Friend" in *Pamela*: A Case-Study in the History of the Family in Eighteenth-Century England', *Social History*, 14 (1989), 289–306.
—— *Family and Friends in Eighteenth-Century England: Household, Kinship and Patronage* (Cambridge, 2001).
TEMKIN, OWSEI, *Galenism: Rise and Decline of a Medical Philosophy* (Ithaca, NY, 1973).
THANE, PAT, *Old Age in English History: Past Experiences, Present Issues* (Oxford, 2000).
THIRSK, JOAN, 'Making a Fresh Start: Sixteenth-Century Agriculture and the Classical Inspiration', in Michael Leslie and Timothy Raylor (eds.), *Culture and Cultivation in Early Modern England: Writing and the Land* (Leicester, 1992).
THOMAS, KEITH, 'The Double Standard', *Journal of the History of Ideas*, 20 (1959), 195–216.
—— 'Age and Authority in Early Modern England', *Proceedings of the British Academy*, 62 (1976), 205–48.
—— *Rule and Misrule in the Schools of Early Modern England* (Reading, 1976).
—— *Religion and the Decline of Magic* (London, 1978).
—— 'Numeracy in Early Modern England', *Transactions of the Royal Historical Society*, 5th ser. 37 (1987), 103–32.
THOMPSON, E. P., *Customs in Common* (London, 1991).
TIGER, LIONEL, *Men in Groups*, 2nd edn. (London, 1984).
TOSH, JOHN, 'What should Historians do with Masculinity? Reflections on Nineteenth-Century Britain', *History Workshop Journal*, 38 (1994), 179–202.
—— *A Man's Place: Masculinity and the Middle-Class Home in Victorian England* (London, 1999).
TURLEY, HANS, *Rum, Sodomy and the Lash: Piracy, Sexuality and Masculine Identity* (New York, 1999).
UNDERDOWN, DAVID, 'The Taming of the Scold: The Enforcement of Patriarchal Authority in Early Modern England', in Anthony Fletcher and John Stevenson (eds.), *Order and Disorder in Early Modern England* (Cambridge, 1985).
USTICK, W. LEE, 'Advice to a Son: A Type of Seventeenth-Century Conduct Book', *Studies in Philology*, 29 (1932), 409–41.
VENN, JOHN, and VENN, J. A., *Alumni Cantabrigienses: A Biographical List of All Known Students, Graduates and Holders of Office at the University of Cambridge, from the Earliest Times to 1900*, 4 vols. (Cambridge, 1922–54).
VICKERY, AMANDA, 'Golden Age to Separate Spheres? A Review of the Categories and Chronology of English Women's History', *Historical Journal*, 36 (1993), 383–414.
WALBY, SYLVIA, *Theorizing Patriarchy* (Oxford, 1990).
WALKER, GARTHINE, 'Expanding the Boundaries of Female Honour in Early

Modern England', *Transactions of the Royal Historical Society*, 6th ser. 6 (1996), 235–45.

WALL, ALISON, 'Elizabethan Precept and Feminine Practice: The Thynne Family of Longleat', *History*, 75 (1990), 23–38.

WALL, RICHARD, 'Relations between the Generations in British Families Past and Present', in Catherine Marsh and Sara Arber (eds.), *Families and Households: Divisions and Change* (Basingstoke, 1992).

———'Elderly Persons and Members of their Households in England and Wales from Preindustrial Times to the Present', in David I. Kertzer and Peter Laslett (eds.), *Aging in the Past: Demography, Society and Old Age* (London, 1995).

WALTER, JOHN, 'A "Rising of the People"? The Oxfordshire Rising of 1596', *Past and Present*, 107 (1985), 90–143.

WARD, JOSEPH P., *Metropolitan Communities: Trade Guilds, Identity, and Change in Early Modern London* (Stanford, Calif., 1997).

WEAR, ANDREW, 'Galen in the Renaissance', in Vivian Nutton (ed.), *Galen: Problems and Prospects* (London, 1981).

———(ed.), *Medicine in Society: Historical Essays* (Cambridge, 1992).

———(ed.), *Health and Healing in Early Modern England: Studies in Social and Intellectual History* (Aldershot, 1998).

WEBSTER, CHARLES (ed.), *The Intellectual Revolution of the Seventeenth Century* (London, 1974).

———*The Great Instauration: Science, Medicine and Reform 1626–1660* (London, 1975).

———(ed.), *Health, Medicine, and Mortality in the Sixteenth Century* (Cambridge, 1979).

———'William Harvey and the Crisis of Medicine in Jacobean England', in Jerome J. Bylebyl (ed.), *William Harvey and his Age: The Professional and Social Context of the Discovery of Circulation* (Baltimore, 1979).

WIESNER, MERRY, 'Guilds, Male Bonding and Women's Work in Early Modern Germany', *Gender and History*, 1 (1989), 125–37.

———'*Wandervögels* and Women: Journeymen's Concepts of Masculinity in Early Modern Germany', *Journal of Social History*, 24 (1991), 767–82.

WILLEN, DIANE, 'Women in the Public Sphere in Early Modern England: The Case of the Urban Working Poor', *Sixteenth Century Journal*, 19 (1988), 559–75.

WOOD, ANDY, 'Custom and the Social Organization of Writing in Early Modern England', *Transactions of the Royal Historical Society*, 6th ser. 9 (1999), 257–69.

———*The Politics of Social Conflict: The Peak Country 1520–1770* (Cambridge, 1999).

WOODBRIDGE, LINDA, *Women and the English Renaissance: Literature and the Nature of Womankind, 1540–1620* (Brighton, 1984).

WOODWARD, DONALD, *Men at Work: Labourers and Building Craftsmen in the Towns of Northern England, 1450–1750* (Cambridge, 1995).

WORDEN, BLAIR, *The Sound of Virtue: Philip Sidney's* Arcadia *and Elizabethan Politics* (New Haven, 1996).

WRIGHT, LOUIS B., *Advice to a Son: Precepts of Lord Burghley, Sir Walter Raleigh, and Francis Osborne* (Ithaca, NY, 1962).

WRIGHTSON, KEITH, 'Alehouses, Order and Reformation in Rural England,

1590–1660', in Eileen and Stephen Yeo (eds.), *Popular Culture and Class Conflict, 1590–1914: Explorations in the History of Labour and Leisure* (Brighton, 1981).
—— *English Society, 1580–1680* (London, 1982).
—— 'Estates, Degrees and Sorts: Changing Perceptions of Society in Tudor and Stuart England', in Penelope J. Corfield (ed.), *Language, History and Class* (Oxford, 1991).
—— ' "Sorts of People" in Tudor and Stuart England', in Jonathan Barry and Christopher Brooks (eds.), *The Middling Sort of People: Culture, Society and Politics in England, 1550–1800* (Basingstoke, 1994).
—— and LEVINE, DAVID, *Poverty and Piety in an English Village: Terling, 1525–1700*, rev. edn. (Oxford, 1995).
WRIGLEY, E. A., and SCHOFIELD, R. S., *The Population History of England, 1541–1871: A Reconstruction* (Cambridge, 1993).

UNPUBLISHED THESES

BOTELHO, LYNN ANN, 'Provisions for the Elderly in Two Early Modern Suffolk Communities', Ph.D. thesis (Cambridge, 1996).
CRESSY, DAVID, 'Education and Literacy in London and East Anglia 1580–1700', Ph.D. thesis (Cambridge, 1972).
DILLOW, KEVIN B., 'The Social and Ecclesiastical Significance of Church Seating Arrangements and Pew Disputes, 1500–1740', D.Phil. thesis (Oxford, 1990).
GOOSE, NIGEL, 'Economic and Social Aspects of Provincial Towns: A Comparative Study of Cambridge, Colchester and Reading, *c.*1500–1700', Ph.D. thesis (Cambridge, 1984).
LORCH, SUE CAROL, 'Medical Theory and Renaissance Tragedy', Ph.D. thesis (Louisville, Ky., 1976).
MORGAN, VICTOR, 'Country, Court and Cambridge University, 1558–1640: A Study in the Evolution of a Political Culture', Ph.D. thesis (East Anglia, 1984).
SHEPARD, ALEXANDRA, 'Meanings of Manhood in Early Modern England, with Special Reference to Cambridge, *c.*1560–1640', Ph.D. thesis (Cambridge, 1998).
SIRAUT, M. C., 'Some Aspects of the Economic and Social History of Cambridge under Elizabeth I', M.Litt. thesis (Cambridge, 1978).
WRIGHTSON, KEITH, 'The Puritan Reformation of Manners, with Special Reference to the Counties of Lancashire and Essex, 1640–1660', Ph.D. thesis (Cambridge, 1974).

INDEX

Adams, Henry 235
Addames, Anthony 204
adultery 81, 83, 119, 120, 121, 152,
    155, 162, 163, 171–2, 180, 240
age 1, 9, 10, 13, 16, 21–3, 49, 51, 68,
    86, 87, 88, 100, 101, 125, 132,
    139, 147, 149, 156, 183, 187,
    206, 210, 214, 217, 221, 222,
    246, 249, 251
ages of man 24, 41, 54–8, 215–16
air 65
Alciston, Sussex 229
Alcocke, John, saddler 102
alehouses 85, 97, 101–3, 114, 130,
    143, 146, 186, 189, 191, 211,
    249, 253
    women in 102–3
Alexander the Great 28
Aley, Edward, merchant taylor 180
Alfriston, Sussex 227
Alfry, Thomas 148
Allaby, Henry 147
All Saints' Day 100
Amore, Thomas 224
Amussen, Susan 128, 186
Andover, Hants. 204
Andrewes, John 207
Andrews, Roger (d. 1635), divine 169
anger 26, 27, 28, 173, 180
Ansty, Edward, tanner 227
apprentices 98, 99, 111, 120, 134–5,
    138, 139, 171, 180, 193, 206–7,
    208, 233
Arante, Helen 197
arbitration 199, 232
    see also informal reconciliation
Archer, Josiah 180
Arcoll, John, husbandman 227
Arely, Staffs. 191

Aristotle 47, 95, 96, 123
Ashley, Sir Francis 114
assault 12, 127–8, 131, 135, 143, 147,
    148, 185, 202
    see also violence
Asser, Befaithful 103
Atkinson, James 178
Attkyns, Katherin and Thomas 202
Averell, William 22
Avery, Edward 228
Avery, Thomas, yeoman 228
Avis, Elyn 234
Aylsham, Norfolk 203

bachelors, single men 9, 87, 99, 111,
    119, 168, 171–2, 206, 207, 213
Bacon, John 241
Bacon, Richard, singing man 112
Bacon, Sir Francis (1561–1626), lord
    chancellor 74, 206
bad company 27–8, 84, 105
Baguley, Hugh (d. 1635) 120, 159
Baker, Robert 233
Baker, Stephen 229
baldness 39, 162, 164, 178
Bales, Robert 120, 159
bankruptcy 162, 164
Barkshire, William, weaver 237
Barnarde, Christopher,
    husbandman 237
Barnes, Thomas, husbandman 192
Barton, Adrian, apothecary 217, 236
Barton, Glos. 216
Batchellor, John 204
Batchiller, Edward, sievemaker 204
Bate, William, tailor 144
Bateman, William 174
Bathurst, Thomas, millwright 241–2
Battle Abbey, Sussex 229

bawdy houses 160, 162, 163, 168
    see also prostitution
Baxter, John 234
Beanes, Thomas 112
beards 93, 146
beastliness, brutishness 25, 28,
    29–30, 60, 67, 84, 86, 88, 94,
    106, 147, 162, 163, 174, 248
bed-sharing 121–2
Beeston, Edmund 190
Beeton, Agnes 197
Belgrave, Mr 177
Bell, Robert, servant 145
Bemont, Helen 234
Benden, Henry, yeoman 237
Benrose, William, servant 168
Beston, Henry, gent. 143
Bewdley, Worcs. 204
Bexhill, Obadiah, physician 217, 236
Bigge, Thomas (d. 1677) 100
Bignor, Sussex 204
Binnes, John 111–12
Bins, Katherine 200
Birch, Thomas 197
Blaker, Richard 226
Blanket, Richard 189
blindness 234, 235, 239, 241
Blomfield, John (1565–1622),
    lawyer 164
bodies, the body 24, 27, 35, 47–50,
    52–3, 59–64, 65–7, 68–9, 76,
    133, 139, 150
Booth, Robert (d. 1657), puritan
    divine 106
Borne, John 196
Boston, Thomas and Ann 164
Botelho, Lynn 220
Bowlting, John, pewterer 177, 212
Bowyer, Richard 145
boy, as term of abuse 127, 142, 162,
    173, 174, 182, 212
boys 23, 85, 117, 120, 138, 142, 146,
    147, 157, 180, 181, 224–5, 226
Brachier, Richard, locksmith 236
Bradley, Ann 199
Bradly, William 235

Brasonet, Edward 239
Brathwait, Richard (*c*.1588–1673),
    poet 22, 30
bravado 93, 100, 121, 126, 136, 149,
    248, 252
Bray, Alan 116, 122
Bray, Margaret 201
Briggs, Richard, chandler 197
Brightling, Sussex 224, 225
Brighton, Sussex 233
Brown, Elsa Barkley 2
Browne, Jone, woman's tailor 202
Browne, Mary 168
Browne, Ralph, barber-surgeon 236
Browne, William, draper 190
Browning, James, tailor 191
Browning, John 181
Bryse, Richard 170
buggery 118
    see also sodomy
Bullein, William (d. 1576),
    physician 54, 55
Bullman, Thomas, weaver 212
Bushnell, Richard, turner 209
Byatt, John 101
Bye, John 208

Callis, John, (d. 1652?) 103
Cambridge 13–15, 93, 96, 101, 107,
    110–12, 118, 126, 127, 136, 141,
    143, 146, 152, 153, 156–73, 174,
    175, 177, 179, 180, 181, 186,
    189, 190, 192, 194, 197, 199,
    206, 208, 211, 216, 231, 232,
    233, 236
colleges in: Christ's 169, 177;
    Emmanuel 103, 106, 110–11,
    119, 121, 160; Gonville and
    Caius 112; King's 112, 177;
    Pembroke 116, 135, 169;
    Peterhouse 135, 147; Queens'
    93, 120, 171; St Catharine's 216;
    St John's 104, 106–7, 120, 122,
    159, 160, 196; Trinity 99, 100,
    106–7, 108, 110, 118, 119, 135,
    145, 160; Trinity Hall 170, 181

fairs: Barnwell 14; Sturbridge 14, 193, 207
Great Gate riot 106–7
inns/taverns in: Cross Keys 93; Dolphin 234; Falcon 93, 167; Half Moon 232; Pheasant Cock 102; Ram 112; Red Lion 112; Sun 141, 142; White Horse 98, 112; White Lion 112; White Swan 112
parishes in: Chesterton 223, 226; Great St Mary's 232; St Andrew's 159; St Botolph's 169
places in: Castle 103, 226; Coe Fen 127; gaol 193; Jesus Lane 232; Public Schools 135; Smoke Alley 98; river Cam 14; spittle house 169; Trumpington ford 169
proctor's watch 93–4, 96, 108–9, 113, 247
town–gown conflict 13, 15
university 13, 93, 94, 103–5, 108–9, 112, 119–20, 121, 145, 168–9, 247, 248
university courts 12–13, 15, 98, 102, 116, 127, 142, 143, 155–6, 160, 167, 170, 185, 195–6, 217, 218, 222
Cambridgeshire 217, 220, 222, 223, 226
cameraderie 96, 109, 112, 113, 125, 126
Canterbury 233
Capp, Bernard 154
Carowe, John, gent. 114, 178
Catlyn, Francis (d. 1624) 177
Caventry, Cambs. 226
Cawdrey, Robert 3
Caxton, William (*c.*1420-*c.*1492), printer 23
Cecil, William, Lord Burghley (1520–98), minister of state 30, 35, 36, 37, 78, 104, 123
Chaderton, Laurence (*c.*1536–1640), master of Emmanuel College, Cambridge 160
Chadwick, Nathaniel, scrivener 208
Chambers, Miles 176
charity 17, 42, 43, 231
charivari 136
Charles I (1600–49), king of England, Scotland and Ireland (1625–49) 104, 119
chastity 10, 26, 32, 42, 96, 121, 153, 168, 172, 184, 186, 213
cheese-making 222–3
Chester 208
Chilcompton, Somerset 203
childhood 34, 40, 44, 55, 57, 214
children 3, 45, 60, 63, 67, 74, 75, 137, 147, 187, 189, 191, 194, 202, 204, 208, 209, 231, 233, 237, 239, 240–3, 245, 250
see also boys; girls; orphans
Chimery, John, yeoman 242
Chipney, Bartholomew, shoemaker 192
Christ 68, 82, 152
Christmas 99, 100
church repairs 222, 225, 226, 227, 229
churchwardens, *see* office holding
Cicero 23, 40, 88, 123
citizenship 174
civility 9, 60, 61, 65, 68, 74, 88, 103–4, 135, 252, 253
see also manners
Clarke, Francis, bailiff 179
Clarke, Henry, innholder 232
Clarke, John, husbandman 224
Clark, Peter 101
class 125, 187–8, 209, 210–11, 212–13, 251–3
Claydon, Barnaby, draper 181
Clayton, Richard (d. 1612), dean of Peterborough 159
Cleaver, Robert, *see* John Dod
Cleland, James 22
climate 65–6
clothing 40, 135, 145, 180–1, 197–8, 201

clothing (*cont*)
  bands 145
  boots 143
  breeches 144
  buttons 181, 202
  caps 93, 145
  cassocks 117, 197
  cloaks 144, 145, 193, 197, 211
  coats 145
  doublets 135
  gowns 96, 114, 145
  hose 127, 180
  kirtles 171
  nightcaps 196
  ruffs 145
  scarves 93
  shirts 135
  shoes 178
  smocks 98
  socks 196
  waistcoats 171
  see also dress; hat-doffing
Cocker, William 238
Cogan, Thomas (1545?–1607), physician 52, 66
Cok, John, worsted weaver 238
Colbrooke, William, husbandman 237
Coldwaltham, Sussex 145
Cole, Benjamin, shoemaker 226
collectivism 203, 213, 249, 252
Collins, Mr 118
comradeship 95–6, 100, 101, 125, 211
  see also camaraderie; male bonding
conduct literature 7, 9–11, 21–2, 25–6, 28, 30, 38, 52–3, 56, 87–9, 105, 106, 137–8, 140, 150, 153, 173, 174, 176, 187, 205, 247
  domestic advice 9, 70–1, 72–3, 77, 78, 80, 81–2, 83, 84–6
  father-son advice 7, 9, 22, 26, 30–8, 78, 123
  parenting manuals 22
Connell, R. W. 5, 249
Conny, John, fisherman 229

conversation 32, 45, 52
  see also speech
Cooke, Bartholomew, labourer 226
Cooke, Robert 145
Cooper, Robert, yeoman 227
copyholders 226
Coton, Cambs. 112, 114
Cotton, Henry, pewterer 160, 232
Cotton, Margaret, wife of Henry 152, 159, 160
Cotton, Thomas 207
Cotton, William, lawyer 160
courage 24, 59, 65, 72, 106
court records 12–13, 131
courts of law:
  borough courts 12, 13, 195, 197, 205
  church courts 12, 154–5, 161, 184, 200
  Common Pleas 178
  Exchequer 12, 217, 220, 222, 223
  Lewes archdeaconry court 217, 219, 222, 225, 232
  London consistory 182
  manorial courts 228, 241
  quarter sessions 12, 13, 134
  see also Cambridge university courts
Coventry 14
coverture 197, 200
covetousness 44, 45, 61
Coville, William (d. 1614?), divine 120, 171–2
cowardice 27, 107, 141–2, 212
Crabb, Richard, husbandman 227
Cragge, John (d. 1605), rector of Coton 159–60, 216
credit 16, 37, 76, 82–3, 84, 101, 123, 157, 159, 160–1, 164, 167, 175, 180, 185, 186–213
Crewe, Sir Randle (1558–1646), judge 105
Crompton, William (1599?–1642), puritan divine 71
Crooke, Helkiah (1576–1635), physician 62
cross-dressing 7, 171

Crowforthe/Crowfoot, Thomas, baker 146, 164
Crystcrosse, Nicholas, cobbler 237
Cuckfield, Sussex 226
cuckoldry, cuckolds 93, 97, 152, 162, 163, 167
Cuffe, Henry (1563–1601), Greek scholar 54
Culpy, John, maltster 198
Curdy, William, yeoman 226
Curtes, Thomas, pewterer 177
Curtes, William, pewterer 177
custom, customary rights 217, 221–30, 245
women's knowledge of 222–4

Dallocke, Luke, yeoman 229
Damet, Thomas, cobbler 239
Dalton, Francis, clergyman 164
Daniel, Robert, yeoman 233
Daniell, Thomas, weaver 228
Dariot, Claude 61
Davenant, John (1576–1641), bishop of Salisbury 94 n.
Davi, John 239
death 38, 39, 67, 214, 242, 244
debt 12, 16, 37, 80, 123, 125, 158, 160, 162, 164, 186, 191–3, 195–7, 198–9, 200, 201, 242
defamation 12, 16, 116–19, 121, 122, 131, 133, 146, 152–85, 187, 193, 234, 237, 250
see also sexual insult; verbal abuse
Devizes, Wilts. 97
Devon 180
D'Ewes, Sir Simonds (1602–50), antiquarian writer 109–10, 122
Dey, William, husbandman 138
Deye, John 189
Dierks, Konstantin 11
diet 32, 64, 66, 68
Diggles, Thomas 112
Dighton, Francis 181
dirt 99, 133, 158
discretion 26, 30, 37, 38, 60, 73, 77, 85, 86, 87

disease, illness 27, 38, 39, 44, 50, 57, 59, 235, 236, 239
dishonesty 61, 94
dissolution of the monasteries 228
Ditchling, Sussex 216, 224
Dod, John, cordwainer 143
Dod, John (1549?–1645), puritan divine 70, 71, 72, 76, 78, 81, 82, 83, 84, 85, 153, 165, 186, 202, 242–3
Dodding, Margaret 201
Dodson, Edward, grocer 232
Doon, Roger, 'poor man' 143
Dorchester 114, 204
Drayton, Norfolk 204
dress 26, 29, 32
see also cross-dressing
drinking rituals 16, 100–6, 111–12, 113, 114, 211, 213, 248
drunkenness 6, 24, 26, 27, 28, 42, 43, 67, 84, 85, 94, 102, 104–6, 111, 144, 145, 147, 155, 162, 163, 165–6, 176, 180, 190, 193, 212, 232
Duckington, Giles 208
Dugresse, Dorothy 102
Du Laurens, André (1558–1609), French physician 41
Durant, John, tanner 127, 131

Eager, Richard 145
Eastbourne, Sussex 148
East Hoathly, Sussex 228
Eccleston, Roger 181
Edmunds, Bridget 120, 171–2
Edwards, Robert, husbandman 216
Edwards, William, yeoman 242
effeminacy 28–30, 59–60, 65, 79, 83, 86, 88, 94, 106, 116, 248
ejaculation 26
Elias, Norbert 128
Elizabeth I (1533–1603), queen of England (1558–1603) 104, 200
Ellwood, Richard 199
Elyot, Sir Thomas (1490?–1546), courtier and humanist 22, 44, 50, 54, 55, 65, 67, 247

Ellyott, John, blacksmith 227
Elwood, Henry, waterman 127, 131, 142
Ely, Cambs. 138, 148, 227, 228
emasculation 79, 146, 188, 213
Emons, Thomas 101
emotion 67
enclosure 150, 223, 225, 227
excommunication 133

false-dealing 44, 161, 162, 167, 176
Farmer, John, yeoman 226
fatherhood, fathers 3, 34, 70, 85, 106, 134, 160, 168, 183, 205, 207–8, 228–9, 240
  see also conduct literature; paternity
feast of purification 100
Feldwick, William, yeoman 224, 227
femininity 8, 250
Field, Theophilus (1574–1636), bishop of Hereford 116–18
Filoe, Joan 199
Fitzherbert, John, yeoman 234
Flamson, Robert 112
Flaxmer, John, tapster 204
Fleete, Edward, clothworker 176
Fletcher, Anthony 120–1
Ford, Sussex 181
Ford, Thomas, servant 114
Foster, Andrew, yeoman 236
Foster, Thomas 148
Fotherby, Charles (*c*.1603–77) 145
Fowler, John 233
Fox, Ursula 102
Freeman, John, yeoman 224
freemen 174, 206, 208, 212
French pox 27, 162, 163
French, Richard 231
friendship 32, 37, 82, 95–6, 115–16, 122–5, 172, 184
  see also male bonding
fugitives 75, 162, 173, 175, 182, 206
Fuller, Gabriel, blacksmith 190
Fuller, William 144
Funell, Garrett, yeoman 229

Galen 47, 50, 51, 57
Gardiner, Samuel 25
Gardner, Hugh 138
Garth, Charles 141–2
Garthesyde, Hugh, gent. 199
Gatens, Moira 49
Gatland, John 224
gender 2–3, 8, 9, 11, 16, 17, 21, 34, 68, 79, 81, 87, 136, 139, 156, 187–8, 215
  convergence 17, 39, 184, 221, 250
  difference 32, 49, 51, 58, 63, 71–2, 96, 103, 127–8, 154, 161–7, 173, 182, 183, 191, 202, 220–1, 222–4, 245, 246, 250, 251
gentility 68, 88
gentlemen 22, 37, 49, 50, 52–3, 64, 67, 105, 114, 140–2, 143, 147, 178, 179, 199, 200, 206, 234, 247
George, Sir Arthur 143
Germany 210
gerontocracy 43, 45, 222, 230
Gibson, John, lawyer 170
Gill, Thomas, draper 158
Girling, Sir 103
girls 23
Gislingham, Norfolk 222–3
Glasse, William, blacksmith 238
Glastonbury, Somerset 134
Goeurot, Jehan 55
Goodwin, Agnes 198
Goodwin, Andrew, innkeeper 178
Gouge, William (1578–1653), puritan divine 28, 40, 70, 75, 79, 80, 81, 82
Goulart, Simon (1543–1628), French theologian 41
Govy, Agnes 223
Gowing, Laura 4, 153, 182
grandparents 233
  grandfathers 229, 233, 240
  grandmothers 240
Graunte, Nicholas 232
Greaves, Richard 174
Greene, Christopher 193
Griffin, Mathias 203

Index

Grime, Henry, labourer 237
Grove, Humphrey, John and Richard 212

Haddenham, Cambs. 223
Haghley, Worcs. 212
Hakewill, George (1578–1649), divine 39
Hakluyt, Mr 106
Hall, Richard, clothworker 189
Halliwell, John, tailor 199
Hammons, John 175
Hamsey, Sussex 229
Hanbury, Worcs. 238
Hanger, Richard 160
Hannay, Patrick (d. 1629?), poet 79
Harrison, Alice 223
Harrison, Robert, shoemaker 228
Harrisons, William, nailer 147
Harrowe, Lawrence, labourer 234
Hart, James (*fl.* 1633), physician 55, 67
Hartlebury, Worcs. 238
Hastings, Sussex 231
Harvey, Francis, carpenter 216
Harvey, John 199
Harvey, Robert, grocer 101
Harvie, Agnes 167
Hassell Smith, A. 203
hat-doffing 145, 177
Haull, Agnes, maid 93
Haymer, Daniel, shoemaker 192
Head, Thomas 227
Heathers, Ann 201
Hedley, William 234
Henry VIII (1491–1547), king of England (1509–47) 228
Hibberd, Peter 211
Hide, John, merchant 231
Hill, Walter 243
Hilliard, Robert 191
Holdord, widow 203
Holles, Walter 239
Holmes, Sir 105
Homes, Michael, brewer 102, 198
homicide 128, 129, 130, 131
  see also violence

homoeroticism 113–14, 126
homophobia 125
homosexuality 115–19, 122, 125–6
honesty 16, 64, 65, 73–4, 78, 87, 110, 119, 149, 153, 154, 156–73, 175, 178, 182–5, 188–92, 194, 201, 213, 234, 244, 246, 248, 253
Hooe, Sussex 233
Hooke, John 233
Hooper, Humfry 235
Horner, Frances, spinster 203
Hornsey, William, apprentice 207
Horsey, George 110
Horsley, George 180
Hother, Thomas, tailor 237
House, Ann, maid 118
household 63, 116, 148, 169
  alternative strategies 16, 187, 195, 203–5, 231, 249
  economy 16, 83, 160, 167, 186–213, 239, 241, 250
  government 3, 45, 70, 75, 136–9
Howard, Walter, soldier 214
Howlings, Martha and William 205
Huitson, James, tailor 160–1, 238
Hull, Helena 200
humanism 50, 52
Humbletoft, Elizabeth 102
Humbletoft, John, alias John Trott, cordwainer 143, 181
Humbletoft, Rachel 102–3, 183
Humfrey, William, apprentice 134–5
humoral theory 24, 50–2, 54, 57, 58, 59, 60–1, 62, 79
Hunstanworth, Dur. 143
Hunne, William, fisherman 233
Huntingdon 14
husbands:
  bad 9, 84–6, 189–90
  duties of 9, 71, 72–3, 75–7, 78, 80–1, 82, 86, 247
Huton, William 181
Hutton, Robert (d. 1623), rector of Houghton-le-Spring, Durham 118

Hyde, Ralph, haberdasher 152
idleness 26, 27–8, 39, 85, 88, 94, 190–1, 211
Ightham, Kent 137
illegitimacy 4, 134, 155, 168, 169–70, 234, 240
independence 34, 36–7, 125, 194, 199, 202, 206, 211, 213, 221
informal reconciliation 101, 199, 232–3
Ingland, Alexander 160
Ingram, George 197
Ipswich 220, 240, 244
Ireland 214
Iverie, John 169
Iverson, Amos and Ann 199

James VI and I (1566–1625), king of Scotland (1567–1625), king of England (1603–25) 22, 27, 62, 143
Jardine, Lisa 124
Jeepe, John 193
Jenner, Richard, bellows-maker 226
jetting 109
Johnson, Arthur (d. 1621), chaplain to Lord Purbeck 177
Johnson, Cuthbert, cook 136
Johnson, Joan, wife of Cuthbert 136
Johnson, John (d. c.1588) 196
Johnson, John, labourer 148
Jones, Hugh 179
journeymen 6, 146, 147, 180, 201, 206, 208–9, 210, 211, 238, 248
judicial punishment 99, 132–4, 139 *see also* violence
Jurdeine, James 136

Kedge, Richard, pipe filler 238
Keepe within Compasse 30–2
Kelly, Theodore 143
Kempton, Elizabeth 170
Kent 190
Keymer, Sussex 226
King, Augustine 175
King's Lynn 14

kin, kinship 114, 137
Knight, Mary 189
Kynge, Richarde 244

labour, *see* wage labour; work
Lane, John 137
Langport, Somerset 134
Lapith, Thomas 199
Lassells, Walter 118
Laurance, Nichollas 211
Lawnder, Thomas 242
Lawrence, Robert 159
Lawson, Christopher, schoolmaster 147
Leeche, Francis, clothworker 142
Leicester 97, 144, 177, 189
Leke, Valentine 240
Lemnius, Levine (1505–68), Dutch humanist and physician 52, 55, 59, 60, 61, 62, 63, 64, 68
Lenton, Francis (*fl.* 1630–40), court poet 22, 28
Levett, Mr 233
Lewes, Sussex 192
life-cycle service 209, 252
Lindfild, George, yeoman 242
Linsey, Joan, widow 169
Litcham, Norfolk 208
Littleport, Cambs. 227
Loader, John, blacksmith 230
Lockridge, Kenneth 6
London 13, 14, 71, 99, 120, 122, 134, 136, 142, 189, 192, 193, 198, 200, 231
  livery companies 12, 134–5; Clothworkers' 138, 146, 176; Coopers' 174; Merchant Taylors' 212; Pewterers' 176–7, 212
  parishes: St Andrew, Holborn 235; St Bartholomew by the Exchange 235; St Dunstan in the West 235; St Martin within Ludgate 194;
  places in: Smithfield 237; Temple Bar 217

Index

Longworthe, Mary 102
Loudham, William 121
love 42, 75, 77, 79, 82, 83–4, 86, 124, 247
Low Countries 214
lust, lechery 26–7, 42, 45, 61, 67, 88, 116, 117, 121
luxury 28, 32
Lyndesley, William 98

madness 27, 32
Magnolls, Gilbert 198–9
male bonding 16, 95, 103, 111, 113–15, 125–6, 248
maleness, as a cultural category 10, 23, 246
manhood:
  alternative codes of 6, 11, 16, 88, 112, 125, 126, 132, 135–6, 148, 150–1, 176, 180, 184, 187–8, 205, 206, 210–13, 214, 231, 248–9, 250, 251, 252, 253
  anti-patriarchal counter codes 11, 15–16, 100, 105, 110–11, 112–13, 121, 125–6, 151, 247–8, 250, 253
  as a phase in the life course 9, 21, 23, 46, 53, 54, 56–8, 87, 215, 246
  normative/patriarchal 6, 7, 8–9, 11, 21, 23, 25–6, 37, 40, 45, 46, 63–4, 72–3, 74–5, 86, 87–9, 96, 106, 113, 125–6, 140, 149, 151, 157, 173–5, 176, 179, 180, 182, 184–5, 187–8, 194–5, 205, 206, 210, 214, 246–7, 250, 253
manners 34, 52, 61, 64, 104, 248
Maphew, William, cordwainer 143
Marefield, Sussex 234
marital status 1, 2, 10, 87, 88, 156, 187, 210, 249, 251
marriage 9, 63, 70–1, 73–86, 116, 124, 204–5, 206, 209–10, 214, 233, 240, 246, 247, 251, 252
  clandestine 119–20; separation 171, 203–5

Marten, John, weaver 227
Martyn, William (1562–1617), lawyer and historian 26, 38
Mary I (1516–58), queen of England (1553–8) 228
Maryne, John, hooper 211
masculinity:
  history of 1–2, 5, 252
  social organization of 249–50
Mase, Henry, weaver 199
Mason, Sir 107
medical literature 7, 9, 22, 42, 43, 47–53, 54, 55, 56, 57, 60, 65, 66, 68, 86, 216
medical practitioners 52
  see also occupations
melancholy 51, 56–7, 61, 62
memory 27, 44, 59, 72, 117, 222, 226–7, 228–30
menopause 220
men's studies 95
Midhurst, Sussex 97
migrants 203, 208
Milton, John (1608–74), poet 110
Mirrour of Friendship 123, 124
misogyny 39, 77, 80
moderation 9, 16, 30, 32, 40, 44, 46, 58, 67, 68, 73, 87, 247, 249
  see also temperance
modesty 32
money 135, 198, 211, 234
Moore, Ann 164
Morley, James 199
Morrill, Parnell 197
mothers 62, 79, 134, 137, 207, 208, 241, 243
Mothers Counsell, The 32–3
Mott, Thomas 232
Mountaigne, George (1569–1628), archbishop of York 94 n.
Muldrew, Craig 191
murder 162, 163
  see also homicide
Mytton, Yorks. 179

Nelson, Mr, clergyman 152

286 *Index*

Newcastle 98, 142
New England 6
Newick, Sussex 211
Newland, Worcs. 203
Newman, Elizabeth 102, 181, 183
Newman, John, cobbler 189–90
Newmarket 14
Newmarsh, Richard 196
Newton, Thomas (1542?–1607), poet, physician, and divine 23
Neyborough, Barbara 201
Nightingale, John 115
nightwalking 93, 94, 96–8, 100, 105, 109, 111, 112, 212, 248
Norden, John 36
Norfolk 200, 242
Norries, Abraham, sergeweaver 209
Norwich 133, 137, 146, 181, 189, 202, 203, 204, 205, 209, 238, 241, 245

obedience 80
occupations:
  apothecaries 160, 236
  bakers 98, 112, 144, 146, 164
  barbers, barber-surgeons 146, 157, 174, 236
  bellows-makers 226
  blacksmiths 133, 190, 227, 230, 238
  brewers 101, 102, 192, 194, 198
  butchers 62, 114, 178, 197, 236, 237
  butlers 99, 181, 183
  carpenters 216, 217
  carters 62
  chandlers 197
  clergy 22, 23, 39, 50, 62, 70, 71, 94, 110–11, 116–17, 145, 164, 175, 177, 180, 181, 208, 224, 229, 233
  clothworkers 135, 142, 176, 189
  cobblers 62, 189, 200, 237, 239
  cooks 62, 133, 179, 196
  coopers 98, 207
  cordwainers 143, 177, 191, 238
  dancers 112
  drapers 120, 135, 158, 181, 190
  fishermen 229, 233
  fishmongers 136, 192, 197
  grocers 101, 135, 232
  haberdashers 152
  hoopers 211
  horse-keepers, stable boys 36, 142, 180
  husbandmen 138, 192, 200, 216, 224, 225, 226, 227, 237, 247
  innkeepers 164, 178, 192, 205, 216
  joiners 208
  labourers 13, 36, 112, 148, 149, 174, 180, 192, 194, 200, 201, 211, 212, 213, 226, 228, 234, 237, 238, 239, 248, 252–3
  lace making 238, 239
  launderers 144
  lawyers 50, 62, 160, 164, 181
  locksmiths 236
  maltsters 190, 197, 198
  mariners 142
  merchants 62, 231
  millwrights 242
  nailers 147
  needlework 202
  notaries 191
  peddlers 183
  pewterers 160, 176, 212
  physicians 50, 52, 61, 62, 111, 217, 236
  pipe-filling 238
  porters 62
  saddlers 102, 174
  scriveners 208
  sailors 62
  servingmen 202
  shermen 142, 157
  shoemakers 192, 226, 228
  sievemakers 204
  singers 112
  skinners 200
  spinning 202
  stationers 164
  tailors 102, 112, 144, 160, 161, 175, 191, 199, 200, 201, 202, 207, 216, 232, 237, 238

Index

tanners 127, 227
tapsters 204
teachers, schoolmasters 102, 147, 186
tinkers 62
turners 193
watermen 127, 142, 190
weavers 189, 199, 202, 212, 227, 228, 237, 238
yeomen 74, 147, 161, 175, 216, 223, 224, 226, 227, 228, 229, 233, 234, 236, 237, 242, 248
occupational status 180, 210
office-holding 17, 45, 168, 179, 181, 182, 217, 227, 231–2, 235–6, 245
   aldermen 144, 231, 232, 244
   assistants 235
   bailiffs 223, 240
   bellmen 97
   borsholders 137
   churchwardens 97, 137, 175, 179, 181, 203, 204, 225, 227, 232, 233
   clerks of the market 177, 181
   constables 93, 127, 130, 133, 145, 146, 178, 179, 181, 216, 232, 235, 236
   headboroughs 244
   justices of the peace 114, 137, 178, 180, 189, 190, 205, 214, 243, 244
   mayors 144, 171, 172, 180, 231, 232
   overseers of the poor 137, 217, 244
   scavengers 235
   sheriffs 180
   sidesmen 144
Office of Christian Parents 24, 26
old age 9, 17, 21, 57, 87, 147, 253
   definitions of 215–21
   experiences of 221–45
   history of 214–15, 245
   representations of 22–3, 38–46, 51
Old Swinford, Worcs. 212
Oliver, Robert, maltster 190
Oliver, Thomas 237
orphans 240
Orton, Robert 147

Osburne, Edward, husbandman 237
Overton, Edward, gent. 200
Oxford 13, 14, 26, 231
Oxley, Christopher 110

Page, Thomas 207
Pahl, R. E. 183
Palfreman, Richard and Henry 148
Paracelsus 51
Parker, Agnes, wife of Edward 196
Parker, Edward, cook 196
Parker, Matthew, labourer 226
Parnby, Mary 201
Parnell, Henry 236
Parr, Thomas 239–40
Parris, Elizabeth 181
Parry, William, waterman 190
paternity 119, 160, 162, 169–71
patriarchy 1, 4–6, 10, 17, 128, 139, 150–1, 201–2, 203, 205, 246–51
patriarchy (*cont.*)
   early modern patriarchal ideology 3–4, 47, 49, 70, 80, 186, 246, 247
   feminist concepts of 3–4, 8–10, 70, 213, 246, 247, 250
   resistance to 4, 94, 126, 210, 248, 251, 253
patriarchal privilege, access to 1, 5, 7, 17, 21, 23, 36, 38, 40, 42–3, 46, 49, 53, 68–9, 85, 87, 88–9, 154, 182, 205–6, 213, 214, 221, 245, 247, 248, 251–3
patronage 115, 123, 233–4
Patson, John 193
Payne, Edward, yeoman 229
Payne, John, draper 168
Pearse, John 177–8
Pearse, William 211
Pecke, William, butcher 237
Peckett, John 188
pederasty 116
Pelling, Margaret 215, 239
pensions 214, 242, 243–4
perambulations 224–5, 226
   see also rogationtide

Perry, Edward 147
Phillips, Francis 101
Phillips, John 144
Pickering, William, brewer 101
piety 32, 42, 110, 191
Pile, John 207
Pinder, Richard 102
pleading strategies 147, 149
Plutarch 22
Plymouth 189
poisoning 163, 164
politeness 252
Pope, John 211
Popley, William, gent. 216
population growth 14, 206, 209
portions 164
Potto, Edward 232
poverty 14, 178, 189–91, 192, 201–2, 213, 236, 237, 238–9
   relief of 17, 204, 232, 243–4, 245
Powell, Edmund, husbandman 237
Powell, Griffin 177–8
Poynter, Robert 240
Prance, Robert, gent. 114, 178
pregnancy 4, 137
Prime, Ann, wife of Benjamin 201
Prime, Benjamin, stationer 164
Prior, Anthony 242
prodigality 32, 85, 88, 210, 213, 248, 252
prodigal son, parable of 25
prostitution 98, 119, 133
provision 77, 83, 86, 186–92, 194–5, 210, 213, 221, 240
   by women 195–6, 197, 201–3, 239, 248
public life 41–2, 45, 239
Pynchin, Wylliam, labourer 238

Raleigh, Sir Walter (1552?–1618), military and naval commander 22, 28, 30, 37
Randall, Mary 146
Ratcliffe, Anthony, gent. 143
Reade, Alexander (d. c.1628), divine 117

Reade, Alice 204
reason 8, 9, 28, 29–30, 32, 52, 56, 58, 60–1, 64, 65, 66, 67–8, 69, 73, 76, 79, 87, 174, 247
recreations:
   archery 236
   bear-baiting 112
   bowls 85, 190, 212
   bull-baiting 112
   cards 111, 164
   dancing 28–9, 134
   dice 212
   dog fights 112
   football 135, 150
   gaming, gambling 16, 84, 212
   hunting 112
   music 28–9
   plays 85, 106–8, 110, 113, 135
   shove groat 212
   stool ball 102
Reddit, Thomas, retainer 160
Rede, John, yeoman 234
rent payments 158, 170, 179
reputation 16, 83, 139, 140, 152–4, 155–6, 157–73, 183–5, 186
respectability 9, 26, 73, 154, 157, 159, 161, 172, 173–4, 175, 183, 184, 187, 213, 244, 246, 248, 253
retirement 214, 231, 235–6
retirement agreements 17, 241–3
Reynoldes, Andrew, labourer 239
Reynolds, Agnes 202
Rich, Barnaby (1540?–1617), soldier 29
Robardes, John, cordwainer 238
Robbes, Mary 183
Robinson, John 233
Robson, Simon 140–1, 147
rogationtide 224
Rogers, Daniel (1572–1652), divine 177
rough music 97, 133
Rowlande, Anne and Petar 240
Rucke, William, husbandman 216
Russell, Quyntyn, worsted weaver 238

Russell, Thomas 207
Rust, Richard, tailor 112
rusticity 66, 69, 174
Rye, Sussex 97, 189

Saintpeere, Owen 164
Salisbury 205, 244
Salehurst, Sussex 227
Sallowes, Robert 244
Salmon, Edward (d. 1681), divine 110
Sander, George, butcher 236
Saville, Francis, butler 181
Saye, Jone and Elizabeth 202
scolds, scolding 133, 163, 165
Scolye, John 193
Scorye, John 101, 167
Scott, John, yeoman 158, 161
Seale, Humfrey 235
seasons 65–6
Sekyn, Robert, husbandman 225
self-control, self-government 9, 16, 26, 28, 29, 32, 34, 37, 38, 46, 70, 73, 78, 85–6, 87, 96, 128, 151, 247
self-sufficiency 9, 16, 73, 87, 179–80, 187, 194, 231, 245, 247, 249
sermons 7, 9, 22, 25, 38, 43, 71, 72, 152
servants 3, 62, 63, 70, 75, 85, 97, 98, 99, 111, 112, 114, 117, 120, 136, 137–9, 143, 145, 162, 163, 165, 168, 175, 179, 180, 181, 189, 197, 199, 206–7, 210, 234
servility 88, 174
see also slavery
sex 116, 120–2, 239–40
bragging of 120, 121, 171, 173
illicit 94, 116, 119, 121, 122, 134, 169–70, 173, 176, 248
see also adultery
Sexton, Rychard 240
sexual insult 97, 98, 102, 153–4, 157, 161, 162, 163, 165–9
see also verbal abuse

Shawe, Agnes, fishwife 171, 180, 197
Shawe, John, brewer/maltster 180, 192, 197
Sheafe, Thomas 25, 40, 41, 43
Sheppard, Robert 190
Sherd, Thomas, notary 191
Shering, John 207
Sherman, John, brewer 194, 230
Shotbolte, Edward, apprentice 135
Shrove Tuesday 99
Simons, Joan, wife of John 161
Simons, John, tailor 161
Simpson, Robert, apprentice 171–2, 180
Singleton, Anne 188
Slack, Paul 50
slavery 37, 38, 78, 79, 106, 123, 162, 173, 174, 181, 182
Slegge, Francis, gent. 179
Smart, Thomas, baker 144
Smith, Bruce 125
Smith, Henry (1550?–1591), puritan divine 71, 80
Smyth, Humfry 146
Smith, Margaret 169
Smith, Margery 200
Smith, Oliver 207
Smith, Robert, butcher 178
Smith, Sir Thomas (1513–77), statesman 74, 174
Smith, Thomas, servant 117
Smith, Thomas, innkeeper 164
sociability 94, 101–3, 113, 114
social description 10, 89, 187, 191, 202, 206, 210, 213
social order 59, 60, 61–2, 63, 68, 73, 87–9, 149, 174, 176, 182–3, 202, 205
social relations 7, 32, 34–6, 67, 110–11, 112, 126, 128, 130, 132, 140–1, 148–9, 150, 154, 161, 167, 211
see also class
social status 1, 2, 9, 10, 13, 17, 21, 23, 37, 38, 45, 46, 49, 68–9, 76, 86, 87–8, 94–5, 100, 111, 149, 157,

social status (*cont*) 172, 194–5, 206, 213, 214, 222, 246, 249, 252–3
  debasement of 165–7, 173–84
  see also occupational status; worth
social polarization 252
sodomy 115, 116, 122, 162
  see also homosexuality
Somerset 134
Soone, William, gent. 206
Soundy, Richard, carpenter 217
Southampton 133, 204, 207, 209
speech 36, 37–8, 45, 46, 76
Spencer, Grace 149, 200
Spering, Anthony 207
Spicer, William, lawyer (b. *c.* 1582) 158, 181
spitting 144, 146
sport, *see* recreations
Staffordshire 97
Standishe, John 236
Stedman, Angela, servant 147
Stiffkey, Norfolk 203
Stockton, Worcs. 204, 205
stoicism 30
Stokes, Edward 239
Stokys, Matthew, gent. 234
Stooks, John 179–80
Stone, Lawrence 128
Stonylandes, William 243
Stowte, Reginald, yeoman 147
Streeke, Richard 146
strength 8, 9, 16, 24, 41, 42, 43, 46, 87, 99, 105, 107, 114, 115, 125, 149, 221, 247
Steyning, Sussex 175
Stodderd, John, schoolmaster 186
Stubbes, Philip (*fl.* 1581–93), puritan pamphleteer 29
Stuckney, Elizabeth 134
Stutfield, John 235
subsidies 200
subsistance migration 238
Suffolk 206, 207
Surrey 178
Sussex 189, 216, 217
Swaffham Bulbeck, Cambs. 228
Swavesey, Cambs. 225
Swayne, Maria, widow 222–3
swearing 93, 110
Swetnam, Joseph (*fl.* 1617), fencing master 141, 144
Swetson, John, apothecary 160
Swetson, Margaret, wife of John 201
Swynney, Beatrice 201
Symcocke, John, servant 180

Tabor, James (d. 1645), university registrar 170
Tancock, Katherine 189
Taylor, William 198
temperance 30, 32, 42, 44, 45, 59, 64, 68, 88
testicles 59
theft 112, 134, 135, 152, 156, 160, 161, 162, 163, 165–7, 172, 173, 176, 184
Thomas, Keith 108
Thompson, E. P. 129
thrift 6, 16, 24, 84–5, 86, 94, 96, 103, 125, 135, 172, 188, 190, 194, 210, 211, 247, 249
Thriplow, John 181
Thurlowe, Richard 203
Tiffen, Rose 157–8
Tillett, Thomas, tailor 175
Tilney, Edmund (d. 1610), master of the revels 71
tithes 222, 223, 224, 225, 226, 227, 237
tobacco 104, 105
Tollye, William, journeyman 238
Tomson, William, tailor 216, 232
Tompson, Frances 190
Tosh, John 5
Toulson, Gamaliel 121
Toulson, Marmaduke, baker 98
Travers, Elias (d. 1641), divine 169
Troye, Ursula 200
Turner, Martin 118
Turner, Nicholas, weaver 212
Turner, Richard 26

Tusser, Thomas (*c*.1524–80), agricultural writer 237
Tutbury, Staffs. 174
Tutt, Edward 234
Twelves, Elizabeth 164
Tyburn, 178

unemployment 239
universities 14
untrustworthiness 61, 73, 161, 165–7, 168, 192

vagrants, vagrancy 62, 85, 88, 134, 170, 175, 202, 203–4, 205, 244
Vaughan, William (1577–1641), poet and colonial pioneer 55, 57
Venner, Tobias (1557–1660), physician 57, 65
Vepen, Elizabeth, wife of John 171–2
Vepen, John 172
verbal abuse 140, 144, 155, 173–82, 185, 190
vestries 194, 235
vexatious litigation 158–9, 161
Vicary, Thomas (d. 1561), surgeon 63
violence 16, 94, 98–9, 100, 108–9, 113, 114–15, 127–51, 157, 184, 193, 212–13, 231, 248
  beard-pulling 146
  brawls 105, 143, 232
  breaking windows 93, 94, 97, 108, 109, 150
  disciplinary 130–1, 132–9, 143, 144, 150
  ear boxing 127, 139, 142, 143, 144, 146
  domestic 6, 81, 130, 136–9, 146, 247
  duelling, challenges to the field 105, 107, 127, 140, 142–3
  group combat 149–50
  interpersonal 131, 132, 140–50
  riotous 106–7, 129, 130
  striking up heels 144, 146
  by women 136–8, 150

whipping 98–9, 133–7, 138, 139, 170, 204, 244
wrestling 43, 114, 115, 144
violent crime 127–8, 129, 130
virility 59
virtue 9, 25, 32, 42–3, 46, 50, 52, 67, 68, 81, 104, 110
Vynsent, John and Margaret 204

wages, wage labour 6, 158, 199, 209, 227, 248, 252
Wakefield, Yorks. 143
Walker, Mary 234
Walkington, Thomas (d. 1621), divine 51
Wallington, Nehemiah, turner 193
Warbleton, Sussex 226, 228
Ward, George 141–2
Ward, Thomas 177
Wardall, Edward, barber 146, 174
Warde, William, yeoman 216
Warren, John, innholder 216
Watson, Margaret 223
weapons 107, 109, 131, 147
  bills 212
  clubs 107, 108
  daggers 107, 141, 147, 212
  halberds 99
  knives 127
  rapiers 93, 108, 141
  staffs, pikestaffs 109, 212
  staves 108
  sticks 127
  swords 93, 94, 98, 107, 108, 144, 193
Wenham, Edward, cook 179–80, 193
Wenham, Lucy, servant 197
Westfield, Sussex 190
West Firle, Sussex 226
West Hoathly, Sussex 224, 225, 229
West Minston, Sussex 227
Westfield, William 147
Wharton, Henry 118
Whately, William (1583–1639), puritan divine 71, 75, 81, 84, 85
Whistons, John 191, 194

Whitaker, Tobias (d. 1666),
    physician 41
'whoredom' in men 29, 240
Wichingham, Prudence 133
Wickliffe, Thomas, yeoman 175
widowers 239, 241
widows 196, 203, 210, 222, 234, 239,
    249
Wiesner, Merry 210
Wilby, Suffolk 226
Wilcockes, Jane and William 205
Williams, Thomas 211
Williamson, Ann 157–8
Willington, John (d. 1643) 145
Willows, Robert 178
Wilson, Agnes 190
Wilson, Margaret 164
Wilson, Robert 204
Wiltshire 194, 207, 212, 214
Winkleigh, Devon 233
wisdom 38, 39, 40, 42, 44, 45, 60, 72,
    73, 75, 81, 86, 87, 247
witchcraft 128, 155
Wittlesey, Cambs. 223, 228
wives' duties 71, 72–3, 75–7, 78,
    80–1
    see also women
Wodehouse, Jamys, lace weaver 238
Wolley, John and Thomas 147
womanhood 7, 10, 39, 246
    see also femininity
women:
    beating husbands 136–7
    banned from male company 119,
        120, 126
    commercial activities of 196–200,
        207, 213
    disobedient, disorderly 32, 34, 78,
        138
    heading households 4

manlike 79, 138, 246
subordination of 36, 70, 72–3, 86,
    87, 137, 182, 199, 206, 250, 251
Wood, Robert, cordwainer 191
Wood, Toby, launderer 144
Woodcock, Jane 200
Woodcock, Peter 208
Woodley, Roger and Samuel 141–2
Woodmancote, Sussex 227
Woods, Thomas, tailor 200
work 85, 190–2, 203, 231, 236–9
    gendered division of 188, 190, 195,
        199–202
worth 16, 123, 160, 164, 179, 180,
    188, 191–5, 200–1, 202, 206–8,
    210, 211, 213, 222, 227, 233,
    237, 241–2
Worth, Sussex 224–5
Wotton Rivers, Wilts. 191
Wratham, John 167
Wright, Walter 203
Wynn, Ellis 105
Wytherly, John 240

Xenophon 77

Yate, Edward, cordwainer 177
Yearle, Francis 199
Yonger, Joan, vagrant 170
York 14, 180, 181
York, Isabel 198
Young, Thomas 28
youth 3, 9, 13, 14, 17, 21, 22, 23–38,
    40, 43, 45–6, 54–6, 57, 74, 87,
    88, 93–126, 182, 208, 210, 213,
    214, 215, 221, 225, 226, 229, 238
    culture 95, 101, 103, 120, 126, 211
youthful misrule 15–16, 93–113, 126,
    150, 206, 248
Yxforth, James, worsted weaver 189